CONTE   ⌐IOLOGY

Editors
JoAnn Miller and Robert Perrucci

The Paths of Glory

The Paths of Glory

Social Change in America
from the Great War to Vietnam

Brian M. Downing

Cybereditions

Cybereditions Corporation
Christchurch, New Zealand
www.cybereditions.com
cybereditions@cybereditions.com

Cybereditions welcomes comments from readers.
In particular we wish to be informed of any misprints
or errors in our books, so that we may correct them.

ISBN 1-877275-58-1

Printed in the United States of America

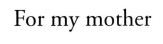
For my mother

You cannot replace the dogma of patriotism, the tradition of courage, and the shrine of honor by the rules of political economy.

ALEXANDER HERZEN, *Complete Works*, vol. 5

"Come, let us go into the forest. We are not here to open old wounds and then to poison them. . . . This meadow," said Bertin, as he slipped his arm through hers; "could be held by one machine-gun against two companies; they could never cross that stream down there. And the edge of the forest would be a first-rate emplacement for anti-aircraft guns." The meadow was a blue sheen of cuckoo flower and stork's bill. "Yes . . . the woods by Verdun looked like that, only much thicker, when we got there."

"I wish you could forget those woods," said Lenore tenderly. Secretly she feared it would be long before this man of hers found his way back out of those magic woods into the present — into real life. Within him the conflict had not died; still it surged and thundered. . . .

Like any pair of sweethearts they passed into the shadowed green splendour of the forest, and the gleam of her yellow frock could still be seen after his blue suit had disappeared from view.

ARNOLD ZWEIG, *Education before Verdun*

Everything a lie. They want you dead or in their lie. Only one thing a man can do: find something that's his . . . make an island for himself. If I don't meet you in this life, let me feel the lack; a glance from your eyes and my life will be yours.

TERRENCE MALICK, *The Thin Red Line*

Contents

PREFACE

*Modern war takes place within a context of cultural "modernism"
and indeed is one of its causes.*
Paul Fussell, *Modern War*

*I think you guys are going to have to come up with a lot of new lies, or
people just aren't going to want to go on living.*
Kurt Vonnegut, *Slaughterhouse-Five*

W. Somerset Maugham observed at the outset of *The Razor's Edge* that a people
is formed by shared experiences:

> For men and women are not only themselves; they are the region
> in which they were born, the city apartment or the farm in which
> they learnt to walk, the games they played as children, the old
> wives' tales they overheard, the food they ate, the schools they
> attended, the sports they followed, the poets they read, and the
> God they believed in.

He went on to describe how another shared experience, the Great War, had
shaped the people of America and Europe, how their confidence and faith had
been suddenly undermined.

For the most part, studies of social change have placed little importance on
war as an agent of change, stressing instead the primacy of domestic, mainly
economic forces. The study of society began in Europe in the wake of the
industrial revolution, as social structures began to move away from rural and
traditional orientations toward urban and modern ones. (Somehow, it has
occurred to only a few that the industrial revolution might have begun with the
Napoleonic Wars.)

Karl Marx conceptualized social change as the result of a new form of
economic organization that was shifting populations from the countryside to the
city, reducing human relations to the cash nexus, altering the state from a feudal
system to an instrument of bourgeois rule, and breaking down old patterns of
community, religion, and authority. All this, Marx was certain, would culminate
in an immense proletariat that would seize the day and a great deal else, thereby
ushering in a new socialist society.[1] By the early twentieth century, very little if
any of this had taken place in advanced industrial countries. There had indeed

been population shifts, but new forms of community and tradition developed. Traditional religions, norms, and other pre-capitalist values persisted despite the force of industrial modernization. The state maintained its prestige and legitimacy despite all these economic changes, at least until 1914.

Émile Durkheim saw the basis of society not in economic systems, but in common beliefs. Societies were coherent wholes, held together by shared norms and respected authorities. Economic changes were, however, important. A changing economy, like that of France in his day, would introduce important changes, but not of the cataclysmic and millenarian nature that Marx envisioned. Dislocations would be appreciable. Some people would experience the collapse of norms and live in "anomie," a condition in which norms no longer govern, despair and confusion reign, and suicide rates increase markedly. But anomie would be short-lived. Social systems have considerable strength and elasticity; they would adapt to change and find a restored order, maintaining social organization.[2]

Durkheim's thought pervades that of Talcott Parsons, the dean of American social science in the 1950s and early 1960s. Parsons's view of society, which became a veritable orthodoxy, blended Durkheim with Max Weber, Herbert Spencer, Sigmund Freud, and other thinkers. He developed a dynamic model of social change stressing gradual adaptation of the economy and value system. Economic change would eventually result in a new equilibrium, restoring balance and maintaining the proper functioning of society.[3]

Few would be so unwise as to ignore the importance of economic forces in history. The various tools of analysis developed by Marx, Durkheim, Parsons, and their followers have provided many insights regarding the workings of society. To borrow Barrington Moore's wonderful simile, they have acted as searchlights, shedding light on obscure historical processes. But, to continue the venerable mentor's simile, searchlights can also blind the observer to the importance of other forces.[4] Early in the twentieth century, Otto Hintze and Hans Delbrück argued that war and military organization are important forces in history, from classical antiquity to their own time, but they found few followers.[5] In the aftermath of World War I, the study of war fell into disrepute. The very subject was painful for many. Furthermore, military history, at least as it was then practiced, was seen as chauvinistic, hortatory, and part of a militaristic culture that had led to the recent slaughter.[6] The interwar period saw the rise of social history and progressive history. Soon, owing to the work of Charles Beard, R. H. Tawney, Marc Bloch, and others, economic forces were the privileged concepts in the study of social change.[7] For the most part, they remain so today. Wars, when they are looked at, are usually considered "time outs," after which the "real" social forces return to the fore.

PREFACE

The argument developed here is that American society was once a relatively coherent whole based on widely shared beliefs and that, although economic forces have brought about fissures and tensions, wars have had much more impact. The World Wars and Vietnam formed the basic contours of much of twentieth-century American history — political, economic, social, and cultural. America in 1917 was a confident, optimistic nation, proud of its beliefs, leaders, and institutions. Less than a year later, this was no longer the case. Leaders lost the aura of romantic infallibility they had long enjoyed. Religious strictures began to fall away. Consumerism and leisure replaced thrift and denial. Two decades later, in 1938, the country was mired in depression, the New Deal was in disarray, and unemployment was soaring once more. The country seemed near collapse. Only a few years later, unemployment was under three percent, beliefs and institutions were once more held high, and authority was revered. This state of affairs continued until the mid-1960s, but was almost completely gone just a few years later. It is difficult to see these sudden and marked changes, taking only a few years, as simply the result of economic forces.

The present study asks to what extent wars brought about these changes. Modern wars lead to bursts of economic growth; demographic dislocations that change patterns of family and community; changes in social structure and gender roles; shifts in nationalism, strengthening or weakening it depending on the outcome; changes in (often inversions of) established beliefs and social relations — again, depending on outcome. The effects of these changes are often so far-reaching as to constitute a break with the past, the closing of an era, and the opening of a new one. Hence, historians speak of the ante-bellum South, Reconstruction, and the interwar period. We now live in post-Vietnam America. Wars of the twentieth century have propelled America from a traditional past structured by families, communities, religion, faith in progress, and integration into a national whole to a postmodern present of atomization, fragmentation, secularization, and normlessness. From the perspective of the late twentieth century, modernity, the object of so much study in the middle of the century, was a brief way station between centuries of tradition and a postmodern present.

Wars have undoubtedly brought many beneficial effects, especially in the lives of minorities and women, in reducing much of the formalism of life, and in opening the way for new ways of thinking in and out of the academy. But there is also malaise, social and political fragmentation, and sharp decline in norms and internal restraints — social problems affecting all. We may see the old beliefs of American culture as good or bad, fair or unjust, universal or hopelessly particularistic; but they served an important integrative role, and nothing has emerged to take their place. They cannot be brought back.

Parts of this study might strike some as sentimentalizing the past. But I have only attempted to convey the sentimentality most Americans once felt for their country — sentimentality whose decline is an integral part of the changes under consideration here. Such criticism is probably unavoidable and perhaps the best that can be done is to point out that any civilization deserves fair treatment, appreciation of its achievements, and understanding of the bases of its coherence.

It is also useful to remember that independent thinking did not always sit well in traditional America. Once again, Somerset Maugham is helpful. Later in *The Razor's Edge*, a veteran of the Great War, dissociated from the world around him, wistfully looks to the past: "I've come too late into a world too old. I should have been born in the Middle Ages when faith was a matter of course; then my way would have been clear to me and I'd have sought to enter the order." Somerset Maugham arches an eyebrow and replies: "I think it's just as well you weren't born in the Middle Ages. You'd undoubtedly have perished at the stake."

***

Several people have helped with this project. I am pleased to thank them: Mary Belferman, Richard Belferman, Sr., Paul Bullen, Randall Collins, Daniel Karasik, Barrington Moore, Jr., William J. O'Connor, Michael Sherry, Robert Stoothoff, and Peter Sweda. Many friends, neighbors, and relatives were kind enough to share their remembrances of depression and war with me: Albert Bracutti, Neil Corey, Sr., Wilbur Dooley, Carmen Gisi, Eva Jekely, Max Royston, William Sausser, and Martha Sweda. And of course any author in the bibliography deserves thanks as well.

Brian M. Downing
Corolla, North Carolina

CHAPTER ONE

TRADITIONAL AMERICA

The meaning of the American experience will remain forever opaque to those who, once they see through the most simple-minded version of American idealism, can find only violence and self-interest in its stead.
ROBERT N. BELLAH, *The Broken Covenant*

Rising Glory of the American Republic!
HEADLINE FROM THE WAR OF 1812

Let us try to view the country's past as most Americans once regarded it, if for no other reason than to establish a starting point, problematic though it may be, to better understand later change. The beliefs and sentiments of past generations will likely now seem provincial and naive, but any traditional society looks that way from a modern perspective, to say nothing of a postmodern one, which likely sees one as dark and oppressive. America was once a coherent nation based on widely shared beliefs and faith in its institutions. Beginning in the colonial period and continuing in later centuries, an array of beliefs and institutions — family, community, nationalism, religiousness, and progress — came into being. Though never universally accepted, they were widely believed in, by people of different social and national origins. They had a mythic, sacred place in people's lives, giving senses of identity, integration, and a basis for judging right and wrong. Traditional America is now largely gone.

FAMILY

The family was perhaps the central part of traditional America, playing a decisive role in the lives of settlers, immigrants, and emancipated slaves. It was a work unit, teacher of basic values, informal welfare provider, and source of affection and idealism. In colonial times, the family was closely tied to local church and community. Family beliefs were often indistinguishable from those of others in the community around them. By the nineteenth century, however, a measure of separation emerged, and borders between family, community, and church were noticeable. Strict discipline, the legacy of Calvinist views of children as wicked and in need of a firm hand, was thought beneficial to all.[1]

Prior to industrialization, the family was a basic economic unit. Family members worked on farms, in small shops, or engaged in cooperative attempts to eke out a living. Making a living in a small business or from a few dozen acres imposed a harsh regimen. The workplace was in or near the home; family members, including wives and children, served as overseers, trainees, and work hands. Just as the peasant's plot had been dutifully worked by the family in the old country, so too was the family business in rural or urban America.[2] Women may have been relegated to the home in the traditional family, but this had a different meaning than it had in the mid-twentieth century. In addition to the management of households, women did piecework in the home, took care of dairy animals and small gardens, ran small businesses out of the home, and even rode shotgun as the family crossed the plains.[3]

In an era of economic hardship and uncertainty, in an unfamiliar land, the family served as a shield for its members. Struggling members could find refuge until better times came, as could those laid off or injured. Similarly, the family felt a duty to care for its aged and infirm. Turning to community relief agencies was a last resort and a rather shameful one, suggesting failure and lack of responsibility. Here too, this protective aspect of the family often drew from old-world folk traditions of family obligation and mutual help.[4]

The family was an important place of education and socialization. Public schools began in some areas during the first half of the nineteenth century, and parochial schools cropped up in later decades, but for many rural and town dwellers, even in the early twentieth century, the family was the main source of education, at best supplemented by a community school. The family, usually women members, passed on the basic skills necessary to become a member of society. Aside from reading, writing, and arithmetic, the family also instilled basic outlooks and dispositions, perhaps even more valuable at the time than the venerable three Rs. The home taught discipline, confidence, and optimism. Life on the farm or in an urban immigrant setting was arduous, but family learning enabled most members to bear up and, with time and a little luck, to prosper. Transmitted by family lore of experiences and deeds, this outlook also conveyed a sense of personal rootedness, generational continuity, and obligation to those around them.[5]

The family provided a basis for affection. Arranged marriages were not common, but they could be found in immigrant communities. For most, however, marriage was based on romantic love: finding a "special someone" and fate bringing the pair together were themes commonly reflected in contemporary songs, poems, and personal correspondence. Courtship rituals stressed the gradual revelation of romantic feeling, and determination of the partner's earnestness and candor. Sentimental attachments predominated over egotistical gratifications, to say nothing of sexual ones. Familial warmth attached romantic sentiments to other parts of American life; leaders, community, nation, and the past, all took on emotional warmth instilled in the home.[6]

COMMUNITY

America was once a patchwork of communities, seemingly isolated worlds unto themselves, but linked by economic ties and common sentiments. Main Street, as the expression went, ran down the middle of America. Many colonial settlements were built by dissident groups, isolated from and often despised by their former countrymen, who settled in groups in the New World. They brought with them strong ties to one other. John Winthrop stated: "We must uphold a familiar commerce together in all meekness, gentleness, patience and liberality. We must delight in each other, make others' conditions our own, rejoice together, always having before our eyes our commission and community in the work, our community as members of the same bond. . . . For we must consider that we shall be as a city on a hill."[7]

Dissenters grew uncomfortable with these early settlements and founded new communities. One of them, Roger Williams, developed a theory of government based not on a state of nature, but on the realities of colonial life, which prized cooperation and consensus as essential to survival in the foreboding wilderness. Local government was a rough democracy in which town members decided matters of common importance such as taxation, defense, magistrates, and the like. Many observers, including Samuel Adams, saw the New England town meeting as the purest form of democracy. Others, in keeping with religious outlooks of the time, saw it as divinely ordained.[8]

Towns spread away from the coastline, driven by dissent from Puritan rigidity, the influx of the Scotch-Irish, and the irresistible attraction of free land. Throughout the eighteenth and nineteenth centuries, new communities spread from the seaboard into the woodlands and trans-Appalachian regions. The shared rigors of the trek, the need to provide common protection by building blockhouses and forming militias, cooperation in building cabins, barns and roads, formed a strong sense of interdependence. A political community emerged, often based on the old town meetings. Common customs and usages enforced by public opinion were far more important than law and contract enforced by sheriffs. This was the America that de Tocqueville saw: a quilt-work of towns and settlements, governing themselves through norms and moral pressures, which he called "habits of the heart." He devotes only a few pages to describing the national government, which was secondary if not largely irrelevant to him, as it was to most Americans until the twentieth century.[9]

Beginning in the mid-nineteenth century and extending into the next, millions of immigrants came to America and established their own communities, primarily in the cities. Again, immigrants brought along Old World traditions. The horizons of European peasants had rarely extended past their village; their character, outlook, and expectations circumscribed by village boundaries. Beliefs, dress, manners, and idioms reflected local particularities. Rural life in the Old World built a cooperative ethic: tilling the local noble's lands, scheming to *avoid* tilling the noble's land, working common pasturage, and periodically redistributing land. From these villages, millions of immigrants streamed into New York, Chicago, and other burgeoning cities.

The prospect of millions of poor peasants leaving their villages and coming to strange industrial cities thousands of miles away alarmed turn-of-the-century social thinkers. Such rapid change in locale and experiences, they feared, would surely result in rootlessness, crime, and moral decay — what Emile Durkheim called *anomie*. Their concerns proved to be largely unfounded. Community and moral order came into being or persisted from older forms. Immigrants from Europe and the South who came north around the turn of the century often settled with people from the same region they left, sometimes even from the old village, retaining important continuities.[10] Unfamiliar and intimidating surroundings encouraged banding together to share news from old homelands, worries of daily life, and information regarding work. They formed mutual-aid societies to help the elderly, the sick, those injured in work accidents, and with funeral expenses. Community stores, aware that most customers lived precariously close to the margins, extended credit until payday, when customers felt obliged to settle accounts, for which they were often thanked with a small gift.[11]

In an effort to maintain their traditions, immigrants held closely to the imagery and values of their religion. Religious artifacts decorated home and workplace. Holy days were important community festivals. Parochial schools, staffed by ethnic clerics, taught the old country's language, history, and customs. In the age before mass media, local theater gave expression to old ways. Neighborhood newspapers figured highly in immigrant communities, often keeping readers better apprised of events in County Cork or Warsaw than of those in New York or Washington. In keeping old ways alive, they built communities that ultimately, and for many, unwittingly, rooted them in America.[12]

Mutual help led to the founding of vital support networks. Welfare was community-based, locally organized, and administered by notables, churches, lodges, and veteran associations. Rural towns supported the elderly and indigent, often grudgingly, and ever suspicious that some recipients were simply not pulling their weight. Because everyone knew everyone else, there was considerable pressure to get off the dole and avoid sanctions ranging from an annoyed glance to an unceremonious send-off. Similarly, in ethnic neighborhoods, religious organizations handled welfare, providing money (often secretly, owing to the shame involved) to the less fortunate. Settlement houses extended an ethos of mutual help from the prosperous middle classes (including the University of Chicago's economics department) to the working poor.[13]

Communities were held together by moral forces. To be a part of a town or neighborhood meant to abide by shared norms. In early colonial times, this entailed a rigid and confining theocratic hand, but harsh Puritan strictures did not always endure. Many chafed under rigidity and left to found their own settlements, which had looser but nonetheless binding norms. Later non-theocratic settlements also needed basic consensus to survive, and refusal to live by them could lead to banishment. What today would be considered intrusive was then considered vital to the community. Breaking norms led to various sanctions. One character in Thomas Wolfe's *Look Homeward Angel*, "wilted under the town's reproveful stare." Stronger sanctions were also present. Feigning infirmity to avoid military service led to one Wisconsin man's virtually complete isolation. One abided by norms or pressed on, often with considerable prodding.[14] Ethnic communities, too, had common norms. Helping each other in the day-to-day effort to get by was routine, one of the rhythms of community life. Refusal to help a neighbor or violation of a moral expectation led to gossip or to loss of credit and social contacts. Community norms were more important than formal legal systems. Courts were slow and costly parts of the strange outside world; but the court of social custom was free and swift, handing out verdicts of public opinion and sentences of shame.[15]

Community life provided senses of rootedness, identity, and continuity. People were part of a living whole, satisfying a basic human need. Each community had its own sounds, sights, and smells (good and bad), which established a rhythm to life. Train whistles, the cries of vendors, and angelus bells conveyed a sense of setting that told people who they were and what was expected of them. Life was flavored by local folk wisdom and superstitions regarding childrearing, propitious times for planting crops, and the causes and cures of illnesses. Local knowledge and customs were passed on to the young, providing a sense of continuity. There was distinctiveness in houses, street signs, and layouts of neighborhoods, which made for a certain homeliness, but perhaps an appealing one, as some might prefer a cantankerous eccentric to an amiable but homogeneous person.[16]

Community life was relatively ordered and comprehensible. Demands and expectations were defined and well understood. These little towns and neighborhoods may now seem confining and narrow-minded, filled with busybodies and ethnocentrics, resistant, indeed hostile to outsiders and change.

However, if we think back to the short-lived rigidity of early Puritan settlements then reflect on the normlessness of much of postmodern life, we might wonder if there wasn't somewhere an agreeable mean.

NATIONALISM

We might also wonder how so many different communities could have formed a unified nation. Unification began with the coalescence of the Atlantic colonies in the late eighteenth century. For most of their history, the colonies had only loose ties with each other, but even looser ones with Britain. The American colonies were far less profitable than the spice and sugar growing ones, thereby drawing British attention to the more lucrative Caribbean — a state of affairs that accustomed Americans to practical independence.

Contacts between the colonies were meager, but the postal system and a few newspapers afforded a measure of communication. Increasing trade, professional associations, and masonic lodges provided a social network. Colonists thought of themselves as a new people who had built a separate identity by taming a vast wilderness. Revivalist movements spread across the colonies, emphasizing common religious fervor and destiny. A loose identity had come into being, which, following British attempts to assert control after the French and Indian War (1754-63), aroused a sense that basic freedoms and liberties were in danger, and that a confederation could protect their cherished autonomy. John Adams roared that there was "a direct and formal design on foot to enslave America." Considerable divisions remained, but a sense of interdependence was coming into being. The experience of war furthered it.[17]

After seven years of war with Britain, victory increased senses of pride, separateness, and destiny. Revolutionary figures were depicted in classical imagery, as if to say that America would one day take its place alongside Rome as a great civilization. A cult of heroes formed into a common mythic pantheon. The War of 1812 gave it several more revered figures. America was distinct from Europe and more advanced in many ways, but this had to be elaborated upon and impressed into the minds of the former colonists. A generation of thinkers saw their duty. Van Wyck Brooks captured their outlook:

> These were the fortunate days of the youthful republic, when the
> good old Anglo-American sang-froid had solid facts to base itself
> upon, — when young men, heirs to the Great Event, knew that
> they had beaten England twice, although they were too well-bred
> to mention it, and felt, if they were students and men of letters,
> that they were volunteers in a nobler war, as builders of a great new
> civilization.[18]

A generation of writers, poets, and painters celebrated the virtues of the young Republic: its natural beauty, gallant leaders, and growing accomplishments. Americans wrote histories of Spain and the Dutch Republic that won the respect of European scholars. Lexicographers set out to standardize a distinctly American form of English with its own spellings and usages.[19]

Between 1830 and 1860, historical societies sprang up throughout the young Republic. Seeking to expand public knowledge of American history, civic organizations constructed memorials to George Washington and the heroes of Bunker Hill; the flag and the *Star Spangled Banner* became widespread. Romantic histories of the Founding Fathers appeared, which were rich in romantic imagery but perhaps a bit lacking in documentation. Accounts of dollars tossed across the Rappahannock and a contrite lad owning up to felling a cherry tree needed no basis in fact. The work was mythic in nature, molding a national identity, constructing a great new civilization out of a breakaway part of an old one. They sought to inspire and build. It was the calling of a generation of volunteers in the cause of creating the myths and sentiments of the new Republic.

Schools began to inculcate patriotism and respect for the new nation's beliefs and institutions. Spellers and readers were filled with patriotic imagery, telling students who they were, what they were a part of, and what duties they had. America was a force of goodness in the world; Europe, a distant and almost irrelevant land, was mired in despotism and chronic war. The Constitution and its institutions were created by great figures guided from above. Local democracy was the wellspring of the nation's political system and everything else that was good. Americans had clearly stipulated rights and duties; citizenship meant active involvement in community and national affairs. The frontier had made the American fighting man second to none; the nation would never lose a war. There was a musical dimension to nation-building as well. Schoolbooks were filled with inspiring nationalistic songs. *The Star Spangled Banner, Columbia the Gem of the Ocean*, and *The Battle Hymn of the Republic* fused æsthetic experience with patriotic imagery in the hearts of children and not a few adults. As millions of immigrants came in, the effort to instill nationalism became more pronounced. More emphasis on patriotic themes was deemed necessary to break down loyalties to the old country and convert newcomers into citizens.[20]

In looking at these sources and instances of patriotism — national holidays, prominent leaders, schoolbook themes — a large amount of military content stands out. It was less than anything that can be called militarism, but enough to call for some exploration. As counterintuitive as it might be to today's sensibilities, to whom war means dissension and guilt, war has generally had powerful unifying effects and provided an array of events and imagery that has shaped generations of Americans. War rivets national attention as nothing else can, involves contributions and sacrifices, and exacts fearful costs that call for a sense of transcendent meaning. A triumphant outcome on the battlefield inspires faith in divine favor. Victory, with which Americans became well accustomed, is a powerful intoxicant that bonds those who contribute to the national effort. Little wonder that when William James identified the ultimate effort by which others might be gauged, he coined the phrase, "the moral equivalent of war."[21]

From the early struggles against Britain to the World Wars, military conflict has played a major role in the development of American nationalism. The Revolutionary War, though fought by a population with many ties to Britain, ended with a powerful sense of pride, unity, and destiny. George Washington, Nathan Hale, Francis Marion, Ethan Allen, John Paul Jones, and others became lionized, mythologized, and immortalized. Their deeds and words were known by all — on the lips of every schoolboy, as an old expression went. Figures such as George III, Cornwallis, and Benedict Arnold circumscribed the limits of American identity, beyond which lay despotism, cruelty, and treachery. Bunker Hill, Valley Forge, and Yorktown were emotionally charged names, infused with passion and reverence.[22]

An important part of the American identity was the satisfying knowledge that they had licked Great Britain, a feat with considerable resonance with the David and Goliath story. The War of 1812 gave a second opportunity. Though highly divisive, indeed to the point of a secessionist movement in the Northeast, the conflict was popular in the rest of the country. Anti-British sentiment, never far from the minds of early Americans, surged once more; provincial sentiment declined. A South Carolinian said, "The War has given strength and splendor to the chain of the Union. . . . Local feelings are absorbed in the proud feelings of being an American."[23] Schoolhouses began the practice of flying the flag. Accounts of daring naval encounters by Lawrence and Perry thrilled the public, as did Harrison's triumph at Tippecanoe, and Jackson's at New Orleans, where miraculously only seven Americans fell in the course of repulsing enemy regiments. Opposition and the threat of secession ended, and the nation celebrated. Victory propelled Jackson and Harrison to the presidency, as it had for Washington, as it would for many others.

The Civil War profoundly affected American nationalism. The Union effort was based on patriotism, and a costly victory solidified it, shaping the moral order for a half century. At the outset of the war, the Union was seen as a sacred, living whole; secession and the firing on Fort Sumter were outrages. The Union had been insulted, dishonored. On Lincoln's call for volunteers, Northern towns debated, formed consensus, and raised regiments for the cause. Grant recalled events in his home town: "As soon as the news of the call for volunteers reached Galena, posters were stuck up calling for a meeting of the citizens at the courthouse in the evening. Business ceased entirely; all was excitement; for a time there were no party distinctions; all were Union men, determined to avenge the insult to the national flag."[24] In the course of the war, speeches and sermons bolstered patriotic sentiment; letters and diaries of Union soldiers exhibit increased devotion to the country; women formed local committees and auxiliaries, for many, entering public life for the first time. It was their duty, as heirs to the Great Event, to show faith with forebears and fight for the Union.[25]

Victory strengthened the sense of national community, at least in the North. The Union's beliefs and institutions emerged triumphant, exalted, and more sacred still. The Civil War was a national war, involving the resources and manpower of the country far more than had any previous war. It involved communities and newly formed civil associations in the national whole in a way commerce and literature never could. The journeys of the local regiment, the heroism of local boys, and the changing tides of war, all focused attention on the nation-state.

Community involvement with the war continued well after Lee handed his sword to Grant. Cannons that roared at Gettysburg and Chickamauga stood in front of courthouses and in public squares, reminders of the noble effort and continuing duty. The dead — "the fallen," as a period given to mythic language called them — were honored: locally, by inscribing their names on monuments; nationally, by cemeteries, battlefields, and holidays. Another Great Event had come into being, taking its place alongside, probably even ahead of, the wars with Britain. The Civil War established a new host of heroes, events, and hallowed grounds that formed a climate of expectations, duties, and reference points, which bolstered confidence in the country for a generation or more, well into the twentieth century, when the old veterans began to pass from the scene.[26]

World War I also increased nationalist sentiment, at least temporarily. Owing to the remoteness of European events, more of it was orchestrated from above than in the past. U-boats occasionally brought the war close to home, but the Somme and Verdun were muffled rumblings of a distant storm, the most recent of a dismal string of European wars, unlikely to affect Americans. When war came in 1917, President Wilson deployed thousands of orators ("four-minute men") around the country, drawing upon martial spirit from an older era and firing patriotic ardor to support a new crusade. The government organized Loyalty Leagues in ethnic communities, where support was questioned. Patriotic marches and spectacles were arranged; dozens of ethnic groups filed past Washington's tomb and swore allegiance. Immigrants were urged to explain America's aims, in war and peace, to relatives in the old country.[27]

Wars, with little warning, throw together people from all regions, backgrounds, and outlooks, turning them into defenders of the nation, their families into unified supporters. Conflicts bring forth an array of imagery, symbols, and heroes, which strengthen patriotism, especially among the young. The venerable McGuffey Readers, with which generations of Americans learned to read and become citizens, were filled with inspirational stories of epic battles and heroic deeds. Schoolchildren read and reread Emerson's *Concord Hymn,* Longfellow's *Paul Revere's Ride,* and William Cullen Bryant's *Song of Marion's Men.* They sang *The Star Spangled Banner* and *The Battle Hymn of the Republic.* They learned by heart the words of Nathan Hale, John Paul Jones, and Oliver Perry, and felt ennobled by them. The more promising could recite the Gettysburg Address. Commager recognizes the old spirit (as well as its later erosion): "The phrases, too vital to be trite, entered into the very fibre of their being, gave them self-assuredness and dignity. . . . It was all to seem naïve to a later generation, but it was not lacking in nobility of inspiration, and it served its purpose."[28] Through war mythology, children came to see themselves as part of a great nation, slow to anger, guided from above, and unbowed.[29]

To a later generation, this cultural current might be seen as evidence of militarism and as a wellspring of imperialism and reckless interventionism. However, martial ardor was restrained by idealism, parochialism, and parsimony. The Mexican War and the Spanish-American War triggered powerful reactions: the former seemed a plot to expand slavery, the latter smacked of the land-grabs that Europeans embarked upon just before another great slaughter. The Civil War's horrendous casualties left no thirst for war. The armies of the North demobilized almost as swiftly as those of the South. Fielding over a million men in 1865, the army comprised only 43,000 a year later; by 1875 it had dwindled to 25,331. Ten years after the Civil War, America's military as a percentage of the population was one-tenth that of England, one twenty-fifth that of Prussia, one thirty-eighth that of France.[30] The casualties of World War I as well as succeeding diplomatic failures left a bitter taste in most Americans' mouths and led to renewed isolationist sentiment. Huge armies were rapidly raised and equally rapidly disbanded at war's end, as Americans preferred to avoid the sordidness of world affairs. Traditional America's military became prestigious and influential, but no more than that of Athens or England, never approaching that of Sparta or Prussia.

RELIGION

Religion was an important force in traditional America. One writer observed, "There is no country in the world where the Christian religion retains a greater influence over the souls of men than in America. . . . It must never be forgotten that religion gave birth to Anglo-American society. In the United States, religion is therefore mingled with all the feelings of patriotism, whence it derives a peculiar force." The passage will likely bring on immediate associations: the immoderate oratory of a sect leader, spoken or shouted in a small rural church, sparsely occupied by simple folk, mostly the elderly and very young, who search for meaning in an increasingly incomprehensible world; or perhaps a polished television broadcast, pharisaically delivered in measured phrases and gestures, informed by little historical knowledge, but calculated to maximize returns on a pledge line.

However, the author of these words was Alexis de Tocqueville, a discerning observer of early America, whose insights have illuminated many thinkers, for many decades and across the political spectrum.[31] When read today, in a highly secularized country, the passage suggests that a momentous change has taken place. The earliest settlements, as even televangelists know, as even the most secular historian must admit, were essentially religious communities. Puritans and Catholics were the best known, but Moravians, Dunkers, and Anabaptists were numerous as well. Intolerance and warfare drove them across the ocean. Colonial administrators saw more economic potential in disciplined religious groups than in freebooters and convicts. A London trade group advised: "A free exercise of religion . . . is essential to enriching and improving a trading nation; it should ever be held sacred in His Majesty's colonies."[32] By the mid-eighteenth century, America comprised numerous settlements with an unmistakably religious character. Quakers and Baptists splintered from Puritan villages; Catholics settled in Maryland, followed by Presbyterians and Anglicans; a variety of smaller sects planted themselves here and there. Doctrinal and ritualistic differences abounded, but a common sense of America as a New Israel pervaded. America was divinely ordained: tolerance and virtue would flourish; leaders followed Scripture rather than prejudice. America, they all agreed, had a great Destiny.[33]

Two religious phenomena grew out of colonial religiousness, the first, a wave of revivalist movements beginning about 1740. The (First) Great Awakening swept the colonies, stressing an immediate, personal variety of religious experience that contrasted (and soon conflicted) with dry, formal religions. This was especially so of the Church of England, which had become increasingly bureaucratic and was part of secular authority in Britain. Religious renewal gave the colonists an important sense of identity as an association of the righteous. Older senses of destiny gained vitality drawn from the surge in religious feelings, setting the stage for the Revolution. Immediate, personal religious experience distanced followers from old religious authority, which brought a portentous sense of political independence and moral conviction. The inner truth they felt was greater than the law of man, especially that of an assembly far away.[34]

A second religious phenomenon important in colonial America was the rise, mainly in educated circles, of an amalgam of religion and science, Christian theology and Enlightenment thought, known as Deism. Its followers saw no conflict between science and religion: science yields an understanding of the divine order, and knowledge of God reveals the nature of the world. Scientific knowledge provides an understanding of natural law, a part of God's mind from which law and rights can be known and, through willing hands, brought into being for the betterment of mankind.

The convergence of popular fervor and Deist thought came at a propitious time. The remote British crown now sought a greater presence in the colonies and advanced plans to raise taxes, quarter troops, and introduce religious hierarchy. In the history of the world's injustices Britain's demands will not figure highly, but at that moment, closely following a religious resurgence, British demands seemed to be sinister machinations. Powerful political and religious opposition followed. John Adams thundered, "Let the pulpit resound with the doctrines of religious liberty. [There is] a direct and formal design on foot to enslave America."[35]

Linked at the outset of the Revolution, politics and religion emerged from it closer still. The pulpit resounded with politically charged sermons, especially in Congregationalist, Baptist, and Presbyterian gatherings. Churches brought gifts of praise to the newborn Republic, imbuing it with religious sentiments and a sense of destiny, which has led observers such as Robert Bellah to refer to an American "civil religion:" a mixture of religious-secular heroes, events, institutions, and expectations that proved divine guidance, righteousness, and mission. Americans firmly believed that God had aided them during the period, by granting patience at Valley Forge, courage at Trenton, mercy at Yorktown, and wisdom at Philadelphia.

A Second Great Awakening electrified the nation during the first half of the nineteenth century. It has often been seen as a reaction to the coldness of Enlightenment thought, or to the violence of the French Revolution; but de Tocqueville and Perry Miller suggest that growing materialism and isolation acted upon the human need for spirituality and brought about new revivalist fervor. Those who associate such movements with untutored bumpkins will be uncomfortable to learn that the principals of this movement included Timothy Dwight, president of Yale University, William Ellery Channing, whose religious teachings influenced Max Weber, and Harriet Beecher Stowe, whose writings spread the anti-slavery gospel.

Religious renewal fueled abolitionism in the decades prior to the Civil War, when religious fervor found a new crusade and a latter-day Saracen. The writings of Stowe and William Lloyd Garrison alerted the faithful to the evil of slavery, the wickedness of the plantation owner, and the complicity of standers-by. Moved by Scripture, Nat Turner began his slave rebellion in Tidewater Virginia.[36] Frederick Douglass's conversion led to his dedication to abolitionism. The flame of Puritanism, dim from years of comfort, flared fiercely as slavery hearkened back to epic deeds of forebears in the English Civil War. Henry Adams (writing in the third person) recalls from his youth: "Slavery drove the whole Puritan community back on its Puritanism. The boy thought as dogmatically as though he were one of his own ancestors. The Slave power took the place of Stuart kings and Roman popes."[37] Van Wyck Brooks saw a similar response in rural communities: "There dwelt, unchanged, the spirit of the Puritans and the Friends, the stiff-necked sectaries of Cromwell's army. . . . The Age of Laud and Charles the First had reappeared . . . ."[38]

Religious beliefs provided an unassailable sense of right and wrong, more cogent and binding than any Supreme Court decision or Congressional compromise made by fallible men. Puritans had left England rather than bow to its inequities; their descendants had broken with Parliament when it became intolerable. John Brown's raid on Harpers Ferry and subsequent trial sharpened the debate. Some saw it as a simple criminal case, while others sided with Emerson, who predicted that Brown's hanging would make "the gallows as glorious as the Cross." When debate finally erupted into war, the Union saw itself as a terrible swift sword, the Confederacy a serpent, Union campfires Pentecostal tongues of flame. After four years of war, Appomattox proved the righteousness of the cause.

Religion had subtler influences than those on the deeds of statesmen and generals. The major universities began as schools of theology, where young men attained breadth and depth in their formation to better guide their congregations. Many leading intellectuals, from the colonial and early republican periods to the early twentieth century, were religious figures. The Mathers, John Winthrop, Timothy Dwight, and Josiah Royce brought religious thinking to issues of the day. The spirituality of Thoreau, Emerson, and Whitman drew upon religious strains. Many of the founders of American sociology were ministers or theology students, who sought to understand the social bases of morality and its decline, the troubling beginnings of which they saw developing.[39] Most of the characters and dilemmas of American literature, from Melville to Steinbeck, though not much beyond, came from well-known Biblical passages.

Religion was present in day-to-day rhythms as well. In the simpler years before radio and television, religious works formed a considerable part of daily life. The Bible, *Pilgrim's Progress,* and *The Book of Martyrs* were read in most every home, and had as much impact on lives as the mass media have today. *Pilgrim's Progress,* which may be described as a stream of moral allegories separated by an occasional preposition, was a powerful literary force that shaped values of individual worth, discipline, and faith in the future. Religion gave special meaning to work. It was more than a means of making ends meet; it was a calling, a way of serving God. Success in one's calling was a sign of divine approval and eternal salvation. Diligence and frugality were praised; sloth and extravagance condemned.[40]

In the colonial period, clergymen were also doctors, lawyers, and other prominent figures. They influenced community life, shaped its routines, and established its priorities. Throughout the nineteenth century, churches were central parts of life: "They counseled the drinker, rebuked the swearer, admonished all vice, and expelled any persistent wrongdoer. Employers who were churchgoers usually imposed their moral standards upon subordinates."[41] Churches in urban neighborhoods ran schools, counseling services, and social clubs, where many met their future mates. Religious rites flavored life from cradle to grave. Baptisms, first communions, weddings, and funerals were important community events and benchmarks in lives, integrating the young with their community and past.

Religious values provided a shared sense of moral truths, a common understanding of right and wrong. McGuffey Readers taught morality on every page. Their didactic stories instilled basic morality through homiletic stories of a child choosing the right path, good triumphing over evil, and the wrongdoer ultimately punished. One reaped what one sowed, pride came before a fall, and though it sometimes seemed to the meek that Rockefeller and Morgan would inherit the earth, neither robber baron nor camel was likely to pass through the eye of a needle.[42] Religious principles were readily applied to the trials of daily life as well as the great issues of the day. Americans were bound together and governed by an invisible but omnipresent regulating system, which settled and prevented disputes without courts or social services, by restraining egotistical, sexual, and destructive impulses.

PROGRESS

Themes of progress were everywhere. Settlers sought to prosper in a new land, free of war, intolerance, and caste barriers. The New World was unburdened by the forces that produced and perpetuated those ills in Europe. America would be pastoral, tolerant, and egalitarian, for Providence was guiding the unfolding of its history. The New Englander felt that John Calvin's mission had been thwarted in Geneva, Holland, and England, but would triumph here. John Adams said, "I always consider the settlement of America with reverence and wonder, as the opening of a grand scheme and design in Providence for the illumination and emancipation of the slavish part of mankind all over the earth."[43] The victory of the War of Independence strengthened belief in progress. Democracy triumphed over despotism; God guided the chosen; and America's triumph would instruct the rest of the world. Shortly thereafter, to no one's surprise, Europe degenerated into the Napoleonic Wars, another internecine bloodletting that confirmed its benighted nature.

Education was an important part of the myth of progress. Through it, Americans felt they could improve their opportunities and those of their children. The interest in education on the part of American rustics astonished de Tocqueville, who first read *Henry V* upon coming across a copy in a frontier cabin. This thirst, he observed, followed from the absence of a rigid class system, which limits potential and stifles the desire to improve one's lot. Perhaps owing to the populism of the Jacksonian era and the ongoing revivalism, the first half of the nineteenth century witnessed enthusiasm for self-improvement. Public school systems began in Massachusetts and spread throughout the Northeast. Public libraries cropped up, as did parochial schools after the influx of German and Irish immigrants in the 1840s. Many religious groups felt it their duty to raise the educational level of the new nation.[44]

This was not limited to the East. As soon as a forest clearing developed into a frontier community, a newspaper, lending library, and other parts of civilization soon appeared. In 1810, Lexington, Kentucky, a modest hamlet of 4,000, had two bookstores and the first college west of the mountains. Seven years later, it was the site of the first American performance of a Beethoven symphony. In 1832, Lincoln's boyhood hometown of New Salem, Illinois, had fewer than 150 people, but it could boast of libraries and a debating society, all before it was three years old. In 1855, San Francisco had more newspapers than did London. Later in the century, shortly before the onslaught of mass media, self-improvement took the form of the Chautauqua movement, which brought lectures to small towns, often in tent meetings similar to the revivalist gatherings. Early women's clubs also felt it their mission to spread literacy and respect for learning. In the early twentieth century, immigrants from Europe and blacks who left the Deep South were happy to find elementary school systems in which their children might better themselves.[45]

Puritan figures such as Mather and Winthrop were talented men of science, as were their successors, Benjamin Franklin, Thomas Jefferson, and John Quincy Adams — this at a time when science was the province of gifted amateurs in their studies and workshops. Science in America benefited from Enlightenment and Deist thought, which held that political freedom would free human reason and expand scientific knowledge. The young country felt destined to become the center of scientific inquiry, surpassing Europe in this regard.

The Revolutionary War stimulated scientific research, as public figures reflected on the immense casualties caused by disease. The confluence of war experiences, Deism, and the Enlightenment led to the founding of science curricula at universities and an academy of arts and sciences — a process that began the transition of science from the avocation of talented amateurs to a professional discipline. In the next hundred years, Americans produced the steamship, the telegraph, the light bulb, and the airplane, as well as countless less notable contributions made by unheralded craftsmen and tinkerers, whose know-how increased the nation's prestige and wealth. By the twentieth century, the prophesy of Revolutionary leaders had become a basic assumption.[46]

Romanticized by novelists, painters, historians, and poets, the West provided enduring parts of the progress myth in the forms of the spread of homesteaders, law and order, and the railroad. Though trivialized by modern media, the settling of the West was once virtually revered. A motley assortment of religious dissenters, rugged individualists, speculators, and freebooters set forth across the Appalachians, through the Ohio valley, and across the Mississippi. Trading outposts became farming villages and towns. Railroads replaced trails, and civilization replaced wilderness. Though, as we acknowledge now, the process entailed the destruction of native peoples, most Americans justified this as the inevitable triumph of a superior civilization. Homesteads replacing empty grassland was a great improvement in which Americans took pride. Law followed the westward movement, replacing a war of all against all with the rough justice of cattle barons and vigilance committees, then with a working legal system. In the tracks of pioneers and homesteaders came shopkeepers and teachers, who brought manners, politesse, and other aspects of civilization to the frontier. Townspeople were eager to emulate eastern towns in order to bolster their prestige and attract more settlers. The extension of railroad tracks across the prairie and through the Rockies fused progress with the nation's growing industrial power.[47] National attention fixed on the unfolding drama. Settling the West was proof that the post-revolutionary confidence in the young country had been well founded. The conquest of the frontier strengthened senses of optimism and confidence; America's resources were limitless; Americans could make their own destiny.

There was a very practical aspect of the progress myth, one that appealed to a very practical people: America was a land of material abundance and prosperity, leading to social mobility unthinkable in Europe. Americans could, through their own talents, improve their lot. De Tocqueville found Americans more interested in prosperity than were Europeans, and looked for a reason. A ready answer for many might be Calvinist doctrine, which saw success as a sign of being one of the elect, predestined for salvation.[48] Perhaps owing to a reluctance to ascribe superiority to Protestantism, de Tocqueville found an alternative to the answer Puritanism suggested. The caste societies of Europe, he reasoned, limited individual potential, leaving a sense of futility regarding self-improvement. Americans, on the other hand, found that work led to advances in material possessions and social mobility. The American could rise from laborer to yeoman farmer or tradesman, entering the middle classes, whereas Europe's class system discouraged social climbing. De Tocqueville also cites a related cultural distinction between the new and old civilizations: aristocratic privilege led to indifference toward possessions, while the poor's deprivation led to resignation — the two converging to form an outlook quite different from the American faith in prosperity.[49]

The theme of material prosperity runs through American history. Material prosperity back then did not routinely degenerate into avarice or materialism. Sybarites there were, but, for most, prosperity was a modest thing. An implement to help planting and harvesting, a Billikens doll, or a hat from a Sears-Roebuck catalog were wonderful additions to life. In time, it meant a radio set for the living room or even a Model T. For most people, religious and community norms prevented the enjoyment of possessions from becoming an all-consuming quest for more.[50] Too many belongings brought greed and avarice, turned the diligent into the slothful. Energies should be devoted to endeavors that helped the common good.[51] Belongings were best thought of as a light cloak that one could shed, easily and without regret.

The colonial heritage, education, science, the frontier, and prosperity coalesced into a broad cultural force. Scratching out an existence in a colony was better than life in an English village; the Revolution brought a more just form of rule; the Civil War ended an atavistic institution; settling the West spread civilization; acquiring foreign lands ousted despotic rule. Extolled from the pulpit, hustings, and lecterns, progress was part of the common stock of knowledge, on Main Street, the Lower East Side, and in Newport. Should one look back to Europe, it was thought of as the place where less fortunate relatives had to live.

SACREDNESS OF TRADITIONAL AMERICA

America was not simply a set of facts, dates, and names. It was a body of deeds, events, and legends. The idea of traditional America was emotionally charged, imbued with myth and sacredness. America was a living whole, its leaders illuminated by a romantic aura. The Declaration of Independence, the Constitution, and Gettysburg Address were held in awe, preserved in august neo-classical buildings evoking the grandeur of ancient civilizations. Washington and Lincoln, Boone and Crockett, Fulton and Edison, all attained mythic qualities. Their burial places became shrines. The year 1776 was emotionally charged, as were 1812 and 1865. This sacred dimension of traditional America made it far more than a list of dry facts and assertions; it was, as Bellah said, a civil religion.

In the days before science dominated the understanding of life, Americans were predisposed to see the world in religious terms. Floods, illnesses, and crop failures might have had bases in material cause and effect, but they were also judgments, acts of God, parts of the Divine Plan. Leaders were naturally likened to Biblical figures, often Old Testament patriarchs, as Lincoln was called "Father Abraham." His death invited comparison to Jesus: each led a great moral cause, each had a premonition of death, and each died a tragic and early death — on Good Friday. The nation saw itself as latter-day Israelites, its enemies as Philistines and Amalekites. Reading national events, they saw messianism, prophecy, and judgment. Government invoked religious symbols to strengthen legitimacy. In God We Trust, opening official acts with prayer, witnesses taking oaths, and belief in God as prerequisite for jurors, all gave rational-legal processes an aura of sacredness.

A powerful means of instilling sacredness came from the family, where maternal affection and paternal authority fused. Familial authority passed on heritage and learning, instilling it with a romantic aura, helping to make politicians into statesmen, policies into deeds, and narratives into sagas. Nationalism, as Christopher Lasch tells us, is built on a fusion of paternal authority and maternal affection, brought together by socialization processes in the family and community.[52] Teachers in the towns and neighborhoods, many of them respected parents in the community, could draw upon the fusion of love and authority, and convey a sense of sacredness in education, ennobling a deal into a great compromise, bull-headedness into steadfastness, and a fiasco into a bold but ill-starred venture. It was all the same mythic process begun by Parson Weems, and even most who saw through it, as an increasingly modern and sophisticated public later would, felt it was nonetheless good for the country to uphold the myth.

War played an important role in this. Military conflict focuses national attention and unites people in a common purpose above the mundane. It entails sacrifice sometimes, as with the Civil War, enormous sacrifice. There is tremendous anxiety and concern for the lives of loved ones, leading people to look to a higher place. God is implored to protect soldiers, guide leaders, and speed victory. Events are embellished by returning soldiers, jingoistic newspapers, and government releases telling of audacious generals and wise statesmen. The experience of victory lifts anxieties and fears, bringing an intoxicating sense of national achievement.[53]

History texts conveyed a sense of sacredness in the nation's past and present. History is rarely a neutral recounting of the events. When written that way, it is usually plodding, lifeless — hardly conducive to mythmaking, or even to finishing the book. Sometimes subtly, sometimes not, history contains an ideological dimension, that is, a body of assumptions and aspirations, commonly held by a group as small as a group of scholars, or as momentous as the beliefs of a nation. This has been seen in the vivid, inspiring tales of great Americans in the primers of nineteenth-century schoolhouses. But at a higher level, an ideological spirit pervades the works of many historians, who stressed the strength of the American character, the hearty frontier folk, and the evolution of the country. George Bancroft's famous works refer frequently to divine inspiration and messianism. Just as English and German historians once romanticized their countries' past, American counterparts attached a sense of sacredness to their own.[54]

The arts, too, have contributed to the romance of national traditions. War epics such as *The Odyssey* did so for Athens, *The Song of Roland* for France, and *Henry V* for England. There has already been mention of patriotic poems such as *Concord Hymn* and *Paul Revere's Ride*, but perhaps one should now try to imagine their meter and imagery enriching a patriotic message, the effect further enhanced by music. Songs praising traditional America abounded — in schoolhouses, lodge meetings, and at national holiday celebrations. *The Star Spangled Banner* and *My Country 'Tis of Thee* served this purpose. *The Battle Hymn of the Republic* conveys this best and merits a rereading after what might have been quite some time.

> Mine eyes have seen the glory of the coming of the Lord:
> He is trampling out the vintage where the grapes of wrath are stored;
> He hath loosed the fateful lightning of his terrible swift sword:
> His truth is marching on.
> I have seen Him in the watch-fires of a hundred circling camps;
> They have builded Him an altar in the evening dews and damps;
> I can read His righteous sentence by the dim and flaring lamps.
> His day is marching on . . . .
> In the beauty of the lilies Christ was born across the sea,
> With a glory in his bosom that transfigures you and me:
> As He died to make men holy, let us die to make men free,
> While God is marching on . . . .

Here we have patriotic, messianic, and military themes artfully commingled with the aesthetics of music and imagery. *The Battle Hymn* was sung in churches across the North, bolstering sagging spirits during the long painful war. It is said to have heartened war-weary Union soldiers on exhausting marches and in

Confederate prison camps. If we can put aside the sentiments and opinion of a later day, and try to intuit the moment of children singing *The Battle Hymn* in their schoolhouse, we might gain a fleeting understanding of the sense of sacredness that once ran through American life.

Literature also played a role in making American life sacred, again by weaving aesthetics with narrative. Hawkeye, the mythic frontiersman in James Fenimore Cooper's stories, embodies the self-reliant American, mastering the wilderness and chafing against civilization. Mark Twain depicts simple folk wrestling with moral issues and, upon seeing the right thing to do, siding with the cause of abolitionism. Countless lesser-known works celebrated small-town life, romanticizing them as the nurturing, formative environment, where America's statesmen, inventors, and generals had learned thrift, honor, and industry — "what made the country great" as the saying once went.

***

Traditional America was not simply a collection of myths and folkways in which a people once believed. It gave a sense of identity, impressing upon each generation a sense of who they were, what their forebears had endured, and what common aspirations they had. It satisfied a vital if largely forgotten need for integration. Americans felt they belonged to a whole, and shared a common past and destiny, which channeled their lives toward a noble purpose. Furthermore, they had a common basis on which they could form a consensus on right and wrong as well as on the proper course for the nation.

Of course, traditional America was never completely homogeneous. It was never universally believed in, and the intensity of belief varied. It was not incapable of wrong, never all sweetness and light. A survey of general trends cannot ignore pockets of discontent and social fissures, especially if they later come to the fore. There were antagonisms between rich and poor, sometimes, as with Shays's Rebellion, extremely sharp ones resulting in violence between debt-ridden farmers and the new government. Similar antagonisms between rich and poor recurred in the Jacksonian period, when widespread debt led to heated protest; as well in the populist and progressive periods of the late nineteenth century, when farmers and urban workers railed against concentrated wealth.

Sectional antagonisms were felt at the outset of the nation's history, as merchants and planters argued, often bitterly and almost irreconcilably, over the form of government, the institution of slavery, and other fundamental questions. Only a few decades later, merchants and bankers, resentful of the growing political power of western regions, threatened to secede. The most important sectional fissure led of course to the Civil War, which preserved the Union but at the cost of rendering the South into a defeated and resentful region for generations, whose faith in traditional America, though considerable, had important qualifications.

The nation's culture and institutions were made by and for European Americans, and though proclaimed to be based on reason and applicable to all, many non-Europeans did not share in the consensus. Free blacks and emancipated slaves were parts of strong families and communities, had their own churches and rites, and believed in progress and a better day for their people, but they could not feel part of the national community. The pride and confidence of most Americans were hypocrisies to poor sharecroppers in the land of Jim Crow. The native peoples who had been dispossessed of homelands and defeated by the American army constituted another alienated sub-group. Driven into reservations, they lived in impotent rage directed at the numerically and technologically superior settlers, whose beliefs and institutions had defeated and almost annihilated them.

These voices, which today enjoy considerable prominence, should not obscure the fact that most Americans believed in traditional America. It was a fundamental part of their lives, something they believed in and worked for. Many today will see this belief in America (or any country for that matter) as quaint, naive, part of a receding past that people have become a bit too sophisticated to fall for any more. And this may be so. Having established a starting point, imperfect though it may be, the present task is to discern how wars have changed traditional life and put dissenting outlooks into the mainstream.

CHAPTER TWO

Tradition and Modernity
in the Great War Era

*The Great War was perhaps the last to be conceived as taking place within
a seamless, purposeful "history" involving a coherent stream of time running
from past through present to future.*

Paul Fussell, *The Great War and Modern Memory*

*Gatsby believed in the green light, the orgiastic future that year by year recedes
before us. It eluded us then, but that's no matter — tomorrow we will run
faster, stretch out our arms farther. . . . And one fine morning —
So we beat on, boats against the current, borne back ceaselessly into the past.*

F. Scott Fitzgerald, *The Great Gatsby*

By the early twentieth century, there was discontent with America, or at least with
the course it had taken since 1865. In many respects, the history of twentieth-
century America is the ebb and flow of these complaints, in war and peace, as
the country moved into modernity and beyond. The Civil War triggered a burst
of industrialization that led many to believe the nation was becoming cold and
materialist, long-standing principles were giving way, and revered institutions
were in the wrong hands. The experience of World War I amplified many of
these complaints, put others to rest, but introduced new ones. The aftermath
opened the door to modernity, through which some scurried and others were
pushed, until 1929, when many looked back.

Discontent in the Gilded Age

There is a striking passage in Sinclair Lewis's *Main Street*, in which an aging Civil
War veteran looks about his town and suddenly comprehends the changes since
his youth. The old fellow quietly takes stock then runs off wildly, shouting for
God's mercy. The world in which he was raised, for which he fought, and which
had been his source of pride and identity, had all but disappeared. The moral
order of post-Civil War America was falling under the weight of prosperity and
the erosion of certainties. The process was slow and gradual, the realization swift
and devastating.

Similarly, though in a more detached manner, Henry Adams, scion of an illustrious family that included two presidents, disliked the changes since his birth in 1838 under the shadow of Boston State House. Returning in 1904 from a stay abroad, he lamented the country's lurch from an orderly traditional society to a graceless modern one, from "unity" to "multiplicity" as he put it. On his return to New York, he looked at the new city and shuddered:

> The approach [was] more striking than ever — wonderful
> — unlike anything man had ever seen — and like nothing he had
> ever much cared to see. The outline of the city became frantic in
> its effort to explain something that defied meaning. . . . The two-
> thousand-years failure of Christianity roared up from Broadway,
> and no Constantine the Great was in sight.[1]

From the perspectives of a humble old-timer to the descendant of presidents, America had changed too much, too quickly.

The Civil War laid the foundations for an economic boom that changed the country in countless ways. The country had once been guided — politically, economically, and culturally — by long-standing elites, mainly from the Atlantic seaboard. The opening of trans-Appalachian lands and the rising political influence of backwoodsmen delivered a blow to that world; the economic boom begun by the war all but put an end to it. The learning and judgment of old elites had served the country well in a more genteel era, but the power of those who had built the railroads, banks, steel mills, and meatpacking houses now surpassed theirs. Traditional notables receded to secondary, if not tertiary roles in national affairs, or left public life altogether for literary pursuits. Adams withdrew to the study of history, searching for a time of order prior to the advent of multiplicity, and found it in the Middle Ages.

Ostentatious displays of wealth, in architecture and fashion, replaced the staid conservatism of traditional tastes. Houses and attire took on forms that broke from previous patterns. Self-made men, former ferrymen and mechanics, amassed enormous fortunes. Independent craftsmen and farmers found themselves reduced to wage-laborers. Charles Francis Adams, head of the Union Pacific (and brother of Henry), lived in both worlds and found the emerging one and its baronage repugnant: "I have known, and known tolerably well, a good many 'successful' men — 'big' financially — men famous during the last half century; and a less interesting crowd I do not care to encounter. Not one that I have ever known would I care to meet again, either in this world or the next; nor is one of them associated in my mind with the ideas of humor, thought, or refinement."[2]

An older America vied with a new one, neither one having the upper hand.

Henry Adams saw the economic crisis in 1893 settling the issue:

> For a hundred years, between 1793 and 1893, the American
> people had hesitated, vacillated, swayed forward and back,
> between two forces, one simply industrial, the other capitalistic,
> centralizing, and mechanical. In 1893, the issue came on the
> single gold standard, and the majority at last declared itself,
> once for all, in favor of the capitalistic system with all its
> necessary machinery. . . . The rest was question of gear; of
> running machinery; of economy; and involved no disputed
> principle. . . . [T]he whole mechanical consolidation of force . . .
> ruthlessly stamped out the life of the class into which Adams was
> born. . . . [N]othing remained for a historian but to ask — how
> long and how far![3]

It would take many decades to answer the question fully, and we may not be able to answer it yet, but by the turn of the century, many Americans felt it had gone on too long and too far.

Discontent was hardly confined to literary figures; it was rife in the heartland and cities, spawning the populist and progressive movements. Farmers and workers felt endangered by industrial forces loose in the country. The size and power of industrial giants reduced the Jeffersonian ideal of a community of farmers and producers to a quaint musing. Politicians and sharecroppers, journalists and authors, spoke out against manipulated commodity markets that caused global disruptions in food supplies, railroad barons who fixed prices and crushed immigrant communities, and meatpacking plants that lacked basic sanitation.[4] It was all part of an eroding moral and social order, which seemed alarmingly advanced at the time.

For most, affluence was beginning — only beginning — to replace scrimping and saving, toiling to make ends meet, with the enjoyment of leisure and consumer goods without pangs of guilt from religious norms. The work ethic began to slacken, just as the Puritan fathers had warned in scolding sermons. Centuries earlier, Cotton Mather had seen affluence as a sign of divine favor but also feared its consequences: "Away to your *Business*: Lay out your *Strength* in it, put forth your *Skill* for it; Avoid all impertinent Avocations. Laudable *Recreations* may be used now and then: But, I beseech you, Let those Recreations be used for *Sauce*, but not for *Meat*."[5] At the outset of the twentieth century, Mather's warning began to sound like a cranky voice from the past.

Along Lake Shore Drive and Park Avenue there grew a leisure class, which eschewed the practical and reveled in the unnecessary. Even outside privileged enclaves, the work ethic was becoming the pursuit of money — what the old sectaries had called Avarice. The middle classes were lured into consumer lifestyles by department stores that promised a new life of comfort and well-being: "[A]s the flood of goods the factories produced flowed into middle-class households, carrying new amenities, overflowing into Victorian parlors overpacked with gewgaws, the values of thrift, diligence, and self-discipline could no more remain unaffected than could the premise of scarcity."[6] Relaxation and consumption were becoming parts of everyday life.[7]

Many women from the middle classes found that economic circumstances had removed them from the day-to-day economic activity of their counterparts on farms and in urban areas. They attended the finest schools and colleges. Educated and able, they were nonetheless confined to a life of being adornments of middle-class men. They (like many of their descendants in the 1950s) found themselves in a middle ground between the hold of tradition and the uncertainty of a future, above both of which stood an almost universal confidence in male authority, which had attained even more preeminence since the Civil War. Some women formed social movements such as those advocating temperance and women's suffrage, but for the most part they remained in that middle ground.[8]

Public life was becoming increasingly sordid. Clouds of sacredness and myth could no longer hide it. As early as 1880, an anonymously published novel entitled *Democracy* depicted the capital as dominated by cliques, intrigues, and vendettas — an "ocean of corruption." The White House was assuming monarchal trappings. Outside the literary realm, in the big cities, political bosses and corruption ruled the day. It was their machinations that got streetcar systems built, controlled the workings of police forces, and led to mayors cutting ribbons at new bridges. Lincoln Steffens saw the decay becoming too prevalent: "And it's all a moral weakness. The spirit of graft and of lawlessness is the American spirit."[9]

Such discontent is usually seen as the product of economic growth, the ineluctable discarding of old ways and the awkward adoption of new ones. But economic growth, at least in American history, has seldom been independent of military conflict. Each war, from the Revolution to the World Wars, triggered economic expansions, some of which lasted for decades and reshaped the country. The Civil War, in many ways the first modern war, was no exception. Iron foundries, meatpacking plants, and textile mills expanded or sprang up from nowhere in response to army contracts. Though Washington tried to include smaller firms in contracts, it found them inefficient and unreliable, and awarded the lion's share to bigger firms, which used their profits to increase mechanization and buy out rivals. The Union's bond campaigns modernized the banking system, which would serve to fuel postwar growth.[10] By 1864, the Union army was a behemoth, armed and equipped by growing industrial might.

The war no longer entailed maneuver and feint before a decisive battle. It was by 1864 the methodical and ruthless deployment of men and material against an inferior enemy that ground the Confederate armies to dust.[11] Appomattox could not halt the momentum; recessions could only slow it down for a while. The war transformed the country. Bruce Catton put it well: "A singular fact about modern war is that it takes charge. Once begun it has to be carried to its conclusion, and carrying it there sets in motion events that may be beyond men's control. Doing what has to be done to win, men perform acts that alter the very soil in which society's roots are nourished."[12] The war pushed the country, unintentionally, reluctantly, but irreversibly, into the industrial age and the beginning of modernity.

The war also contributed to the declining moral climate that many lamented. Prosperity itself brings temptation to cut corners and elide basic principles, as Mather had warned. Perhaps more importantly, victory created an atmosphere of confidence and sanctimony that made the moral order less restraining. In the years following the war, the nation, at least outside the South, was exultant. Its trials were over, the Union preserved. Grant, Sherman, and Sheridan entered the pantheon of the nation's military heroes alongside Washington, Decatur, and Jackson. And when the jubilant parades down Pennsylvania Avenue and Main Street ended, and the last regiments furled their colors and stood down, people returned to their daily lives, more confident and assured of their righteousness and place in heaven than ever before. As Merle Curti expressed it, "the old sense of destiny confirmed by a new sense of military and economic competence."[13]

After a few decades, as the Great Event receded into the past and prosperity reworked the nation, many wondered if the noble effort hadn't had regrettable consequences. Carl Schurz, a soldier and statesman, saw the war's idealism degenerate over the years into materialism: "Is it really true that our war turned the ambitions of our people into the channels of lofty enthusiasm and aspirations and devotion to high ideals? Has it not rather left behind it an era of absorbing greed of wealth, a marked decline of ideal aspirations?"[14] H. L. Mencken thought the Civil War had produced a sense of presumptuousness and infallibility that led to hypocrisy and unctuous insincerity, which he called (alluding to a Dickens character) "pecksniffery."[15]

Robert Penn Warren said this postwar spirit was governed by "the doctrine of the Treasury of Virtue." The Civil War, he wrote at the time of its Centennial, was a

> consciously undertaken crusade so full of righteousness that there
> is enough surplus stored in Heaven, like the deeds of the saints,
> to take care of all small failings and oversights of the descendants

40

of the crusaders, certainly unto the present generation. From the start America had had adequate baggage of self-righteousness and phariseeism, but with the Civil War came grace abounding, for the least of the sinners.[16]

As the forces of industrialism raced through the country, Americans could invoke the Treasury of Virtue against all critics and remain assured of their righteousness. The people who had crushed the serpent and abolished slavery could now and then ignore laws and norms. Religious strictures could be bent, rendered into rationalizations, reworked until they had little to do with original meanings. The Treasury of Virtue allowed Americans to feel assured of their place in heaven, listen less to their consciences, and marvel as the economy expanded.

The decades between 1865 and 1917 saw the country take its first steps toward modernity, but traditional patterns still predominated. Literature expressed concerns with big business, corruption, and the plight of women. Populists and progressives mounted spirited but short-lived political movements, before blending into the main political parties and going into dormancy. But neither in rhetoric nor in policy were these voices hostile to the basic principles of America. On the contrary, they saw themselves as embodiments of traditional America, its defenders from industrial Goliaths, the faithful believers of Jefferson's ideal of equal farmers and producers.[17]

THE EXPERIENCE OF THE GREAT WAR

Ill-ease with moral strictures, small-town confinements, and much of traditional life became more pronounced and widespread after World War I. Leisure and consumerism became important parts of people's lives. After the Great War, the old world no longer made sense, and a new one had yet to take hold. The past and future were no longer certain. Social change took on a new dynamism, free from old restraints. Louis Brandeis observed (with a good measure of overstatement), "Europe was devastated by war, we by the aftermath."[18]

Myth and Authority on Trial

To understand the impact of the Great War, the importance of war romance prior to 1918 must be considered. War mythology had been a mainstay of the Republic since the Revolution and the War of 1812, providing many of the nation's leaders, beliefs, and symbols. The triumph of 1865 added to this. Various elites, northern and southern, wrapped themselves in the mantle of military glory and built careers and fortunes upon their service in what, in time, became remembered as a noble cause. Military service was virtually a prerequisite for high elected office until the turn of the century. Every president from Grant to McKinley (except for Cleveland) had been an officer in the Union army, all but McKinley had been generals. The ideal of America was once again imbued with victory, more so than ever before.[19]

War romance pervaded American life. Town celebrations honored veterans of the war a half century after the Confederacy fell. Memorial Day came into being to honor the fallen of both sides. Literature abounded with stories of great deeds, youths finding courage, and the rising glory of the Republic. Every authority figure, social norm, and institution assumed greater prestige by invoking memories of Shiloh and Gettysburg. The Union celebrated for a generation; the South joined in by commemorating a noble but lost cause. Later American conflicts were relatively uncostly, often spectacular, and always victorious. The drive West and the demise of Spanish tyranny in Cuba and the Philippines were seen as beneficial to all, political and military leaders as wise, far-sighted, and generous to defeated foes. Beliefs and institutions emerged with enhanced prestige and sacredness.

The romanticization of the Civil War, and of war in general, became an ordering principle. As the country became increasingly materialistic and hedonistic, veterans looked back on their war years, somewhat selectively, as a contrasting epoch of selflessness and honor.[20] Oliver Wendell Holmes, wounded three times, left for dead at Antietam, was reluctant to discuss the war in the decade or so following the war. Later in life, he spoke of it proudly and romantically:

> I do not know the meaning of the universe. But in the midst of
> doubt, in the collapse of creeds, there is one thing I do not doubt,
> that no man who lives in the same world with most of us can
> doubt, and that is that the faith is true and adorable which leads
> a soldier to throw away his life in obedience to a blindly accepted
> duty, in a cause which he little understands, in a plan of campaign
> of which he has no notion, under tactics of which he does not see
> the use.[21]

General Sherman once warned schoolboys that war is hell, but he later saw it in Arthurian terms:

> Now my friends, there is nothing in life more beautiful than the
> soldier. A knight errant with steel casque, lance in hand, has always
> commanded the admiration of men and women. The modern
> soldier is his legitimate successor. . . . Now the truth is we fought
> the holiest fight ever fought on God's earth.[22]

America was not an empire, and bread and circuses were not instruments of rule, but here it had its equivalent of the Roman adage romanticizing death in war, *Dulce et decorum est pro patria mori*, and of the British verse, "Theirs is not to reason why . . . ." War was glorified as a rite of passage into manhood, the true test of virility and patriotism, a safeguard against excessive materialism, and a sure means of winning the hand of a fair lady. Of course, none of this would have occurred to anyone at Shiloh or Gettysburg, but over the years, cultures, as well as many aging veterans, have uncanny ways of creating romantic memories of war.

In 1917, Americans found themselves drawn into the conflict then raging in Europe for three years. It went against common sense and provincialism, but the idealist exhortations of political and religious leaders prevailed. It would strengthen the forces of democracy, enhance the prestige of the country, and make the world a better a place. Washington, mindful of Civil War draft riots, feared unrest when the conscription system was put into effect, but the intervening years had glorified military service and the draft went smoothly. Millions of youths, volunteers and inductees, enthusiastically went off. At train stations and embarkation points, aging Civil War veterans, blue and gray, cheered the boys on, waved flags, and seemed to promise a quick path to manhood and glory.[23]

World War I, unlike the recent conflict with Spain, was neither splendid nor little. The war ended the days when individual valor, inspired charges, and spirited athleticism could determine a battle's outcome, who won and who lost, who lived and who died. Visions of glorious charges across verdant fields and capturing the foe's colors did not last long in front of machine-guns and poison gas. Bull Run and Antietam were distant events, so sentimentalized over the years by poems, picnics, and parades, that their horror had been obscured by a fog of myth and cant. But Chateau-Thierry and the Argonne were immediate, appallingly close, and beyond cultural capacities to soften and romanticize. Americans did not arrive over there in strength until early 1918, but by autumn over one-hundred thousand lay dead. One doughboy, exhibiting the alienation and bitterness of many of his generation, noted the disjuncture between official pronouncements and frontline realities:

> It will never do to let the people at home find out the truth about
> this war. They've been fed on bunk until they'd never believe
> anything that didn't sound like a monk's story of the Crusades.
> Every time I get a paper from home, I either break into a loud
> laugh or get mad.[24]

The people at home never saw the war as he did, but they did see the casualty lists, and many recognized a few names. Officials had deceived them — and for what? The sacred view of war, in which the nation had prided itself since 1865, lost much of its appeal.[25]

The impact was far greater in Europe, where war myths based on Jena, Waterloo, and Sedan had long been sources of legitimacy for kings and nobles, and where casualties were far greater.[26] Defeat brought down established beliefs and institutions across the continent. Russia and Germany collapsed into anarchy and revolution. Britain and France were badly wounded but managed to limp ahead. As Churchill put it, "a death knell rang in the ears of the victors, even in their hour of triumph."[27] Kings and nobles could no longer invoke the old way of life based on tradition and chivalry. Old moral truths that had governed for centuries lost their hold and were now referred to ironically or sarcastically.[28] Literary forms, whose meter and imagery once graced paeans to Mars, now turned on him and the nations over which he had reigned. Wilfred Owen wrote just before the end of the war, just before his death:

> To children ardent for some desperate glory,
> The old Lie: *Dulce et decorum est pro patria mori.*[29]

And Rudyard Kipling, who had romanticized the thin red line and heroic skirmishes on the Empire's frontiers, felt quite differently after his son was killed in the war. Burdened by guilt, he reasoned why:

> If any question why we died,
> Tell them, because our fathers lied.[30]

Siegfried Sassoon threw his Military Cross into the Channel, an act unthinkable to one of Wellington's lieutenants, but an understandable one to one of Kitchener's.

Pessimism replaced the confidence that reigned only a few years earlier. Toynbee and Spengler saw the centuries-long rise of Western Civilization as having stalled and begun to decline. Toynbee surveyed the history of the world from Mesopotamia to the present, and concluded that war was the principal destroyer of civilization:

> Militarism has been by far the commonest cause of the breakdowns
> of civilizations during the four or five millennia which have
> witnessed the score or so of breakdowns that are on record up to
> the present date. . . . In this suicidal process, the entire social fabric
> becomes fuel to feed the devouring flame in the brazen bosom of
> Molech.[31]

Military success — "the intoxication of victory" — has been an important step on a path that leads but to the grave:

> Our survey has revealed the suicidal importunity of a sword that
> has been sheathed after having once tasted blood. The polluted
> weapon will not rust in its scabbard, but must ever be itching to
> leap out again — as though the disembodied spirit of the would-
> be-saviour who first had recourse to this sinister instrument could
> now find no rest until his sin of seeking salvation along a path of
> crime had been atoned for by the agency of the very weapon which
> he once so perversely used.[32]

Ezra Pound saw Europe as a "botched civilization." To T. S. Eliot, the splendor of the continent had become a wasteland, its Fisher King mortally wounded, no Grail in sight, none believed in any more. A half century earlier, the loss of six hundred on a disastrous charge could be mitigated, even turned into a part of war romance. But sixty thousand British soldiers were killed or wounded one morning on the Somme, advancing only a few hundred yards, and not even Tennyson could have turned that into an ode to king and country.[33] During the war, Freud observed a "compulsion to repeat" in war trauma patients, and began to suspect a dark force in the human mind, a death instinct, affected human behavior.[34]

Malaise was not confined to literary figures. The same message was conveyed, less artfully but more powerfully, in the blank stares of millions of disillusioned and maimed veterans. Religious and moral beliefs declined:

> Life was less than cheap; it was thrown away. The religious teaching
> that the body was the temple of the Holy Ghost could mean little
> or nothing to those who saw it mutilated and destroyed in millions
> by Christian nations engaged in war. All moral standards were held
> for a short moment and irretrievably lost.[35]

A way of life had been undermined:

> For many, Europe died in the valley of the Somme, its beauty
> enhanced in retrospect but its corruption final. Beside the horror
> of an ancient civilization destroying its young, the daily life of the
> family, religion, and career, inspired by the old ideals, had become
> a macabre jest, recognized only by the surrealists.[36]

Gloom spread from literary elites into mainstream culture, into popular forms of entertainment, the conversations of average people, and into schools. Simone Weil noted that in interwar France it was widely thought that "the schools at the beginning of the century had formed a generation for victory, and that those after 1918 turned out a beaten one."[37]

The Great War's role in European social change is a subject for another study, and attention should return to less dramatic effects across the Atlantic. America emerged chastened and disillusioned, but able to go on far better than could Britain or France, to say nothing of Germany and Russia. We had in some sense won, and crowds cheered the returning boys, but there was a sense of lost times, disenchantment, and betrayal. It was more pronounced among cultural elites than in American Legion halls, but Americans entered a new era of change and reappraisal. Trends idling before the war got a green light.

New forms of literature emerged. Henry Adams's *Education*, describing America's unhappy but unstoppable transformation, was published in 1918 and struck a chord with a younger generation newly estranged from their upbringing. It remained a bestseller for over a year. *Civilization in the United States,* a critical and sometimes caustic assessment of American life was also popular.[38] The war brought about or spread new critical styles of history, indisposed to the romantic styles of older history and recent presidential orations. Historians rejected Wilson's justification for intervention. Germany was not solely to blame for the war; decades of diplomatic maneuvering and militaristic cultures were guilty. America had hardly been neutral in the early years; it had been arming Britain and France. Intervention came to ensure repayment of vast sums that New York banks had extended to the Entente powers. Corporations, banks, and other diabolical parts of American capitalism had conspired to reap huge profits. A young intellectual, Randolph Bourne, saw the exhortations to go to war as lies put forth by an official propaganda mill. War led to the manipulation of the "herd" and an ominous growth of state power, which was used to squash dissent.[39]

Mencken, as might be expected, went further, ridiculing virtually every aspect of authority and tradition. In an unrelentingly cutting essay, in which he compared American elites to the recent enemy, he asserted that America had been governed by "moral Junkers." In the decades after the Civil War, they had become increasingly arrogant and intolerant, adopting a domination mentality (*Herrenmoral*), and directed a passive public on a course of imperial expansion (*Wille zur Macht*). The common folk, he went on, had adopted a slave mentality (*Sklavenmoral*): "Their moral passion spent most of its force in self-accusing, self-denial and self-scourging. They began by howling their sins from the mourners' bench; they came to their end, many of them, in the supreme immolation of battle."[40]

It was the beginning of the end for a charmed relationship between government and governed, as well as for mythic history in the tradition of Bancroft, Parkman, or for that matter, Woodrow Wilson. Reflecting the spirit of the time, and embarrassed by their profession's recent foray into propaganda, historians began to debunk the romanticism surrounding the past, which had played no small part in the country's eagerness to go to war. The concept of historical objectivity came into question, if not disrepute, opening the door to new historical interpretations.[41] This "new history" actually began just before the war, when Charles Beard argued that the framers of the Constitution had been motivated by self-interest rather than religious or philosophical principles. The Constitution was an instrument of upper-class domination, designed to reduce the influence of the lower sort in the new Republic. Madison and Hamilton had no more moral purpose than did Morgan and Rockefeller.[42]

Beard was severely (though unfairly) criticized as a Marxist bent on fomenting unrest amongst the working classes. Religious and literary figures attacked him as well. A midwestern newspaper expressed its outrage in a headline:

SCAVENGERS, HYENA-LIKE, DESECRATE THE GRAVES
OF THE DEAD PATRIOTS WE REVERE[43]

After 1918, however, voices of patriotic rectitude were less confident, and an increasingly literate public, jaded by recent experience, was open to new historical views. A generation of new historians, many of them colleagues and disciples of Beard, who had come of age during the Great War, looked back on the past and revolutionized the field of history. The lofty ideals of august figures were exposed as having deluded the public, and often tricked them into wars from which only the wealthy benefited. The founders broke from England only when it seemed that further association hindered the growth of commerce. America had built an empire on the continent, all the while developing any number of high-minded rationalizations. The Civil War resulted not from abolitionism or any moral issue, but from a conflict between manufacturers favoring protective tariffs and planters preferring free trade. Alternately, scholars saw the war as the result of blundering politicians.[44]

Literature formed the vanguard of the attack on traditional beliefs. The effort was most passionate among a generation of young writers, best exemplified by John Dos Passos, many of whom had once been inspired by the war's idealism. A contemporary said of him: "The excitement which Dos Passos seems to have felt when he conceived of war as a great adventure and crusade has apparently been transformed . . . into an immense energy of denunciation."[45] His *Three Soldiers* tells of naive youths, initially confident in victory and glory, but dehumanized by military brutality, then pushed into the slaughter. One embittered soldier kills a sergeant with a fragmentation grenade. In *Company K*, William March attacks war mythology as well as government officialdom by parodying a letter of condolence:

Your son, Francis, died needlessly at Belleau Wood. You will be
interested to hear that at the time of his death he was crawling
with vermin and weak from diarrhea. . . . A piece of shrapnel hit
him and he died in agony, slowly. . . . He lived three full hours
screaming and cursing. . . . He had nothing to hold onto, you see:
He had learned long ago that what he had been taught to believe
by you, his mother, who loved him, under the meaningless names
of honor, courage, patriotism, were all lies.[46]

Faulkner and E. E. Cummings also weighed in with denunciations of the old
mythology of war and manhood, as well as much that had surrounded it. As Paul
Fussell notes, the language of war changed. Romantic, feudal usages gave way to
realist, modern ones.[47] The novels of this disaffected generation were widely read
by an increasingly literate public eager to make sense of the events in Europe and
uncomfortable with the residual war cant in popular culture.[48]

Europe's disillusionment found numerous literary voices that became popular
in America. The poems of Owen, Sassoon, and Eliot, as well as the novels of
Remarque, Zweig, and Manning, found audiences here.[49] The postwar mood
was ably captured in Somerset Maugham's *The Razor's Edge,* in which the
characters seek new forms of spirituality in eastern mysticism, or indulge in
self-destructive pursuits, or become absorbed in materialist quests. The newly
burgeoning cinema presented audiences with works of postwar disillusion in
The Big Parade, What Price Glory?, and of course *All Quiet on the Western Front*
— the latter, in conjunction with the book, helping to form an international
peace movement.[50]

Assault on Puritanism

Of all the basic influences on the American mind, surely one of the most
important was Puritanism. It pervaded every aspect of national life, from day-
to-day routines to matters of state. Complaints against Puritanism had begun
to emerge before 1918, but the experience of the war sharpened and popularized
them. Prewar discontent found voice in Van Wyck Brooks, whose *The Wine
of the Puritans* (1908) criticized much of traditional America, including its
religious foundation. Brooks suggested that America, while undoubtedly a great
civilization, was, alas, a one-dimensional one. Its focus on logic and self-denial had
produced industry and wealth, but at the expense of creativity and spontaneity.
Puritanism had molded the American "to feel suspiciously toward ritual, pleasure,
light-heartedness — all the things which an established civilization can support,
as symbols of opposition to the stern economic world. . . . He doesn't believe
in impulses and intuitions, because they interfere with the silent, regular and

inexorable grinding of the machine."[51] There was too little appreciation of art, beauty, spirituality, and the enjoyment of life; too much emphasis on getting ahead, making money, and becoming cogs in the machine. Soon after settling in the United States, immigrants lost their warm spontaneity and lively customs. College students learned only how to become parts of stale, dehumanizing processes, not how to raise important questions and search for meaning in life.

Such criticism found only a limited audience prior to the war, but after 1918 it reached a broader part of the public. Puritan strictures had been mobilized and sent off to France; they returned wounded and unsure of themselves. A Calvinist president sought to impose his strict principles on the slackers of the world, but accomplished nothing. His simplistic division of the world into good and evil brought on blunder and slaughter. Unwillingness to compromise led to failed peace negotiations and the triumph of the old ways that brought about the war in the first place. Religious thinkers reinterpreted scripture and orchestrated public sentiments to suit the purposes of the state.[52]

The Puritan critique was sharper and more prevalent in literature. Mencken, seeing no sacredness around the presidency or the dead, mocked Wilson as "the Archangel Woodrow," "the late Messiah," and "the deceased Moses."[53] The rigidly moral figure was now depicted as pompous and fraudulent. George Santayana's *The Last Puritan* (1935) portrays the life of a young Brahmin, who comes to see through the haze. He learns that his father had committed a murder in his youth, and though justice was said to be blind, family money and influence covered it up. He travels to Europe and discovers a world of sensuality, art, and new lifestyles that his upbringing had condemned. In England, he sees the Puritan order on the wane, its last believers killed on the Western Front.

For Mencken, Puritanism was from the outset a misfortune; the Massachusetts colony was governed by "sour gatherings of hell-crazed deacons."[54] Puritanism constituted the basis for a domination mentality; its sanctimonious elders became the "moral Junkers," ordering a subservient herd on quests for national power. One author saw his generation's duty in ending the harsh religion's hold: "Puritanism is the great enemy. The crusade against puritanism is the only crusade with which free individuals are justified in allying themselves."[55]

Progressive historians gave the most systematic analysis of the role of Puritanism in American history, concluding that it was a "misfortune," an obstacle to political progress that had to be broken down. Behind every high-minded principle lay self-interest and disdain for the masses. Vernon Parrington asserted that misanthropic Puritan forebears had instilled in us their dark view of human nature: essentially wicked, needful of constant supervision by harsh secular and religious authority. The Puritan colonies were "tyrannies" that opposed the menace of egalitarianism at every turn: "The Saints must not have their hands tied by majority votes." It was for the better that Calvinism failed in Geneva and England, for in New England, "by virtue of its rigid suppression of free inquiry, Calvinism long lingered out a harsh existence, grotesque and illiberal to the last."[56]

Beginnings of the Mass Leisure Class

Many of the social changes of the period came from the combination of weakening moral strictures and increasing affluence among the public — both products of the war. The boom of the war years brought consumer goods and leisure time to large portions of the population, vaulting America into a period of new orientations — what Leuchtenberg called "the perils of prosperity." People began to enjoy a measure of the good life previously confined to privileged upper strata. Dire warnings by religious authorities against sloth and leisure became less relevant to a prosperous, modernizing country, as unlikely to be heeded as another call to arms against the Hun. Disillusionment with war served as a green light, signaling all to go ahead with material pursuits and self-indulgence.[57]

As prosperity continued, a shift in values took place. Since the days of the early colonies, when settlers eked out a living in the wilderness, Americans valued thrift, parsimony, saving — denying themselves enjoyment of leisure and luxury, either because it was simply beyond their reach or because it was thought wiser to save. By the 1920s, productivity and wealth began to wear down the ethic of thrift. With pay higher and workdays shorter, abundance and leisure came to the general public. The economy had long depended on thrift to expand, but now things were turned upside down. An economist warned that "People may ruin themselves by saving instead of spending."[58] Bankers complained that farmers were taking out their savings to buy automobiles.[59] Once considered dangerous, even a sign of failure, debt was now an indicator that one had risen from humble origins and entered the middle classes. Success in one's calling depended less on one's character — thrift, discipline, and honesty — and more on a pleasing personality, the ability to persuade, sell, and induce others to part with their cash. As a later salesman put it, success came from a shoeshine and a smile.

Americans, more the young than the old, began to enjoy the fruits of prosperity. They bought, borrowed, and bought more, laying the foundations of a new leisure society.[60] Tastes in clothing, housewares, and the like were no longer circumscribed by local customs or what the family could make. Newspaper and radio ads made new things attractive and irresistible, as though nothing could be more normal than buying, as though nothing could be more old-fashioned than saving. The new advertisement industry learned from wartime propaganda efforts that the public's thought and behavior could be channeled in desired directions. Radio and movies pushed out the old self-improvement societies; jazz began to replace folk melodies; the automobile introduced change to slow-paced, self-contained towns.[61]

The Great War introduced changes in the lives of women. For decades, many women had been pressing for opportunities to work in more areas, for access to education, and for the right to vote, but made little progress. The war forced matters. Labor shortages brought women into the industrial workplace and government bureaus in large numbers, making their abilities and importance to the national effort clear to other women and a few men. After the war, recognition of their efforts mingled with the hope that feminine influence in public life might weaken militarism and make the world more peaceful.[62] Traditional arguments against women's suffrage were less forceful in a period of deflated male authority, and in this context women won the right to vote in 1919. In the following decade, amid change and uncertainty, many women became more independent, assertive, and sexually aware.[63]

The interwar years saw the beginning of youth culture. Previously, the ken of young people had been limited to the local community, rural and urban. Few had any opportunity or interest in looking beyond. A Sears-Roebuck catalog, a visiting relative, a promising son returning from college — these were exotic contacts with the larger country. But now, radio and film presented young people with an array of new experiences and sensations. Adolescents — the term "teenager" hadn't been coined yet — adopted faddish styles of dress and rapidly learned slang, linguistically setting themselves apart from older generations. Old styles of courtship on the front porch, never far from watchful adult attention, gave way to youth clubs, automobile rides, and consumer-based outings called "dating."[64] The Lynds' study of Muncie, Indiana, noted a trend toward more sexual experimentation, with youth quick to see that automobiles provided a handy means of evading adult supervision.[65]

Weakening Religion

The disaster of the Great War led some to fall back on traditional forms of religion. Others, resentful of the role of traditional religion in war romance, explored new forms of religion, mysticism, and popular forms of psychology. The more literary read Freud and saw religion as an illusion or paged through Jessie Weston and suspected it was the residue of primitive cults. But most simply felt the hold of religion slip away and indulged in the consumerism the war boom made possible.[66]

Indeed, consumerism appropriated some of the language and imagery of religion. Henry Ford averred that "machinery is the new Messiah;" Calvin Coolidge that "the man who builds a factory builds a temple, the man who works there worships there." Bruce Barton, the father of advertising, preached that Jesus "picked up twelve men from the bottom ranks of business and forged them into an organization that conquered the world," in part thanks to Jesus' parables: "the most powerful advertisements of all time."[67] Such expressions, which a few decades earlier would have been widely condemned as blasphemy, convey something about the cult of prosperity as well as the changing religious norms of the period. Pursuit of leisure came at the expense of religious duties. Ministers noted a decline in church attendance by automobile owners or members of sports and social clubs. Leisure was pushing aside religion and duty. Accordingly, many churches became less rigid and more like recreation clubs.[68]

The consciences of Sunday motorists were eased by popular reappraisals of religion. Invocations of religion in 1917 had been intemperate works of propaganda that harmed both political and religious authority. The postwar mind knew that our allies were not blameless victims, Belgian babies had not been impaled on German bayonets, and no war like that could have been God's will. Postwar religion also suffered from a streak of hucksterism, or at least preexisting trends became more noticed. Revivalism had once been based on genuine spirituality and sincere evangelists, but by the 1920s it had taken on some of the era's methods and goals, resulting in crassness, exploitiveness, and profitmaking. Billy Sunday mixed Christianity with lower-class resentments and pugnacity. Aimee Semple McPherson's tent revivals drew big crowds and large profits until her personal indiscretions invited unwanted comparisons to Mary Magdalene's earlier career. Sinclair Lewis lampooned evangelists in his characters Mike Monday and Elmer Gantry. They were unscrupulous opportunists, more akin to snake-oil salesmen than to latter-day apostles. Mencken thought that "any literate plowhand, if the Holy Spirit inflames him, is thought to be fit to preach." His theological training was held in a "single building in its bare pasture lot, and its faculty of half-idiot pedagogues and brokendown preachers."[69] Scandal and satire assuaged the Sunday motorists' pangs of conscience and allowed them to motor happily down the road, perhaps even past the church.[70]

Declining norms led to increased crime rates. The First World War, adumbrating greater changes during the Second, altered the social structure and moral environment. Mobilization led to sizable population movements and dispersals of neighborhoods and towns, reducing moral pressures that communities had exerted. A looser-knit social setting was emerging. Millions of young men were uprooted from their upbringings and exposed to the soldierly world of hard-drinking and coarse revelry — experiences that, upon demobilization, were not without effect on society at large.[71] After 1918, rates of murder, robbery, fraud, and prostitution shot up. Sexual awareness increased, too, as widely different material from popular notions of Freudian theory to racy movies found audiences. Decrying the plummeting morality of the nation, ministers and politicians pressed for censorship of the mass media and new laws to restore the old order. Many crimes became federal offenses. Movies had to conform to a code of morality.[72]

Criticism of consumer society came from non-traditional sources as well. Ministers railed against defiling the Sabbath, while Sinclair Lewis and H. L. Mencken fired off secular jeremiads against the rise of Babbitry and the Booboisie. The 1920s, they lamented, was the decade of amoral egotists, who, casually or ruthlessly, pursued their business, unrestrained by community or personal principles. Less interested in the offerings of cultural elites, people now plunged into mass-market writings, which were churned out in great numbers — "mush for the multitude," as Mencken put it in a moment of alliteration. Americans still professed to be religious, but they were becoming more secular and egocentric. Church attendance provided the appearance of propriety, as one might decorate a drawing room with a piano that no one played.[73]

The Small Town Reconsidered

Small towns enjoyed a sacred position in traditional America. They were communitarian nursery that taught virtue, honor, and steadfastness. They gave the nation its presidents, captains of industry, and inventors. William Jennings Bryan and countless other politicians proclaimed that American civilization rested on the sturdy shoulders of small towns, and that without them it would fall. Popular culture once abounded with tales of earnest youth, reared in idyllic towns, working hard and making their mark in the world.

Critics of the small town were not unknown before the Great War. One of the first was Edgar Lee Masters (1869–1950), who grew up in rural Illinois — Lincoln country. His *Spoon River Anthology* (1915) is unsparingly critical of small-town life, attacking every sentiment ever attached to it. In a series of short poems, the deceased of Spoon River speak out. With more candor than they ventured in life, they voice their discontent, despair, and delusions. A few express regret for dying for their country in the Civil War. Referring to the inscription on his tombstone, one character wonders what *Dulce et decorum est pro patria mori* means. Others lament hidden shames and infidelities, or confess that greed had been their main motivation. Life wounds and confines, until youthful ideals become hypocrisy and cynicism. Only two characters seem to have been happy. A blind girl extols the decency of human nature; but readers learn her blindness was caused by a venereal disease her father contracted from a prostitute. A scholar speaks proudly of his father's guidance; readers soon learn, though he never did, that his mother was a servant his father raped. Behind every myth there is an unseemly or tragic reality. Toward the end, we see a few who found a measure of meaning in life

— oddly for the time, through eastern religion and philosophy.

Discontent with small towns was rife in the new era, which one historian called "the debunking period."[74] To a new generation, it was better to be from a small town than to be in one. Many bases of rural community had weakened, if not disappeared. Threats of attack and lawlessness had once bound townspeople together, but with the closing of the frontier, militias and posses faded into folk tales and tall tales. Wartime prosperity brought a four-fold increase in farm machinery, reducing the need for mutual help in planting and harvesting.[75] New fortunes were made during the war, eclipsing the wealth of older notables. Long-standing residents left, entering the service or seeing opportunities in cities. In 1920, for the first time, urban dwellers outnumbered rural ones. In the next decade, six million people left the countryside for the city.[76] Community composition changed markedly and rapidly. Small towns no longer limited tastes and expectations; radio and magazines exposed the prairie to new, fast-paced urban life. In comparison, towns seemed dull, confining, incapable of further growth. The complaint was echoed in popular literature. Sinclair Lewis's *Winesburg Ohio* and Sherwood Anderson's *Main Street* showed the town as stifling, close-minded, and petty, its homely patterns dreadful mummery. Children fortunate enough to attend college or find better pay in the city left and hoped never to return.[77]

Debunking small-town life came mainly from urban or urbanizing writers, often influenced by the impact of war or a college education. Their creativity burst out of Springfield and headed for Chicago, bolted from Sauk Centre and beat a path for New York. They could no longer understand anyone who did not share their cosmopolitan outlook. Accordingly, it is important not to overstate change in the towns. There was no mass migration to the city, no catastrophic economic or moral collapse, no boarded-up windows and graffiti-covered walls on Main Street. Despite the message of literature, most townspeople stayed and lived contentedly, though with less of the old romance. But there was the lingering appeal of urban life promising better pay, greater opportunity, and fewer restraints. Many would occasionally look into the distance in a moment of reflection and wonder if life wasn't passing them by.[78]

The Family

By the late nineteenth century, the family was becoming less important as an economic unit. Family farms were still quite common, but in the cities and towns businesses were growing and centralizing, reducing the importance of small businesses. Changes in domestic life accelerated after the war. The hold of tradition weakened, and divorce rates rose. Prosperity reduced the need for parents and children to devote themselves to scrimping and saving. They could begin to relax and enjoy a part, maybe just a small part, of the lifestyles shown in magazines and movies.

But leisure activities of young and old seldom coincided. Each generation pursued its own form of recreation. The advertising world, seeing the weakening of the family and higher divorce rates, proclaimed that the automobile would counter this troubling social trend:

> Holding the family together is with many families one of the strongest arguments that can be advanced in these days when the divorce mill is grinding overtime. . . . It is an argument that has sold thousands of cars and will continue to sell tens of thousand more, even if salesmen never mention it. Any force that makes stronger the family ties is bound to be a potent force; it is bound to be an enduring force. With the middle classes it is a very strong force.[79]

Disconcerting though it is to challenge the veracity of advertising, and to suspect the industry of less than altruistic motives, the evidence suggests the automobile's effects on the family were different. Increased mobility simply allowed children and parents to spend leisure time away from each other, often quite far away. Family evenings together and supervision of courtship were less common.[80]

Paternal authority declined along with most other forms of authority after 1918. Traditional fathers were seen as out of date, stultifying, and unable to accept change. Youth culture made inroads into family solidarity, but was not an alternative to family life, nor was it yet cynical or hostile to it. Prosperity and cynicism raised the importance of the individual and reduced that of traditional senses of family duty.[81] Many younger people moved away from their families, either upon returning from France, or on seeing greater opportunity in the city. Faith in progress had always had material aspects — getting ahead, obtaining land, acquiring a few consumer items from a mail-order catalog — but religious freedom, education, and civic advancement had been present too, and had been more important. But this changed, and progress came to mean simply better pay, a house or a bigger one, a Ford, and so on and so on. It also came to mean letting go of the old and grabbing hold of the new. Higher meaning receded to the back of the mind, where it might nag but could no longer govern.[82]

Despite all this dynamism and discontent, political life was conservative, more so than before 1917. With energies devoted to the war, progressivism took a back seat, a phenomenon that Franklin Roosevelt would later know well and encapsulate in his "Dr Win the War" remark. Vilified before the war as ruthless exploiters and dangerous monsters, big business emerged with a better public image. They were not the patriarchal benefactors of Gilded Age sentiment, and though some thought that Wall Street devils had started the war, most admitted that large corporations, by churning out ships, planes, and weapons for the doughboys, had proved themselves important parts of the nation, and so merited respect. Economic growth set in motion during the war continued well after it. Factories expanded and churned out consumer goods. Farmers benefited from unprecedented demand for foodstuffs.[83] The system was working fine.

The war saw a decline in the idealism upon which progressive politics had relied. Wilson wanted to make the world safe for democracy and professed noble principles; theologians invoked Christian duty to mankind; and other honored authorities promised glory. However, as the peace negotiations played out in Versailles, old-regime politics demonstrated remarkable persistence. Economic privileges were established, provinces traded hands, and overseas territories were carved up. The estate of the recently deceased sick man went through a dubious probate, where estranged relatives in London and Paris became benefactors. One American statesman left in disgust and headed for the Riviera "to watch the world go to hell in a handbasket." A British officer observed, "After 'the war to end all war' they seem to have been pretty successful in Paris at making a 'Peace to end Peace.'"[84]

In less than a year, the idealism of 1917 seemed naive and manipulative, quaint prose from an era the war had closed. The experience of the war "was itself profoundly corrupting, for it transformed citizens into cynics, filled free men with self-loathing and drove millions into privacy, apathy, and despair."[85] Americans no longer wanted energetic administrations seeking to right all wrongs and end all injustices. They wished to be left alone, to return to everyday life. Bryan and Roosevelt were replaced by Coolidge and Harding.

The war, then, changed the country. While much of the nation felt fairly comfortable as they drove away from traditional life, there were elements of unease, regret, and hysteria. Concern over change manifested itself in anti-immigration frenzies, the resurgence of the Ku Klux Klan, opposition to Darwinism, and Prohibition — all short-lived efforts to preserve the past or some conception of it.[86] But moderate voices, including some who had taken part in the revelry, felt that change was too fast, directionless, and reckless. As the 1920s came to a close, the indulgence had become quite advanced, in some quarters dangerously so. Suicide rates, which had declined during the war, went up fifty percent in the decade after 1918.[87] Fitzgerald saw the best minds of his generation damaged by the green light:

> By this time contemporaries of mine had begun to disappear into
> the dark maw of violence. A classmate killed his wife and himself
> on Long Island, another tumbled "accidentally" from a skyscraper

in Philadelphia, another purposely from a skyscraper in New York. One was killed in a speak-easy in Chicago; another was beaten to death in a speak-easy in New York and crawled home to the Princeton Club to die; still another had his skull crushed by a maniac's axe in an insane asylum where he was confined. These are not catastrophes that I went out of my way to look for — these were my friends; moreover, these things happened not during the depression but during the boom.[88]

Fitzgerald sensed an impending fall, a "crack-up" following a long joyride. The end came, not with a revivalist movement or totalitarian political party, but with a crash. People looked around at the debris and felt confused and defenseless. Many turned backward.

The Great Depression

While many Americans rushed into the modern world, many of the elderly saw great folly, even sin, in it. The nation's value system had been tossed aside, and dire consequences would surely follow. However, few would listen as long as jobs were plentiful, pay was good, and average people could make a buck on Wall Street. The Depression, the one still capitalized, changed all that, seemingly irreversibly. To many whose outlook was still shaped by religion, it was a Judgment intended to return a sinful people from wickedness and idolatry.[89] The downturn brought on a return to parts of traditional life, but also to a weakening of others.

Americans had endured depressions in the 1870s and 1890s, but none like the one beginning with the Crash of '29. Fortunes and savings vanished. Margin calls forced frenzied selling of stock, then luxuries and necessities. Factories closed and unemployment shot up from four to twenty-five percent. Natural calamities combined to form an almost preternatural phenomenon. Droughts and plagues of locusts struck the plains. Dust storms kicked up topsoil and deposited it far away in New York and Philadelphia, even on ships hundreds of miles out to sea. The faces of those begging in cities or making their way across the country looking for work show hunger, desperation, and fear. The system had collapsed, and there seemed no prospect of restoring it. Thoughts that had receded into the background during prosperity reemerged. The root of all evil had been forgotten, and pride had surely come before this fall. In many respects, there was a return or a reluctant retreat to traditional ways.

As unemployment soared, many who had moved away to find new lives in the city had to return home. Hard times placed strains on the family, but there were some unifying effects. The family again became a cooperative unit, as it had been a generation or so earlier. Adults and children worked odd jobs, pooled resources, and eked out a living as best they could.[90] Poverty ended many leisure activities, leaving families with more time together. Divorce rates began to decline.[91] The small town's prestige and enchantment had fallen throughout previous years, but its virtues were appreciated anew, if only by necessity. Communities gave a sense of belonging and continuity in bewildering times. The return to the family and hometown was praised in local editorials:

> More families are now acquainted with their constituent members
> than at any time since the log-cabin days of America. And those
> who are going back to the farms also are returning to homes and
> home life in a simpler and more direct way than was possible for
> them so long as they were city dwellers. . . . City folk had grown
> far away from the soil from which their grandparents wrested a
> living.[92]

Sentimental themes ran through Depression-era popular culture. Andy Hardy, Henry Aldrich, and Deanna Durbin films showed the charms of family and small-town life — a comforting vision of affection and security. In a famous film of 1939, a young girl, upon returning to Kansas from a strange journey, concluded there was no place like home. Thornton Wilder's *Our Town* and Richard Llewellyn's *How Green Was My Valley* depicted warm havens held together by norms and rites. Norman Rockwell's homely depictions of Americana became popular. Even Sinclair Lewis (yes, the author of *Babbitt* and *Main Street*) found much to admire in small-town life after all in his *The Prodigal Parents* and *Home Town*.

The great rebuke saw many return to religion, where solace, meaning, and hope could be found. One Okie recalls: "Did we need the church in the Depression? You bet we did. What else did we have? We had no one else to turn to."[93] Popular magazines abounded with stories of rejecting frivolities and getting back to thrift, hard work, and perseverance — the old ways would see you through.[94] Suicide rates continued to climb steadily until 1932, when, perhaps owing to re-integration with traditional life, they fell off sharply.[95]

This is not to say that the Depression was ultimately a good thing during which resurgent family, community, and religious life made up for economic privations, a harmless interlude that brought people back to their senses. People went hungry, despaired, and went mad. The country came close to collapse. Not everyone who returned home was happy to do so, nor, sentimental editorials notwithstanding, did everyone share in the appreciation of home life. For many, return signified lost opportunity and failure. Many experienced mental difficulties from the conflict between the new identity built during prosperous times and the one that re-emerged as they got off a bus or hopped from a truck that helped them out hitchhiking.[96] Town life wasn't functioning smoothly. Local relief agencies couldn't cope with such unemployment levels; schools, parks, and other public goods suffered as municipal revenues fell; the wealthy were resented and suspected of skimming from the Community Chest.[97]

For millions of unemployed men, traditional senses of manhood were reminders of their inadequacies. American men had prided themselves as breadwinners whose hard work brought respect and progress. Laid off from the plant, idled after losing the family store or farm, men found themselves at home, a locale with troubling connotations of sloth, failure, and effeminacy. For many, home life was no refuge from the heartless world around them, and tensions surfaced there as helplessness continued. No longer able to prove themselves in the workplace, to feel that their efforts made a difference and brought rewards, many men fell into despair, left home to search for work, or just left.[98]

Early in the Depression, clergymen noticed an increase in people returning to the congregation, seeking solace, finding comfort in old ways. Many ministers thought the country was on the verge of a new awakening such as the ones that had reverberated in earlier centuries. But after a few years, it was clear that anecdotes of religious renewals were plentiful and some fundamentalist churches enjoyed growing membership, but there was no widespread return to religion.[99] Furthermore, the clergy noted that people came to religious services for consolation, but looked increasingly to the government for information and hope.[100]

As the economic crisis deepened, a political and social one emerged. Faith in authority and in basic myths, still weakened from the war, became macabre jests. In the year after the crash, the Hoover administration and captains of industry confidently assured the public that events on Wall Street affected only a lunatic fringe of speculators. The economy was sound, and full employment would soon return. Prosperity was just around . . . well, everyone soon tired of that line. Trust in political and economic institutions wore down as each confident prediction failed to come true.[101]

Political and business elites had been the objects of criticism and derision in the past. Twain satirized the scandals of the Grant administration. Grover Cleveland endured ridicule when suspected of fathering an illegitimate child. The press vilified robber barons a generation earlier, and numerous scandals damaged the Harding administration. However, the Depression was not a transient scandal involving a handful of incompetents or scoundrels. Basic political and economic institutions — "the system" — were questioned. One gibe converted a psalm into a bitter expression of disaffection: "Hoover is my shepherd, I am in want, He maketh me to lie down on park benches."[102]

Business leaders, aside from a few robber barons, were once widely considered patriarchal figures whose vision brought jobs and wellbeing. Their image suffered during the progressive era, but, during the Great War and ensuing boom, they enjoyed a measure of prestige once more. The Depression brought anti-big-business sentiment, even anti-capitalist sentiment. The public saw the wealthy as manipulators who had caused the crash. Behind their fortunes doubtless lay sordid crimes, though the people would never know. The Beards' popular history, a mixture of scholarship and outrage, argued that business leaders had treacherously invested American money abroad, and instituted reckless margin policies, which led to the collapse. Page after page outlined stock swindles, insider deals, and other skullduggery. These "lords of creation" wielded undue influence in Washington, especially in foreign policy, which had been exploited to build financial empires overseas. In the middle of the crisis, despite such intolerable social injustice, their media subsidiaries obediently churned out escapist entertainment, lulling the public into political passivity.[103]

Many forms of popular entertainment did in fact contain harsh social criticism. The Great War converted Dos Passos into a strident critic of American life; the Depression deepened his alienation and anger. In his famous trilogy, he eschews the use of the term "America," preferring the cold, corporate-sounding *USA*, in which he presents a thoroughly bleak look at a soulless, valueless land of exploitation and lies. Dos Passos takes his readers into a netherworld of bars, brothels, and menial work — for him, the essence of the country.

The best-known novel of the era is John Steinbeck's *The Grapes of Wrath*, the saga of the Joads, a family of dispossessed Okie sharecroppers. The grandparents (alive at the outset, dead by the end) had settled the land, fought off Indians, and earned a humble living from the uncharitable land. As the Depression worsens, the bank ("the monster") evicts them in order to build a mechanized corporate farm. Hearing of work in California, the Joads pack up as much of their belongings as their rickety truck can hold, but must leave behind many things, including the family copy of *Pilgrim's Progress* — the moral compass of pioneer families, which no longer provides direction or solace. Similarly, the local preacher has lost faith in God, and chooses to accompany them. Their trip recalls basic myths of heading West to find opportunity and self-sufficiency. However, on reaching the promised land, the Joads find only lies and repression. Ranch owners have lured thousands of desperate Okies to drive down wages. Those who complain or attempt to unionize are beaten or killed. A happy ending was once obligatory in American literature, but no longer. At the end (of the book, not the film), the Joads are split apart and near starvation. A glimmer of hope is afforded by the suggestion that folk traditions can serve as a basis for a socialist future.[104]

Rejection of myth also stands out in Steinbeck's *Of Mice and Men*, in which two workers drift from job to job, ever hopeful of saving enough money to start their own business and live off the fat of the land. But this is a delusion made by the economic order to con the poor and keep them in line. Belief in the American lie ends in tragedy, with a bullet in the back of the head. Similarly, Erskine Caldwell depicted characters believing, against all evidence, that a bumper crop is coming (*Tobacco Road*), or imagining that there is a cache of gold somewhere on the property (*God's Little Acre*). People cling to ideology to stave off despair. Many of these works became important films, enjoying critical and popular acclaim. Another film looked at the other extreme of the social order, the phenomenally wealthy head of a publishing empire. In *Citizen Kane*, success entails loss of principles, even if penned and sworn to in the presence of a close friend. Pathology motivates the pursuit of wealth, the end of which is personal destruction and an unmourned death in a resplendent but empty castle.[105]

The high-culture critique of American values echoed the experiences of average people. Americans had long believed that hard work would better their lot, but now the myth was hollow. Work became a desperate struggle to avoid hunger. There were few if any signs of progress; unemployment remained high throughout the 1930s, often well over twenty percent. There were moments of general despair during which every institution, custom, and law had exhausted itself, no longer able to inspire or command respect. Lawlessness was right around the corner. Myths of latter-day Robin Hoods, robbing the rich to help the poor, attached themselves to vicious criminals. When bankers threatened to foreclose farm properties, a midwestern governor invoked a higher moral law and advised, "Shoot the banker if he comes on your farm."[106]

In 1931, the Hoover administration was reluctant to trim military spending for fear it would "lessen our means of maintaining domestic peace and order,"[107] which is to say, it feared a rebellion, if not a revolution. When a mass of veterans marched on Washington to demand early payment of a bonus, many saw it as the vanguard of revolution, or as Brown Shirts who might bring an indigenous fascism. General MacArthur deployed the army against them. Colonel Patton led a saber charge into the throng, during which a veteran who had saved his life in 1918 was gruesomely slashed across the face. Something had gone wrong if Cossacks were needed to uphold the system.[108] Troubling questions abounded: Could current institutions handle the problem? Were new, socialist ones needed? Or could darker aspects of the past provide a basis for an American form of fascism?[109]

In 1933, Herbert Hoover, visibly embittered, left the White House, reluctantly turning over the presidency to Franklin Roosevelt. The public demanded something be done, and soon. In the first hundred days, the new administration embarked on a series of programs to get the country back to work and restore faith in America. Roosevelt brought in many of the leaders of the war mobilization effort of 1917 to get the country moving again. In many respects, the National Recovery Administration used the War Industries Board (1917–18) as a model: fighting the Depression, like mobilizing for the war, was a matter of the state redirecting the economy in the appropriate direction.[110] He declared bank holidays, began work programs, and sought to reorganize the economy to prevent future collapses. A president trying new things, exuding confidence, was a tonic for the public.

In a few years, America seemed to be on the move again. The banking system stabilized, factory gates reopened, and many found work again. In 1937, however, the economy collapsed again, and unemployment jumped from fourteen to nineteen percent in a year. Business leaders who had gone along with the New Deal and workers who had expected much from it began to grumble.[111] The administration was unable to agree on a new course. Roosevelt had inured himself to harsh words from the *Chicago Tribune*, but now even *The Nation* observed: "FDR now realizes that the New Deal is stopped, that he is not making a dent on the unemployment situation, that the present tremendous spending is doing very little to restore prosperity and that he has lost control of congress."[112] The slump worsened and people began to refer to the new downturn as the "Roosevelt Recession." The system was once again on trial.[113]

***

Meanwhile, in Germany and Japan, the Depression had brought portentous changes that were leading to another immense war. The global economic crisis overwhelmed Germany's young democracy and ushered in the Nazi regime, which increased government expenditures and in a few years brought full employment, popular support, and a powerful war machine.[114] In Japan, state ministers, ever wary of foreign powers in the region, saw the Depression as affording a singular opportunity to create an empire for the Rising Sun.[115] The colonial powers, they calculated, were weakened and distracted; their populations looked inward and questioned the utility and morality of colonies. The world was headed for war again, but Americans felt sure they would stay out of this one. They were wrong. The crisis in America was not solved by new policies or soothing chats. The greatest depression the country ever endured was ended by the largest and bloodiest war in history. Fortunately, America had enough coherence for the immense national effort ahead.

CHAPTER THREE

CROSSCURRENTS OF TOTAL WAR
1941–1945

*Total war sets into motion certain forces tending to unify the nation under
the stress of external threat to its existence, although their total net effect
is probably less important than those forces making for the interruption
of normal social relationships. Total war in general makes for social
disorganization.*

FRANCIS E. MERRILL, *Social Problems on the Home Front*

*For those children of the Depression who survived the war with body and
mind intact, the experience of seeing the world from the cocoon of Uncle Sam's
Army must have left most with a new sense of the wealth and power of the
United States. In a new way, they were American and proud of it.*

DAVID REYNOLDS, *Rich Relations*

In the year before Pearl Harbor, Americans slowly and reluctantly put aside
the wistful illusion that they could remain distant observers of another major
war. Events moved the country toward involvement, and President Roosevelt
encouraged a rendezvous. The war was a tremendous effort, as great a national
achievement as any in history. It churned through America like the propellers of
a great battleship through a school of fish. Traditional life weakened. Parts of life
that had slowly and grudgingly loosened over the previous half century now did
so quickly and willingly, though most Americans thought that changes were only
for the duration. Older Americans remember December 7th not only because of
events in the Pacific, but also because it was a watershed, before which all seemed
fixed and recognizable, after which all became impermanent and new.

AMERICA GOES TO WAR

As Europe slid once more toward war, Americans resolved to avoid the mistakes
of 1917 and to stay out. Congress forbade American merchant ships from
carrying war matériel to Europe and the navy from escorting foreign cargo ships.
Japanese aggression in China met with strong notes and stern warnings, but
the public mood allowed for little more. The fall of France in May 1940 altered

public opinion. When deployed against Eastern Europe, Hitler's war machine seemed unthreatening. But when it turned west and quickly overwhelmed France, leaving only Britain standing against it, realities dawned on all but the staunchest isolationists, and sympathy grew for the embattled British. Roosevelt convinced the nation that lending Britain a fleet of old destroyers would bolster a first line of defense and make American involvement unnecessary. He justified this action in the homely and unthreatening analogy of lending a neighbor a garden hose to put out a spreading fire.[1]

Soon thereafter, Congress allowed American ships to transport war supplies to England, escorted by American destroyers — a change of policy likely to result in engagements with German submarines. Shots were fired, ships sunk. By October 1941, over a hundred American lives had been lost in the North Atlantic. Mindful that impassioned responses had plunged them into the Great War, Americans held their breath. Telling the nation that its sons and neighbors had been attacked by a dangerous aggressor, Roosevelt argued for firing first on Nazi subs. After all, he counseled, no one waited for a rattlesnake to strike first. By the fall of 1941, it was the administration's unstated policy to escalate naval engagements in the North Atlantic until war was declared. Meanwhile, relations with Japan deteriorated as its expansion in China and Indochina continued. Warnings grew into embargoes, which in turn led to Tokyo's decision to cripple American naval power in the Pacific and seize its empire.[2]

Drawing upon extant senses of justice and duty, events and leaders slowly drew the country back into world affairs. The 1940 election saw no dispute over foreign policy, as the Republicans fielded Wendell Wilkie, an opponent of isolationism (and later author of a widely-read internationalist tract). Sensing the changing public mood (and probably contributing to it as well), films began to stress military adventure and moral obligations in *Sergeant York, The Fighting Sixty-Ninth*, and *They Died With Their Boots On*.[3] Opinion was still ambivalent, and though isolationists such as Burton Wheeler warned that Lend-Lease would lead to a war that "will plow under every fourth American boy,"[4] the public was stepping back from isolationism. Sounding increasingly interventionist, *Life* and other parts of the press asked why the navy hadn't sunk any Nazi subs yet. Seventy percent of Americans wanted to stay out of war, but the same percentage felt that Germany had to be stopped, even if it meant war. By late 1941, two-thirds felt war with Japan was imminent.[5]

On December 7th, far away at Pearl Harbor, the blow fell. Congress declared war the next day. Shortly thereafter, Hitler, incensed by naval exchanges in the Atlantic, declared war on America. The ambiguous state between war and peace, the debate over the proper course, and the discontent and fissures of previous years ended in an instant. Wheeler put it in straightforward terms: "The only thing now to do is to lick hell out of them."[6] Secretary of War Stimson expressed the same thought in terms befitting his Brahmin caste: "[I] never doubted that the central importance of the Pearl Harbor attack lay not in the tactical victory carried off by the Japanese but in the simple fact that the months of hesitation and relative inaction were ended at a stroke. No single blow could have been better calculated to put an end to American indecision."[7] Total war had come.

THE FAMILY AT WAR

The war was felt in every part of life. Prior to the nineteenth century, war had been the affair of nobles, mercenaries, and dregs, with little effect on the population at large. Few families felt the impact of war unless armies actually came to their village to pillage and burn. With the rise of mass armies, however, states mobilized their human resources, economic potentials, and moral energies. The greater the war, the greater the mobilization. Americans would have to make enormous efforts, far more than any previous war had required. Every family became part of the effort.

Families pulled together as they lived with anxiety over the fate of loved ones serving overseas and over that of the nation should the struggle against the Axis fall short — an unspeakable but real possibility early on. Family members shared the common experience of various parts of the effort: work in war plants, scrap metal drives, saving and rationing, and making do with ersatz products and older goods. Families engaged in common effort as they had in the days of the settlers and immigrants, as they had to once again when the Depression ended consumerism for most. Scrimping and saving, harnessing energies for the national effort instead of personal gain, became the basis of daily life. Children took part too by writing encouraging letters to GIs, following unfolding events in school, scanning the skies for Messerschmitts and Zeroes (their silhouettes known from cereal boxes), recreating gallant deeds in backyard play, and comforting families suffering all too real casualties. In many respects, the family pulled together.[8]

The image of the family as a vital part of the effort became the stuff of army lectures, magazine stories, and more than a few movies, perhaps the most exemplary of which was *Since You Went Away*. Its opening scene is a hearth with a cozy fire blazing, over which appear the words:

> This is a story of an Unconquerable Fortress:
> the American Home . . . 1943.

The Hilton family adapts to wartime: they display a star in their front window, indicating that a family member is serving overseas; the mother has gone to work in a war plant and a boarder is taken in to help make ends meet; the daughters volunteer in a hospital and on scrap drives. The issue of fidelity is broached on more than one occasion, but the faithfulness of the wives and sweethearts is of course above question. *Since You Went Away* is an interesting and poignant artifact from the period, conveying the experiences of many families, but in many respects it is pat, contrived, and may be seen as a rejoinder to enemy propaganda of the "Your-sweetheart-is-seeing-a-4F" variety. It was useful in the war effort, but less so in understanding important social trends.

Raised in a more orderly world in a midwestern town (and probably still harboring opposition to the war), Charles and Mary Beard saw the family in danger:

> [F]amilies were undergoing disintegration; for men were being
> drafted for war, women drawn into the auxilliary armed forces,
> war production and civilian defense, children of school age
> crowding into war industries, adolescents left to roam the streets
> for excitement, and the energies of parents distracted from
> the care of homes and children. The fact was indisputable and
> its social import was recognized by leaders in public affairs.
> It was discussed in newspapers, in meetings of organizations
> concerned with public welfare, in journals devoted to surveys of
> social and economic conditions, and in popular magazines. . . .
> Yet no generally accepted and workable plans were devised for
> successfully countering disruptive effects of war activities and war
> regimentation on the homes and family life of the nation.[9]

The war would have to take priority, but would the country ever return to normal family life as the Beards and much of the country knew it?

Mobilization meant disruption, transience, uprooting — shocks to patterns of family life. The war caused one of the largest internal migrations in history, with over thirty million out of 140 million Americans leaving home. Induction into the military or relocation to war-related jobs brought unprecedented horizontal mobility. Over fifteen million civilians moved to another part of the country, leaving behind familiar settings near relatives and neighbors.[10] Over sixteen million Americans, mostly men, served in the military, usually far from home. Though induction of fathers didn't come until 1944, defense jobs and military service combined to bring about an immense number of family separations and dislocations.[11]

Millions of women also took part. Over a quarter million served in the armed forces and in jobs such as ferrying planes from plants to port facilities. They were more frequently found in the workplace, where by 1943 there were labor shortages. World War I had seen many women enter the workplace, but U. S. involvement was relatively short and social change less pronounced. With the Second World War, their participation in the effort was on a far greater scale and for a longer duration. Women found themselves outside the confines of traditional roles and in workplaces that had been male-dominated. In some sectors, women as a percentage of the workforce went from five to twenty-five percent.[12] Work gave them new feelings of independence and efficacy, not simply from working outside the home, though that was important too. Women learned that they could make planes and tanks and participate in solving workplace problems, that they had abilities they would never have dreamed of a few years earlier. They could do the jobs of men. Furthermore, women became active participants in an event of overwhelming national and historical importance that broadened their outlook and planted the idea that women could do more than prewar opinion admitted. The denouement of these experiences was not immediate — after all, most women later returned to prewar roles — but women's outlook on those roles would never be the same.[13]

In 1940, there were over eight hundred thousand working women with children under ten. Four years later, the number had almost doubled. Although the war gave family members common efforts and aspirations, it also reduced contact with one another.[14] In many households, paternal authority — heretofore the basis of discipline — went away. The role of instilling discipline shifted from fathers, relatives, and neighbors and came to rest on the shoulders of women. This constituted an unparalleled and burdensome transferal to which many women were equal. But for many, alone and in new environs, working long and odd hours, it was impossible to perform both parental roles. The family, upon which the teaching of norms and values had rested, was less able to do the job. The process of transmitting discipline and values, though hardly in collapse, was working less effectively. Most thought that the disruption was just for the duration, like doing without coffee, and that with peace all would be set right again.

The war had consequences for children that set into motion dynamics of later decades. Many older children, especially boys, quit school in their mid-teens to take factory jobs or split time between school and work. Not surprisingly, the number of secondary students dropped eleven percent between 1940 and 1944, far more than demographic changes account for. Handsomely paid at a young age, these young people constituted a prematurely independent group, who, though still members of families, were less and less meaningful parts of them. Their work was outside the family, and so increasingly were their leisure time, consumption habits, expectations, and plans. Magazines and other forms of entertainment came into being, catering to this young group, further redirecting their attention.

Many children found themselves growing up outside stable family settings.

They were sometimes left in movie theaters or playgrounds until the parent's shift was over. The term "juvenile delinquency" came into common usage to describe a new phenomenon covering a range of behavior more serious than soaping windows or stealing garden gates on Halloween, but almost trivial by later standards. Most cities, especially the ones with large population influxes, experienced sharp increases in youth crime. Young girls sought the attention of soldiers on leave, often feeling that it was contributing to the war effort. Few GIs argued the matter.[15]

Despite unity of purpose and other centripetal forces, war mobilization weakened the family. Transmitting values to the young was no longer proceeding smoothly. A youth group — the term "teenager" came into use then — began to coalesce, which, though supportive of the war, indeed enthusiastically so, was becoming more attuned to war service and mass entertainment than to family life. Its members were distant from and consciously distancing themselves from the family and the traditional patterns of life it represented. In the flux of the period one can see the dissolution of one part of traditional America and the origins of later generations of youth.

DISPERSAL OF COMMUNITY

Local communities suffered from the post-1918 cynicism and prosperity, but with the onset of the Depression regained appreciation and prestige. With the Second World War, they regained even more. Every community went to war, putting aside old concerns, sending its young overseas, and producing goods to back the attack. But the thousands of Middletowns across the country experienced extraordinary migrations, both in and out, which tested coherence.

After Pearl Harbor, towns held meetings to determine how best to do their part, much as they had on hearing of the firing on Fort Sumter eighty years earlier. Previous antagonisms seemed petty compared to the enormousness of the war. Communities found purpose and vigor in scrap drives, blood donor programs, and blackouts along coastlines. The national conscription system had extensive local involvement, in part in order to deflect potential resentments away from Washington.[16] Prominent citizens were charged with the sobering and agonizing task of determining who was needed back home and who would be sent to war, a decision that of course meant sending some to their deaths. Communities found new life in various forms of volunteer work: in USOs, in hospitals, in honoring the dead, and in comforting their families.[17]

The hometown angle was part of war reporting. Stories about the Screaming Eagle from Orange, New Jersey, the tanker from Cohoes, New York, the nurse from Springfield, Massachusetts, the B-29 gunner from Braddock Heights, Maryland, the intelligence officer from Oak Park, Illinois, and the general from Abilene, Kansas, enlivened ties between hometowns and distant fronts. The index of Ernie Pyle's *Brave Men* lists all the towns mentioned in the book as well as the GIs who came from them.[18] News stories boasted that the local community had instilled discipline and courage that helped in the fight with Hitler and Tojo. Local teachers, coaches, and neighbors had all built the character of the American fighting man. Everyone in the neighborhood knew of others with family members overseas, shared their anxieties on hearing of sharp engagements, and felt part of a common effort: "You just felt that the stranger sitting next to you in a restaurant, or someplace, felt the same way you did about the basic issues."[19] Today, veterans might not readily recall a platoon member's name but still remember his hometown.

The most important parts of the community were the local manufacturers whose products changed from agricultural implements to tank turrets, from fertilizer to high explosives, from colorful textiles to olive drab issue. Towns enjoyed the prestige of making rifles, mosquito netting, boots, and landing craft. (It is unclear if anyone took credit for C-Rations.) One woman recalls going to work this way: "If you ask me what are my most vivid impressions of the war years, I'd have to go back to the factory, driving down and seeing the antiaircraft guns on the roof and the lights and the feeling of just being involved."[20]

Townspeople felt a sense of identity and unity of purpose. The war effort sometimes had the quaintness of a folk rite. The people of Seneca, Illinois, on completion of an LST landing craft, would all turn out as it rolled into the river on its way to the Mississippi and ultimately to Anzio, Kwajalein, or Normandy. Senecans celebrated their hard work, then, after a religious service and a speech from a wounded serviceman, returned to work on the next LST, many more of which were needed. From a bridge over the river, children tossed flowers on to the vessel and offered prayers for those who would go into battle from her.[21]

The impact of the migration of over thirty million people has already been noted in regard to the family; its impact on local communities was probably greater. The town had never been a completely self-contained world. It had known periods of population movements, in and out, but nothing like that which came with the war. Many small towns were hurt as people entered the service or found better paying work elsewhere, usually in bigger cities. The movement was especially pronounced in the interior South and Midwest, where businesses could not compete with booming cities along the coasts and in the Northeast. Between 1940 and 1945, the rural population declined by an average of 1.6 million each year.[22] Capital and skilled labor left the Middletowns. Neither returned in large numbers following the war.

Seeing greater efficiency in economies of scale, the government tended to award contracts to large businesses, typically in urban centers. In the course of the war, over half a million small businesses went under, and the percentage of workers employed by big business soared[23] — trends that alarmed New Dealers like Adolph Berle as well as old-line Republicans like Robert Taft. The antagonistic pair could at least agree that the common man and the small town, bedrocks of traditional America, were in danger. A Senate inquiry warned: "If we continue destroying America's small businesses and uprooting small communities, and many of our large ones as well, we shall not recognize post-war America."[24] But there was a war on, you know, and national priorities understandably lay elsewhere. FDR admitted that he listened less to Dr New Deal than to Dr Win the War. That meant welfare was second to warfare. In earlier years, anti-big-business rhetoric had thundered from Washington, but now the rhetoric declined and captains of industry such as Kaiser, Stetinius, and Knudsen were welcomed in the White House, where industry and government forged a newer and more lasting deal.[25] Reflecting changing public attitudes, *The Saturday Evening Post* proclaimed, "If Free Enterprise had not flourished here, the cause of world freedom might now be lost for centuries."[26]

Many small towns had serviceable mills, mines, and foundries that benefited immensely from government contracts and did not experience population loss. In others, such as Richland, Washington, Oak Ridge, Tennessee, and Willow Run, Michigan, large new defense industries sprang up in the blink of an eye. The war transformed such towns. Many were no longer communities in any meaningful sense. A thriving factory or mine in a sleepy hamlet might attract tens of thousands of new workers, unfamiliar with and often resentful of local folkways, unrestrained by the proximity of neighbors and family. Earning good money for the first time, they were eager to spend it on Saturday night.[27]

Many small towns were like boomtowns of the old West. Cacophonous migrations overwhelmed the rhythms of local life. Ramshackle housing sprouted up for workers, many of whom were single and felt even less need to conform to local usages than did newly arriving families. Where factories ran two or three shifts, round-the-clock bars sprang up. The disruption worried W. Lloyd Warner:

> In some communities the whole system of control that formerly
> prevailed has ceased to function or has been suspended by outside
> authority. The influx of population has been so great that the
> schools can teach but a small portion of the children. The police
> force is inadequate. The usual recreational life has disappeared
> to be supplanted by the taxi dance, juke joint, beer hall, and
> gambling dive. Institutions such as the church and lodge have
> almost ceased to function. In some towns one can drive through

> miles of trailer camps and small houses pressed against each other,
> all recently assembled, where the inhabitants are living in squalid
> anonymity with, but not of, the thousands around them. They are
> an aggregate of individuals concentrated in one area, but they are
> not a community.[28]

Many sizable cities underwent rapid growth. Between 1940 and 1944, Mobile grew by sixty-five percent, Norfolk by forty-five percent, San Diego by forty-four percent, San Francisco by twenty-five percent, and Los Angeles by fifteen percent. City neighborhoods lost their identity. Younger men and women went wherever the war pushed them. The old stayed and wondered if the others would ever return once the job was finished. We know now that fewer than twenty percent did.[29]

RELIGION AND SOCIAL NORMS AMID TOTAL WAR

Throughout history, wars have increased religiousness. This is not to say that wars transform sinners into saints, or that they are the true path to salvation, or that they are a desirable thing. However, in time of war, social and psychological forces come into play that strengthen religion. This was true of the American experience during World War II, but disruptive forces made themselves felt on the country's moral order as well.

Western civilization has long associated war and religion. The association has been impressed on generations of Europeans and Americans, who then interpreted later wars through this tradition. Much of the Old Testament is a narrative of an embattled people seeking and gaining God's help in smiting enemies. Many passages read like a war epic, replete with heroes, martial prowess, and miraculous deliverances. David slew the seemingly invincible Philistine giant. Joshua's horn crumbled the defenses around Jericho. The destruction of Pharaoh's army in the Red Sea delivered the nation from foreign domination, leading Moses to proclaim, "the Lord is a man of war" (Exodus 15: 3).[30]

Greek and Roman armies carried images of gods on campaigns and looked to them for auguries of an impending battle's outcome. Victorious generals became emperors, and emperors gods, commemorated with awe-inspiring arches and enshrined in the Pantheon. Constantine, according to legend, converted to Christianity on the eve of a decisive battle, promising to end religious persecution and unite his empire under the new faith. The newly converted emperor vanquished the enemy, creating a myth of divine support for the righteous that became an enduring part of Western culture.[31] Centuries later, the Crusades, though fraught with base motives, strengthened the association between war and religion, as Christendom fought to free the Holy Land.

Arthurian legends, *The Song of Roland*, the myth of El Cid, the tale of Joan of Arc, and countless other war epics immortalized the association between war, religion, and heroism. Early Russian chronicles depicted the Muscovite princes as valiant defenders of Christianity.[32] Händel and Haydn composed religiously inspired works to bolster wartime morale, and with victory wrote moving Te Deums. Making an obvious allusion, countless aspects of culture, high and low, stressed the sacredness of shedding one's blood in war. The link between religion and war became part of the Western mind, almost as much as life after death and the fall from grace. One military historian has called Christianity "one of the great warrior religions of mankind."[33]

The theme of war and religion runs through American history as well. The War of Independence enjoyed support from the pulpit as a just war against tyranny, as shortly later did the War of 1812. The Civil War grew out of revivalist-based abolitionism and became a crusade against wicked rebels; the stars and stripes were the sign under which Lincoln triumphed and reunited the nation. Indeed, during the war, as each side invoked Biblical symbolism, revivalism pulsed through army camps of both sides.[34] The Indian Wars were thought of as Christian civilization pitted against pagan hosts. The experience of World War I damaged the association of war and religion, but when America found itself in another World War, the embers of religiously sanctioned war were warmer than elsewhere and the country fell back upon a long-standing part of its past.

Aside from cultural currents, emotional forces tied World War II to religion in the minds of Americans. The war brought great uncertainty, even dread — over one's fate, that of loved ones, and that of the nation. Uncertainty called for comfort and assurance, not all of which, needless to say, could be provided by official statements and cheery films. David Reynolds captures the moment of soldiers about to assault Normandy: "Although some GIs derided 'fox-hole religion,' the religious services on ship, as in the marshaling areas, were well attended. Young men in their early twenties confronted, often for the first time, the fact of their own mortality."[35] Americans suffered more casualties during World War II (over 400,000 dead) than in any previous war except the Civil War; almost four times those of the First World War; seven times those of Vietnam (and in a far shorter period). The sinking of a large ship, an assault on a well-defended beachhead, or a bombing mission deep into Germany or Rumania sent shock waves back home as telegrams arrived in large numbers. Owing to the deployment of national guard units, groups of friends joining up together, or a group of brothers serving on the same ship, death sometimes hit certain locales with appalling force. The Virginia town of Bedford lost nineteen young men on D-Day when the 29th Infantry Division (the Maryland and Virginia national guard) assaulted Omaha Beach. The Sullivan family of Waterloo, Iowa had five brothers killed in a single day.

Faced with death, people looked for spiritual comfort and transcendent meaning. Individual and nation searched for something after a close call: for the serviceman, a mortar round hitting close by or a sister ship sent to the bottom; for the nation, an improbable victory against superior forces or a decisive battle portending a turning point. Providential aid was more convincing than pure chance, as after Midway (1942), where American planes caught Japanese aircraft on their carrier decks in the vulnerable position of refueling and rearming. Three enemy carriers went down in less than an hour, a fourth was later scuttled. Inasmuch as all four had struck Pearl Harbor, vengeance was ours. The tide of war had shifted, and victory in the Pacific was all but ensured. Many Americans felt that guidance from above had led them from the dark days of early 1942. Perhaps not since Appomattox had the nation felt so confident in the old founding belief that America was God's nation.

Political and military leaders encouraged religious sentiment. At every juncture, from the declaration of war to V-J Day, leaders called for national prayer and otherwise invoked religious sentiments. Churchill and Roosevelt sang *Onward Christian Soldiers* ("marching as to war") after forging the alliance against Hitler off the Canadian coast. Roosevelt spoke frequently of the nation being guided from above, and never hesitated to ask for prayer or to pray himself. On D-Day, he offered a lengthy prayer gathering all these themes:

> The spirit of man has awakened and the soul of man has come
> forth. Grant us the wisdom and the vision to comprehend the
> greatness of man's spirit that suffers and endures so hugely for a goal
> beyond his own brief span. Grant us honor for our dead who died
> in the faith, honor for our living who work and strive for the faith,
> redemption and security for all captive lands and peoples. Amen.[36]

Eisenhower saw his task as a "crusade in Europe;" MacArthur his in the Pacific, a "holy mission." Such invocations were especially forceful in a war against enemies whose acts and ideology could, with little if any hyperbole, be called evil.

Religion was everywhere: in speeches, at the launching of a new ship, in magazine advertisements, and at battalion aid stations. People, in and out of the military, who had rarely if ever prayed now found themselves attending services. The cinema, working closely with the Office of War Information, stressed religious themes in *Since You Went Away, A Wing and A Prayer*, and *God Is My Co-Pilot*. An article in *Readers Digest* popularized the expression "There are no atheists in a foxhole." Mothers gave their sons small, iron-plated Bibles to place in their breast pockets before going into battle. The evidence, admittedly anecdotal, suggests they stopped thousands of bullets. Fortunately, we have more reliable evidence of the importance of religion among combat soldiers. When asked what helped most during the stress of battle, combat soldiers mentioned (in ascending order) the rightness of cause, hatred of the enemy, desire to get home, duty to fellow soldiers; but between seventy and eighty-three percent of respondents stated that "prayer helped a lot." After the war, seventy-nine percent of combat veterans stated that war experiences had strengthened their religious faith.[37]

The war had both positive and negative consequences for family and community, and, lest anyone think it a rapturous moment of pentecostal renewal, attention should turn to less spiritual aspects. Beneath the religious sentiment, there were portentous changes in norms.

Coarsening of Traditional Sensibilities

Military service deliberately promotes coarsening. Turning millions of civilians into servicemen, farmhands into riflemen, clerks into tankers, consisted of a well-calculated program of hardening and desensitizing through which a large portion of a generation passed. Geographic separation, close-cropped haircuts, and uniforms uprooted recruits from their past, and then they were herded like cattle through medical exams, chow lines, training programs, embarkation depots, and short-arm inspections. Cadence calls, ribald limericks, and barracks doggerel depicted women as invariably unfaithful, joked of killing and dying, and ridiculed sentimentality. The civilian world was untrustworthy; commanders and fellow soldiers alone deserved trust.

The recruit was reoriented into a new moral environment to reduce individuality, accept hard realities, and put aside religious and family beliefs. After initial indoctrination, army life continued to be rough and vulgar, wearing down sensibilities and inculcating obedience. The job is at least half done when soldiers call themselves "GIs" — Government Issue — and wear "dog tags." Paul Fussell ably describes the outcome of this process as "boys turned by training into quasi-mechanical interchangeable parts. . . . You might as well be an inert item of Government Issue, like a mess kit or a tool, entrenching."[38] Standing up is useless: "Everything broke you down, until in the end you were just a little goddam bolt holding on and squealing when the machine went too fast."[39] James Jones, with caustic irony (a souvenir of the war, this), captures the thought of soldiers as dehumanized instruments. Amid an assault on a heavily defended ridge on Guadalcanal, one character observes:

> They thought they were men. They all thought they were real
> people. They really did. How funny. They thought they made
> decisions and ran their own lives, and proudly called themselves

> free individual human beings. The truth was they were here, and
> they were gonna stay here, until the state through some other
> automaton told them to go someplace else, and then they'd go. But
> they'd go freely, of their own free choice and will, because they were
> free individual human beings. Well, well.[40]

There is a grim functionalism here, the consequences wholly intended. Soldiers must put aside much of their past and pull the trigger at the appropriate time. They must distance themselves from family and community to become parts of a vast impersonal apparatus of destruction. They are taught to obey the commandment engraved into every part of military life, in its cadences, posters, and uniforms: *Thou shalt kill.* General Leslie McNair attempted to harden inductees by telling them, "We must lust for battle; our object in life must be to kill; we must scheme and plan night and day to kill."[41] The final episode of Frank Capra's *Why We Fight* series depicts photographs of Axis leaders and exhorted: "If you see one of these men, KILL HIM!" Troops near Admiral Halsey's headquarters saw his motto in large letters: "Kill Japs, kill Japs, then kill more Japs."[42] They were not just slogans. Many GIs did just that, and millions of others steeled themselves to do the same.

There is no more hardening experience than combat, especially on the ground. What folks back home had to read about and accept in the abstract, hundreds of thousands of soldiers had to endure in reality, for months and years. Endless marches with backbreaking packs, living in mud and rain, and continuous exposure to enemy fire wear away humanity. Many units suffered over fifty percent casualties in just a few weeks, some, as at Tarawa or Omaha Beach, in a few hours. Nervous breakdowns were commonplace;[43] wounds not neat incisions; neither prisoners nor corpses always treated respectfully; and the dead did not look natural or as if they were sleeping. Bombs were dropped on cities; bullets shot into enemy soldiers; information extracted from prisoners; satchel charges (with gasoline cans) thrown into caves; and flame-throwers fired into bunkers. Shocking instruments brought the glory of victory.

The experience of combat is dissociating. Many soldiers become estranged from the conventions and sentiments of traditional life, no longer parts of a family or community or civilized society, but now parts of an immense killing machine stretching across whole continents and oceans, incredibly effective at its work. One of Mailer's platoon members, Red Valsen,

> had been through so much combat, had felt so many kinds of
> terror, and had seen so many men killed that he no longer had
> any illusions about the inviolability of his own flesh. He knew
> he could be killed; it was something he had accepted years ago,

and he had grown a shell about that knowledge so that he rarely
thought of anything further than the next few minutes. . . . Red had
accepted all the deaths of the men he knew as something large and
devastating and meaningless. Men who were killed were merely men
no longer around; they became confused with old friends who had
gone to the hospital and never come back, or men who had been
transferred to another outfit. When he heard of some man he knew
who had been killed or wounded badly, he was interested, even a
little concerned, but it was the kind of emotion a man might feel if
he learned that a friend of his had got married or made or lost some
money. It was merely something that happened to somebody he
knew, and Red had always let it go at that. . . . Guys came and guys
went, and after a while you didn't even remember their names.[44]

Though often read merely as comedy, albeit a dark one, Kurt Vonnegut's
Slaughterhouse-Five tells of a veteran permanently dissociated from the routines
and conventions of civilian life. He has become "unstuck in time," continuously
drifting back and forth between unassimilated events of the war and escapes into
fantasy, where he feels more comfortable. He is no longer able to feel horror or
sadness, no longer able to see any reason or morality in life. With every random,
senseless death, he simply notes in laconic resignation, "So it goes."[45]

In Burns's *The Gallery*, an infantryman, in a moment of introspection
afforded by a pass, breaks down and weeps. He weeps for the dead and wounded
of course, but also for the millions back home living in a charmed delusion,
seeing the war in terms of ideals, innocent of the knowledge that it is systematic
slaughter on an incomprehensible scale. Fussell has spent much of his life trying
to understand war and the pall that hangs over combat veterans' lives. He found
words that expressed the war's impact on his life in the reflections of a veteran
of the Great War:

Life was good and easy, and I called life "friend." I'd never hidden
anything from him, and he'd never hidden anything from me. Or
so I thought. I knew everything. He was an awfully intelligent
companion; we had the same tastes (apparently) and he was awfully
fond of me. And all the time he was plotting up a mass murder.[46]

Through their experiences of uprooting, standardization, regimentation,
coarsening, and subjection to impersonal forces, GIs may have formed the
vanguard of modern mass society.[47]

Though slight in comparison to that of front-line troops, coarsening was
felt back home too. The fearful resolve that followed Pearl Harbor mobilized

dark aspects of human nature and American culture. A society normally keeps hatred and violence in check, but in wartime it reorganizes itself to wage war, an abstraction that obscures the reality of killing young men and setting cities ablaze. However just the cause and noble the intentions, America did not win the war through persuasive arguments, majority votes, scrap drives, or prayer. America defeated Germany and Japan by teaching a large number of its citizens to hate and kill, or at least to condone hating and killing, and to become supporters of, if not cogs in, an immense killing machine. Americans hoped and prayed for the violent deaths of millions of the enemy, and when those deaths came, they were welcomed.

The war legitimized and even honored properly channeled hatred. A *New York Times Magazine* article, written by an OWI official (Rex Stout), was titled "We Shall Hate or We Shall Perish."[48] No room for debate here. Such hatred was all the more easy to develop given the treachery of Japan and the monstrosity of Germany (though only a part of the latter was known until late in the war). Common parlance, from the ladies auxiliary to a front-line unit, adopted cruder words for the enemy — Japs and Krauts, often preceded with an expletive or two that came more readily now.[49] Speeches, movies, posters, and accounts from returning soldiers portrayed them in unrelentingly sinister light, making killing them less offensive. In many films, to the public's delight, enemy soldiers (especially Japanese ones) were savagely killed by lengthy machine-gun bursts, massive explosions, and spectacular immolations — the latter connoting sanitization and providing catharsis.[50] Such were the popular passions unleashed that by 1944 complaints were heard that the war was transforming the American people into "mad dogs," and that "perhaps the most marked forms of undemocratic, pro-Fascist mentality are today to be observed in certain traditionally liberal circles when they discuss the treatment of the enemy."[51] But calls for moderation were drowned out and seemed tinged with pacifism.

Other losses of social sentiment are clear as well. In 1917, Wilson feared the Great War would hurt the country:

> Once lead this people into war, and they'll forget there ever was
> such a thing as tolerance. To fight you must be brutal and ruthless,
> and the spirit of ruthless brutality will enter into the very fiber of
> our national life, infecting Congress, the courts, the policeman on
> the beat, the man in the street.[52]

Though coarsening there was, the war's effects were less than Wilson feared. The experience was relatively brief, and the media could not present the war as graphically as later technology would allow. Perhaps more importantly, war romance clouded the minds of most Americans, limiting their grasp of combat to sentimental images of heroic charges and capturing the foe's colors — that is, until the casualties hit home and rudely pointed to a chasm between myth and reality.

The next war brought a franker depiction of combat. Reporters eschewed the romantic language of previous wars. The public didn't read of noble lads answering the call and winning the day on the field of battle. Such depictions ended in 1918 and could no longer be relied upon to rally the nation. Ernie Pyle, Margaret Bourke White, Vincent Tubbs, Richard Tregaskis, John Hersey, and others adopted a writing style drawn from Depression-era realism, in which soldiers — average guys, not latter-day Rolands — experienced terror, suffered ghastly deaths, saw eviscerations and decapitations, and ate C-Rations next to corpses.[53]

Government censors certainly could have insisted on nothing but uplifting stories of high-spirited boys boldly moving forward, eager to give the foe a black eye, but they cleared many blunt stories and photographs to brace the public for a long and bloody war. Popular books by Tregaskis and Hersey spoke of grisly beheadings and the sickening smell of decaying flesh.[54] One *Yank* story reads like an autopsy:

> The rifleman presses the trigger, and the bullet passes through
> the helmet, scalp, skull, small blood vessels, membrane, into the
> soft sponginess of the brain. Then a man is either paralyzed or
> he's blind or he's an idiot with his memory gone, or he's dead. If a
> medic picks up a man quickly enough there's a surgeon who can
> pick out the bullet, tie up the blood vessels, cover up the hole in a
> man's head with a metal plate. Then, sometimes, a man can learn
> things all over again, whether it's talking, walking, or smelling.
> But if the bullet ripped through the medulla region in the back of
> a man's head, or if it tore through a big blood vessel in the man's
> brain, then he's had it. In Sicily or on New Guinea, it all depends
> on how a man was holding his head when the bullet hit.[55]

The usually affable Bill Mauldin learned hard lessons in Italy and tried to convey to the home front that war was neither heroic nor fair:

> Many celebrities and self-appointed authorities . . . say the
> American soldier is the same clean-cut young man who left
> his home; others say morale is sky-high at the front because
> everybody's face is shining for the great Cause. They are wrong. The
> combat man isn't the same clean-cut lad because you don't fight a
> Kraut by Marquis of Queensbury rules: You shoot him in the back,

you blow him apart with mines, you kill or maim him the quickest
and most effective way you can with the least danger to yourself.
He does the same to you. He tricks you and cheats you, and if you
don't beat him at his own game you don't live to appreciate your
own nobleness.[56]

Ernie Pyle made the same attempt. Here, he writes of an ordnance company that
rebuilds damaged rifles:

As gun after gun comes off the stack you look to see what is the
matter with it. Rifle butt split by fragments; barrel dented by a
bullet; trigger knocked off; whole barrel splattered with shrapnel
marks; gun gray from the slime of weeks in swamp mud; faint dark
splotches of blood still showing. You wonder what became of each
owner; you pretty well know.[57]

In the underappreciated novella, *A Walk in the Sun*, a soldier approaches a
damaged German half-track:

[The GI] hopped to his feet, his tommy gun at the alert, and
trotted out to the armored car. He put the gun in the driver's eye
slit and pulled the trigger. Lead smashed against the car's interior as
he moved the muzzle up and down. He put about thirty shots into
the car. Probably the two men who made up the crew had been
alive when he started shooting; if so, they were not alive now. The
platoon had no time to take prisoners.[58]

The matter-of-factness of the last line merits a moment's attention.

Far away, civilians, perhaps for the first time, began to understand something
about war. Early in the war, with Washington's approval, newspapers published
a photograph of dead GIs strewn across a New Guinea beachhead, their arms
and legs sprawled grotesquely, indicating instant death. The waves have partially
buried them in sand, suggesting little attention for them even in the tropic heat.
Another photo showed several dead marines, lifeless in the sand and bobbing
in the surf off Tarawa — a jarring departure from the old imagery of the fallen
soldier peacefully slumbering in the arms of the Lord that had once consoled
families.[59] Considered shocking and disrespectful, the photographs caused a
furor at home. Generals and policymakers received angry letters and even some
threats, but most GIs had seen far worse and couldn't understand the fuss. After
a year or so, as casualties mounted and the costs of war became painfully clear,
neither could most civilians.[60] Soon the public would see newsreel footage
of countless corpses littering scores of battlefields and a famous still of an

incinerated head protruding from a burned-out tank, the remnants of its face frozen in a death-scream. In 1940, Americans were horrified that anyone — *anyone* — would bomb population centers like Warsaw and Rotterdam. Shortly thereafter, they cheered the fire-bombings of Hamburg and Tokyo.

Many films dealt with the brutal aspects of war in a surprisingly frank manner.[61] Powerful depictions of death, wounds, amputations, and nervous breakdowns appear in *Thirty Seconds Over Tokyo, Pride of the Marines, A Walk in the Sun,* and just after the war in *Twelve O'Clock High* and *The Best Years of Our Lives. The Fighting Sullivans* traces the lives of five brothers from their boyhood. We see them playing pirates, sneaking a smoke, receiving their First Communion, and growing into young men. Shortly after Pearl Harbor, they join up together and ship out on the *Juneau.* In the last few minutes of the film, all five are killed when their ship is torpedoed and its magazine explodes. Emotionally devastating, it was pulled from theaters for fear it would weaken morale. The charmed and innocent world of Andy Hardy was an early casualty of the war, and a world of sentiment and Victorian propriety retreated.[62]

Mars and Venus

The moral thinking with which a society determines right and wrong is transmitted through the expectations of family members, neighbors, officials, and institutions, especially local ones. Prior to the war, most Americans lived in relatively stable moral environments held together by local pressures. The war changed this, dispersing families and communities throughout the country. Millions found themselves removed from the moral pressures that had shaped them. They were cast into strange new environments, some in bigger towns, some in military garrisons, others on the line. Flux and transience replaced traditional patterns. Old influences gone or weakened, people changed. Norms regarding decorum and violence were giving way, and the same can be said of sexual ones.

The 1960s are thought of as the time of a far-reaching sexual revolution that transformed the country's views on sexuality. The Second World War, however, contained an opening upheaval that extended into the postwar era of Kinsey, Hefner, and Presley, and set the stage for the later revolution. Transience and uncertainty loosened sexual norms. Separated from loved ones and feeling loneliness, stress, perhaps even a sense of impending doom, many looked for intimacy. One serviceman described a wartime dalliance this way: "She wasn't a whore, she was a girl from Toronto and we'd met in London among six million people. We'd found each other."[63] Another, in a manner that might initially seem ribald, recalls the fears and need for companionship:

> My God, but it was easy to fall in love in those two months before
> D-Day. . . . There was the feeling that these were the last nights
> men and women would make love, and there was never any of the
> by-play or persuading that usually went on. People were for love,
> so to speak. It was so easy to fall in love. . . . I won't describe the
> scenes or sounds of Hyde Park or Green Park at dusk and after
> dark. They just can't be described. You can just imagine, a vast
> battlefield of sex.[64]

The Andrews Sisters' song notwithstanding, many did sit under the apple tree with someone else.[65]

Young couples married hurriedly to have some element of permanence before shipping out, though many such marriages didn't last much past V-J Day. Other moral changes were baser in motivation. Army life, despite or because of isolation from women, was rife with sexual tension. Cadence calls, jokes, limericks, even propaganda broadcasts, contained sexual themes, invariably vulgar. One limerick, though laced with WWII-references, could, perhaps owing to its witty commingling of crudity and misogyny and understanding of GI life, still be heard in the army during the Vietnam War:

> Don't back the attack
> By screwing a WAC
> Or grabbing the tits of a WAVE.
> Just use your own hand
> As you lie in the sand
> And buy bonds with the money you save.

Young men away from home for the first time, paid at the end of the month and imbued with notions of soldierly virility, sought out female companionship. And in the juke joints and bars that thrived around military bases, they found it. Indeed, female companionship, of a sort, sought them out as well. Prostitution flourished around military bases as well as in war-ravaged areas overseas, where a pack of smokes went a long way. As a wry observer put it: "The effect of wars upon chastity has always been known. That this one will accelerate the abandonment of chastity in those who still possess it is as certain as moonlight."[66] Effects were not limited to Americans. The deployment of millions of allegedly overpaid and oversexed GIs led to loosening sexual norms in many parts of the world. One Yank boasted, "I like to say the Victorian era in England ended when we arrived."[67]

Crackdowns on prostitution only led to less organized forms of it, which had the unintended result of increasing venereal disease rates. Accordingly, officials in and out of the military placed a higher priority on winning the war than on fighting vice. Perhaps with a shrug, perhaps with a wink, authorities condoned organized prostitution. Though he might not have scrawled his trademark face and tag line there, Kilroy was in the seamy parts of Rome and Manila too. Military commands set up units devoted to ensuring a modicum of hygiene in local prostitution. Combat units were especially likely to organize brothels, replete with prophylactic dispensaries and medical examinations. One of the first things done by occupying troops in postwar Japan was to organize prostitution centers. Inasmuch as efforts to prevent VD were not always successful, we might wonder if the father of penicillin has been given his due in winning the war. This unheralded chapter in military history, rarely mentioned outside veteran circles, awaits its chronicler.[68]

The point is not that prewar America was genteel and chaste, or that the war made it vulgar and promiscuous. Movement along a continuum took place, though it might be more appropriate to say that the actual movement was less important than a *loosening*, which allowed the country to move away more noticeably in later years. Movement along the continuum, as shall be seen, began in the following decade, and took on a greater pace in the next.

FAITH IN PROGRESS RESTORED

Americans have long expected material, scientific, and spiritual progress, in their own time and especially in their children's. World War I damaged much of this faith, leaving an emphasis on materialism and self-indulgence. As the Depression wore on, even this was undermined, and long-standing trust turned into a sense of betrayal. The New Deal began to restore faith, but in 1937 it faltered badly. Bewilderment and despair returned.[69]

The outbreak of war in 1939 hauled the country out of an economic morass and pushed it into sustained prosperity. As war loomed, European defense orders breathed life into American industry, as did modest domestic defense programs. Unemployment rates, on the rise in 1937, flattened out and began to decline. Government expenditures rose eleven-fold between 1939 and 1945, pumping billions of dollars into the economy, the equivalent of thousands of Civilian Conservation Corps, pushing GNP from $90.5 billion in 1939 to just over $210 billion by war's end. Seventeen million jobs were created; unemployment fell from seventeen percent in 1940 to under two percent in 1944. Market forces that had driven down wages ten years earlier now lifted them to unprecedented levels. Crop prices increased one hundred fifty percent. Industrial wages went up eighty-six percent.[70] Smokestacks belched smoke once more — back then, a welcome sight. Workers could choose from a number of well-paying jobs. Sugar, coffee, and other items were scarce, but plenty of food was on the table, and many enjoyed a partial return to consumer lifestyles. Had Clausewitz lived then, he might have observed that war is Keynesian economics by other means.[71]

The West has always been an important part of the myth of progress. It was a bountiful place where one could obtain land and build a future. By 1940, however, the frontier had long been closed. The open expanses that lured settlers hadn't been available for over fifty years. The war against Japan made the West the land where aircraft and shipbuilding industries thrived. Okies had fled the dust bowl only to find menial work, but when aircraft carriers and bombers were being built, they found good pay with a future. Someone with ability could build a new life in a new land with limitless potential. It wasn't a hundred and sixty acres, but, after more than a decade of hard times, a steady paycheck was just as good. The West would no longer be the supplier of raw materials to the "true" economy back East; its own industrial might emerged, luring huge amounts of money and talent, both during the war and for decades thereafter. Greeley's old recommendation once again rang true.[72]

The war boom altered the structure of American society. Widespread poverty ended and the middle classes expanded into a huge majority. Between 1941 and 1945, the lowest fifth of American families saw their incomes rise an astonishing sixty-eight percent; the next fifth enjoyed a fifty-nine percent increase; the middle segment thirty-six percent; the next thirty percent; the top fifth of families saw a twenty percent increase. (Note that price controls held inflation down and also that over sixteen million adults were in the service, where pay was, to say the least, quite low — about sixty dollars a month for most.) Farm income soared, allaying the fear that the family farm was disappearing. People could once again expect their children's lives to be better than their own.[73]

Scientific and technological advances abounded. In 1943, an economist commented: "In the space of two or three years, you are getting as much scientific progress in this country as you ordinarily get in 40 or 50 years."[74] The Garand rifle increased the firepower of American infantry. Sulfa drugs, penicillin, vaccines, and pesticides saved countless lives. The computer was developed to calculate artillery trajectories. Radar and sonar tracked enemy craft in the air and under the sea. Numerous lesser technological innovations modernized every factory and mine in the country. Plastics became substitutes for rubber that normally came from the East Indies, then occupied by Japan. The public hailed nuclear weapons as a miraculous scientific breakthrough that brought a swift end to the war and precluded a costly assault on Japan.[75]

The war itself gave an important emotional sense of progress. Mired in despair and directionlessness for the previous decade, the nation once more felt potent and purposeful. People were involved in a crucial historical event that restored meaning to life. Suicide rates had gone up sharply throughout the 1920s, and reached a peak in the early 1930s before receding somewhat. With the beginning of the war, suicide dropped sharply, reaching the lowest levels of the twentieth century.[76]

The war had unmistakable signs of progress, from the tentative offensives at Guadalcanal and in North Africa, through the middle periods of increasing confidence, to the beginnings of the end at Normandy and Leyte. The public could follow the war in lines moving regularly on the front pages of morning papers: the Solomons, Gilberts, Marianas, Philippines, Iwo Jima, and Okinawa; Tunis, Sicily, Rome, Paris, the Siegfried Line, and the Rhine. A shrinking black expanse on the map and photos of cheering French and Filipino civilians conveyed more than statistics could. Three years into the conflict, Jack Benny could quip that Japan was a group of islands completely surrounded by Nimitz. In early 1945, Joe Rosenthal's famous, almost mythic photograph of marines raising the flag atop Suribachi became an enduring symbol of progress and national will. It all culminated in 1945, less than four years after Pearl Harbor, at a headquarters in Rheims and aboard the *Missouri* in Tokyo Bay.

NATION BUILDING AND POWER PRESTIGE

The response to Pearl Harbor is often seen as a nationalistic frenzy, a re-emergence of the flag-waving patriotism that inspired boys to march off to previous wars. There is some truth here, but it does not really capture the moment. The memory of the Great War and the inevitable and depressing slide to war since 1939 prevented many from responding with old-fashioned idioms. *Yank* told of a soldier scheduled for discharge in a few days, who on hearing of the Japanese attack slumped back in his chair and muttered, "I'm screwed . . . I'm screwed."[77] Resigned determination was more common than spirited jingoism.

Though there were ditties about slapping Japs and throwing pies in Hitler's face, they were not in keeping with the general mood. Polls from 1940–41 showed increasing concern about involvement but also growing realization that Germany and Japan had to be stopped — unfortunately by us. William Manchester remembers, "Unlike the doughboys of 1917, we had expected very little of war. We got less." Robert E. Sherwood said of the period, "Morale was never particularly good nor alarmingly bad. There was a minimum of flag waving and parades. It was the first war in American history in which the general disillusionment preceded the firing of the first shot."[78]

The war effort nonetheless entailed a degree of dedication and sacrifice that is almost incomprehensible today. Though only fifty years apart, the people who fought the war are in this respect almost unrelatable to their children and grandchildren. At Tarawa, troops waded over seven hundred yards under murderous fire before reaching shore. B-17 crews suffered five percent casualties per mission, and were required to fly twenty-five of them. One needn't be an actuary to realize their odds weren't good. Eisenhower had estimated that paratroopers would suffer horrendous casualties at Normandy, and on the eve of D-Day was reluctant to face them. Nonetheless, he felt an obligation to meet with them — to exhort them of course, but also to spend a few moments with young men he was sending to their deaths. Hours later, in total darkness, they leaped out of aircraft and parachuted into Normandy, where the estimates proved accurate. Indeed, the five American divisions that landed on June 6th suffered seventy-five percent casualties in the next few weeks. Ten months later, on the other side of the world, another assault force was told to expect high casualties in the first few hours. They climbed down into amtracs, attacked the beach, and, after three months and almost fifty-thousand casualties, finally secured the small island of Okinawa. Though kill-ratios weren't reported or relevant then, it has been estimated that for every two Germans killed by American troops, three GIs were killed. And there were thousands of nameless hills and crossroads that were taken at high cost without being noted in a dispatch or history book, remembered only by those who were there. Over the years, countless films have trivialized these events by turning them into action stories and dull clichés ("We're all scared kid." — "Even you, Sarge?"), but if we can see past what Hollywood has done to the memory of the war, there is something remarkable here, and, to look ahead briefly, it underscores some of the changes since the war.

What motivated them? Perhaps the myth of glory, but the romantic sentiments that motivated young men for centuries had weakened after the Great War. Though not entirely absent among interwar youth, many of whom read *All Quiet on the Western Front* as an adventure novel,[79] the call to glory was an initial motivation that peaked at the recruitment center and faded quickly during boot camp. The first exposure to combat rendered romantic myths into objects of ridicule. Many analysts of the present day would look to a system of incentives and sanctions. Incentives have been important at least since the Roman soldiers who looked forward to the reward of a plot of land, the seventeenth-century mercenaries who hoped for loot from a conquered city, and the soldiers of the Revolution and War of 1812 who were promised land and bonuses.[80] But sixty bucks a month and a souvenir flag were little incentive, especially when others made much more in war plants. The GI Bill was not passed until 1944 and in any event couldn't have meant much under artillery and machine-gun fire. Many armies have used sanctions, from running the gauntlet to executions, to maintain discipline and efficacy. This was the case in Swiss mercenary units, the Prussian army, and even in the American Civil War, in which provosts and cavalry stood behind front-line regiments with orders to shoot deserters. However, there was little of this during the Second World War.

The most commonly encountered explanation for combat efficacy is primary-group dynamics, that is, loyalties built into small groups during training and combat. But in the course of many battles, casualties mounted swiftly and personnel changed rapidly, thereby destroying primary-groups. Many units lost over fifty percent in a few days, but still went on. Replacements came in and within a short period became effective parts of the unit. If combat efficacy depended mainly on these primary-group dynamics, *any* army, simply by following established models, would be able to train effective combat troops, but countless examples (including a later ally) show this not to be the case.[81]

A famous study of combat motivation found that only a small percentage of frontline soldiers mentioned idealism, patriotism, or revenge. Almost none felt their officers' leadership was a factor. The most important motivations were based on a general sense of duty: the need "to finish the job" (39 percent), group solidarity (14 percent), and a sense of obligation and self-respect (9 percent)[82] — much of which, according to many veterans, was based on ingrained character traits predating military service. The war drew from a deep reservoir of duty, drawn from various sources in American life, based on thousands of small and seemingly insignificant inflows. Though virtually gone now, this reservoir was quite large then; it formed an important basis for the bonds between individual soldiers, between them and their immediate leaders, between citizens and statesmen, and between a four-star general and a band of paratroopers.

One of the foundations of this broad-based sense of duty was the family: in routine chores, in taking care of an elderly or sick relative, in sacrificing for a child's education. It was also inculcated in the community: trusting fellow members of the neighborhood, helping a neighbor during planting and harvesting, performing charity work, doing volunteer work. Religious principles bolstered this cultural trend and tinged abrogation with sinfulness. Senses of tradition and honor were embodied in the aging veterans of Antietam and Chateau-Thierry honored in local Memorial Day services. Traditional views of manhood stressed honor, duty, seeing things through. Scions of the upper crust held a sense of noblesse oblige — with privilege came obligation. In 1942, this translated into service in the OSS, with the air corps, and as infantry officers, which by most accounts entailed very high casualties. A strong ethic of duty, of reciprocal rights and obligations, pervaded American life then and was mobilized into the war.[83]

The 1920s witnessed a decline in the sense of duty, as postwar cynicism eroded long-standing attitudes regarding war and duty, and as prosperity and mobility took a toll on community and family. The Depression had the fortuitous effect of reversing this trend. Families once again had to struggle to get by; sloughing off could mean losing the small margin enabling survival; older ways dismissed in care-free years were once again respected as first principles, or at least as something to hold on to.[84]

This raises the unsettling question whether America could have fought for four years and suffered over two million casualties had the self-indulgence of the 1920s not been reversed by economic collapse. The question is probably unanswerable, but Manchester offers some thoughts. After several agonizing pages recounting the deaths of fellow marines and his own near death on Okinawa, he observes:

> To fight World War II you had to have been tempered
> and strengthened in the 1930s Depression by a struggle for
> survival. . . . You had to remember your father's stories about
> the Argonne, and saying your prayers, and Memorial Day, and
> Scouting, and what Barbara Fritchie said to Stonewall Jackson. . . .
> And seen how your mother bought day-old bread and cut sheets
> length-wise and resewed them to equalize wear while your family
> sold the family car, both forfeiting what would be considered
> essentials today.[85]

The images Manchester recalls may seem trite today, but amid the Depression and war, people clung to them, and made it through the most difficult years in the country's history. Less benignly, the Depression also led to senses of frustration, bitterness, and powerlessness that, in many, turned into hatred, an emotion that could be channeled into the war effort. Hatred of a landlord or a banker could readily be redeployed against Japs and Krauts. Senses of powerlessness that nagged during the Depression disappeared on becoming part of a powerful war machine.

National Integration

During the war, an image emerged of the nation as one, the American people unified to end tyranny. We see it in broadcasts and posters, but perhaps most often in the cinema. Countless films depicted an assortment of college boys, urban ethnics, and farmboys, united by training and experience into a fighting unit — the melting pot at war. Though a national myth asserts that America has always been a melting pot, it would be more accurate to say that wars have lighted the fire under the pot, reducing ethnic and local ways, imposing standardized uniforms, food, experiences and aspirations, and converting disparate youths into American soldiers. One might be tempted to dismiss this as a tedious bit of propaganda, the creation of an unimaginative functionary with well-intentioned but dreary ideas on keeping up morale. However, it contains a measure of truth that should not be lost.

The American mainstream, from which came political, industrial, and cultural leaders, comprised mainly English and Scottish groups, outside of which there were large numbers of Irish, Italians, Jews, Blacks, Hispanics, American Indians, and other people, who, though contributing to the nation, were considered "others," not "real Americans." They endured various levels of alienation, ranging from subtle restrictions to overt contempt. Total war entailed mass mobilization, and this gave others the opportunity to prove themselves alongside real Americans. Previously unassimilated or partially assimilated groups became better integrated by the cult of GI Joe.[86]

Black Americans sought to win a "double victory," against domestic prejudice as well as foreign totalitarianism. Their contribution became apparent as early as Pearl Harbor, where Dorie Miller, a mess steward on the *West Virginia*, shot down several Japanese planes and earned the Navy Cross. His heroism (and later death off Tarawa), though mentioned in many papers, did not lead to proper recognition of his people's contributions, most of which remained invisible. In 1942, J. Saunders Redding wrote, "I do not like the world's not knowing officially that there were Negro soldiers on Bataan with General Wainright."[87] Government officials eager to avoid racial conflict, and black leaders eager to advance their cause, campaigned to make them more visible. When naming a parade ground on Fort Knox after a black soldier (Robert Brooks, killed in the Philippines shortly after Pearl Harbor) caused controversy, the post commander attacked the issue frontally: "For the preservation of America, the soldiers and sailors guarding our outposts are giving their lives. In death, there is no grade or rank. And in this, the greatest Democracy the world has known, neither riches nor poverty, neither creed nor race draws a line of demarcation in this hour of national crisis."[88]

Blacks served throughout the war, on all its many fronts, but almost always in segregated units. There were two black infantry divisions, the 92nd in the Solomons and the 93rd in Italy.[89] The black 2nd Cavalry Division, before ever reaching the front, was judged unreliable and disbanded on orders from General Patton, whose slaps in the face were not confined to figurative ones. (In fairness, when later assigned a black tank battalion, he told them: "I don't care what color you are, so long as you go up there and kill those Kraut sonsabitches."[90]) Black fighter squadrons and tank units saw action and won honors — and respect. Following the heavy losses of the Battle of the Bulge (winter 1944–1945), black volunteers served in previously segregated infantry units, foreshadowing the desegregation of the services a few years later.[91]

Back in the States, the NAACP prevailed upon the White House to ensure that defense jobs were open to all.[92] The OWI, in an effort to publicize the importance of black troops, saw that documentaries and short features showed their participation.[93] The dislocations of the war served to advance the cause as well. Population shifts drew blacks away from the rural South and into the industrial regions in the North, bringing many whites and blacks into the same workplace for the first time. Rising wages brought new outlooks and opportunities. As blacks saw the importance of organization during the war, membership in the NAACP went up ten-fold.[94]

Blacks realized that they too were contributing to the war effort, and so did many whites. America was beginning — only beginning — to change, and the change is reflected in the films of the period. Newsreels made an effort to show blacks in the service, as did Hollywood. *Lifeboat* (1944) portrayed various classes, races, and ethnic groups thrown together after their ship was sunk by a U-boat. They were all — it was not a time for subtle symbolism — in the same boat. *Since You Went Away* and *God Is My Co-Pilot* show blacks following war news and pulling for hometown kids, just as everyone else was. *Sahara* and *Bataan* depicted blacks serving and dying in combat, in North Africa and on the legendary holding action in the Philippines. When Americans went to theaters to get some understanding of the war, they saw black participation in it.[95]

Paul Fussell, not one to sentimentalize war experiences, admits that before the war, like most whites, he did not consider blacks to be Americans. On seeing black corpses strewn across a field, he realized, "The lucky among us, black or white, survived; the unlucky, black and white together, died in the open air or under trees or at the bottom of slit trenches. Where it mattered at all, we were quite the same."[96] When black replacements entered depleted infantry companies in 1945, there was grumbling and trepidation. But after a few months, seventy-seven percent of white veterans of integrated units stated that their view of blacks had become more favorable. One sergeant (perhaps it is relevant he was from South Carolina) said of integration: "When I first heard about it, I said I'd be damned if I'd wear the same patch they did. After that first day when we saw how they fought, I changed my mind."[97]

Jewish contributions to the war effort stemmed from the desire to demonstrate their loyalty and worth, but also to fight the Nazis, whose destruction of European Jews was becoming known. Jews served in many different branches, including combat units, as the Stars of David in the cemeteries of Normandy and Okinawa silently attest. Many other minority groups served as well. The 45th Infantry Division (drawn from national guard units in the Southwest) had many American Indians and Hispanics in its ranks. Bill Mauldin, who served in this division, modeled Joe of the famous "Willie and Joe" sketches after an Indian, who was later killed in action in Italy. An awkward but well-intentioned journalist observed, "A red man will risk his life for a white as dauntlessly as his ancestor lifted a paleface's scalp."[98] As much as we might wince here, his point is that all who serve in the war are real Americans, a discernible change from the opinion of earlier generations. While their relatives lived in internment camps, many Japanese-Americans served in the 442nd Regimental Combat Team in Italy and France, and with intelligence units in the Pacific.

This is not to say that all served harmoniously and cheerfully, thereby ending once and for all a dark part of traditional America. There was, however, at least for many Americans, a gradual if belated realization, born of eating the same C-Rations, enduring the same privations, loathing the same non-coms, and living through common hardships, that America was a more complicated and perhaps even a more powerful nation than prewar outlooks had acknowledged.

Regional, ethnic, and class antagonisms declined as well. The integrative effects were more pronounced overseas, where British, French, and other people saw the Americans not as various separate groups, but as a homogeneous bunch of Yanks.[99] Southerners, many of whom had lived in brooding resentment since 1865, felt like parts of the American whole for the first time. Impoverished Okies had been treated like animals when they fled to California from the dust storms, but found acceptance after the war: "Very few people suggested any more that [Okies] were 'of the lower fringe of humanity.' Those that served were simply American veterans — at least those who lived through it were — and many of them were heroes."[100] An ethnic Italian who served at Anzio recalled, "When we marched on Rome and I was continually greeted as an 'Americano' like all my buddies, I realized for the first time that I was not a 'dago' or 'wop' Italian but a real American."[101] This should underscore the fact that many people — Okies, Irish, Italians, Poles — had not been considered real Americans prior to the war. That we consider them so now stems largely from the integrative effects of the war. No one would claim that prejudices disappeared during the war or that postwar America solved the matter. The country was late in realizing its race problem, and the resolution might today be unsatisfactory, but where marches and editorials and petitions had failed, the exigencies of war forced the issue and, as shall be seen, put civil rights on the postwar agenda.

Norman Mailer's platoon in *The Naked and the Dead* may serve as a useful corrective to (though not a refutation of) the pat image of the infantry platoon melting pot. In the course of a harrowing patrol across a formidable mountain range, the platoon is rent by ethnic and personal animosities, at one point to the brink of mutiny. However, on securing the island, they look back on the rugged mountains, reflect upon their shared hardships, and, though bitter and exhausted, as far from the red, white, and blue image as possible, experience "a startled pride in themselves." They begin to joke and boast about their accomplishment.[102]

Restoration of Authority

Unifying effects were not limited to the integration of ethnic groups and minorities. The war, more precisely its victorious conclusion, restored confidence in various forms of authority, which emerged with greatly enhanced credibility, legitimacy, and sacredness, able to draw from a vast reservoir of prestige for decades.

The Depression had been a political as well as economic crisis, during which beliefs and institutions were as bankrupt as the local thrift. Confident predictions of good times just around the corner and continuous invocation of perky sayings only worsened matters. Roosevelt's common touch played well for a while, but the New Deal's success was short-lived, and a legitimacy crisis loomed once more.[103] The war, however, gave political leadership, from local councils running scrap drives to the planners of grand strategy, enhanced prestige and trust. (It is sobering to speculate on the consequences that a series of early defeats and blunders would have had on already weakened political institutions, but happily that was not the case, and America remained stable and committed to the war.) The Doolittle raid, Midway, Guadalcanal, and Tunisia reversed the gloomy trend of early 1942 and provided confidence and hope. Only a year after Pearl Harbor, the seemingly unstoppable Axis powers had been halted on all fronts. Two years after the fall of Bataan, people could speak confidently of victory in a year or so.

Business leaders had faced public hostility during the 1930s. They were widely thought of as grasping swindlers whose greed had brought on the Depression. Traditional principles of individualism, hard work, thrift, and free markets seemed to be delusions, folklore, self-serving myths foisted on average people by the rich. Many in the Roosevelt administration were openly hostile to what they saw as a discredited economic system. "Big business" became a term of abuse, and FDR looked for ways to bring the "economic royalists" to heel.

During the war, cooperation replaced confrontation, and "dollar-a-year" men from business replaced reformers. As Roosevelt listened increasingly to Dr Win the War, Ford churned out bombers, Kaiser rolled out ships, and Stetinius produced steel at record levels, before becoming Secretary of State.[104] Business leaders were once more respected members of the national community, because they too backed the attack by providing the GIs with the material to do the job. Big shots and average Joes were now on the same team. The virtues of the old order were appreciated anew. In previous decades, prosperity and cynicism had eroded the work ethic, until it was little more than the ghost of an old religion. But dedication to one's calling took on new importance when it involved making planes and bullets for the troops. In the fight against fascist evil, religious sentiments attached themselves once more to work.

The adaptability of industry allowed a rapid conversion to war-footing, developed countless innovations, and introduced new technologies, which greatly outstripped those of the enemy. Zeroes and Messerschmitts that had once ruled the air were, by 1944, blown out of the skies by Hellcats and Mustangs. The character traits that the system impressed upon the public — initiative, cooperation, adaptability — gave GIs advantages over their rigid authoritarian enemies. American productivity won the war, a fact celebrated in documentary footage of busy assembly lines, crowded marshaling yards, and bustling ports. We produced more planes, more tanks, more ammunition, more of everything, until the war resembled Grant deploying his vast resources against Lee's ill-supplied army.

Prior to the war, the military had been respected, but not especially so. It had produced a number of illustrious soldiers and statesmen, and following the Civil War enjoyed a great deal of prestige, but rapid demobilization and the passage of time returned the military to middle status. During the Second World War, the military trained sixteen million men and women, developed strategic plans, and defeated Imperial Japan and the Third Reich. The military, from buck private to five-star general, emerged victorious and lionized, ascending to the same august position it enjoyed after Appomattox.

From the perspective of the home front, the military seemed to work smoothly and harmoniously, but from within, from the perspective of the ordinary GI, it had more than its share of blunders, incompetence, and idiocy, all of which come across repeatedly and often bitterly in postwar literature. Rapid expansion necessitated promotion of the unqualified. Beef-witted corporals became sergeants and lieutenants, inept captains were thrust into regimental commands, and so on up the chain of command. (Little wonder the "Peter Principle" was identified after the war.) Where a civilian saw a stern but able sergeant, many GIs saw an illiterate bigot, resentful of the intellectualism of high school graduates. Where a civilian saw a bold commander, soldiers often saw a martinet who forced them to wear helmets, even far behind the front, "to keep them on their toes." As one veteran noted, with lingering acidity, "It was the hired help, not the 'professionals,' who won the war."[105]

Blunders were either kept under wraps (there was a war on) or seemed trivial in the big picture. Miscalculation of Tarawa's tides forced marines to wade ashore over seven hundred yards under heavy fire. American anti-aircraft guns near Sicily killed hundreds of GIs, as did bombers at St. Lô. The

7th Infantry Division trained long and hard for jungle warfare before being sent to the Aleutians. Omaha Beach was a catastrophe, as were the airborne landings inland. Utah Beach was relatively easy, in part because troops landed in the wrong area. Sherman tanks presented a high profile — a fact not lost on German eighty-eight crews — and were so prone to fire that they were nicknamed "Ronsons" because, like the lighter, they were "guaranteed to light every time." Military chiefs determined that the invasion of the Palaus was no longer necessary but felt it was too far along to cancel. There were ten thousand American casualties.[106]

The list could go on and on, but suffice it to say that the war gave us the word *snafu*, an acronym for *Situation Normal: All Fouled Up* (though some claim the *F* stood for another word, heard with numbing regularity in the military), and countless variations such as *tarfu, fubar,* and *janfu*.[107] Despite all the martinets and blunders, the military did win the war, perhaps not efficiently, but Germany and Japan surrendered, and in a period of time that did not leave the public looking for light at the end of the tunnel. Enjoying more prestige than at any time since Grant's army paraded down Pennsylvania Avenue, the military ascended to prestigious heights from which it influenced the country for decades. Most veterans looked back on all the snafus and incompetents much as Mailer's platoon looked back upon the mountain range of the small island they took. Despite all the snafus, it was a tremendous accomplishment.

The restoration of confidence in political, business, and military leaders spilled over to become an extensive and intensive faith in what might best be called "the system." The same system that had collapsed in the early 1930s now worked astonishingly well. In the years after the war, leaders of the system, school teachers, cops on the beat, parents in the home, business leaders, and elected officials from local councils to Commander-in-Chief enjoyed an infusion of prestige from a proud public, which saw in the various loci of authority continuities with the ideals and leaders that had won the war. They were stewards of the American way who had saved the world. In the eyes of many, leaders could do no wrong, nor even be suspected of less than the highest motives.

***

America had forged another Great Event. Those who cheered Eisenhower's ticker-tape parade on his return from Europe were certain that America had reached its greatest heights, and that, unlike previous great civilizations, it would remain there. In that proud and exultant moment, when a rendezvous with destiny had come about and the American century seemed assured, many must have felt as the young Arnold Toynbee did at the zenith of the British Empire:

> I remember watching the Diamond Jubilee procession myself as a
> small boy. I remember the atmosphere. It was: Well, here we are on
> the top of the world, and we have arrived at the peak to stay there
> — forever! There is, of course, a thing called history, but history is
> something unpleasant that happens to other people.[108]

For Britain, the two World Wars figured highly in that unpleasantness. The pride
and confidence of Victorian Britain dissipated after the carnage of the Great
War, and further eroded when it emerged from the next one, on the winning
side, but surpassed — politically, militarily, economically, and culturally — by
a former colony. The confidence with which it conquered and ruled an empire
was gone.[109]

For America, too, there would be a fall from the lofty heights of victory. But
that was later, and few at Ike's parade looked for historical analogy, or thought of
hubris or Gibbon or Spengler, or thought the war's disruptions would be lasting.
Few could see how much of America had changed, how the country had been
thrust into modernity, or how rapid changes would continue, or how another
war would acquaint Americans with a thing called history. But allusion to later
events intrudes and detracts from the moment. It is as out of place as bringing up
Spengler to a sailor kissing a nurse in Times Square. It is best simply to say that
in 1945, when America saved the world, when GIs drank wine in Berchtesgaden
and samurai surrendered their swords to guys from the neighborhood, when
millions knew they would return home alive, when after years of hardship the
nation could rejoice, America had its proudest moment.

CHAPTER FOUR

THE LID IS OFF
1945–1965

*Had they been Tyrian traders of the year B.C. 1000, landing from a galley
fresh from Gibraltar, they could hardly have been stranger on the shore of a
world, so changed from what it had been ten years before. . . . How much its
character had changed or was changing, they could but partly feel. For that
matter, the land itself knew no more than they.*

HENRY ADAMS, on returning to America after the Civil War

*Since the beginning of World War II, American society has been changing
continuously. All of the major characteristics of American society and culture
are changing so rapidly that it is more and more difficult to recognize older
American institutions and life styles. The older styles were defined in the first
half of the nineteenth century by, among others, de Tocqueville, and in the
first half of the twentieth century by Robert and Helen Lynd. This revolution
is so deep and pervasive that all traditional analyses of American society no
longer hold.*

JOSEPH BENSMAN AND ARTHUR J. VIDICH, *The New American Society*

After the war, there was little impetus to return to prewar patterns. Revitalized
by the war, the economy stood high above the rest of the world's, many of
which were in a shambles. Confidence in institutions was high, again in
contrast to most of the rest of the world. Dynamic change had been set loose.
Modernization surged through the country. Covered by a sacred aura of victory,
the country felt it could do no wrong. Anyone expecting the country to go back
might just as well ask it to become a Puritan colony once more.

BREAK WITH THE PAST

Americans have long defined themselves by change — throwing off British
rule, leaving old homelands, and pushing across frontiers — and wars have
been engines of change. Historians speak of the ante-bellum South, the
Reconstruction era, and the interwar period, all of which suggest that military
conflict has demarcated historical periods and brought changes that differentiate
them from previous eras. Each war brought movement, transition, and

dynamism. Victory provided or opened up new regions, expanded the economy, and invigorated the nation.

Veterans figure highly in postwar change. After the Revolution and the Civil War, many were awarded land grants. Consequently, veterans moved into the South and trans-Appalachian lands, bringing new regions into the Republic's domain. The incentive of free land provided a pull, while military experiences provided a push. Wars, especially modern ones, dissociate soldiers from their upbringings. Standardized food, clothing, and thought replace familial and community orientations. The military brings together people from various parts of the country and from differing social levels. Habits, beliefs, and accents encounter and often conflict with those of others, creating awareness that they are not fixed in stone, only conventions, local usages, or familial quirks. The military transports people into unfamiliar places, far from home, often far from America, where extraordinary experiences alter their lives. Skills are learned and opportunities present themselves. The scale of war, especially World War II with its enormous campaigns, huge logistical systems, millions of participants, made prewar life almost insignificant. Unskilled workers became engineers; soda jerks became bomber pilots; callow youths in 1941 commanded a hundred men or more a few years later.[1]

Soldiers had had enormous responsibilities placed on them, more than they would ever have again or want to have again. Friends and settings of just a few years earlier seem puerile and alien, and many veterans could never feel comfortable with them again. It was easy to be put off by civilians' pat talk of "action" and "heroism," and common to ponder the chasm between them and those who had remained abed. A ditty from the Great War asked if the doughboys would return to the farm after seeing Pa-ree. But reluctance to return to prewar life was probably stronger among those who had seen Chateau-Thierry or the Belleau Woods. It was no less so for those who had seen the Hürtgen Forest or Okinawa. There is nothing enchanting about war, but there is something broadening.[2]

Many found that home had changed during their absence, an experience nicely dramatized in *The Best Years of Our Lives* as returnees flying over their hometown note the differences. Even where outward appearances hadn't changed much, old rhythms had. The close-knit nature of small-town life was largely gone. Many veterans resented those who had stayed home, making lots of money and advancing their careers, while they were overseas on sixty bucks a month. Many felt that home was no longer there.

A further impetus to breaking with the past stemmed from its less than endearing nature. Memories of hard times, dust storms, malnutrition, and despair often countered sentimental aspects of life. The insularity and lack of opportunity of the old home compared poorly with opportunities opened by the war. Many towns and urban areas had been built around the turn of the century and were now decrepit. Many rural areas were still without electricity or hot water, and only barely and grudgingly integrated into the national economy. Americans had glimpsed a promising future of prosperity, technology, and modernity. Few pasts, however sentimentalized, could compete with that. As Marx (Groucho, not Karl) noted, "How ya gonna keep 'em down on the farm after they've seen . . . the farm."[3]

The whole country was still in flux following an event in the Pacific a few years earlier, and nothing could slow it down or restore things. Change was in the air. Philip Roth remembers it:

> [T]he upsurge of energy was contagious. Around us nothing was
> lifeless. Sacrifice and constraint were over. The depression had
> disappeared. Everything was in motion. The lid was off. Americans
> were to start over again, en masse, everyone in it together. . . .
> — the miraculous conclusion of this towering event, the clock of
> history reset and a whole people's aims limited no longer by the
> past.[4]

Probably at no time in American history had so much of the nation been so eager to break from its past and leap into a seemingly bright but essentially unknown future.[5]

THE FAMILY IN CONTINUED FLUX

The war put immense strains on the family. Fathers went into the service, across the country, around the world; mothers worked in defense industries and often served in the military. Extended family networks, which had never been especially strong in America but had begun to coalesce before the war, disappeared. Sociologists, religious authorities, and politicians were alarmed. During the war years, children grew up parentless, leading to increased teen-crime rates, which boded ill for the next decade or so. Returning fathers would be resented. Juvenile delinquency would skyrocket. Respect for authority and the sanctity of the family would fall apart. Experts predicted that the family would collapse in a decade or so.[6]

Looking back, these concerns were much overstated. In any case, the idea that family changes after 1945 were the consequence of dad's absence for the duration should be regarded with caution. Ties between fathers and children were not irretrievably broken: most GIs served about two and a half years, and most were not parents. Those who were, found no vast breach upon return and soon restored their position in the family. Restoration was all the more easy as dad returned home victorious, with a row or two of ribbons across his chest, the pride of the neighborhood. Of all the discontinuities the war brought, this was one of the most easily bridged. Wartime juvenile delinquency might have become more problematic had the war ended in defeat and malaise, but with victory it was contained by postwar respect for authority, including fathers.

An important family discontinuity was caused by accelerated bureaucratization. Throughout the previous half century, an economy of farmers, shopkeepers, tradesmen had been giving way, sometimes gradually, sometimes rapidly, to one based on organizations, management teams, and white-collar workers.[7] An economy based on individual skill and merit had given way to one based on corporations and bureaucracy. The transition began around the turn of the century, sped up during World War I, but slowed and even reversed itself during the Depression, when at times it was unclear if there was any economy at all. During World War II, over a half million small businesses went under as owners were inducted or lost contracts to large enterprises. Others had key people taken into the service or were based on consumer products such as automobiles and washing machines that were no longer made. These too went under.[8]

The rise of white-collar jobs was perhaps most noticeable in the federal government, where they increased from one million to three and a half million between 1940 and 1945, and only declined to two million after the war.[9] By the mid-1950s, Americans could look around and see just how far-reaching bureaucratization had become. Everywhere, there were layers of management, vice-presidents and partners, research and development divisions, regional offices, legal and personnel sections. Earlier, there might have been more concern. Corporate giants had been seen as threats to the common man and as responsible for the Depression, but they were now seen as essential parts of the nation. People had to adapt to them. Wartime ideology placed a premium on teamwork, cooperation, and subordinating personal interests to those of the nation. Individualism smacked of egotism, selfishness, and disloyalty. Such people dealt on the black market, sloughed off at the plant, or could not be relied upon under fire. In this respect, wartime experiences made the transition more acceptable.[10]

Fathers no longer worked near the home, on the farm, or downstairs in the store — a more significant separation than that entailed by war service. The father's work became abstract to children, as did many fathers. Children could hardly relate to work in corporate accounting or personnel as readily as they could to work on the farm or in the shop. Many sociologists noted that paternal authority, though strong, was no longer above question.[11] Ironically, the war weakened male identity in many ways. Men had focused their energies on the war effort, either in the service or in civilian work, but with peace the focus was gone, replaced by the quotidian, unheroic activities of going to work and paying bills. Making money was the new supreme commander — and a rather uninspiring one.

Appearance and reality were troubling. The civilian view that all who wore the uniform had performed countless acts of valor made most veterans uneasy over their important but mundane service in, say, the quartermaster corps. Who wanted to let on that he had never seen combat and that he had bought that Luger? Limited though it was, the independence women and children experienced during the war years made men uneasy about their roles and identities.[12] Many television shows of the time, today criticized for inculcating patriarchy, actually depicted fathers as less than certain, sharing decisions with the mother, bewildered by their children and new environs, though somehow getting through the day. Only in depictions of the past (*Bonanza, The Rifleman*) were fathers self-assured. (Perhaps significantly, Messrs Cartwright and McCain were also widowers.) The original title of one highly popular series of suburban family life, *Father Knows Best,* had a question mark at the end.

Family life based on shared work and the passing on of skills was a thing of the past. The transmission of values from one generation to the next was less smooth. Children looked for direction from an array of figures in popular culture. James Coleman expressed it this way:

> [A]dolescents today are cut off, probably more than ever before,
> from the adult society. They are still oriented toward fulfilling their
> parents' desires, but they look very much to their peers for approval
> as well. Consequently, our society has within its midst a set of small
> teen-age societies, which focus teen-age interests and attitudes on
> things far removed from adult responsibilities, and which may
> develop standards that lead away from those goals established by
> the larger society.[13]

Even in redoubts of tradition such as rural areas and ethnic neighborhoods, where family, community, and religion were stronger, young people were uncomfortable with the hold of the past.[14]

Suburbanization is relevant here. Families moved away from kinship ties and the influences of old ways. Everything was different now — locale, income, status group, outlook — and questions naturally arose regarding the effectiveness or even the desirability of continuing old patterns of family life, including child-rearing customs. As David Riesman put it, "The loss of old certainties in the spheres of work and social relations is accompanied by doubt as to how to bring up children."[15] Child-rearing had been an amalgam of religious adages, local folklore, family tradition, and old-country customs. They had once enjoyed great respect but now seemed groundless folkways, quaint lore from dear but unsophisticated people who believed in superstition, folk remedies, and the righteousness of Billy Sunday.[16]

Traditional child-rearing practices seemed as out of place in modern America as a horse-drawn cart. Americans, especially middle-class ones, looked to experts for modern methods based on the latest scientific research. One sociologist found that "middle-class mothers often mention experts, other mothers and friends as their sources of ideas about child-rearing. If they mention their own parents, it is usually as a negative reference."[17] Experts knew the modern ways of socializing children, teaching them to adjust and become productive members of society.[18] Relying on old ways could bring incalculable harm by undermining the children's confidence and stifling their creativity.[19] Alternately, one could simply look about the subdivision to see how others were raising their kids. This might well have been the first time in history that a people doubted something as basic as traditional child-rearing practices and entrusted the matter to people they never met.

Into the gap between the generations streamed numerous agents of change, from low and high culture, from popular media as well as from the universities. Postwar affluence meant greater access to movies, but it also brought new forms of entertainment such as television and hit music. An earlier time presented Andy Hardy, the hard-working judge's son, faithful to family and community, starry-eyed over the girl next door. Though only a decade or so old, the series was now hopelessly out of date. New stars of youth culture had little in common with him. Holden Caulfield, the anomic boy in J. D. Salinger's *Catcher in the Rye*, struck a chord with postwar youth. Perhaps drawing from the archetypes of the disillusioned soldier and the swaggering, leather-jacketed flyboy, figures such as James Dean and Marlon Brando — loners, victims of circumstance, men who despite their youth had seen or seen through too much — became popular among the young. They were hipper than and at odds with their surroundings, eager to break away. Many protagonists, such as Yossarian in Heller's *Catch-22* and McMurphy in Kesey's *One Flew over the Cuckoo's Nest* initially seem mentally ill, but the reader comes to see them as sane and their environments crazy.[20]

Affluence brought greater emphasis on education. Given free tuition and a decent stipend, GIs enrolled in college in huge numbers. Parents with high school diplomas or less, new entrants to the middle classes, sent their children to college. The curriculum was for the most part practical, geared to preparing the young for a place in society and, numerous complaints notwithstanding, only rarely and obliquely criticized American beliefs and institutions. Still, there were aspects that contributed to distancing youths from traditional orientations. The modern outlook held that every social system, from the Trobriand Islands to the United States, adopted certain beliefs and customs, Samoans and Middletowners had their rites of passage, and America as well as Russia had its own national character. One textbook stressed that parochialism was an obstacle to a modern career:

> Because we were born and reared in one culture, it is difficult for
> us to understand the customs and ways of life in another culture.
> Only one's own way seems right and proper. In many occupations,
> however, it becomes very important to understand a culture
> different from one's own. Agricultural missionaries, employees of
> our government's technical assistance program, Armed Services
> personnel, corporation employees stationed in foreign lands,
> all need to understand the culture of the area in which they are
> located.[21]

For many, more the young than the veterans and their peers, an assertion of undisputed superiority of one's social system was a bit provincial, unsophisticated, the sort of outlook to which the elderly and rustics clung.[22]

The family had once performed numerous roles, but by the early 1960s most were gone or receding. Formerly, a person was born at home, educated there, worked there, recovered from illness there, died there, and even eulogized there. No more. Most families no longer had to struggle to make ends meet. Films such as *A Tree Grows in Brooklyn* and *I Remember Mama* depicted old family life, but did so as nostalgic homage to a passing way of life. Riesman observed that children no longer did family chores out of a sense of duty. They had to be paid.[23]

The family was still a center of affection and warmth, yet more and more it was a unit of consumption, sampling the array of goods the nation produced. After years of Depression and war, Americans wanted to retreat into the haven of a family. Popular psychology, magazines, films, and television presented the family for the most part in those terms, and constructed an idealized model based on prewar forms of family life and postwar consumerism.[24] The disjuncture between a myth manufactured by popular media and a reality of continued weakening would someday become apparent.

CONTINUED LOSS OF COMMUNITY

The war shook up virtually every community. As a popular book put it, the winds of war scattered Americans across the continent. The ethnic neighborhood changed greatly or began to disappear. Suburbs sprouted up around every city but did not form meaningful communities, at least as prewar Americans knew them. Life became more individualistic, less governed by local norms. European visitors were quick to notice the absence of community and the cult of mobility.[25]

Local communities once guarded against marauding outlaws and raiding parties, but these threats were long gone. Lively legends remained and had binding effects, but the community no longer had to unite against outlaws and hostiles. Mechanization of agriculture in previous decades led to greater crop yields, but also to less need for cooperative planting and harvesting, as well as to migrations to urban areas. Between 1945 and 1965, net migration from rural areas averaged 874,000 people per year.[26] Rising affluence and leisure time reduced civic-mindedness. The war injected new vitality into communities but also ended stability and insularity. The composition and rhythms of local life changed suddenly and continued to do so well after V-J Day. The war created new wealth that surpassed that of old notables. The importance of founding families receded. Prosperity let many acquire land and property in their locale, further rooting them there, but most people looked elsewhere. In one rural New York village studied in the late 1950s, only twenty-five percent of the population had been born there.[27]

To remain the same was to stagnate and miss out on tremendous opportunities. One sociologist estimated that twenty percent of the population changed residence every year.[28] Continued defense spending and attendant growth on the West Coast ensured that migration there would continue. The career paths of many in the new middle classes entailed routine relocations. Eager to broaden their experiences and move up the corporate ladder, they moved every few years. Managers of one large corporation joked that its acronym stood for "I've Been Moved," then called the van line, knowing that *not* being asked to relocate boded ill. Even those staying in an area nevertheless usually moved to better housing as soon as incomes allowed. The military remained quite large and moved its members even more frequently than did IBM.[29] Children went to college in unprecedented numbers, moved to new areas, found new opportunities, and rarely returned home. Senior citizens, who we might think least likely to move about, left for retirement developments in warmer climes. Affluence of course was a factor, but deteriorating community life played a part as well. One study found that seventy-five percent of such people no longer had children in their old hometowns.[30] People came and people went, and after a while you didn't even remember their names.

Rural America had been giving way since the late nineteenth century. The First World War had led to a decline in rural population, and the Second led to an even more precipitous one: down twenty-seven percent between 1940 and 1955.[31] Mass media penetrated the heartland as never before, noticeably reducing regional accents and ways. Primary-group relations declined as people went their way; churches and schools closed in large numbers; shoppers preferred modern stores in bigger towns.[32] Suburbanization delivered the most serious blow. Young people, often veterans with new jobs and GI benefits, left old communities for suburbs, the most famous of which, the Levittowns, were built by an entrepreneur who had honed his craft building wartime housing near Norfolk.[33] Bright and cheery, replete with good schools, nice parks, and the promise of a new way of life, suburbia drew millions away from towns and cities.

Criticism of suburbia erupted scarcely before the sod took hold and the first supermarket opened. Much of it was based on snobbery and prejudice — how could suburbia compare to the genteel images in *Town and Country*? Critics complained of banality and standardization; but most older neighborhoods were hardly aesthetic visions. There were also complaints of conformity; but there had certainly been far more in small towns and ethnic neighborhoods.[34]

More thoughtful objections pointed out that there was something lacking there, something that made suburbs less than meaningful communities. Suburban tracts lacked senses of organic whole, belonging, continuity, and common involvement. Older neighborhoods had a workplace as a center of life — a plant, a mill, a stockyard, a produce market. But in suburbia, one commuted to a distant place of work, only rarely that of neighbors. There were no factory whistles, freight trains, or produce carts to provide rhythms and reminders of who you were and what was expected.[35] Neighbors once felt free to stop over, especially on Sundays and holidays, without calling first, in many places without knocking. This gave way to the new value of privacy, a legacy of years of intrusions in military life and the hurly-burly of the times. Most suburbanites wished to live without outside impositions.[36] Older people were generally absent in suburbs. Children were separated from family lore of men and women crossing prairies and oceans, building new lives on frontiers and in cities, and slogging through the mud of Petersburg and the Argonne. Whatever links children had with the past came from the proximate experiences of their parents, or, more importantly, from small screens in their living rooms.

Suburban tracts were less able to enforce norms. In prewar communities it wasn't improper to discipline the mischievous children of neighbors; parents felt gratitude for the help and shame for their shortcomings. But the old neighborhoods had changed too much. The composition was too different, primary ties and the assumption of trust were absent. Suburbs lacked the intimacy, shared experiences and hopes, and consensus on proper behavior in which old neighborhoods had prided themselves. An observer of suburbia noted increasing reluctance to meddle in the concerns of others, including scolding others' children.[37]

A further erosion of community came from rising bureaucracy. Suburbs were only rarely incorporated and self-governing. Most left matters to county and state governments, relinquishing a vital part of community life. This was felt in older communities too. The Depression had overwhelmed local charities and shifted responsibility to extra-local agencies; the war saw federal supervision of housing standards and hiring practices. The trend continued well after 1945 as new roads, schools, sewage systems, and the like had to be built. People shrugged it off — costs had gotten too high, let the experts handle things — but an important part of community had been lost. One study called this, "the surrender of jurisdiction."[38]

The 1920s saw the beginning of mass media. Movies, magazines, and the radio began to draw Americans, especially the young, away from their locale and orient them to mass culture. The Lynds and numerous others noted an accompanying decline in church attendance, volunteer associations, and other parts of local life. The Second World War saw a large increase in public attention to the mass media, as people eagerly followed war news in newspapers and on the radio.[39] Following the war, the mass media added the new force of television, which figured highly in loosening community. People once gathered during evenings, to share experiences, play cards, and talk politics — to socialize. Now they watched television.[40] Old community life could not compete: local newspapers, fifty-watt radio stations, amateur theaters, social clubs, and self-improvement societies lost audiences. Modern Americans were content to stay home, detached from neighbors, passing away the time with the new medium.[41]

Many books and films showed the problem of declining community. Though usually seen only as sentimental holiday fare, *It's A Wonderful Life* is a look at a community struggling with postwar change. The town shows the strains of demographic change and new wealth stemming from wartime production, especially plastics. The charming hamlet of Bedford Falls is becoming the cold Pottersville, whose raucous juke joints, austere and antagonistic social relations, and primacy of the cash nexus constitute the bleak end-point of forces put into motion a few years back. Small-town community wins out in the end, but only through divine intervention.

Another genre from the period, wholly lacking in Capra's nostalgia, drew from earlier criticisms of small-town life by Sinclair Lewis and Sherwood Anderson and contrasted with the sentimentalization of that life during the Depression and war. Close-mindedness and hypocrisy are once again the hallmarks of town life. These themes filtered down from the highbrow literature of *Babbitt*, *Main Street*, and *Winesburg, Ohio*, and reached the mass market, both in book and movie form, with *Cat on a Hot Tin Roof*, *Peyton Place*, and several imitators. In this genre, the town's upright pretensions are debunked. The town is rife with adultery, unhappiness, and other dark secrets, almost invariably associated with prominent families whose Puritan exterior is revealed as sham. Creative individuals cannot survive there. Related themes recur in *The Long Hot Summer, Baby Doll, Written on the Wind, Bad Day at Black Rock,* and *This Property Condemned,* in which an outsider arrives and exposes hypocrisy, an aging or dying patriarch is plagued by irresponsible children, an eldest son is incapable of siring an heir, lively night clubs and racy sports cars disrupt old ways. It all signaled senses of discontent and discontinuity, and probably strengthened and disseminated them as well.[42]

Clergymen and sociologists, journalists and old-timers, noted postwar changes to community life. Volunteer associations lost members; civic mindedness and senses of interrelatedness declined; materialism and privacy became prized; senses of belonging were weaker. The ability of society to provide rootedness and continuity and to pass on basic values was breaking down. A malady had developed in local communities during the 1920s. They found new strength during the war but emerged exhausted. By the early 1960s, they were again in failing health.[43] For many young people, the small town had to be escaped from — Fairmont to Hollywood, Tupelo to Memphis. Cities and suburbs were the new centers of life, often in California, the state most dramatically affected by the war, where the hold of tradition was weakest. On the West Coast, openness to change was greater than in the rest of America, to the point of ridicule in the rest of the country. To many, California was a cautionary example of directionless change, fortunately confined to a distant coast.

PROGRESS AND PLENTY

The war revitalized the myth of progress. The economy rebounded, social mobility returned, and the ordeal ended in glorious victory. Though tarnished by later events and trivialized by sports usage, the word "victory" then connoted more than an agreeable end to war. It was positively incandescent, charged with pride, confidence, and unity. It meant relief from anguish and suffering, solace for the tremendous sacrifice, reunion with loved ones, senses of wellbeing and purposefulness, and confirmation of once questioned truths. Democracy triumphed over fascism, good over evil, the American way over European and Asiatic archaisms. Buoyed by the experience, America strode ahead, confident that heaven was in its place and that the nation that had vanquished the Wehrmacht had a special place in the world and would stay there, forever.

Renewed faith in progress was only somewhat diminished by deteriorating relations with the Soviet Union and the start of the Cold War. Five years after Americans and Russians embraced at the Elbe, mistrust intensified and positions hardened. Former allies, each recently imbued with power prestige and more confident than ever, now pointed increasingly deadly weapons at each other. The effect, at least in the first decade or so, was less to undermine faith in progress, than to engage the nation in a new cause, another contest between good and evil. There were signs of progress here, too: lifting blockades, forging instruments of containment, rebuilding shattered nations, maintaining technological superiority in arms and industry, and leadership of the free world.

In 1950, the Korean War broke out. Fighting moved rapidly up and down the rugged peninsula in the first year, but then stabilized near the old demarcation line, where, for the next two years, the war raged over hilltops and negotiating points. The war had an air of unreality: borders and legal distinctions had to be respected; battle lines scarcely budged in two years. Meanwhile, the casualties mounted, with over fifty-four thousand Americans dead in three years.[44] The public, seeing no signs of progress, grew restless. In 1952, Americans placed their trust in Ike, the hero of the European theater, who soon succeeded in bringing about a truce. It was neither victory nor defeat, but anything forged by Ike was okay. Soldiers, statesmen, and the general public all agreed that America would never again involve itself in a land war in Asia.[45] Korea was a break in a steady stream of progress to which the country soon returned. The Cold War led to competition for control of outer space, which provided clear indications of progress, scientific and military. Radios, dogs, primates, and humans were launched into space, to gain an advantage in prestige in the earthly contest. The space race became a showcase of American technology, know-how, and courage, fulfilling the need for continued signs that the nation was moving forward and, at least in some respects, beating the Soviet Union.

Education had been a key part of American life, with each generation generally attaining higher levels of education. During the war, millions of people learned navigation, engineering, oceanography, logistics, communications, medicine, and foreign languages. After the war, the GI Bill sent millions to trade schools, colleges, graduate and professional schools. The children of the war generation followed their lead, often with incentives provided by the Cold War. Political and military leaders called for greater emphasis on science and technology, and subsidized those fields. Foreign languages, too, were deemed critical for the new global power, and the study of defense-related languages such as Russian and Chinese received federal grants.

Higher incomes and more possessions had always been part of the myth of progress. The Depression rudely ended a general trend of economic growth, and the myth was close to collapse. The war swiftly returned the country to full employment, bringing good income to most, but with so much of the economy producing war matériel, there were few consumer goods to purchase, and what could be found was usually rationed. It was widely feared that with peace unemployment would return to prewar levels. A GI rhyme foretold of coming home from a long war only to find another depression:

> The Golden Gate in '48
> The breadline in '49

But GIs are seldom an optimistic bunch, and neither prediction came true. The following decades saw enormous prosperity and an immense consumer binge. Prosperity reshaped the lives of Americans and, after Depression hardships and wartime shortages, materialism became more important than ever before. By the late 1940s, after industry reconverted to consumer goods, the country was eager to bask in the satisfaction of a job well done and satisfy two decades of pent-up demand. As Averell Harriman put it, Americans simply wanted to relax and drink Coca Cola.[46]

A further impetus to consumerism lay, strangely enough, in wartime propaganda. In the pages of *Life* and *Look*, between stories of battles and bond drives, there were prominent advertisements for consumer products. What is remarkable here is that, regardless of one's income, ration card, or connections, the items couldn't be bought — they weren't being made. Businesses proudly noted the radios, uniforms, medicines, bombers, and trucks they were making, and, in the same ad, promised that victory would bring unprecedented prosperity, technological marvels, and labor-saving devices. The *Saturday Evening Post* thought it had hit on an important morale booster when it chided the forces of totalitarianism in a curious way: "Your people are giving their lives in useless sacrifice. Ours are fighting for a glorious future of mass employment, mass production and mass distribution and ownership."[47] (Unpersuaded, the Axis fought on.) Wartime propaganda promised that the sacrifices of today would be rewarded with refrigerators, houses, automobiles, an abundance of clothes and food, luxury items, and other things that seemed equally exciting and magical. Some electronics firms promised that every household would have a television, but few believed it. There were, after all, some limits to the public's credulity.

After the war, people bought and bought. If it cost too much, they got credit. Concern with craftsmanship diminished: if something broke, they bought another. Roadsides and intersections were transformed. Shopping centers shot up in the blink of an eye, unlike anything most Americans had ever seen, unlike anything many older people had ever cared to see. A popular history saw material abundance as a defining theme in the nation's history.[48] The concept of the American dream had once had a rich meaning of political and religious freedoms, wondrous opportunities, and much more, but it soon placed primary importance on material goods.[49]

RELIGION AND NORMS

The First World War brought on cynicism, but not so the Second, at least not in America. Other countries, even those on the winning side, emerged devastated, seething with animosities over collaboration and ineptitude, or sensing that their days of greatness were over. The war had brought about increased religiousness, but when America emerged triumphant and war anxieties disappeared, the intensity of religion, though probably not its scope, waned.

Postwar Religion

With the end of the war, after a respectable period of thankfulness, religiousness declined. The trials were over, the dead buried. The triumph over evil had proven the righteousness of Americans, just as it had after the Civil War, and a similar sense of complacency set in.[50] Ironically, wartime mobilization of religion contributed to its weakening. Previously, each denomination had erected walls between it and others, underscoring differences in doctrines and rites, often vilifying rivals. Wartime ideology, however, stressed common elements and purposes. Differences seemed insignificant and petty while fighting the Third Reich and the Japanese Empire. Religions were united and tossed together until, after the war, the differences were difficult to reassert. An amorphous religiosity emerged.[51]

Modern families and communities affected religion. Spiritual and moral practices are not independent of surroundings. They are ethereal parts of culture, based on the edifices of family and community, which after the war, as noted, lost vitality and thence no longer reinforced religious sentiments.[52] Furthermore, much of modern life had a decidedly secular tone. Nature and society were governed by observable scientific laws, cause and effect. Divine direction and intervention — the stuff of earlier forms of history — were rarely openly denied, but neither were they openly professed much either.[53] The war added to the secularizing process. The public focused on military campaigns, political dynamics, and material production, which though accented with a prayer or two, nonetheless had the effect of riveting national attention on armies, generals, statesmen, planes, and ships. Attendant with this was greater confidence in secular leaders, the military, scientists, experts, and the rational application of resources to human problems.[54] The war conferred, perhaps transferred, a great deal of sacredness to the military and the state. History was less the unfolding of fate or divine will than the work of governments with powerful armies and navies. The power and glory of the American state became central to the postwar outlook.[55]

Polls showed that Americans were still quite religious. Attendance at services was high; churches sprang up in the suburbs; and, apart from the occasional fashionable atheist, almost everyone professed to believe in God, the Ten Commandments, heaven and hell, and so on.[56] But many observers noted important changes. Congregations were different, more heterogeneous, and less involved with one another. The relationship between ministers and their congregations was not the same. Clergymen no longer played vital roles in people's lives; pastoral visits declined or became formal in nature, little more than dinner engagements. People looked less to spiritual figures for guidance than to psychologists, teachers, social workers, and other secular experts. Ministers still preaching the old-time religion irritated their congregations and had to change their message or move on.[57]

Psychologists held that religion might be based on nothing more than primitive needs or neuroses.[58] The religion of old, fiery certainty, direct relationship to God, inner retrospection, searching for spiritual guidance, were no longer parts of most people's lives. The view of man's inherent wickedness and need for constant religious supervision was no longer readily applicable to a people who had just rid the world of evil. Faith in God, as Cotton Mather or Dwight Moody had understood it, was relegated to backwaters, but even there many young people complained that participating in Sunday meetings would make them old.[59] Religion was replaced by what has been called "faith in faith," amorphous beliefs, which, though based on religion, were largely devoid of meaningful religiousness.[60] The force that had energized the colonies into breaking from Britain, ended the evil of slavery, and helped to sustain the nation through its trials had lost vitality and become another status symbol, like the automobile displayed in the driveway.

William Dean Howells noted a similar decline in religiousness among the upper crust of the nineteenth-century:

> Religion there had largely ceased to be a fact of spiritual experience,
> and the visible church flourished on condition of providing for
> the social needs of the community. It was practically held that the
> salvation of one's soul must not be made too depressing, or the
> young people would have nothing to do with it.[61]

By the 1950s, this form of religious experience had spread to the mainstream. The wave of religious television shows and Biblical epics of the period might be cited as evidence of religion's strength, but they would better be seen as evidence that it was becoming a form of entertainment.[62] Amid this dilution of religion, various forces and desires, held in check in earlier generations, began to push against social norms, which slowly retreated.[63]

The Acquisitive Society

Frederic Wakeman's *The Hucksters* noted the rise of material pursuits during and after the war. Shocking in its day, it tells of a young man who leaves the Office of War Information for the advertising world — not a great change in the author's view, merely an exchange of one form of propaganda for another. After all, the director of WWI public information referred to his work as "the world's greatest adventure in advertising."[64] And as a later observer put it, "The postwar power of 'the media' to determine what shall be embraced as reality is in large part due to the success of the morale culture in wartime."[65] In Wakeman's novel, though the war is still on, its urgency is over. The ad agency is seeking to capitalize on Japan's impending surrender by allying V-J Day symbols with advertising copy for a brand of soap. In this world, the dollar is almighty, one learns to rise above principle on a daily basis, and everyone knows the score.[66]

Though received as social satire, it became clear over the years that *The Hucksters* offered valuable insights. Similarly, the popular film, *The Best Years of Our Lives*, showed returning veterans having difficulty adjusting to the materialism created by the war. Every suburb, commuter train, and office building had thousands of people whose eyes were fixed on the output of consumer goods, which Americans had once been admonished to regard as a light cloak they might easily shed. Postwar prosperity eroded that old principle as people found V-8 engines, kitchen luxuries, televisions, and all the rest more appealing than an old cloak. Much of life became "a bland ritual of competitive spending."[67]

The war boom went on for decades. Throughout the 1950s and early 1960s, the children of the Depression eagerly purchased more and more new products. Cars were bigger, clothes more colorful. By the mid-1960s, a critical junction in the contest between tradition and modernity was reached. National holidays such as Memorial Day and George Washington's Birthday were changed from their original dates to moveable ones, on Mondays, which gave the public three-day weekends and more opportunity to shop. Though largely unnoticed, the change was perhaps one of the most important of the century, signaling a triumph of consumerism and leisure over tradition and heritage.

Coarsening of Culture

The coarsening effects of the war did not end in 1945. Coarsening had become ingrained; people had changed. Toward the end, as the workings of the Nazi death camps became known, the public discovered depths of human malevolence few could have imagined. After so much death and destruction, it was difficult to see the world in sentimental and romantic terms. Coldness, amorality, cruelty, and violence became more prominent in culture. Mechanisms that once limited them no longer worked well after being all but suspended during the war.

War novels showed a pronounced disdain for prewar sentiments and conventions, even more than avant-garde novels smuggled into the country in the interwar years. In this respect, the war had a double coarsening effect: the war itself as well as the later books with which the public came to terms with it. Literature abounds with themes of the destruction or impotence of idealism. In *A Bell for Adano*, a well-intentioned military governor is relieved of his command by his boorish, authoritarian superior. Mister Roberts, whose decency merited portrayal by Henry Fonda, is killed by a kamikaze. Billy Pilgrim in Kurt Vonnegut's *Slaughterhouse-Five* is an innocent youth until he witnesses the Battle of the Bulge and the bombing of Dresden.[68]

In Norman Mailer's *The Naked and the Dead*, decency is overwhelmed by the brutality of Sgt. Croft, the embodiment of America's frontier past, and Gen. Cummings, the same of its militaristic future. One soldier rises against Croft but ultimately knuckles under; another discovers Croft's murderousness but is powerless to do anything about it. After expounding his martial world-view, Cummings sadistically orders the naive Lt. Hearn to pick up a cigarette butt or face court-martial. He picks it up. When Hearn takes over a platoon, Croft, resentful of his loss of authority, arranges his death (as, in a way, did Cummings). Another character's wholesome upbringing is the object of derision ("no apple pie today"), as though Andy Hardy had suddenly been put into combat in a Pacific jungle.

The protagonists of Irwin Shaw's *The Young Lions* direct inexperienced GIs into a suspected ambush — better them than us. It concludes with a soldier expressing hope for the postwar world, but an embittered German soldier, whose hardening has been mirrored in the narrative, kills him, even though he knows the war is nearly over. Another GI hunts down the now disarmed German and kills him. A character in Burns's *The Gallery* observes, "I thought that all humanity had gone from the world, and that this war had smothered decency forever."[69] Mailer uses his unparalleled descriptive skills to convey, in horrifying detail, the reality behind a communiqué reporting a "mop-up operation:"

> It was simple, a lark. [T]he mopping up was comparatively
> pleasant, almost exciting. The killing lost all dimension, bothered
> the men far less than discovering ants in their bedding. . . . Certain
> things were SOP. The Japanese had set up many small hospitals in
> the last weeks of the campaign, and in retreating they had killed
> many of their wounded. The Americans who came in would finish
> off whatever wounded men were left, smashing their heads with
> rifle butts or shooting them point-blank.

But there were other, more distinctive ways. One patrol out at dawn discovered four Japanese soldiers lying in stupor across a trail, their ponchos covering them. The lead man halted, picked up some pebbles and flipped them into the air. The pebbles landed on the first sleeping soldier with a light pattering sound like hail. He awakened slowly, stretched under the poncho, yawned, groaned a little, cleared his throat, and stretched with the busy stupid sounds of a man rousing himself in the morning. Then he poked his head out from under the poncho. The lead man waited until the Jap saw him and then, as he was about to scream, the American sent a burst of Tommy-gun slugs through him. He followed this by ripping his gun down the middle of the trail, stitching holes neatly through the ponchos. Only one Jap was still alive, and his leg protruded from the poncho, twitching aimlessly with the last unconscious shudders of a dying animal. Another soldier walked up, nuzzled the body under the poncho with the muzzle of his gun, located the wounded man's head, and pulled the trigger.[70]

The Naked and the Dead, with surely some of the most cold-blooded passages in English literature, could never have been published before the war, but in the changed culture of the postwar years it found a publisher and became a bestseller.

Postwar literature is crude. The use of obscenities was as common in military life as an early wake-up — indeed, they went hand in hand. No honest depiction could avoid using rough language, and, accordingly, vulgar slang for body organs and functions found their way into print. Convinced that his publisher would never allow the actual words, Mailer created "fug" and "fuggin" for *The Naked and the Dead*.[71] Soon thereafter, perhaps with the publication of *From Here to Eternity*,[72] and in part owing to public acceptance of Mailer's creative diction, vulgar language began to abound, practically becoming obligatory. As might be expected after so much exposure to decidedly unromantic relations, the depiction of sex was often coarse, mechanical, and soulless. For every girl waiting back home, there were three or four waiting on the street corner. Syphilis and gonorrhea are routine occurrences, whereas before the war they had only been mentioned in whispers or in hidden pamphlets. *The Naked and the Dead* contains numerous references to soldiers getting a dose of the clap; *The Gallery* contains a whole chapter on the travails of a GI who contracts VD.[73]

More banal effects of coarsening manifested themselves in the content of Western and detective genres, most of which became more violent and sadistic. Fighting, killing, and prominent display of weapons were everywhere, signaling that violence was part of life and essential to resolve matters. Of course, violence had been part of American culture at least since Cooper's tales of Natty Bumpo fighting the Iroquois, and the dime novels of frontier life. But the war greatly strengthened the trend, and the media eagerly beamed out the message in film and television. A Ford Foundation study in the 1950s found that television viewers saw almost three thousand acts or threats of violence per week.[74] Many postwar films show a changed country. Often, a character returns to find, not a familiar neighborhood, but a dark, amoral environment, in which the old expectations of a society held together by norms no longer hold, in which law and order are upheld by dishonorable means.

Many films and television shows were peculiarly fascinated with weaponry: Thompsons brandished in a manful way that made veterans laugh; grenade pins pulled with teeth (it can be done, but few soldiers and fewer dentists recommend it); prominently displayed sidearms to convey unmistakable virility. The titles of movies and television shows suggest obsession (*Winchester '73, Springfield Rifle, Colt .45, Carbine Williams*), as did the defining weapon of choice of heroes. Popular television stars sported exotic weaponry such as Buntline Specials, derringers, Bowie knives, Winchesters, Winchester wranglers, sawed-off Winchesters, and even a bat that fired bullets.[75]

Changing Sexual Norms

During the war, many people sought intimacy amid the stress and uncertainty. Millions of GIs became familiar with the prostitution trade flourishing around military bases and overseas. Dislocated people looked for companionship in new environs. Signs of changing sexual norms abounded in the next few decades. Academic books, as any scholar will attest, only rarely enjoy widespread readership, but an entomologist's study of human sexuality swept the nation. Alfred Kinsey interviewed thousands of people over a number of years and published his findings in the late 1940s and early 1950s. The public read his findings on such previously taboo subjects as the percentage of men and women who were virgins at marriage, the frequency of sexual relations by age group, incidence of adultery and masturbation, and the number of homosexual contacts.

Literature and film tested limits and found them flexible. Publication of *Lolita, The Naked Lunch,* and other "racy" books led to celebrated court cases, most of which ended with benchmark decisions asserting the value of free speech over old restrictions. Needless to say, interest in sex took on less erudite and literary forms. Mainstream magazines of the 1930s had some sexual content: Vargas girls, Gibson girls, candid photos, spicy stories, and the like. During the war, pin-ups were in lockers, GI magazines, and painted on tanks and aircraft. In

1953, Hugh Hefner began publishing *Playboy*, which was bolder in its depiction of the female anatomy, more frank in its discussion of sex, and geared to men of the new middle classes. It also had a world-view, a "playboy philosophy," advocating a freer approach to sex and attacking prevailing sexual mores, which had been imposed by dour Puritan forebears. Responding to strengthening demand and weakening norms, countless imitators appeared.[76]

By the mid-1950s, popular music took on a markedly sexual content. Rock 'n roll was based on black music from the rural South, that is, from a minority group distanced from mainstream norms. When they migrated north during the war, blacks brought along their musical forms, which found resonance with less inhibited postwar youth of all races. Slang, innuendo, and double entendres abounded. "Rock 'n roll" was of course slang for sexual intercourse; references to "ballin'" (Miss Molly's preoccupation or occupation) and "one night with you" (Smiley Lewis's hope) were thinly veiled terms; and, search as one might, the "House of Blue Lights" is not in the phone book, but a cabby might know it. Performers played before rapt audiences, in roadhouses, juke joints, movie theaters, and eventually on television, where censorship gave way to ratings. Crowds seemed to be electrically charged, like nothing before, except possibly, oddly enough, a revivalist tent meeting.[77] To older people, rock 'n roll seemed to be a threat to established norms, adult authority, indeed authority in general. Many groups sought to stifle it, to nip it in the bud before it led to moral collapse, but in a society welcoming change in almost all its forms, little could be done. Cries of indecency led only to the realization that old norms no longer held sway.

Similar processes were at work in the cinema, which took on previously taboo subjects. Films of the 1920s certainly had sexual content and pressed against norms, but public dismay led to a system of self-censorship, the Hays Office and Production Code Administration, which supervised the depiction of sex, violence, unconventional political beliefs, and anything else it thought injurious to public morals. By the 1950s, however, many people, both in and out of Hollywood, saw the PCA as old-fashioned, even silly, like crinoline on the legs (limbs?) of a table. The public wanted frankness, sophistication, and freedom to explore new social issues. By the late 1950s, weighing potential sanctions against potential revenue, Hollywood released a few films without approval, foreshadowing the PCA's demise a few years later.[78] Ministers and politicians could rail against it but, their influence on the wane, little else. They became scolding voices from the past, echoing across a yawning gap opened by the war. Efforts to counter the trend seemed purposeless, old-fashioned, the sort of thing a Puritan colony might have tried.

NATIONAL COMMUNITY AND NEW POWER PRESTIGE

Victory brought a powerful sense of unity and purpose that vitalized the country for decades. It provided an infusion of sacredness and legitimacy for the nation, what earlier times called "rising glory of the Republic." Every part of American life was imbued with prestige. Every figure of authority, cops and teachers, fathers and elders, corporate chiefs and heads of state, stood taller. The public, or at least a great preponderance of it, thought they could do no wrong.[79]

Since the Revolution and the War of 1812, military success had been a pillar of nationalism. Victories over the British blended with pride in natural beauty, scientific and literary accomplishments, and democratic processes to form the nationalism of early America. The Union's triumph in 1865 greatly strengthened patriotic sentiment. After World War II, pride in military success and world power became more important than ever before, aiding considerably in maintaining coherence in a changing country. In romantic language hearkening back to the nineteenth century, the New York Herald Tribune proclaimed in 1945, "The Great Republic has come into its own; it stands first among the peoples of the earth."[80] Postwar America was a rapidly modernizing country above which prevailed national myths and institutions that enjoyed new strength, ironically from the same event that pushed away much of tradition.

The End Of Isolationism

Newspapers of August 7, 1945, ran banner headlines telling of the atomic bomb dropped on Hiroshima the previous day. Other stories told of continuing fighting in the Pacific, the death of a famous fighter pilot, and hopes for a swift end to the war. Beneath the fold, a story noted the passing of Senator Hiram Johnson, an isolationist who had vociferously opposed involvement in the war prior to Pearl Harbor. The coincidence of the news from the Pacific and Johnson's death suggests that the muse of history is not without the gifts of irony and metaphor. In 1948, Charles Beard published a volume arguing that FDR had deceived the public in regard to his intentions to stay out of the war.[81] Ably documented and rather persuasive, the book was as irrelevant to the public as if it had argued for a silver standard. Isolationism had been a guiding principle since the country's inception. In the years prior to Pearl Harbor, defense expenditures passed Congress, but only barely, and only after much arm-twisting and disingenuousness. Shortly before December 7th, extension of the draft law passed by a single vote. Ten years later, six years after the war, America prided itself for its vast power around the world.

How did the country move from isolationism to internationalism so quickly? The war of course began the process. It mobilized traditional senses of morality and duty and sent them across the globe. News reports, government pronouncements, and Hollywood films depicted foreign countries as gallant allies with families like ours, endangered by a common enemy. British and Russian armies, French and Filipino undergrounds, Polish and Chinese civilians, all played roles in the great international effort. "V for Victory" was not just a publicity gimmick; it was an inspiring symbol of international resolve. It was flashed by leaders in public speeches, displayed on posters, and, in occupied countries, tapped out in code to annoy German soldiers.[82]

Popular culture took up the cause. A film biography of Woodrow Wilson (Best Picture of 1944) blamed isolationism for the failure of a lasting peace in 1918. Other films suggested that isolationism was tinged with foreign subterfuge or anti-semitism and that American common sense saw the foreign peril. Beneath the melodrama, *Casablanca* told of an average American, Rick, who claimed he stuck his neck out for no one, but who, we learn, had fought fascism years earlier in the Spanish Civil War. Isolationism made the country sleep while evil was on the march. And it was time to wake up. Rick puts private concerns aside — they didn't amount to a hill of beans during war — and helps a resistance leader escape to Lisbon, after which he teams with the French underground, the beginning of a beautiful friendship.

Outside the cinema, everyone had neighbors and loved ones in the service, deployed around the world in places no one had ever heard of in 1941. They fought and died in distant places like Bougainville, the Kasserine Pass, Buna, Peleliu, and Houffalize. For the first time, events thousands of miles away affected people in the most ethnocentric neighborhood, in the most remote hollow, and in the sleepiest whistle-stop. The change was as striking and revolutionary as learning that the universe does not revolve around the earth. Americans no longer thought in terms of a self-contained locale.

Victory played a critical role in reducing isolationism. The suffering and privations of the war ended in overwhelming victory, in contrast to the stalemate and diplomatic failures of the Great War. Images of Yanks greeted by Parisians and the flag raised over Suribachi were stirring sights that no isolationist plea could match. American troops remained across the globe for decades, garrisoned in Germany, North Africa, across the Pacific, and involved in training armies from Greece to Vietnam. America was a world power. It had really been one for decades, but now Americans knew it. More importantly, they liked it, and adopted it as a defining characteristic. Walter Lippmann saw it in epochal terms: "What Rome was to the ancient world, what Great Britain has been to the modern world, America is to be to the world of tomorrow."[83] Charles Beard died in 1948.

Militarization

The end of isolation was accompanied by a significant degree of militarization. Caution is needed when using this term. America never became the Sparta of the Western Hemisphere; it never became (as Voltaire said of Prussia) an army with a country, instead of a country with an army. In 1938, America had the nineteenth largest military in the world. By 1941, it had moved up a few places, in part because of increased defense spending grudgingly allowed by Congress, but mostly because Germany had adroitly removed the Czech, Polish, and French armies from the list. The war was not without concerns and opposition: conscripts resented military regimen, constitutional experts watched in dismay as civil liberties were eroded, many felt uneasy as hatred became an integral part of life. Most felt, however, that it was necessary, a price to be paid for defending the country and saving civilization.

Militarization continued well after the stars and stripes went up over Berlin and Tokyo. Millions of GIs had been discharged, countless ships had been decommissioned, but huge numbers of troops and equipment remained in the U. S. and around the world. For the first time, conscription continued in peacetime. Servicemen were everywhere, at train stations and airports, in the audiences of television shows and ball games, and on college campuses. They wore their uniforms into town and hitchhiked home in them as well. It was easier to get rides that way, and they usually got free meals along with a little nostalgic boasting ("I was in the big one, you know"). For many, the service was a bridge between high school and adulthood or between college and career. A hitch in the service became part of career development, a feather in one's cap at a job interview.

Following Pearl Harbor, the economy converted to war production. Considerable reconversion followed V-J Day, but not every sword was hammered into a ploughshare. In fact, countless new swords were made. Weapons were modernized, made more powerful, nuclearized. Propeller-driven planes became jets; Sherman tanks became Pattons; M-1s became M-14s then M-16s; Essex-Class carriers gave way to nuclear-powered ones; B-17s and B-29s became B-36s and B-52s. New equipment came into being: missiles, satellites, infrared scopes, Claymore mines, and so on. A considerable portion of the economy devoted itself almost entirely to weapons development. Industry eagerly placed retired generals and admirals on their boards of directors: not only to gain their managerial experience and to garner some of the prestige surrounding the military, but also to forge ties with business partners in the Pentagon. There was some concern with the pace and seeming endlessness of it all, but most felt it was necessary. Besides, to people for whom the Depression was a recent memory, defense spending meant good jobs.

When, in the late 1930s, plans were made to build the Pentagon, objections were raised to its enormousness. It betrayed the administration's desire to build a huge military and enter the war. The administration countered (disingenuously) that it would be used by other government bureaus. In just a few years, however, not even the world's largest office building could contain the military bureaucracy. Its offices sprawled across the Washington area and elsewhere. The New Deal had created an alphabet soup of bureaus (CCC, NRA, WPA), but most of them disappeared during the war. The national security state created its slew of acronyms (CIA, NSC, NSA, DIA), which lasted far longer. Often secret, not even shown on detailed maps of Langley or Laurel, they were seen by most Americans as silent guardians, staffed by graduates of elite universities and service academies. Their work was above question, even above discussion, as had been the planning for the Doolittle Raid, Overlord, and the Manhattan Project. Founders of the nation had warned against standing armies and foreign entanglements, but the world was far different now, and cautions from the eighteenth century had little value in the twentieth.

The construction of the National Defense Research Council in the early 1940s brought the best scientific minds into the war effort. Biology, medicine, engineering, physics, and chemistry reoriented themselves toward producing weaponry, electronics, and medicines. Elsewhere, especially in the Office of Strategic Services, social scientists studied the psychology of fascism, the traits of German and Japanese national character; and used their findings in propaganda campaigns. Universities became part of the war effort, teaching navigation, engineering, foreign languages, and public affairs for future administrators of occupied territories. A few engaged in secret research on rockets, jet engines, and other new weapons.[84]

Science and the state maintained their alliance after the war. Washington continued to fund military-related research. The social sciences studied the Soviet system, economic development, nation building, brainwashing (especially after Korea), and nuclear war scenarios. An enterprising professor of literature might well have received funding to study the relationship between Dostoevsky's similes and Soviet propaganda. By the late 1950s, Washington had charged Michigan State University and the RAND Corporation with solving the problems of economic and political development in a new Southeast Asian republic facing a growing insurgency. It was simply a matter of devoting sufficient resources to the problem.[85]

One of the more prominent aspects of militarization in the universities was the expansion of ROTC, a program that trained students to be the next crop of junior officers. ROTC existed before the war, but in the 1950s it grew rapidly, becoming a part of most college campuses, mandatory at many land-grant colleges. Drill and ceremony took place on the quads; uniformed students ambled to and from classes; and honor guards performed at halftimes. It filtered down to many high schools, where Junior ROTC was taught, drum and bugle corps proliferated, military-style haircuts were in fashion, and sports took on martial trappings. The ubiquity of the military at schools helped to reinforce what political rhetoric, church leaders, and even scout leaders insisted: we were still at war and may at any moment be in a shooting war. Many boys looked forward to the day.

Military Culture

The decades after 1945 had common themes with those after 1865. The post-Civil War era saw the romanticization of war and the military. The nation exulted in its glorious achievement, confident that it could achieve other great things and do no wrong. The memory of the fallen as well as the tragic death of Lincoln added to the religious significance of postwar culture. From the end of the war to the outset of the twentieth century, almost every president had been a Union officer. No achievement in business or the letters could measure up to having faced down Pickett's Charge or having stood with Grant as he crushed the rebels outside Richmond. The celebration went on and on.

The same could be said of the decades following 1945. Memory of the war permeated life: politics, fashion, films, television, and the play of children. Virtually every thought was influenced by the certainty that America was powerful and good. The memory of the fallen and FDR's death added a certain poignancy and tragic dimension that made the experience more sacred. Military service, both during the war and after, was considered highly desirable in corporations, police forces, and public school systems. Almost every president and serious contender had served in the war, as commander of a theater of operations, PT boat skipper, or bomber pilot. The imagery and prestige of war service, even if inflated a bit, were formidable advantages over a candidate who had not worn the uniform.

The war shaped the cinema, sports, styles, expectations, and almost everything else. Following World War I, the cinema depicted war in dark tones. Gloom and pessimism, disillusionment and death, stand out in *What Price Glory?*, *The Big Parade*, and *All Quiet on the Western Front*. The post-1945 mood was upbeat. Hollywood sensed it and depicted it — repeatedly. Scores of films, most of them made with Pentagon assistance (gratefully acknowledged in the credits), depicted courage, resourcefulness, and sacrifice. They all culminated in the Big Win, usually relatively painlessly, with a little melodrama thrown in for good measure. *What Price Glory?* was remade in 1952, and though war was heck, there were enough mademoiselles and hi-jinks to make it entertaining. *The Naked and the Dead* was transmogrified into action fare in which key events of the book were turned on their heads. They all celebrated the Great Event, but in a manner that cheapened it into mere entertainment.

A notable exception was *Victory at Sea* (1952), the renowned series that avoided Hollywood gimmickry and instead relied on documentary footage. Week after week, viewers saw U-boat predations in the North Atlantic, destroyers crashing determinedly through heavy seas, broadsides silhouetting huge battleships in night battle, immense task forces stretching across the horizon, scores of fighters gracefully lifting off carriers to mete out rough justice, and relentless kamikaze attacks repulsed off Okinawa. The myths were all there: a peaceful nation stirred to action; average Yanks achieving the extraordinary; the national virtues of courage, diligence, and ingenuity; good triumphing over evil. Each episode ended with calm seas, the famous leitmotif, and victory.

The emotional effect was enhanced by a moving musical score and an austere narration, which conveyed the gravity of the war, the uncertainty of its outcome, and, as much as any medium can, the reality of death. Several episodes showed poignant scenes of burials at sea, the faces of gravely wounded servicemen, and badly damaged fighters careening out of control or, in a horrifying instant, exploding into a fireball on the flight deck. In contrast to a short film or television show, the twenty-six part series depicted the war not as action or melodrama, but as an agonizing ordeal that had annealed the nation. Americans watching *Victory at Sea* observed, in every frame, proof of their goodness and power. They were on top and sure to remain there, forever.

Martial messages were also in less formal places, and always appealing to youth. Almost everyone's father had served. Some would tell stories of the war, some would tell war stories, others would only smile wryly or look away blankly. In each case, it had the powerful effect, intended or not, of romanticizing the war in the minds of young people, needless to say, mostly boys. Many veterans had brought back samurai swords, Lugers, helmets, flags, or lighters, which, when occasionally displayed, were viewed by kids with awe and reverence, as though they were in a past century looking upon a Saracen sword brought home by a victorious knight.

A considerable portion of boys' time, at least until they developed the motor skills for sports, was spent reenacting the war, or "playing guns." It was a natural enough response to the victory, but it received additional vitality from television programs depicting boys playing small but valorous roles in wars past. Johnny Tremain did his part in the War of Independence, as did the intrepid lad who helped the Swamp Fox outwit the Redcoats, and Johnny Shiloh, the Union drummer boy who found courage under fire. They made military service identifiable and desirable. After school and on Saturdays (it was not appropriate to play guns on Sunday), neighborhood youths would assemble, armed with a panoply of plastic Thompsons and Colts that industry, in an ironic form of reconversion, mass produced a few years after making the real things. Backpacks and divisional insignia could be had cheap at surplus stores, which, with aisle after aisle of artifacts from the war, were more interesting than museums. Backyards and fields became the battlegrounds of France. Suribachis were made out of small hills. In winter, a few kids in a tool shed became the beleaguered garrison of Bastogne, and imagination allowed for an occasional kamikaze to swoop down from the Belgian sky. Bold flanking maneuvers took place on neighbors' lawns, carefully avoiding the flower patches, lest a good scolding mandate a cease-fire. Nicks and cuts were inevitable, but they were borne with the same bravado of a GI in a battalion aid station. Only a Lucky dangling from the lips was missing.

Girls who accepted prevailing gender roles tended to the wounded; others, perhaps anticipating later social change, put them aside, at least for the afternoon duration, and became combatants. Classmates became crack elements of the German army until the sides were changed — a necessity because no one wanted to be the Krauts, who, though demonstrating admirable tenacity, invariably lost. There were important debates on the way to school or at recess: Were marines tougher than paratroopers? Was Anzio more glorious than Iwo Jima? Whose dad was the biggest hero? How did he get the Luger? There were variations — the Civil War (especially during its centennial), the venerable cowboys and Indians — but World War II was the favorite. They were all calls to glory based on military culture. Shortly after V-E Day, Patton thrilled a Sunday School class by telling them, "You are the soldiers and the nurses of the next war. There will be another war. There always has been."[86] It was inspiring back then.

It was very powerful and meaningful, fusing play with history, past with present, sons with fathers. Great victories were won; greater victories were hoped for, far from the backyard, somewhere in one of the world's many trouble spots — Berlin, the Congo, or perhaps Korea again. Much of American youth marked time and looked forward to the day when it could prove itself and return home, festooned with ribbons, greeted by a hometown crowd and a girl who had been true. The Roman saying that had gained currency after the Civil War, but scorn after the Great War, was restored to an honored position: *Dulce et decorum est pro patria mori.* The thought of a glorious death was appealing, but few thought they would really get killed, and no one thought America would ever lose a war.[87]

Militarization contributed to the rising popularity of football after the war, all but unseating baseball's privileged position as national pastime. Contrasts between the two sports are obvious but perhaps worth noting. Baseball is leisurely and placid, suggesting the pastoral. Football is more intense and violent, evoking war. The game parallels armies battling over territory: frontal assaults, enveloping tactics, ground and air operations. A goal-line stand was likened to Guadalcanal; a touchdown tapped into the mythic reservoir in which memories of the flag raising on Suribachi were stored. Harsh authority in training camp paralleled that of DIs at Parris Island and Fort Bragg, complete with short haircuts and psychological abuse.[88] A player's invocation of teamwork recalled the self-effacing phrases of combat soldiers. Football became an ideal of American youth, a path to manhood, the builder of discipline, honor, and sacrifice, a training ground for the next generation of soldiers. It was both a response to a militarizing society as well as an agent of socializing youth with the values the era prized. Future generations, it was thought, would look upon the gridiron much as the Duke of Wellington had the playing fields of Eton.[89]

Shortly after the Civil War, General Sherman chided a group of schoolboys who thought of war as adventure and glory. Seeking to disabuse them of this, he told them that war is hell. In 1963, American boys were watching an action movie entitled *War is Hell.*

Unifying Aspects of Militarism

Reviewing the militarization of life from the play of children to the high councils of government might seem like watching a great ship steaming heedlessly into the path of an iceberg. And it might appear like a destructive process that led only to a debacle. As understandable as this is, as much as it might resonate with themes in today's discourse, it might prevent appreciation of integrative effects that victory and military culture had on a rapidly changing country. Whatever relationship war had to the unmaking of America in the late 1960s, in the quarter century after Pearl Harbor, war culture had important unifying effects that countered many opposite trends.[90]

Though the war had set into motion forces generally weakening the family, postwar militarism infused parental authority with legitimacy and prestige. Most fathers, and many mothers as well, had served in the war or otherwise contributed. Children saw parents (not only their own) as legitimate authorities of a great nation that had proven itself and had to be ready for another conflict. This aura from the past and urgency in the present made parents more respected than they might otherwise have been in an increasingly consumer and media-oriented society. While much of modern life made fathers rather abstract, children could more readily idealize and respect a parent who had been part of the Great Event.

Military culture somewhat countered the decline of community. Americans, though increasingly atomized, could still look upon each other as fellow participants in the war, who had worked and sacrificed together, who had basic agreements on many important things, and who shared a sense of pride and accomplishment. Even in the most demographically altered town or the newest suburban development, veterans, whatever their social backgrounds or ethnicity, could, on noticing a lapel pin or a slight limp, find an important bond with someone who might have remained a stranger, with whom one might only have exchanged pleasantries. Veterans could form ties among themselves, create chapters of veteran and other organizations, and otherwise establish a measure of primary-group ties amid a general pattern of formal relations.[91] Communities took pride in their members who had gone off to war, in their industries that made the matériel, and in their young now serving overseas. W. Lloyd Warner notes the sociological importance of local observations:

> Memorial Day is a cult of the dead which organizes and integrates
> the various faiths and national and class groups into a sacred
> unity. It is a cult of the dead organized around the community
> cemeteries. Its principal themes are those of the sacrifice of the
> soldier dead for the living and the obligation of the living to
> sacrifice their individual purposes for the good of the group, so that
> they, too, can perform their spiritual obligations. [92]

The recent memory of over four hundred thousand dead brought new meaning, senses of sacredness, and integration, to commemorations of Memorial Day, Veterans Day, and V-J Day, where those who served under Ike and Nimitz stood alongside those who had been with Teddy or Blackjack, and even a few bent old-timers who had stood with Grant or Lee.

Postwar culture provided a sense of integration, of being a part of an ongoing historical process — important orientations in an otherwise mass society. Owing to recent memory, distant historical events, especially the sacrifices in war, were more meaningful and sacred in people's lives. There was a sense of involvement, of being part of an effort above individual preoccupations that provided a sense of purpose. Principles of duty and honor might well have receded into the past and the country might have been even more consumer-oriented than it was, but the imperatives of commemoration and vigilance countered this. It conveyed a sense of responsibility, especially to the young: to be an American, though in a purely legal sense a birthright, meant certain duties and obligations, seeing things through, living up to what was expected — this at a time when little else conveyed the same message.

CHAPTER FIVE

DISCONTENT AND ALIENATION
AMID THE CELEBRATION

In this period of rapid growth and change, uncertainty and instability rather than calm and security were the norms; men commenced to subject ancient religious and social standards to searching analysis, to evolve new political doctrines, and apply new deductions from the new science to their lives and problems.

CARL BRIDENBAUGH, *Cities in Revolt*

The uneasiness, the malaise of our time, is due to this root fact: in our politics and economy, in family life and religion — in practically every sphere of our existence — the certainties of the eighteenth and nineteenth centuries have disintegrated or been destroyed and, at the same time, no new sanctions or justifications for the new routines we live, and must live, have taken hold. So there is no acceptance and there is no rejection, no sweeping hope and no sweeping rebellion.

C. WRIGHT MILLS, *White Collar*

The war set into motion changes unthinkable only a decade or so earlier. Older minds reeled. Many younger ones saw modern America as natural and went along; other youths found it sterile and crass. Unable to differentiate between the traditional and the recently arrived modern, they felt alienated from anything American. Sub-groups coalesced and sometimes found voice. Nonetheless, most Americans thought of their society as intricate and mellifluous musical pieces, performed by those faithful to the composers and respectful of the conductors. But, attentive listeners could hear players out of time, out of tune, some playing different melodies, some refusing to play at all.

ALIENATION AMID CONSENSUS

Much as the 1950s might appear as stable and conformist, many contemporaries were alarmed by rapid change and feared the country was falling apart. Millions relocated into new towns and suburbs. Formerly isolated locales became integrated with the outside world and exposed to new media. Local customs gave way to modern influences. Parts of the old middle classes lost out to a growing corps of white-collar workers. The increasing importance of sales-oriented work placed a premium on flexibility and adaptability, so much so that basic personality types had changed. Older America receded into enclaves surrounded and encroached upon by mass society.[1]

Owing to the decline of extended family networks and the rise of youth culture, families were no longer what they had once been. Settled community continued to wane, replaced by transience and suburbia. The newly educated saw old ways as folklore, superstition, or ethnocentrism. Schools stressed a more secular and rational outlook, more in step with the times.[2] It was far less rich and satisfying, but it had science and government on its side. Incomes soared during and after the war, propelling people into abundance, turning the old culture of thrift into the eccentricities of grandparents and recluses. Opportunities and spending power grew each year. Horizons that a few years earlier had seemed narrowly circumscribed now seemed limitless.

The American mind had once been shaped by cultural elites, mainly Protestant, whose writings, sermons, and speeches conveyed basic heritage and outlooks. The cumulative effect of Hawthorne and Cooper, Twain and Mencken, Royce and Moody, Beard and Parrington, had once percolated through high and low culture alike. But they could not hold their own against the popular media's message of consumption and melodrama. The masters of the new media, with little deference to or even knowledge of older influences, scanned and polled, plumbed the depths of target audiences, and began to reshape the American mind.[3]

By 1960 or so, older and middle-aged Americans decried declining moral standards. In private and public conversations, in films and music, in school subjects and dating patterns, there was a fascination with subjects previously kept private. Kinsey's study of human sexuality found so much putative deviancy that in hip circles the concept of normal sexuality came into question.[4] There were trends of drug use, juvenile crime, and alienated subgroups, none of which seemed overwhelming or capable of becoming so, but which nonetheless worried those raised in older times. Previously, there had been essential continuity between generations, with the young eventually and perhaps grudgingly adopting parental values. Popular music, fads, and consumer goods became wedges between the generations. The transmission of norms and beliefs was no longer assured. Divisions were forming between those who came of age before the war and those growing up after it.[5]

America was becoming city-oriented, rationalized, secular, formal, and modern. It was losing much of its aura of enchantment and sacredness. Earlier, beliefs and institutions were imbued with sanctity, charisma, and folk mysticism, as though ordained from on high and chosen to serve an historic role. The First World War and the despair of the Depression made the sacred aura seem more of a smoke screen. The Second World War had ambivalent consequences. Leaders, institutions, and beliefs enjoyed renewed sacredness: Eisenhower and Kennedy, Congress and free enterprise, the family and the hometown. But the war eroded many sources of the sense of the sacred. Family and community sentiments — warmth, idealism, romance — had been wellsprings, but they now were trickles. The experience of war hardened public sensibilities and made them less receptive to sentimentality. A secular outlook was prevailing. One believed in observable phenomena and mistrusted or even ridiculed views based on folk wisdom. Much of life revolved around the decidedly unromantic activities of buying and selling, paying loans, and acquiring things, none of which was conducive to enchantment.[6]

The mass media played no small role in this. Traditional forms of entertainment such as folklore and fairy tales, handed down to the young by parents and grandparents, had instilled senses of enchantment, wonder, and morality.[7] They were replaced by mass-media products that turned great leaders and events into banalities. By the early 1960s, World War II had itself been trivialized by a steady output of movies and television programs depicting the war as action, adventure, melodrama, even comedy. Compensating for Mailer's inability to see the bright side of combat in the Pacific, Hollywood processed *The Naked and the Dead* into war fare, complete with a happy ending. It was easy to find courage under fire; a friend's death was quickly forgotten; stars seldom died (though the Duke did buy the farm in *The Sands of Iwo Jima*); and the resourceful Yanks quickly found a way to win. A few highly decorated veterans parlayed fame into B-movie careers, turning authentic heroism into mass entertainment. The urgency, immediacy, and agony of the war became a set of clichés that could not inspire, only entertain for a while. The war became as trite as a posse heading 'em off at the pass or a lonely librarian finding true love.[8] Years earlier, Nathanael West identified the trivializing effects of the mass media: "Although dreams were once powerful, they have been made puerile by the movies, radio and newspapers. Among many betrayals, this one is the worst."[9] A few decades later, the process reached full stride.

There were numerous voices of concern. Religious leaders and the elderly decried the dissolution of long-standing norms. Such things, they inveighed, are timeless truths that do not change with the times. There was too much materialism, too much licentiousness, and too much secularization. Sensationalist events such as the Starkweather murder spree and a motorcycle gang's donnybrook in a California town boded ill.[10] In the past, only a half century earlier, revivalist movements erupted and spread like wildfires across the country, rekindling religious commitment and becoming important historical forces. However, a people that had been shaken about and rearranged since then was unlikely to respond in traditional forms. In any case, there was enough religion in the movies and on television.

One of the most famous books of the period, David Riesman's *The Lonely Crowd*, argued that a fundamental and worrisome change had taken place in the American character. Americans were breaking free from traditional moorings and adrift with neither rudder nor compass. They were no longer rooted in religious beliefs and personal convictions. They were increasingly "other-directed," constantly looking to opinion leaders, peer groups, and the media for cues on how to think and behave.[11] Riesman was troubled by the rise of other-directedness but did not sketch where it was leading. Many fellow social thinkers did. According to them, Americans had lost ties to the past and to community, long-standing certainties had disappeared, resulting in isolation, malaise, and dread. They saw troubling problems in urban and suburban locales, among white-collar workers, college students, and among those who had experienced high degrees of vertical and horizontal mobility. Essential human needs for community, efficacy, authenticity, and integration were no longer fulfilled. People were vulnerable to manipulation by demagogues and the mass media. They would have unrealistic expectations from marriage, leading to disappointment and high divorce rates. Others would languish in despair and isolation, or search for meaning in popular religion and social movements. Crime and suicide rates would soar. The country would unravel.[12]

A different line of analysis could be heard as well, a soothing, optimistic voice heard above the warnings. It was delivered by legions of psychologists, school principals, self-help advocates, personnel administrators, and social workers. Attuned to the times, they preached a secular message of comfort. People needed to change, keep in step, adapt to their surroundings. Society was modernizing, and people needed to change as well, molding themselves to its contours. Adapt. The message was spread high and low, in every school, corporation, and rotary club. Seemingly engraved into the façade of every modern building and proclaimed by every organization man, it became a veritable catchword of the age. There was a change on and everyone needed to do one's part. But no one knew the duration, what it would cost, or what victory would bring.

SOCIAL PROTEST AT THE CELEBRATION

Most Americans celebrated the victory of 1945 for twenty years or so. The celebration was widespread and long-lived, but there were many who tired of it, many who didn't celebrate at all, and many who felt they hadn't been invited. Like the Civil War, World War II ushered in a "Treasury of Virtue." Robert Penn

Warren's description of post-Civil War America also describes the country eighty years later and so bears repeating. The war was a

> consciously undertaken crusade so full of righteousness that there
> is enough surplus stored in Heaven, like the deeds of the saints,
> to take care of all small failings and oversights of the descendants
> of the crusaders, certainly unto the present generation. From the
> start America had had adequate baggage of self-righteousness and
> phariseeism, but with the Civil War came grace abounding, for the
> least of the sinners.[13]

In the decades after Appomattox, voices of protest could occasionally be heard above the jubilee, but only barely. Most celebrants thought the voices were shrill and lacking in proportion, perhaps even half-mad. Critics insisted that emancipation wasn't enough, industry was too powerful, and sharecroppers were being robbed. Others despaired that the idealism of the war had degenerated into greed, materialism, grabbing with both hands. Such complaints received only brief attention during a monetary crisis or depression, or were opposed as a new threat to the Union, especially if (like the populist movement) they came from the South.[14]

The second Treasury of Virtue also pushed much social criticism to the background. The post-1945 celebration became for many a frustrating environment that made critics more alienated and radical than they might otherwise have been. For them, it was complacent, self-congratulatory, and hypocritical — a childish sentimentalization of a country that no longer existed, if it ever had. Subgroups saw the war as ending progressive politics, militarizing the country to a disturbing extent, and imposing stultifying standardization. But what was to be done as long as the celebration went on? They met in coffee houses, lecture halls, or at political rallies of one sort or another. They complained of the stifling sanctimony around them and looked forward to the day when perhaps a crisis of some sort would arrive or a unifying cause would arise.[15]

During the Depression, only twenty years earlier, domestic matters of poverty, unemployment, malnutrition, and income inequities had been at the fore of public attention. The Roosevelt administration created a number of bureaus charged with solving social problems, but with the outbreak of war priorities shifted and Dr Win the War reigned. The CCC, NRA, and WPA gave way to CINPAC, SHAEF, and WPB. The administration concentrated on mobilization, foreign policy, and national security. The postwar years saw little change; in fact, new military-oriented agencies emerged, grew, and entrenched themselves.[16] Though supportive of the war as well as of postwar containment,

New Dealers felt that the opportunity for progressive reform had slipped away. The momentum and sense of urgency were gone. When Henry Wallace, an old voice of progressivism in the administration, spoke out against aggressive confrontation with the Soviet Union, he was fired.[17] To add to the frustration, the mainstream refused to recognize many serious problems in the land of the free and the home of the brave. Where most saw a land of plenty, others saw a large other America, where, though no longer one-third, far too many remained ill-fed, ill-clothed, and ill-housed. There were pockets of dire poverty in Appalachia, inner cities, and throughout the South. Meanwhile, prosperity brought an aberrant concern with buying things. America had become an acquisitive society that was losing its senses of humanity and justice.[18]

Various sources of discontent tried to coalesce. One was the early environmental movement. Popular books such as Rachel Carson's *Silent Spring* warned that industry was polluting the air, soil, drinking water, and oceans.[19] Factory smoke, petrochemical runoff, power plants, and automobile engines contributed to the problem, the consequences of which ranged from health problems to the possible extinction of life.

Another source was the growing disaffection among women. The war and its aftermath changed their expectations and outlooks. Many had gone to work for the first time in war plants, done volunteer work, or served overseas in the military or USO. Most left the work force in 1945, but memories of efficacy and independence lingered. They had participated in the war but were back in subordinate and comparatively dull roles. Most women moved away from old neighborhoods, where traditional norms had dictated gender roles, and resided in suburbia, where the hold of tradition was weaker, where the grandmothers and church groups of the old community, in which women were regarded only as mothers and housewives, were far away.[20] Even in working-class neighborhoods, where traditional roles were still respected, times were changing: "Whatever lip service is paid to the importance of the home, the housewife herself notes that social esteem and economic rewards go to women who achieve success in careers outside the home."[21] Across the social scale, many women began to seek work, if only part-time, outside the home.[22] A growing number of women attended college, became familiar with new opportunities and outlooks. Some entered law, medicine, and other professions.[23] There was no sweeping rejection or revolution, but the hold of the past was less firm. Many women felt themselves in an uncomfortable middle ground between tradition and something that had not yet been defined.[24]

During the war, Americans saw the contribution of blacks in news releases, documentaries, and movies. After it, the issue of civil rights was on the national agenda. Though integrated into families, communities, and churches, and in many other respects sharing basic beliefs of mainstream Americans, they were second- or third-class citizens. At the outset of the Second World War, not content with promises of postwar attention, the NAACP and other groups pressed for desegregation in war industries. Concerned with maintaining a united home front, the Roosevelt administration ordered industry to hire minorities. Things began to change: "In a real sense, the watershed of African-American history occurred during the 1940s." C. Vann Woodward called the postwar era a "Second Reconstruction."[25]

In 1900, seventy-five percent of blacks lived in the rural South, but fifty years later, after two World Wars, only fifty percent did. During the Second World War, the number of blacks in industrial jobs went from 500,000 to 1.2 million.[26] Black factory workers listened to labor organizers, who underscored long-standing grievances and the need to organize. Membership in the NAACP rose during the war from 50,000 to just under a half million.[27] The social climate outside the South was by no means benign, but it was less malignant than the Mississippi Delta. The hold of hatred and prejudice was weaker. Jim Crow was not absent, but he was generally less brutal. The law in the South was in the hands of The Man, but elsewhere it provided a measure of protection.

Over a million blacks served in the armed forces, in every branch of the service, in every theater of operation. Black soldiers in England found the local people welcomed them as allies, a view not always shared by white GIs.[28] In previous wars, they had served under white officers, but once again war needs brought change. Though full integration of all units might have been desired, separate black units, especially infantry, armor, and air units, made the point that they fought and died in the national effort. This led to greater recognition of racial injustices as well as a measure of optimism for postwar progress. Bigoted NCOs and officers gave white servicemen a glimpse at life in the South, and a measure of sympathy for blacks stayed with them well after separation. During the war, forty-three percent of black soldiers were optimistic that things would improve for them after the war.[29]

As black GIs returned, they were well aware that they had contributed more to the country than had white civilians. Farmhands in the Deep South were irrelevant to the mainstream, but not so soldiers who fought on Bougainville or in Italy and came home with campaign ribbons, Purple Hearts, and Silver Stars. As one put it,

> I spent four years in the Army to free a bunch of Dutchmen and
> Frenchmen, and I'm hanged if I'm going to let the Alabama version
> of the Germans kick me around when I get home. No sirreee-bob!
> I went into the Army a nigger; I'm comin' out a man.[30]

One black soldier on furlough encountered an injustice of astounding irony. He was barred from entering a restaurant that

> was doing a rush business with white civilians and German
> prisoners of war. There sat the so-called enemy comfortably seated,
> laughing, talking, making friends, with the waitresses at their beck
> and call. If I had tried to enter that dining room the ever-present
> MPs would have busted my skull, a citizen soldier of the United
> States. . . . Nothing infuriated me as much as seeing those German
> prisoners of war receiving the warm hospitality of Texas.[31]

Black soldiers saw countless injustices in wartime experiences, but they also learned the importance of leadership and organization in getting a job done, and, upon demobilization, they developed both.

Important events of the civil rights movement had origins in the war. Rosa Parks worked on an airbase in Alabama during the war, where public transportation had been integrated by executive order, allowing her to ride, seated, with whites. Off base, to her growing irritation, buses remained segregated, a daily contradiction that contributed to her joining the NAACP in 1943. Following the war, she noted the injustice of blacks, especially veterans, barred from the front of the bus. Eventually, she refused to give up her seat.[32]

In late 1945, the Brooklyn Dodgers, whose fortunes had waned in recent years, looked to improve their lot by hiring players from the Negro Leagues. Wartime criticism of segregation provided a somewhat favorable climate for integration, but there remained the question of which player to bring into the major leagues. They selected Jackie Robinson, in part because of his athletic skill, but there were others such as Satchel Paige and Josh Logan who had more. The Dodgers chose Robinson because he had been a lieutenant during the war, which would certainly help acceptance. But also, they knew he had refused to give up his seat on a supposedly desegregated bus on Fort Hood. Acquitted in the ensuing court-martial, Robinson demonstrated the resoluteness the Dodgers knew would be needed by whoever broke the color line.[33]

Though officially integrated in 1948, the armed forces dragged their feet and remained largely segregated. The sharp casualties of the first year of Korea and personnel shortages throughout the military, forced the matter, especially in combat units. Practical needs effected change where idealism and politics had failed. General Anthony McAuliffe noted, "We didn't do it to improve the social situation. It was merely a matter of getting the best out of the military personnel that was available to us."[34] Despite concerns, integrated units performed well, as they had after the Battle of the Bulge a decade earlier.[35]

The Cold War, often seen as having a chilling effect on social progress, aided the civil rights cause. In 1952, in the landmark Supreme Court proceedings on segregation in public schools, the attorney general argued,

> It is in the context of the present world struggle between
> freedom and tyranny that the problem of racial discrimination
> must be viewed. . . . Racial discrimination furnishes grist for
> the Communist propaganda mill, and it raises doubt even
> among friendly nations as to the intensity of our devotion to the
> democratic faith.[36]

Advances came within the context of a dynamically changing society, whose mainstream saw the irony and injustice of treating soldiers and veterans as second-class citizens, and of maintaining racist domestic relations after recently ending Nazi racial hatred.[37]

To progressives, women, and minorities change was needlessly slow. Demonstrations and essays could achieve only so much. The principal cause of delay was the Treasury of Virtue, which assured Americans that they were virtuous and righteous, incapable of wrong, and needed no more proof than the Great Event. To most Americans, critics were out of touch, or the time wasn't right, or perhaps they were dupes of foreign powers trying to weaken the country. To others, the Treasury of Virtue was a frustrating obstacle to change, a cloying web of myths, half-truths, and lies that deluded the country.

UNEASE WITH MILITARISM

Following the war, Americans bestowed countless accolades on the military, awarding it great prestige and unprecedented importance in national life. Many Americans found this disconcerting, even dangerous. Criticism ranged from light-hearted satire to dire warning. Unease was barely perceptible in the early 1950s, but a decade later, events gave it strength.

One source of unease with the military was a considerable number of veterans whose service memories had not softened into nostalgic anecdotes and backslapping at legion halls. Many veterans had memories of gormless NCOs, inept junior officers, and arrogant senior ones.[38] Though proud of their service, they disliked military institutions and were uncomfortable with their influence. Their novels, diaries, letters, and remembrances describe abuse of power, prejudice, and incompetence up and down the chain of command. Military intelligence, they liked to quip, was an oxymoron, as was military justice.[39]

Reasons for lingering hostility are not long to seek. The army expanded over thirty-fold during the war, the navy twenty, and the marines sixteen, necessitating the rapid promotion of many unqualified personnel, whose prewar numbers were not insignificant. The armed forces minted NCOs and officers almost as rapidly as factories did Garand rifles, but not always with the same quality control. A PFC at the outset of the war might easily have become a platoon sergeant a couple of years later. A young lieutenant before the war might have risen to major or lieutenant colonel. A major in a lackadaisical national guard unit might later command a regiment. Results were not always fortunate, and many men were placed in positions for which they had little qualification.[40]

GIs respected many generals, but others were remembered as haughty, elitist, lusting for fame and power. Contrasts might be instructive. Eisenhower and Bradley were widely admired as modest and unassuming, the very embodiment of the decency of average Americans. Ike and Brad looked more like high school principals or hardware store owners than commanders of millions of soldiers. Ernie Pyle, the wartime voice of the average Joe, said of them: "Surely America made its two perfect choices in General Eisenhower and General Bradley. They are great men — to me doubly great because they are direct and kind."[41] By contrast, MacArthur and Patton strutted and preened like characters in a comic opera. They wielded authority and commanded troops imperiously, sought publicity as though running for office, and threw tantrums when their judgments were questioned.

MacArthur was widely (though falsely) rumored to have lived in luxury on Hollandia during the war. Patton led the Third Army from a ducal palace, where he once upbraided Bill Mauldin for lacking the understanding of GIs, which he, amid so much rococo splendor, had cultivated.[42] Veterans remember Eisenhower and Bradley as fine men. On hearing that a young private from his hometown had asked to see him, Ike found a few minutes to chat with him. He is said to have wept as he watched paratroopers take off for Normandy. MacArthur is often remembered as "Dugout Doug," avoiding exposure to hostile fire but taking all the credit; Patton as the Junker who slapped a soldier hospitalized for battle fatigue, or as "Old Blood and Guts" — his guts, GI blood.

Postwar literature abounds with unflattering descriptions of the military. In John Hersey's *A Bell for Adano*, a general (said to be modeled after Patton) shoots a peasant's horse obstructing his way. The skipper in *Mister Roberts* is a petty tyrant resentful of college boys. James Jones's *From Here to Eternity* and *The Thin Red Line* show authority as inept and arrogant, though first sergeants are presented as having a measure of paternalism. Mailer's *The Naked and the Dead* bristles with hostility to military authority. The platoon sergeant is a sadist who tyrannizes his soldiers and has a rival killed. The lieutenant sees himself as a decent guy, concerned with his men, but he is a feckless nullity, disliked by privates and generals alike for pretenses of virtue and camaraderie. The general sees the war as an opportunity to advance his career and for America to establish itself as a world power, which, by an ineluctable law of history he has discovered, will come to blows with Russia. Similarly, Irwin Shaw's *The Young Lions* describes a general who admires power, despises weakness, and envisions the historical necessity of America's rise to global power.[43]

Aversion to the military was also portrayed light-heartedly. The squadron commander in Joseph Heller's *Catch-22* is a bungling, obsequious, publicity hound. A general orders a man shot for showing disrespect for his nubile "aide." His life is spared when the general's attaché (by chance, his son-in-law) points out potential repercussions. Other works lampooned military professionals as oafs, blowhards, dilettantes, and sycophants, obsessed with rules and promotions.[44] They all conveyed something about the military that the Pentagon would categorically deny but many veterans would readily confirm.

Concern also came from intellectuals and average citizens who felt that militarization had perverted American values. While most Americans looked upon their tanks, jets, and atomic bombs with a sense of awe, and enjoyed the power prestige, others were dismayed. A pastoral nation had become a garrison state; the military had become a power elite:

> The military order, once a meager establishment in a context of
> civilian distrust, has become the largest and most expensive feature
> of government. Behind smiling public relations, it has all the grim
> and clumsy efficiency of a great and sprawling bureaucracy. The
> seemingly permanent military threat places a premium upon high
> military personnel; virtually all political and economic actions are
> now judged in terms of military definitions of reality.[45]

Many Americans had become accustomed to hate, feel pride in destruction, and distort enemies into sub-humans. The war had stirred up a nationalist frenzy, filled with bluster, hokum, and cant; and revitalized violent and cruel parts of American culture that had been on the wane.

A few films of the period expressed this sentiment. *Hail the Conquering Hero* depicts a town's ebullient welcome for a returning soldier who, after being honored with a statue and urged to run for mayor, confesses that he was discharged because of hay fever and never even went overseas. Such was the lack of proportion that the war had ushered in. *The Ox Bow Incident*, though set in the old West, portrayed mob hatreds, similar to those stirred up by the war, which swept away respect for law. *Bad Day at Black Rock* tells of a Japanese-American murdered by an angry mob shortly after Pearl Harbor. *Crossfire* and *Suddenly* saw the war turning some soldiers into dangerous killers, who continued to hate and kill back home.[46]

The Cold War and continued conscription underscored fears of perpetual international tension and of the country becoming a garrison state — fears that ranged across the political spectrum from progressives like Henry Wallace to Republican isolationists like Robert Taft. In 1947, adumbrating later events, four young men burned their draft cards. Too much of the country was under arms, marching to drumbeats, perversely looking forward to the next war. The glorification of the military sometimes took on disturbing similarities to the sort of adulation against which the country had just fought. Anyone who expressed opposition was branded disloyal, a pacifist, a threat to national security, or regarded as someone whose manhood was questionable. Some generals indoctrinated their troops with views that went beyond conservatism into the radical fringe of the John Birch Society.[47]

In 1942, civilians went into the service reluctantly, despised the harsh regimen, but did their duty. Postwar youths were eager to become warriors and awaited their war. Military training became even harsher and more brutal than during the war, in part because studies found that training had not adequately prepared soldiers for combat.[48] But it also stemmed from the changed culture from which recruits came, and from the aura surrounding drill instructors, who, having won their spurs at Normandy and Iwo Jima, were held in awe by postwar boys. Marines memorized an ode to their rifle and recited it before lights-out:

> This is my rifle. There are many like it but this one is mine.
> My rifle is my best friend. It is my life, I must master it as I master my life.
> My rifle, without me, is useless. I must fire my rifle true.
> I must shoot straighter than my enemy who is trying to kill me.
> I will.
> My rifle is human, even as I, because it is my life. Thus I will learn it as a brother. I will learn its accessories, its sights, its barrel. I will keep my rifle clean and ready, even as I am clean and ready. We will become part of each other.
> We will . . .
> Before God I swear this creed. My rifle and myself are the master of our enemy. We are the saviors of my life. So be it, until victory is America's and there is no enemy but peace!
> Amen.[49]

To many, this was a glorification of war mixed with messianic psychopathology.

To symbolize the death of youthful innocence and the birth of the manly warrior, basic training sometimes ended with a ritualized slaughter of a rabbit or puppy. In 1956, six marine recruits drowned while on a disciplinary march on Parris Island. The incident was widely condemned and the responsible sergeant court-martialed, yet the "Ribbon Creek Massacre" became an appealing legend.

Apparently, it was sweet and fitting to die for one's country even in boot camp. Hazings and beatings were common and became part of youth folklore; trainees on leave *boasted* to rapt friends of mistreatment at the hands of drill sergeants. It was a rite of manhood, garduation from backyard play and football.[50]

To many, it was a troubling break with traditional moderation and a large step in the direction of institutionalized militarism that would ensure another war somewhere. Especially disturbing was the fascination with atomic weapons. The general public thought the A-bomb had ended the war and later compensated for the manpower advantages of the Soviet Union and Red China. Nuclear technology spread into naval propulsion, tactical weapons, power plants, and medicine. Surely atomic energy was making life better. One early critic observed: "Most Americans looked upon the atom bomb as a self-starting magic lamp; even without being rubbed it would produce their long-sought City on the Hill in the form of a de facto American Century embracing the globe."[51]

Mushroom clouds were symbols of national power, demonstrated to the world by spectacular detonations. Diners, motels, and supermarkets adopted the word "atomic" or the image of a mushroom cloud as advertising gimmicks. Two-piece swimsuits took their name from a recent atomic test at Bikini atoll. Some high schools even took on atomic-inspired mascots: cheerleaders from Richland, Washington (where plutonium was processed) rooted on their team, the *Atom Bombs*, with cheers of "Kaboom! Kaboom!" Countless movies, most eminently forgettable, showed nuclear weapons saving civilization from Martians or, in a display of some ambivalence, from dangerous mutants caused by radiation.

Many found this repugnant. Hiroshima and Nagasaki, they held, were among the greatest atrocities in human history, needlessly incinerating tens of thousands of civilians and leaving others to die slowly from radiation sickness.[52] Nuclear fallout spread around the world. Rainwater contained an isotope so similar to calcium that humans absorbed it into bone tissue. Scientists had relegated the bombs of 1945 to virtual firecrackers. Critics could only look on in incredulity as statesmen, generals, and political scientists spoke dispassionately of "mega-deaths" as "acceptable losses," and developed plans to collect taxes and deliver the mail after a nuclear war.[53] Ban the Bomb movements and groups of concerned scientists spread. (The former's symbol later became better known as the peace symbol.) The policy of massive retaliation seemed to place the world on the path toward destruction, the extinction of life, the fulfillment of the Armageddon prophecy.[54]

The military-industrial complex — a term that of course entered common usage after President Eisenhower's 1961 farewell speech — was another source of anti-military sentiment. Government and industry had been at odds during the 1930s, but during the war they forged a solid partnership. Close ties between industry and government alarmed many, from average citizens to the commander in chief. During his first term, Eisenhower vetoed a military budget, leading to a storm of protest, not only from contractors, but also from the Pentagon and Congressmen whose districts stood to benefit. Despite the opposition from the admired military leader and chief executive, there was little doubt who could mobilize more resources for this battle.

For the rest of his presidency, Ike looked on with dismay and sometimes anger as Congress funded project after project he knew to be unnecessary or overpriced. There was no end. In a supreme irony, a presidential hopeful accused him of allowing the Soviet Union to develop superiority in ballistic missiles. On the eve of handing the torch to a new generation, Ike expressed traditional American sensibilities facing an anguishing dilemma. New generations of missiles, planes, and other armaments meant less spending on schools, hospitals, and housing. He was concerned with the growing power of the military-industrial complex, but at the same time thought it necessary. It was a threat to American democracy, but vital to its security.

Critics saw less a dilemma than a distortion of national priorities that squandered billions of dollars. Seeing peace as a threat to its interests, the complex seemed to ensure that tensions would remain.[55] Some even held that the war-partnership had conspired to begin the Cold War in order to prop up a failing socio-economic system. Progressives saw Roosevelt's death in April 1945 as a double tragedy. Not only did it deprive the nation of a great progressive leader, dedicated to solving social ills and ensuring world peace, but it also left the nation in the hands of a machine politician, unduly influenced by generals and business leaders whom FDR had brought in only for the duration. The war transformed the country into a national security state, obsessed with secrecy, mistrust, espionage, and all too eager to forge alliances with any enemy of our enemy. Pearl Harbor ended many things — isolationism, the Depression, a stable social order — but it also ended a period when gentlemen didn't open other gentlemen's mail, when covenants were openly arrived at, and when ideals could prevail over national security.

No one doubted the need for secrecy during the war. Strategy and troop movements were kept secret. Only a handful of policymakers knew of code-breaking abilities or the Manhattan Project. (Truman, it is well known, found out about the bomb only after FDR's death.) GIs had their mail censored. Many disasters, blunders, and miscalculations were not fully known until after the war. The kamikaze devastation of ships off Okinawa was hushed up. The debacle of Slapton Sands, where hundreds of soldiers were killed through error, remained secret for decades.[56] Pacts were made with partisan strongmen, Latin American dictators, and, in order to prevent sabotage in the dockyards, even the Mafia.[57]

Internally, suspect groups of Japanese (as well as some Germans and Italians) were interned. Spies were put in front of secret military tribunals and quickly executed. Through official communiqués, documentary films, and publicity events, the state controlled public knowledge of the war.

The relationship between government and governed changed. Of course, it was generally accepted as necessary to win the war. Loose lips, as everyone knew, sank ships. Civil libertarians and constitutional experts complained and filed suits, but the Supreme Court, which only a decade earlier had struck down many government powers, now allowed them to expand virtually unchecked. Though the government remained for the people, when it came to war, it was no longer as truly of and by the people as it once had been.[58]

The secrecy and pragmatism of the war years continued into the Cold War era, taking on the names of "national security" and "reason of state" — mysterious and vague terms that could justify almost anything. The Central Intelligence Agency grew out of the wartime Office of Strategic Services and engaged in espionage and related matters that old OSS hands would never have dreamed possible or even desirable, perhaps most notably the recruitment of the Nazi intelligence network in Eastern Europe. The National Security Agency was born, too, but few knew it existed, let alone exactly what it did. Military assistance and counter-insurgency programs set up around the world, in Greece, Latin America, and Southeast Asia. U-2 reconnaissance planes flew over the Soviet Union and other areas. The CIA was confident that Soviet missiles could not bring down a U-2, but in that unlikely event, the public would be satisfied by a cover story (a lost weather plane), and the nettlesome matter of the pilot would be solved by issuing him an injector with which he could nobly commit suicide rather than embarrass the country. Most Americans thought the new national security state was all for the best and didn't look into the matter; others thought quite differently but, owing to national security, were unable to do so.

George Washington, in his oft-quoted farewell address, warned of foreign entanglements, and for the most part henceforth American foreign policy aimed to keep Europe out of the hemisphere and to stay aloof from its periodic bloodlettings. The experience of World War I reinforced old outlooks and made entrance into the war against Nazism more difficult. After 1945, America assumed the burden of leading a global coalition against Communism. As European countries, bankrupt and demoralized, withdrew from far-flung empires, they left indigenous populations embittered from decades of misrule and open to appeals from the Soviet Union. In response, America entered into numerous treaties, executive agreements, and secret understandings with countries around the world. Any enemy of the Soviet Union had merits.

Older Americans yearned for a simpler past when politics was more understandable. Others were less troubled by global commitments than by the sordid characters and regimes with whom we allied. An occasional embarrassing ally is part of the compromises of politics, domestic or foreign; but in the postwar years, there seemed to be an uncomfortably large number of them. Junta leaders, cliques of landowners, and a Shah could be seen smiling for the cameras as they stood next to our statesmen and generals beneath a White House portico. Matters worsened when a band of guerrillas descended from the mountains and toppled the Cuban government. Military assistance and counter-insurgency programs received larger funding. American soldiers and case officers increased their efforts to train foreign troops, intelligence services, and police forces.[59]

The Cuban missile crisis (1962) broadened and deepened these concerns. The presence of Soviet missiles on the Caribbean island brought the world perilously close to nuclear devastation. The growing influence of the military had been easy enough to dismiss when it was mostly rhetoric and posturing, but it was a different matter when the world came close to annihilation. When the crisis ended — when the other guy blinked, as it was put — there was elation, but not from victory, rather it was from getting a last minute reprieve or, better expressed, a last minute stay from an execution that might still take place.[60]

After the crisis, there was no widespread demand for disengagement or disarmament. There were no defense cuts; indeed, quite the opposite took place. There was, however, increased concern with the military's influence. Previous wars had given clear signs of progress. By 1965, the Cold War had gone on for twenty years, five times the length of World War II, without any such sign. Commitment remained but enthusiasm waned. Grumbling was heard on college campuses and in coffee houses as student groups and professors spoke out more stridently. More importantly, one could hear it in the general public.

Unease was discernible in books and films. Heretofore, most films had depicted the armed forces as vigilant defenders and miraculous deliverers. A few deviated from this trend (*War Hunt, The Victors*) but did not enjoy popular success. *On the Beach* was set in Australia after nuclear war has destroyed the Northern hemisphere. Though daily activities go on, they all know they will soon be enveloped by radiation and slowly die. Daring for its time, the film did not address the cause of the war, and so held back from blaming politicians and generals. After the Cuban missile crisis, such reluctance disappeared. In *Seven Days in May*, an impending arms control treaty precipitates an attempted military coup. The film mentions Douglas MacArthur, whose disdain for civilian leadership was well known, and also Edwin Walker, who had recently been relieved of his command for teaching Birchite views to his troops.[61] Both generals, the film suggested, had dangerous senses of duty and mission that were threats to the Constitution.

Several books and films expressed concern over the danger of systemic error and flaws in the military character. They counterpoise decent American civilians — presidents, doctors, journalists — against caesarist or deranged generals. Perhaps expressive of concern with the recent integration of Germany into NATO, perhaps muted commentary on our own military, leaders in these films often have German advisers who had served the Third Reich. In *Fail Safe*, a computer mistakenly sends bombers on a nuclear strike against the Soviet Union. The war plan does not allow recall; humans are no longer in control; mistrust prevents cooperation that could stop the bombers. Moscow is annihilated, forcing the president to destroy New York to prevent all-out war.[62] In the dark comedy *Dr. Strangelove* (based on a non-comedic novel[63]), General Jack Ripper, convinced that a communist plot (fluoridated water) has rendered him impotent, orders a nuclear attack on the Soviet Union. Aside from the insane general, other military figures in the film are sex-crazed buffoons or reckless cowboys eager to go toe-to-toe with the Russkis. *The Bedford Incident* deals with an American destroyer skippered by an aggressive officer who stalks a Soviet submarine during a period of international tension. Annoyed by civilian meddling, he wishes to provoke an incident to force his government's hand. Holding the crew at general quarters leads to strain, nervous breakdown, and an accidental missile firing.[64] All three films end with official films of nuclear explosions. The same footage once watched with pride and wonder was now looked at more soberly.

Unease with the military was stronger in Boston than in Muncie, stronger at Berkeley and Columbia than at Ohio State or the University of Texas. Student groups previously dedicated to social ills and school problems found a more urgent, more passionate cause. But average Americans felt uneasy as well. A call to arms, an invocation of the rallying cries and symbols of 1945, would face more ambivalence and opposition than it would have a few years earlier.[65]

ORIGINS OF THE COUNTERCULTURE

Alienation was more pronounced in young people, especially those from the middle classes, suburbia, and the better schools. They felt like outsiders, distanced from the mainstream, unable to communicate with those in it and increasingly unwilling to try. This was both liberating, in that it gave greater freedom, and frustrating, in that they didn't know what to do with it. They had no blueprint, home, or coherent belief system. Much of their complaint, largely unbeknownst to them, was with modern elements of the country had only recently taken on. Knowing little of prewar America, they looked about, saw extensive sterility and artificiality, and concluded that this was the USA. For the most part, they defined themselves negatively: they were not materialistic, not suburbanites, not future organization men or housewives, not holes in a key punch card, not numbers on a roster, not rats in a giant Skinner Box. Their parents had been defined by the Depression and the war; their forebears by the Great War, the Gilded Age, and the Civil War. They felt an ill-defined yearning for authenticity, a measure of spirituality, and a cause of some sort. But who were they?[66]

Anti-materialism

In the years following the Civil War, Carl Schurz lamented growing hedonism. His words bear repeating: "Is it really true that our war turned the ambitions of our people into the channels of lofty enthusiasm and aspirations and devotion to high ideals. Has it not rather left behind it an era of absorbing greed of wealth, a marked decline of ideal aspirations?"[67] Many felt the same change had taken place after 1945. A generation that had endured twelve years of depression, then four years of war, felt that it had sacrificed enough and earned the right to relax. There was considerable merit in this feeling, but many of their children could not see it. Raised in unprecedented comfort, many young people thought that material indulgence had become a stupefying endpoint in American history that pushed spirituality, morality, and social justice to the background or merely chiseled them into a façade.

Materialism, they held, was corrupting. Money had become the one true god of America and hucksterism the essence of the USA. Sinclair Lewis noticed the trend in his day, but thirty years later everyone seemed to be a Babbitt, exulting in acquisitiveness and pretensions of virtue. Bending the rules, compromising, helping a crony, rising above principle, greasing the wheels were by-words. That's what made the world go 'round, and the sooner you learned it the better. If pulled over for speeding, handing over a fiver with your license settled the matter. Quiz shows could be rigged to make for better viewing pleasure. (It didn't hurt anybody.) You didn't get that contract simply by giving the lowest bid. (What they don't know won't hurt 'em.) And no one knew who wrote the rules, but that's how the system worked.[68]

Anti-conformity

An abiding dislike of suburbia and conformity were important parts of this outlook. Suburbia promised a new way of life away from aging cities and towns, but many of those raised there found them stale, homogenous, and stultifying: houses made of "ticky-tacky" that "all looked the same," as a popular song put it. Today, we still commonly hear fond recollections of urban neighborhoods and small towns, places that might have been poor and lacking in opportunity, but nostalgic recollections of Levittown or Park Forest, Chevy Chase or Winnetka, are rare. Accounts of suburban upbringings, though not devoid of affection for friends and ball teams, are often tinged with sarcasm, or are simply recitations of schools attended and stores patronized, with little if any affection.

To some extent, this simply reflects the spirit of our day, but it is also due to the different natures of the two forms of neighborhood. The old communities, for all their material wants, provided a rich array of experiences, sights and sounds, people and buildings, which gave a sense of wholeness and integration, of common involvement. Suburbs lacked this. Their modern looks were bland and uninspiring. People didn't develop roots; there was no sense of interrelatedness or integration. Alienated youth saw life there as contrived, lacking a sense of integration and purpose, as artificial as plastic and polyester. They yearned for some authenticity, a genuine, original experience uncorrupted by the profit motive or media programming.

Many young people thought that the unimaginative sameness of tract houses, schools, and office buildings came from a conformist society and went a long way in reproducing it. Schools and office buildings were graceless edifices, devoid of art and vision, as mass produced as products on a store shelf. Inside the suburban house, one found not crafted furnishings of earlier periods, but mass-produced, modern furniture or similarly produced pseudo-colonial products. Television, schools, and bureaucracies drummed into the heads of the young that there were standards before which all must bow. Parents were shaped and conditioned by the corporate world for which they worked. For all its talk of rugged individualism, the country really wanted people to shut up and toe the line. The idea of an external thing called "society" imposing its values on the young came into question; individuality meant the absence of restraint and distance from authority.

From the perspective of earlier American history, this reaction against conformity is puzzling. Surely any society that popularized the Kinsey Reports, rock 'n roll, *The Village Voice*, Sidney Poitier, Betty Friedan, *Playboy*, *Mad Magazine*, *Catch-22*, Ernie Kovacs, Rachel Carson, Jackson Pollock, *The Twilight Zone*, beatniks, birth control pills, and Tom Lehrer, cannot meaningfully be called overly conformist. Compared to urban or town life at the turn of the century or to any other part of the world, past or present, postwar America was bubbling with dynamism, change, experimentation, eccentricities, and weirdness. Why then this complaint of conformity?[69] Growing hostility toward conformity in a society signals that acceptance of governing beliefs and conventions is dwindling. Such a society is loosening up, fraying, becoming elastic, changing into something else. *Conformity is breaking down.* Values are no longer passed on smoothly and new ones struggle to assert themselves. Younger people are only partially socialized; others say "no" or ask "why?"

Another key to understanding discontent with conformity lies in recognizing that much of it had not been part of older America at all. Complaint was mainly with conventions recently adopted by people newly situated in the middle classes, in suburbia, in a modernizing country. Millions of people, raised in prewar communities, from poor or working-class backgrounds, now found themselves in new settings. They tried to create manners for the new modern era, customs, routines, and the like. Hence the superficial neighborliness, concerns with appearing ostentatious or tightfisted, looking to others for cues as to proper behavior, trying to fit into something that no one quite understood, looking for new standards of behavior where older ones no longer seemed appropriate. Trying to fill the void, schools and businesses showed films on manners, decorum, appropriate behavior, civic-mindedness, filial duty, and other familial and societal practices. To adults, this was an attempt to establish new ways and a semblance of continuity, but to many young people, it was trite and artificial. In this respect, their disaffection with America was in many ways disgust with modernity.

Disaffected youth loathed the popular media — movies, magazines, hit music, and especially television — regarding them as agents of conformity, marching in step, doing what the system wanted happy young Americans to do. The media imparted, or attempted to anyway, a saccharine morality in which fathers were all-knowing, women and children looked on deferentially, optimism and hard work always won out. It beamed a soothing message of all's well in our age of constant improvement.[70] The residual content was trivial and witless. As the media brought history into the living room, the alienated saw their country in those same terms. Seeking to capitalize on the postwar celebration, the media rushed to present American history to the public. The past came across in the form of telegenic leading figures, action scenes, a simple moral thrown in, a happy ending, then a quick cut to the soap ad. Davy Crockett, Wyatt Earp, Bat Masterson, Jim Bowie, homesteaders, and the cavalry were uniformly virtuous and had an uncanny ability to solve the problem of the week within the allotted half-hour. And the merchandising: coonskin hats, six-guns, and long knives for throngs of kids![71]

A generation of young people came to see American history largely through television. The hardships of frontier life and the complexities of historical figures were lost. Legends, folklore, historical works, and a few well-made films conveyed the difficulties and ambiguities of earlier days. They also showed the less wholesome side of historical figures who, in addition to admirable qualities, were not above ruthless, vindictive, or mercenary actions, which made them more interesting to generations who had learned about them from traditional sources. Davy Crockett had a conniving and self-aggrandizing side (one source called Crockett a "hero of the Munchausen-Eulenspiegel breed"[72]); Judge Roy

Bean was a tough cattle baron who ruled with an iron fist; justice and revenge were often indistinguishable in Wyatt Earp's mind.[73] This was too complicated for the modern media, and history thereby lost much of its power to inspire. It came to be seen as simple-minded propaganda designed to herd youth in socially useful directions.

The educational system seemed to serve this function as well. Schooling was no longer in the hands of prominent members of the community or revered church figures. Americans formerly learned from figures with an aura of reverence and a feel for the subject, or from old folk who had acquired learning informally (to say the least) and passed it on the same way. Teachers were now the products of formal training and certification, utilizing scientific methods, data processing cards, statistics, and standardized tests. Education became soulless and bureaucratic. It bored and alienated many students, especially the talented.[74]

College Life

Higher education was an ambivalent experience. The scientific teaching methods of primary and secondary education were created in university laboratories and their influence there was naturally widespread, especially at large state universities. Many classes had over a hundred students, not from student interest, but from administrative policy. Registration, testing, and grading were done with data-processing machines. Science departments worked closely with the military, and ROTC was prominent on many campuses.[75]

Progressive views of history and society that had once flourished fell into disfavor during and after the war. Though their continued postwar decline is often attributed to McCarthyism, it was due more to broader postwar trends. Renewed nationalism looked unkindly at the reassessments begun by the Beards. The skepticism and relativism of progressive history were blamed for preventing earlier recognition of the danger of totalitarianism. Pride in the nation was more in tune with the times than debunking its myths.[76] Furthermore, the appeal of social programs and government planning had suffered. There were doubts about the effectiveness of the New Deal, which was in a shambles by 1938. A few years into the war, government planning, though part of the war economy, was seen in an unflattering light. It was the essence of totalitarianism, a feature of those political systems that crushed freedom and converted people into tools of the state. Planning was, in the words of a popular book from the period, "the road to serfdom."[77] The system that appeared to be moribund during the Depression had sprung back to health and, to most Americans, seemed to be working just fine.[78] Most social scientists looked upon it as a model of political and economic development for the world.

Many social science courses were, for the most part, dry and formal, committed to the prevailing orthodoxies of systems theory, structural-functionalism, and modernization theory, which demythologized human events, stripped them of sacredness, and processed them into flow charts, organizational tables, and equilibrium models.[79] They purported to be value-free and scientific, eschewing passion and moral judgment as though they were medieval dogmas that had long burdened mankind.[80] There were important exceptions, and certain students naturally gravitated there. Academic figures such as Theodore Adorno, Erich Fromm, and Herbert Marcuse had fled Europe in the 1930s, bringing few personal belongings but many critical theories of society. Another source of interest was the group of American thinkers who came of age during the Depression, became influenced by progressive ideas of the period, and maintained positions in the academy. There was also a handful of younger professors such as C. Wright Mills, Barrington Moore, Jr., and William Appleman Williams, who shared the discontent with mainstream America, and developed critical lines of thought, complete with passion and moral judgment.[81]

For estranged young people, this assortment of European émigrés, New Dealers, and young mavericks constituted an intellectual and emotional oasis in the arid expanses of American academia. Certain themes stand out in their teachings: the urgency of social ills; activism and engagement over scholasticism; the danger of the military-industrial complex and other power elites; the West's exploitation of the wretched of the earth; resistance to the forces stifling the human spirit; breaking down repressive sexual mores; conflict and repression as ordering principles of society; the conviction that meaning in life was not passed down from the past, but had to be made in the present. They constituted an underground of sorts and a training ground giving rigor and focus to educated young people. The university setting gave them the opportunity to come into contact with kindred spirits and develop organizations.[82]

Other Alienated Sub-Groups

The disaffected gathered in coffee houses and bohemian neighborhoods. They coalesced into ersatz communities, too loose and transient to constitute real ones, but finding fellow seekers was like finding a band of the faithful beneath Diocletian Rome.[83] The most extreme of these ersatz communities was the Beats, a group of artists and freethinkers whose rejection of materialism ("moneytheism") and conformity was almost total. They avoided a nine-to-five routine, dabbled in the arts, and read socialist thought and eastern religion. Their clothing came from Salvation Army stores and food from no particular source, though panhandling figures highly in their memoirs. They embraced almost any unconventional experience — marijuana, mescaline, poetry, open sexuality, Zen — and drifted about in search of new experiences, often in Greenwich Village,

Berkeley, Mexico, and other unconventional places. Drifting, moving about, searching for new experiences, getting away from the confines of American conventionality, these were the credos of the Beats. Kerouac, Ginsberg, Burroughs, and the rest attained a cult status. Their writings spread the word to those attracted to the life-style, but not yet willing to break away.[84]

Many young people found meaning in political activity. Organizations speaking out against racism, poverty, and nuclear weapons gained national prominence, and disaffected youth joined these movements, often passionately and completely. They participated in civil rights demonstrations, volunteered to register voters in the South, staffed social centers in inner cities, and denounced the waste of resources on the military. Perhaps more importantly, they formed their own movements on campus, distinct from the Democratic Party and the NAACP. The Berkeley Free Speech Movement, Students for a Democratic Society, and the Student Nonviolent Coordinating Committee pressed university officials on national issues and protested the absence of democracy on campus, irrelevance in the curriculum, Pentagon research, and other aspects of the university, which they saw as a microcosm of the country. By the early 1960s, student movements formed national organizations, held conferences, and issued manifestoes, trying to become a national force and awaiting a defining cause.[85]

Political engagement among the disaffected young was not yet widespread. The Beat lifestyle, though intriguing, was too dangerous for most. A more popular and safer sense of community came from alternative musical trends. Rock 'n roll had once been a creative and spontaneous force led by raw performers who transfixed young people and frightened older ones. By the early 1960s, however, scandals and corporate management had neutered it. Elvis was in the army and went into the movie business afterwards. It became predictable, devoid of the energy, spontaneity, and appeal of the taboo of earlier years. Many parents now thought it was harmless.

Folk music and the blues appealed to those too sophisticated for the mainstream music on hit music stations in every city and town. Folk music had a spirituality hearkening back to pre-modern rural dwellers and working people. Its closeness to the people and the land gave it an attractive authenticity. The lyrics often involved issues of injustice, constant sorrow, poverty, the plight of common people such as coal miners, union activists, and other members of the working class. Folk festivals were placid and often involved audience participation, providing them with a sense of community. Blues music was earthy, spontaneous, intense, and also drawn from the lives of the downtrodden such as sharecroppers from the Delta and migrants to Chicago's South Side. The esoteric sounds of guttural voices and bent strings conveyed a world of sorrow and pain commingled with perseverance and hope of eventual triumph.[86]

The arrival of the Beatles in America in 1964 tapped into this discontent, but appealed to a much broader segment of youth, including those not dedicated to social change or even attending college, yet ready for change nonetheless. Their music was highly creative, with complicated chord progressions and clever lyrics. Their long hair mocked the military-style haircuts of the time. Boys grew their hair a little and enjoyed reproveful looks from parents and teachers. Unease with conformity, poking fun at authority, and weariness of the war generation's cant are all contained in their 1964 film *A Hard Days Night*. After invoking "the rules" to shut off their radio, a stuffy businessman reminds them that he fought in the war for their like. One playfully retorts, "I bet you're sorry you won!" Later, British and German soldiers are extras in a stage production of a war story, suggesting that a young generation saw it as a hackneyed form of entertainment (a sentiment later expressed: "I saw a film today. Oh boy . . . the English army had just won the war"). The Beatles intermittently antagonize, good-naturedly of course, authority figures around them. An expert on youth-marketing points to statistics on teen trends, but the boys ridicule them. Stodgy managers and directors are outwitted. The message of the film, as well as of the Beatle phenomenon, was that youth no longer found the adult world intimidating, creativity and spontaneity could no longer be repressed, and youth was now a force in the world.[8]

***

Only rarely was discontent hostile to American principles and institutions. Although alienated youth saw hypocrisy and failure to live up to the promise, they were, like the progressives of the turn of the century, for the most part believers. There were, however, subgroups of virtually complete disaffection who found the whole system corrupt and reactionary — beyond reform. But as long as most people believed in the Treasury of Virtue, there was little to be done. They marked time and waited for some event — a cause, a crisis of some sort — that would wake up the country, that would provide a hammer with which they could knock down the old edifice. Fortune did not refuse them.

They were polar opposites of many of their classmates and neighbors in the broader strata of youth, with whom they still had something in common in 1965, but not much later. This broader group comprised, among others, the boys (many now young men), raised in the postwar celebration, who longed for a war of their own, so they could have the experience of glory and victory their fathers had known, the goal toward which their culture had long been guiding them. In a curious quirk of history, both groups, though profoundly different, got what they wanted when America went to war in Vietnam.

CHAPTER SIX

VIETNAM AND THE FALL

How has accelerating historical change altered the nature of psychological experience and the extent and form of human development? And how do young men and women with a new psychological orientation affect the history of their time?

KENNETH KENISTON, *Youth and Dissent*

We're stuck over here God knows how long, just waiting and sweating it out, and finding out things about yourself that, by God, it don't pay to know.

NORMAN MAILER, *The Naked and the Dead*

The country that went to war in 1965 was very different from the one that did so a brief generation earlier. The war in Vietnam lasted for years, longer than any previous American war. Opposition grew out of pockets of discontent and spread into the general public until beliefs and institutions were on the verge of collapse, more so than during the Depression. Years of warfare and internal strife ended in shameful defeat. In 1965, the country was confident and optimistic, but only a few years later, it was embittered and pessimistic. America experienced a thing called history.

THE PATH TO VIETNAM

Vietnam first figured in American history during World War II. Germany's defeat of France in 1940 left its colonies vulnerable to conquest, a situation not lost on Japan, which quickly occupied Indochina and eyed adjacent territory. The Roosevelt administration, already opposed to Japanese aggression in China and worried about nearby American possessions, protested sharply, leading to further tension and ultimately to the attack on Pearl Harbor. Japan used bases in Vietnam to conquer Malaya, Singapore, and the Dutch East Indies.[1]

The war led to immense changes in Vietnam, perhaps as momentous as those in the United States. The Japanese demonstrated that westerners could be defeated — and by Asians. They further showed that Asians also could be ruthless masters. French rule had been moderated by political pressures back home and by the ideology of a civilizing mission, but Japanese generals ruled as emissaries of an Asian master race.[2] Nationalist movements gained in strength, and guerrilla forces banded near the border with China. Directed by Ho Chi Minh, the future leader of North Vietnam, the guerrillas forced Japan to allocate resources against them, rescued downed American pilots, and even established contact with American intelligence officers. By 1945, Ho's movement had considerable organization and confidence.[3] The war had brought a break with the colonial past. The days of colonization and subordination were gone, and Vietnamese of various political stripes resolved to prevent their return. They looked for a way to achieve independence; Ho and his movement fitted the bill.[4]

France, humiliated by defeat and occupation, and delegitimized in the eyes of much of its population, sought to regain power prestige by restoring its empire. Negotiations went nowhere, and war broke out in late 1946. America had pressed for decolonization throughout the World War,[5] but realities of the emerging Cold War (France made American support in Indochina a prerequisite for NATO participation) argued for accommodation with colonial powers. Despite US aid, the French fared poorly, controlling the cities but little of the countryside, where most of the population lived. The war dragged on for eight years, and support for it in France flagged.

In late 1953, French paratroopers and Foreign Legionnaires fortified Dien Bien Phu, a remote valley in northwest Vietnam. Soon it was besieged by the Viet Minh, who choked off resupply efforts and silenced the garrison's artillery. When Dien Bien Phu seemed doomed, France requested American air support. President Eisenhower sounded out military and political leaders but found little enthusiasm.[6] "No land war in Asia" had been all but engraved on Pentagon entrances since the truce in Korea the previous year. Eisenhower, in a draft of his memoirs, observed:

> The jungles of Indochina . . . would have swallowed up division
> after division of United States troops, who, unaccustomed to
> this kind of warfare, would have sustained heavy casualties. . . .
> Furthermore, the presence of ever more numbers of white men
> in uniform probably would have aggravated rather than assuaged
> Asian resentments.[7]

Dien Bien Phu fell the day before peace negotiations began, leaving France little bargaining power. After a few months, an agreement was signed, dividing Vietnam in half: a communist north under Ho, and a separate country to the south under non-communist rule. There were promises of a unifying election in a few years, but almost no one thought it would take place, and refugees streamed north and south. As though to foreshadow later superpower involvement, refugees going south traveled on American ships, those heading north on Soviet ones.[8]

Training South Vietnam's military and government was in the hands of French and American advisers, but when France pulled out to deal with the insurgency in Algeria, the burden fell solely on the United States. Policymakers in Washington were confident that economic aid and military training would place Vietnam on the proper path of development.[9] They were equally sure that French failures stemmed from the same cultural and institutional flaws that allowed the Nazis to triumph so swiftly in 1940. By the early 1960s, it was clear that the Saigon government was corrupt and unpopular. Much of the population wanted land reform but received only promises or wasteland. They responded to communist assurances of reform, which, upon running off an ARVN garrison, was put into effect.[10] The military, too, was venal and incompetent. Peasants hid their belongings and daughters when soldiers ventured out from garrisons, usually only during the day.

American largesse made it unnecessary for the Saigon government to become popular or even competent. A government that had engineered meaningful land reform, a fair civil service, and a professional military might have garnered popular support, thwarted the rise of the Viet Cong, and established a viable alternative to communism. However, the Saigon government was a coterie of isolated dilettantes, out of touch with the times and with political and military realities. Such a regime is a rich source for satire, but it is also ripe for insurgency. Communist cadres were winning support from the peasantry, organizing guerrilla bands, and assassinating government officials. The South Vietnamese government began a crackdown, which, predictably, was ineffective. Police beat and tortured suspected Viet Cong, but they frequently arrested the wrong people. Troops went into villages and looted, avoiding as best they could any fighting with the guerrillas.[11]

Experienced observers of foreign affairs — Hopkins, Stimson, Kennan, and their generation — might have observed unfolding events and recommended cutting losses, letting the South fall, and making a stand elsewhere. An old saying in Chicago politics advises, "Don't back no losers," and if its grammatical faults had been overlooked, it might have been invoked here, avoiding a debacle. But the torch had been passed to a new generation, a less experienced generation, idealistic and unpragmatic, which thought they could solve any problem by applying resources. They were willing, even eager, to pick up any burden and fight any foe. Humiliated by a reckless adventure in Cuba, the Kennedy administration searched for a place to show resolve. The deteriorating situation in Vietnam and neighboring Laos called for a firm stand: more resources and more advisers would solve the problem. More GIs and shiploads of equipment would bring the communists to their senses.[12]

In August 1964, North Vietnamese torpedo boats attacked an American destroyer. The administration, sparing the public the minor details of its proximity to a commando raid as well as recent intrusions into the North's waters, sent a second destroyer into the area. Shortly thereafter, amid the confusion of a violent thunderstorm, a second attack might have taken place, though no one on either ship was sure. President Johnson, himself unconvinced of a second attack, nonetheless ordered a retaliatory air strike. Americans congratulated themselves for their firm and proportionate response, confident that they had taught the communists a valuable lesson. The following November, they elected Johnson, the candidate of peace and moderation, over his intemperate adversary. The situation in Vietnam continued to deteriorate. In March 1965, marines had to be deployed around Danang, and paratroopers patrolled outside Bien Hoa (near Saigon). The show of force neither intimidated the communists nor heartened the ARVN. The Viet Cong attacked in larger units and with greater confidence; ARVN units began to disintegrate. When two North Vietnamese divisions arrived in the Central Highlands, it was certain that without immediate US intervention the South would soon collapse.

In July 1965, American policymakers confronted a dilemma which Kennedy had hoped to avoid, but one to which he had led the country. His successor had either to send hundreds of thousands of troops to South Vietnam or to withdraw and allow it to fall. Opponents of intervention argued spiritedly that it would be a quagmire and a misallocation of resources in the global struggle with the Soviet Union. They even had sobering CIA estimates to support their arguments.[13] The opponents of escalation were listened to, but in the end a consensus in favor of large-scale intervention was reached. In his address to the nation on the decision, President Johnson proclaimed, "America will stand in Vietnam."[14]

LIMITED MOBILIZATION FOR A LIMITED WAR

There was no Fort Sumter, *Lusitania*, or Pearl Harbor to galvanize support. There were only puzzling attacks on ships and remote outposts halfway around the world. Nonetheless, after the victory of the Second World War and the vigilance of the postwar years, many Americans reflexively answered the call. The word of the president went far back then. On the matter of war and peace, it carried honor, integrity, and virtual infallibility.

Many young men saw it as their opportunity to do what their fathers had done and what their upbringing had urged. There were many familiar images: lines outside recruiting offices; recent boot camp grads home on leave; GIs posing confidently with their rifles, helmets at jaunty angles and Marlboros dangling from their lips. They had seen it all in the newsreels and movies, and reenacted it in their backyards; now they were doing it themselves, and trying to bridge the gap between boyhood dreams and what they would soon face — what they could only partially conceptualize as "the real thing." Many boys under eighteen were disappointed: the war would surely be over soon, and who knew when the next chance would come. Veterans of past conflicts saw it as passing on the baton, a shared duty and heritage that ensured generational continuity and national greatness. American Legion posts hailed local boys heading off to Parris Island, Fort Bragg, or to the big show itself.

There was imagery from World War II everywhere. Renowned units of the Great Event went over with their guidons and battle streamers: the First Marines of Guadalcanal, the Big Red One of Omaha Beach, the 101st Airborne of Bastogne. News reports, almost invariably upbeat, invoked the past as well: marines hitting the beach, a platoon moving down a jungle trail, interviews with a young soldier from a small town, medics inoculating grateful civilians, and GIs handing out candy bars to smiling kids. Reporters flew along on Hueys and tagged along with ground patrols, ending their reports with hearty thumbs-up.[15]

Cultural Reflexes

In the months after Pearl Harbor, popular culture rallied to the cause. Songs, movies, and television programs did their part. Many stars joined the service or helped out at USOs. There was a little of this early in the Vietnam War. A popular song romanticized the Green Berets. Bob Hope called up his troupe and went overseas for a third war. On variety shows, the houselights would come up to honor servicemen, and the audience would cheer when an entertainer expressed support for the boys overseas. However, on the whole, popular culture showed only limited enthusiasm for the war, though not necessarily for political reasons. The public thought the war would be over quickly, a misconception that the Johnson administration was not eager to correct, even though its confidential studies saw a long war. A brief conflict didn't warrant the planning and production time required of movies and television shows. The events overseas would soon be over, and in any case were for most a distraction from the good life.

Even at the outset, there was ambivalence and opposition. Isolationism persisted in some parts of the country, especially among rural dwellers, the elderly, and those smarting from Korea. Others, including many retired generals, had no quarrel with internationalist policies or with fighting communism, but saw Vietnam as an irrelevant sideshow, another land war in Asia that would draw away resources from Europe. Our allies would be puzzled, if not alarmed, by our policy in Vietnam and would have doubts about an ally that had made such a miscalculation. Hans Morgenthau, a conservative foreign-policy expert, expressed misgivings: "And what will our prestige be like if hundreds of thousands of American troops become bogged down in Vietnam, unable to win and unable to retreat?"[16]

There were also people, neither isolationists nor realists, who saw no reason to send our troops off to an obscure foreign land with no strategic importance. Then there were many young people, who were breaking from the socialization system. For them, the USA was a dilapidated building that had to be repaired or torn down. Vietnam, they hoped, would provide the cause for which they had longed.

Support and Attrition

The war, even at the outset, never had especially high levels of public support. In the early months, before the fighting had really begun, and when it promised to be a short war, support was only at sixty-five percent, with much of that rather tepid. Ominously, before there were any bloody engagements or troubling footage on the news, fully twenty-five percent of the public opposed the war. In early 1966, after a few hundred battle-deaths in the Ia Drang battle, support fell to fifty percent, and opposition climbed to thirty-seven percent.[17]

Earlier wars had seen the government go to great lengths to mobilize support. In 1917, legions of "four-minute men" were deployed around the country to stir popular passions for the war against the Kaiser. Following Pearl Harbor, the government orchestrated news, documentaries, publicity events, and bond drives. It helped to keep up morale in dark periods, as well as toward the end, when it was feared high casualties would weaken resolve to finish the war in the Pacific. The Johnson administration, however, avoided stirring up popular passions. They might get out of hand, transforming Vietnam from a limited war to a larger one that might draw in China (as Korea had in 1951) or the Soviet Union. Furthermore, concentration on the war might provide opponents of civil rights and welfare policies with a rallying cry. Dr Win the War might prevail over Dr Great Society.[18]

A war with only moderate levels of support and firming opposition would have to be over and done with quickly. Alternately, it would have to provide important victories, indicators of progress that would buoy public support, as Midway and North Africa had and as Gettysburg and Sherman's March to the Sea had. Failing that, support would likely deteriorate.

In November 1965, an air cavalry unit set down in the remote Ia Drang Valley to search for the North Vietnamese units whose detection the previous summer had led to Americanization of the war. The few hundred GIs were almost immediately surrounded by over three thousand NVA, and one of the fiercest battles of the war raged for several days. Though it was a near run thing, American firepower and airmobility dealt a punishing blow to the NVA regiment, which had to flee into Cambodia to reorganize and rethink tactics.[19] Confident, even elated, the Johnson administration looked forward to a long string of Ia Drangs, which would wear down the enemy's manpower and morale, and force them to call it quits — the strategy of attrition.[20] In the months that followed, however, there were no more large battles, only hundreds of skirmishes and countless mines and snipers.[21] Policymakers in Washington were publicly confident but privately dismayed. The enemy was able to determine the time, place, and duration of engagements. They controlled casualty levels, the length of the war, and, indirectly, the American public's support for the war. And they knew it.

America was once again at war. Parts of the population supported the effort, parts were determined to use it to expose the country's flaws, but most people simply went on with their lives. As the war stalemated and dissent grew, it was clear that the war had placed American beliefs and institutions on trial. America had sent along with its troops and supplies its history, power prestige, sacred traditions, and, by 1968, its viability as a social system. Into the war went basic American myths: the system of authority; the faith that policies were based on principles of justice; the idea of America as a beacon of light for the world; and the assurance that America would never lose a war.[22]

EROSION AND CRISIS, 1967–1968

A half million troops, mountains of supplies, and billions of dollars poured into Vietnam — an impressive feat that only the US could have accomplished. The military constructed huge port facilities and sprawling logistical centers stocked with everything from jet engines to cases of beer. It built support bases in remote jungles in a day and conducted operations from them the next. Firebases sprang up in a matter of hours, from which artillery fired into the continent. Formidable achievements all, but they were not victories, and support for the war waned throughout 1966 and 1967.

Opposition among the young spread, becoming more intense and confrontational. But it wasn't just the young: average people, true believers in America, and veterans of earlier conflicts saw a stalemate and became disenchanted. For every image of Vietnamese greeting our troops, there were others showing them dismayed by their presence. When GIs set fire to villages, it was rarely seen as part of an intelligible counterinsurgency program, but more often as an act of wanton destruction. The use of technologically sophisticated weapons, the enormous expenditure of ordnance, and the deployment of a battalion to chase a handful of ill-equipped Viet Cong struck many as absurdly disproportionate, needlessly destructive, wasteful, and maybe even unfair.

Disquieting news images might not have undermined support had our Vietnamese allies been perceived as worthy and had there been signs of progress. There was little doubt about the worthiness of allies during World War II. They had spirited civilians and formidable armed forces; they pulled their weight, inflicted heavy casualties on the enemy, and suffered high losses themselves. By contrast, the South Vietnamese government was unstable, unpopular, and untrustworthy. Lacking discipline and fighting spirit, its military left the burden of fighting, and dying, to Americans. There were few signs of progress. Comparisons to World War II, the public's template for war, are once again instructive. By late 1943, the public could see that victory was not far away. The Japanese, defeated at Midway and Guadalcanal, were being steadily driven from island after island. Rommel had been expelled from North Africa; Sicily had been taken and a foothold in Italy established; U-boats no longer ruled the Atlantic. The Russians were advancing on Berlin across a huge front. The sinister black expanses centered in Berlin and Tokyo shrank steadily.

There were no major victories in Vietnam. Try as the administration did to make a recent operation sound like a turning point, the public remained unconvinced. The nature of the war (or at least its strategy) did not call for taking enemy territory and shrinking dark red expanses on the map, but for grinding down its forces, "attritting" them, until they could no longer fight. Body counts, kill ratios, and hamlet evaluations were the only indicators of progress. But there is nothing heroic or inspiring in statistics, nothing that captures the public imagination and lifts flagging spirits. They were abstract numbers that, in time, became doubted along with so much else.

If television played a role in eroding support for the war, it was not by showing the death, suffering, and other realities of war; it was by showing, night after night, straightforward footage of operation after operation, air strike after air strike, and briefing after briefing. Television showed the petty pace of the war, which led more people to conclude that it was a mistake. Doubts were reinforced by returning GIs disillusioned if not embittered by their year of trigger time, numerous casualties inflicted by an invisible enemy, populations (home and abroad) indifferent to their sacrifice, and shattered myths of heroism and adventure.[23] The sight of veterans criticizing their leaders and the wisdom of the war itself was unprecedented.

The Johnson administration responded with confident reassurances and invocations of trust in institutions. There had been doubters during the War of Independence; Madison faced secessionist threats during the War of 1812; and Lincoln wrestled with considerable opposition in the North.[24] In each case, the administration told itself, victory ensued — Saratoga, Tippecanoe, Gettysburg — silencing doubters, restoring faith, and rallying support.

By late 1967, the administration itself was beset by doubts and divisions. No one could find a way to halt infiltration from the North. McGeorge Bundy, the national security adviser, had stepped down, and Robert McNamara, the coldly analytic defense secretary, broke down in public and had to be replaced. The administration was in crisis, as was the whole nation. With each day, each troop deployment, and each public reassurance and invocation of the nation's past, the administration delved into a reservoir of trust, which after 1945 seemed expansive and deep but which was now draining away, with little prospect of replenishment.[25]

Fissures and Opposition

Vietnam brought conflict to many families, typically along generational lines. The older generation, from a more fixed world, was inclined to accept and believe; the younger one, raised in transience, more prone to question and reject. Though television filled the air with programs about wholesome families like the Bradys and Partridges, it was more an attempt to soothe fears than to reflect reality. Family members argued over the war, often bitterly, making many gatherings unpleasant, vituperative events. Paternal authority and domestic comity eroded, and any family discussion was now likely to include contumely.[26]

The war hurt local community too. Draft boards, which decided who went off to war and who was exempt, came under criticism for protecting those with connections. Public school systems came under attack for providing local boards with the names of draft-age boys. Differeng views on the war strained friendship networks. The passions of the war affected voluntary associations and local boards that decided the contentious issues of jobs, race, housing, schools, and the like. Staid administrators and anyone opposed to change became proxies of Lyndon Johnson pitted against the advocates of reform and peace. Civility in discourse about the war, as well as in public life in general, suffered.

At the national level, public life became dominated by the single question of where one stood on the war. Everything else was secondary or easily deduced from the all-defining question. In late 1967, support for the war had declined and opposition had risen until each side was roughly even. (Some polls showed opposition slightly higher than support.) Fissures were deepening and new ones appearing. Positions hardened and tempers flared. Blue-collar workers ("hardhats") held lunch-hour rallies, condemned young opponents of the war as traitors and cowards, and sometimes went after them. There were streetfights in New York and other cities.[27] Many poor people saw the burden of the war falling unfairly on them, all the while, the rich got richer from war profits. Blacks held that they were suffering disproportionately high casualties — more proof of the country's racism. Conspiratorial thought saw the war as a plot to thin out a newly assertive black population. Moderate leaders of the civil rights cause who were reluctant to criticize the war openly — after all, LBJ was their ally — lost support to radical firebrands with no such reluctance.[28] Emerging feminist voices blamed the war on patriarchal institutions predisposed to use force.[29] Many who went to war unquestioningly in 1941 could not understand the lack of faith and conscience in the young; those who refused the call to arms in Southeast Asia could not understand blind faith in institutions, and were not willing to die in an immoral, unwinnable war.

The Spread of the Counterculture

For years, a counterculture had been developing out of the rapid social changes and disrupted socialization process of the postwar period. The war gave it greater numbers and prominence. Its members were usually middle and upper middle-class, typically suburban, and had at least some college education, often at the better schools. They came from groups that had experienced the most disorienting changes over the last few decades: the new middle classes, quasi-communities in suburbia, and a generation more educated than its parents. Vietnam coalesced them, energized them, and gave them their cause. The days of folk singing and poetry readings, of bending, folding, spindling, and mutilating, were over. History now gave them their opportunity, and they would use it to bring down the old regime and forge a new one. They were, for the first time, committed.

Communities sprang up in college towns (Berkeley, Ann Arbor, Cambridge), in bohemian sections of cities (Haight-Ashbury, Greenwich Village, Perry Lane), and in rural and urban communes, where kindred spirits reinforced each other's beliefs. Using blueprints from progressives and Beats, they wanted to build an alternative culture with its own ideals, leaders, heroes, myths, views of history, tastes, and styles. The passions of the times made their beliefs inversions of those of traditional America. Worn clothes were preferred to mass-produced new ones. If they could not be found in the attic or at Salvation Army stores, they could be deliberately distressed to avoid appearing conventional. They might complement worn attire with a top hat or a suit jacket to accentuate the absurdity of conventions. Old furniture and rugs were preferred, in part because they were affordable, but also because they had craftsmanship and richness that had been lost with mass production. Counterculturalists moved about in search of authentic experience, on the road, among artisans and bohemians, at teach-ins, anywhere one could begin to undo the brainwashing.

They saw formal education and careerism as part of the rat race. It was better to learn through activism, from the arts and humanities, or from all-night discussions, where upbringings were lampooned. They struggled to see through the lies of their socialization and accept radical ways of thinking. Though the work ethic was rejected as inculcating self-denial over enjoying life, the counterculture was not composed of layabouts. Many toiled in the civil rights movement, in political campaigns, and on communal farms, or learned some sort of artisan skill. Many dropped out of middle-class trajectories and worked in blue-collar jobs, where a more authentic life could be found and where ties could be forged with an important social class.[30]

Their main work, their great event, was the antiwar movement. Whereas the mainstream had doubts about the war, the Left had a fiery certainty. They defined themselves by their inversion of mainstream views on the war and everything else: white was black, cops criminals, sinners saints, and heads tails. The good guys wore peasant garb, the bad guys olive drab. The war was not a crusade against Soviet expansion; it was an attempt to repress a people seeking to build a progressive society. American troops were racist and destructive; as products of Amerika, they could be little else. They burned and pillaged across Southeast Asia like a mercenary army of centuries past. Alternately, they could be pitied as poor, deluded cogs of a machine, the dupes of a militarist society.

The Left's view of the war took on many themes of alienated youth. The Vietnamese, by defending their ways, could avoid the fate of modern America with all its crassness and injustice. In the villagers banding together to feed guerrillas, make booby traps, hide weapons, and gather intelligence, they saw an egalitarian community replete with the participation of women. The Vietnamese people stood as one in an historically important moment, and forward-thinking Americans stood with them. The counterculture built its own pantheon of heroes and bestowed upon them an aura of sacredness. Fidel, Mao, and Uncle Ho were men of the people, visionary nation builders. Giap and Guevara were military geniuses who, in humiliating modern armies, had revolutionized warfare and shown the way for the weak to defeat the mighty, the young to overthrow the old.

Though most opposition to the war was peaceful, the rightness of the cause made many feel above civility and propriety. Extremism in the name of justice was no vice. Neighborhoods near draft boards and anything related to the war were attacked. Policymakers were shouted down by chants branding them murderers and lauding the Viet Cong. On campuses, they closed access to ROTC buildings and recruiters from war industries such as Dow Chemical (the manufacturer of napalm). Military-funded research facilities were vandalized. Professors who supported the war were interrupted, hooted, and occasionally driven from the forum. Administration buildings were seized to bring the system down. Large numbers mobilized in Washington to shut down the command centers of the war.[31] The counterculture's size and militancy grew steadily during the war. Every autumn, more young people entered college and assimilated the exciting new ideas there.[32]

THE TET OFFENSIVE

By late 1967, a crossover point was reached, one that the administration dreaded, but saw coming all year. In November, for the first time, more Americans opposed the war than supported it. Many public officials remained confident. General Westmoreland proclaimed that a corner had been turned. Walt Rostow, who had replaced Bundy as national security adviser, saw light at the end of the tunnel — an unfortunate phrase used, no more prophetically, fifteen years earlier by a French general. The erosion of support as well as the leadership's buoyancy stemmed from the enemy's return to large-scale engagements at Dak To and Con Thien in late 1967, which analysts interpreted as a sign of desperation. Large battles offered hope that attrition would work, but they also meant higher American casualties, and public support fell to forty percent, while opposition was just under fifty.[33]

The large-scale engagements were actually preparation for a major offensive in January 1968. The Tet Offensive aimed to shatter the South Vietnamese military, trigger a popular uprising against Saigon, and set the stage for a decisive defeat at Khe Sanh, which would knock the Americans out of the war, as Dien Bien Phu had the French. Though enemy plans had been detected and US troops redeployed, the offensive was greater in scope and intensity than predicted. The American public, recently assured of important progress, was unprepared.[34] The offensive exploded on 31 January 1968, with coordinated attacks on every city, district capital, and military base of any size. Even small firebases in remote areas came under attack. A handful of VC penetrated the American Embassy in Saigon, where they fought a sharp firefight before being killed or captured. Most attacks were repulsed in a few days, but in some places, notably Hue, fighting raged for weeks. The offensive was spectacular and made for dramatic news stories, but it fell far short of what the communists had envisioned. The South Vietnamese army was expected to collapse, but it performed surprisingly well. Civilians showed little enthusiasm for rising up in support of the communists. On the contrary, they were appalled by the destructiveness the communists had brought, as well as by the massacre of thousands of civilians at Hue and elsewhere.

As the offensive subsided, there was room for optimism, politically and militarily. Many South Vietnamese, alarmed by the Viet Cong's methods, gave half-hearted support to Saigon, and even half-hearted support was an improvement. They organized local militias to defend against further communist attacks. The Viet Cong, the southern insurgents, lost almost seventy thousand of their most experienced soldiers, and were now beset by high desertion rates and recruitment difficulties.[35] North Vietnamese soldiers had to be put into

Viet Cong units, which, owing to long-standing regional resentments, led to conflict in many units. The presence of northerners hurt combat efficacy and made southerners see the war as a northern invasion. American leaders were again upbeat.[36]

The American public, however, was aghast. The scope and intensity of Tet as well as the casualty figures horrified them. It was incomprehensible that a ragged guerrilla army, said to be in extremis, could pull off a massive, coordinated offensive that sent our forces reeling and even held the Embassy grounds for a while. Doubts about our Vietnamese allies had long troubled Americans, but they grew after seeing graphic images of a police intendant summarily executing a Viet Cong on a Saigon street. The film of the execution opened the evening news; the photograph was on the front pages of most newspapers. Americans had already known the Saigon regime to be corrupt and unstable, but now it was also brutal and murderous.[37]

Americans had endured years of pointless operation after another, week after week of body counts, and countless confident but vague predictions. Tet underscored the absence of progress and the unworthiness of the South. The war would surely drag on for years. Pessimism set in. A few months before Tet, fifty percent of Americans saw progress in the war and only eight percent thought the war was being lost. After it, only thirty-three percent saw progress while twenty-three percent thought the country was losing the war.[38] The opposition had heretofore come mainly from figures easily dismissed by the public. After Tet, authoritative voices that had held back spoke out. A prominent news reporter observed the war was probably unwinnable. It was not a question of a liberal media. The *Wall Street Journal* observed:

> We think the American people should be getting ready to accept,
> if they haven't already, the prospect that the whole Vietnam
> effort may be doomed, that it may be falling apart beneath our
> feet. . . . We believe the Administration is duty-bound to recognize
> that no battle and no war is worth any price, no matter how
> ruinous, and that in the case of Vietnam it may be failing for the
> simple reason that the whole place and cause is collapsing from
> within. . . . [E]veryone had better be prepared for the bitter taste of
> a defeat beyond America's power to prevent.

Nor was it a question of eastern elites. The *Salina Journal* expressed pained voices from the heartland:

> It is hard for a proud nation such as this to admit defeat and error.
> But if we are a moral, honorable nation with a sense of duty and

destiny, we cannot go on killing and destroying to perpetuate an error and deepen it. . . . The only honorable and wise course is to de-escalate the war and prepare to withdraw from Vietnam in the best order and with the fewest casualties possible. If President Johnson finds his personal pride too stubborn, the weight of defeat to grievous, the Congress should reassert its Constitutional authority, if necessary remove him from office, and put this nation back on the paths of peace.[39]

Tet impressed countless images upon the national mind. There was footage from Khe Sanh of an ammunition dump exploding, airstrikes only a few hundred yards outside the wire, cargo planes dropping supplies then taking off before NVA mortars found the range. In Hue, marines fought block by block across acres of rubble recalling Stalingrad. And of course there was the infamous execution in Saigon. A less famous news report captures the mood. A GI, hunkered down as bullets hum overhead, is asked if the war is a good cause. His initial response, true to his upbringing, is affirmative, but then he pauses, realizing, perhaps for the first time, that he no longer believes this. He was taught that America is always right, and that it always fights for democracy; but hard experience compels him to rethink things. His face etched with skepticism, he answers, "Well, they say it's a good cause . . . but now . . . I just don't know anymore." Back home, there were millions of Americans, long faithful to the American idea, whose upbringing and reflexes also told them to support the war, but who, after Tet, no longer could.

Agonizing Reappraisal

Public opinion aside, members of the elite, in and out of government, were turning against the war. Johnson's national security adviser, McGeorge Bundy, had already left government and his secretary of defense, Robert McNamara, soon followed. Clark Clifford, the incoming secretary of defense, asked the generals, How much longer could the communists wage war? Would more troops break the enemy's will? Would more bombing cut off supplies from the North? The generals had once spoken confidently, but now they were less so. Clifford concluded that the war could not be won and sought to build a consensus, within the Pentagon, for disengagement.[40]

Throughout the war, Johnson sought the advice of a group of jurists, retired generals, bankers, and former statesmen. These Wise Men were old hands in war and foreign policy, present at the creation of the American century. Many of them had guided the country through World War II, after which they became architects of containment policies. They had convened several times during the war and each time had expressed support, as recently as the previous November. Johnson had been heartened by their counsel, which was based on long experience, not public moods. In the aftermath of Tet, Johnson convened them once more.

The Wise Men listened to official briefings for several days, studied the reports, then gave their judgments. Four expressed strong doubts about the war; seven favored fundamental change of some sort. Only three expressed confidence in the current policy. Johnson had withstood flagging public opinion, stacks of letters calling for peace, and jeering crowds, but now the most experienced hands, privy to the best information, the same information he had, suddenly no longer supported his war policy.[41] Johnson was stunned and began a reappraisal, of the war as well as his presidency. Shortly thereafter, in an address to the nation, he announced a bombing halt and a new effort to seek a diplomatic end to the war. In a few sentences, added unbeknownst even to close advisers, he announced he would not seek re-election. The nation, then somewhere between a receding era of confidence and an emerging one of cynicism, felt, perhaps for the last time, a shared sense of tragedy.

RESURGENCE AND DEFEAT

Few can look back on 1968 without at least some sadness. The violence of Tet and the fall of a president were opening acts in a yearlong tragedy. Only a few days after Johnson's speech, Martin Luther King was assassinated, triggering riots in several cities. Paratroopers had to be rushed in to guard the White House and Capitol. Many people saw the country on the brink of collapse and placed hope in a Kennedy Restoration, a return to a mythic past of optimism, unity, and idealism that ended in Dallas and Vietnam. But only a month after King's murder, another lone deranged gunman, for which the country seemed a breeding ground, killed Robert Kennedy as he neared winning his party's nomination and taking his rightful place. The Democratic convention in Chicago was turbulent and divisive. Violent fights broke out between young demonstrators and city police. Hundreds were injured and arrested.[42]

The country was tearing itself apart. Malaise and disgust, no longer confined to pockets of students and intellectuals, were everywhere. The charm of America gave way to the view that it was a "sick society," plagued by violence, racism, and militarism.[43] Vietnam was seen as neither an aberration nor an error. The country's culture and institutional framework, from the earliest encounters with Indians to the present, had been geared toward hatred and war. Richard Hofstadter described the mythic frontier man as "an almost monstrous archetype of aggressive masculinity."[44] William Appleman Williams acerbically observed: "Empire is as American as apple pie. Or as American as the ever westward moving frontier. . . . Or as American as saving the world from the devil. Or as American as the veils that Americans have woven to obscure the harsh reality of their imperial record." He goes on to outline violent expansionism from the colonial period to the conquest of the West, culminating in the ongoing disaster.[45] Many people felt that no matter what arguments could be marshaled for the war, it was not worth destroying the country's beliefs and institutions.[46]

Nixon and the Faithful

By the middle of 1968, public opinion began to swing back. Looming anarchy caused many to reach for anything promising stability. The antiwar movement's confrontational and scatological tactics led to disgust and a yearning for law and order. The Soviet Union's invasion of Czechoslovakia in August crushed a democratic movement there, giving credence to old warnings of communism's danger. Support for the war actually increased somewhat in the second half of the year.[47]

The Democrats were seen as the party of a disastrous war and brutal police repression orchestrated by a big-city boss. The Republicans presented themselves as the party of unity that would "bring us back together," by restoring faith in America and respect for the law. They would end the war honorably, just as Ike had with Korea — and who better to do it than the venerable general's vice-president? The millions still faithful to America, as well as the millions of others who needed something to hold on to, placed their hopes in Richard Nixon.

Pity is not the first emotion that comes to mind on mentioning Nixon's name. However, a measure of pity might be in order for any president in 1969. Later events might make this somewhat difficult in Nixon's case, but the country's problems that year were formidable. He inherited a war he did not begin, one that was now impossible to wage, at least as it was being waged. Polling data were exasperating. Fifty-five percent of the public opposed the war and only forty supported it, with that figure declining. Perhaps the most interesting (and from the perspective of the White House, frustrating) data showed that only nine percent would support ending the war if it meant a communist victory, as it surely would have.[48] A rapid pullout and ensuing collapse would have caused a vicious backlash, damaging the party in power for a decade and poisoning civil-military relations for even longer. The framework of containment would have been undermined. Whatever the consequences, polling data suggest that the public simply wanted the ugliness to disappear — and they wanted it, somehow, to happen right away.

In late 1968 and early 1969, as the communists rebuilt, there were fewer engagements, and US casualties dropped. In early May, however, American paratroopers trapped a sizable NVA force in the A Shau Valley, setting the stage for a ten-day battle that became known as Hamburger Hill. In purely military terms, Hamburger Hill might be roughly compared to Sugar Loaf Hill in 1945, where a similar number of troops attacked a Japanese position on Okinawa. The casualties at Sugar Loaf were staggering — over seven thousand killed and wounded — but it was seen as a necessary sacrifice. Twenty-five years later, amid an unpopular effort, one that with every passing day was less a national effort, the assault on Hamburger Hill stirred anger. Fifty-six Americans were killed, another four hundred wounded, less than seven percent of the casualties at Sugar Loaf. The public saw the battle as another senseless operation aimed at racking up a body count. After ten days, the paratroopers took Hamburger Hill then hopped into their Hueys to search elsewhere for the elusive enemy. Their departure made sense from a strategic point of view, but, from the public's, it proved the operation's folly. Outrage was intense. The public would no longer tolerate high casualties; the big battles earlier hoped for now had to be avoided. Nixon ordered a reduction in ground operations.[49]

The Nixon administration developed a plan to disengage as best as circumstances allowed. It forced the South Vietnamese army to assume the combat burden, allowing reductions in American troop levels, casualties, and draft levies. Vietnamization would not be easy. The ARVN had to build confidence; coordination between ground and air forces had to develop; logistical skills would have to be mastered. Time would be bought by attacks on communist sanctuaries in Cambodia and Laos, disrupting their supply system and timetables. Diplomatic efforts would attempt to weaken support for the North in Moscow and Peking. It was a masterful plan, displaying formidable strategic vision, but it required time and patience, neither of which was in good supply. Events would do nothing to increase it.

Rise and Fall of the Antiwar Movement

There had long been rumors of American atrocities in Vietnam. To the general public, they didn't seem possible: our boys didn't do such things. If a Viet Cong was tortured, or a civilian inadvertently killed, it was dismissed as one of the horrors of war. Now there was talk of something else. Members of Congress received letters from recently discharged veterans about a massacre of civilians in March 1968. At Congress's request, the army began an investigation, which, after several months, issued a report. An American infantry platoon entered My Lai and, without drawing fire, slaughtered hundreds of unarmed civilians, mostly women and children. In November 1969, the army indicted Lt William C. Calley and several others for murder.

Wire services and television networks carried the story, but it wasn't until *Life* published a series of nightmarish photographs that the enormity of the massacre was felt. Americans were appalled by the pictures and accounts of slaughtered peasants and babies. They were convinced more than ever that the war was a mistake, and that there was something fundamentally wrong with the country.[50] Opponents pointed to the massacre as proof that the war was immoral, America was racist, and the Vietnamese people supported the communists and feared the Americans. Many were convinced that My Lai had been a typical or at least common operation. Hysteria existed among supporters as well. Calley was widely defended as an unfortunate lad trying to do his duty in a war in which friend and foe were not easily distinguished. Veteran organizations contributed to his defense fund and organized petition drives to free him. A popular ballad portrayed him as simply doing his job under difficult circumstances. Such were the demented polarizations of the period that opponents of the war thought the average soldier was a Calley, and supporters thought Calley was an average soldier.[51]

My Lai gave more credibility and momentum to opponents. Though the air-war over North Vietnam had been halted in 1968, and casualties had declined, frustration continued to mount. The change of presidents had not brought an end to the war, as many had hoped. Democratic opponents of the war held their fire while their party was in the White House, but felt no such reluctance with a Republican there.[52]

On college campuses, opposition to the war became part of life. Despite the growing numbers — perhaps *because* of them — the movement was weakening. The deeply committed noticed with dismay that most people at antiwar gatherings cared little for the cause. They were there because it was the thing to do or it was a convenient place to meet people and listen to music. They were just following a fad, joining the movement for the same reasons they had bought Hula Hoops a few years earlier. Their dorm rooms had Viet Cong flags and posters of Che, they listened to songs about revolution, they spoke glowingly of "the people" and darkly of "the pigs," but they had none of the leadership's convictions or vision. The counterculture, too, had its other-directed crowd.[53]

The massive demonstrations in Washington and elsewhere brought the cause to the public's attention, but achieved little of consequence. The movement had become large and unwieldy, comprising a mass of disaffected and merely adventurous youths opposed to the discipline and organization needed to bring its numbers to bear on the political system. The movement had limited access to the Democrats; no contact at all with the Republicans. They had neither the hope nor the inclination to build a third party, especially when twenty-one was the minimum voting age. Among the intelligentsia, radicalism had become in style, part of the affectations displayed at fashionable dinners — it had become chic.[54] Madison Avenue was using the rebellious spirit of the day to sell Dodges. The capacity of American culture to absorb, deflect, and co-opt was boundless. As the movement faltered, the establishment regained strength from the crisis of 1968. The Nixon administration, with its attacks on the movement, invocation of American values, publicity events featuring wholesome youths and sanctimonious preachers, re-invigorated the Treasury of Virtue that had been moribund a year earlier.

A portion of the movement's leadership concluded that revolutionary violence was needed. Taking their nom de guerre from a Bob Dylan song, the Weathermen embraced the code and methods of a revolutionary sect to do the people's will. A secret band of disciplined revolutionaries was needed to bring the system down, to "bring the war home," as the saying went. Remembering the destruction of Tet and the shock it had on the public, the Weathermen concluded, "We've got to turn New York into Saigon."[55] They engaged in street battles and robbed banks to fund the cause, but might best be remembered for a series of bombings. One target was a major bank headquarters on the West Coast, another the Capitol building. A plan to bomb an army base in New Jersey went awry when a basement lab in Greenwich Village exploded, killing a number of the group. A like-minded group failed in an attempt to destroy a munitions plant, but were able to detonate a fertilizer bomb outside a military research building at the University of Wisconsin, killing a young physicist and wounding several other people.[56]

The conventional antiwar movement went on, at least for a while. There were candle-lit processions from Arlington National Cemetery to the White House, prayer vigils, petitions from professional organizations and average citizens, and thousands of local events conducted by an array of people from members of the Old Left of the 1930s to mothers of those killed in the war. The chief American prosecutor at the Nuremberg war crimes tribunal wrote a book outlining parallels between Nazi and American atrocities. No one could any longer argue that the antiwar movement was then the product of pampered middle-class youth.[57] Polling data had heretofore fluctuated, with each side experiencing ups and downs, but after 1970, the year of the Cambodian incursion and Kent State, opposition shot up steadily and support plummeted, with both trends continuing, unabated, for the rest of the war.

By mid-1971, opponents of the war were more than twice as numerous as supporters, roughly sixty-six percent to twenty-seven. Yet the movement fell apart. A large mobilization in Washington had taken place in the Spring, but it was a last hurrah. After years of passionate involvement, many militants were simply exhausted — "burned out" as the expression went. Others threw up their hands in despair, concluding there was nothing they could do to end the war. For many others, for whom the movement was less a calling than a lark, the sense of adventure and romance had worn away. Furthermore, the terrorism of the Weathermen caused many to step back and realize that revolutionary talk in the dorms, when put into practice, was not a pretty sight. It was one thing to talk idly about smashing the state and offing pigs, but quite another to see burning buildings and grieving widows.[58]

There is a more important reason for the movement's decline. Amid all the turbulence since 1968, there had been a remarkable reduction in American troop levels and battle casualties. Nixon had coerced the South Vietnamese to assume more ground operations, and, by mid-1971, a little more than two years into office, he had reduced troop strength in Vietnam by sixty-three percent. By the end of that year, the military was relying mainly on incentives rather than conscription to meet manpower needs, allowing for reduced draft levies.

Troop Levels and Battle Deaths in Vietnam, 1968–1972[59]

Year	Troop Level	Change	American KIAs	% Change
1968	536,100		14,589	
1969	475,200	- 60,900 (-11%)	9,414	-35%
1970	334,600	-140,600 (-30%)	4,221	-55%
1971	156,800	-177,800 (-53%)	1,381	-67%
1972	24,200	-132,600 (-85%)	300	-78%

The most surprising figure here might be the number of Americans killed in action. In 1971, the death toll was down sixty-seven percent from the previous year, down *ninety-four percent* from 1968. Though not as precipitous as other candidates had suggested in the '68 campaign, and not as rapid as many in the public wanted, in the less heated atmosphere time has mercifully provided, it is clear that American involvement wound down rather quickly. Vietnamization was easing disorder in America, but it remained to be seen if it could ensure the independence of the South.

Few looking back on those years will remember them for the rapid reduction of troop levels and deaths. They are generally remembered with anger and disgust, often accentuated by expletives and epithets, as years of continued war and sordid revelations about it. The My Lai massacre and subsequent trials were the most shocking, but dozens of lesser stories came out, one after another, undermining faith in government, myths of decency and justness, and every aspect of American life. Bombing campaigns were taking a fearful toll on innocent civilians. Sometimes, as in Cambodia, they were of questionable legality and in any event were unknown to the public until newspapers broke the story. Chemical defoliants were causing birth defects among the Vietnamese. A CIA campaign to assassinate Viet Cong cadre (the Phoenix Program) was thought to be killing innocent people. The war was turning a traditional Asian society into a sprawling black market and tawdry whorehouse.

In early 1971, newspapers began to publish a series of classified documents, spirited out of the Pentagon, which outlined the unseemly road to Vietnam. The Pentagon Papers showed a pattern of deceptions, half-truths, and lies.[60] Presidents had sanctioned clandestine and often illegal operations, backed a coup d'état that killed leaders they once praised, misled the public on the Gulf of Tonkin Incident, and manipulated events and opinion to justify escalation. In the next year, two books critical of the war became bestsellers.[61] A dark mood was spreading out across everything American. Nothing could be believed and everything had to be doubted.

POLITICAL CRISIS AND DEFEAT

A weary and demoralized country welcomed a peace agreement in January 1973. The last American troops left South Vietnam two months later. Prisoners of war, some held for more than eight years, came home. A few kissed the ground as they deplaned and exclaimed "God Bless America," gestures from an older America that, unbeknownst to them, had disappeared during their captivity. Charts of support and opposition were now moot; Nixon's popularity soared. An outsider might have concluded that the turbulence was over, that Nixon had restored the faith, and that America would resume the pleasant normalcy of the early 1960s. There was, however, lingering hostility toward the country in general and Nixon in particular. The war had not truly come to a close, only American combat in it; a final judgment on the war, and America itself, rested on the fate of South Vietnam.

The administration asserted that the South's army would be able to hold its own and maintain independence. Those who trained and advised them were far less confident. The Laos operation in 1971, they knew, had been a disaster, and the communist offensive of 1972 had been blunted mainly through American airpower. A few months before the peace agreement, a young corporal asked a ranger captain, an old hand with more combat decorations than the corporal had years, how long the South would last after the last GIs left. The question was not *if* the South would survive — any corporal could see it wouldn't — but how long it had, how long until the inevitable fall. It was a simple question, but to a man who had dedicated his life to training the South's army, had been wounded several times, and had once believed in the cause with the faith of a crusading knight, it was personal and painful. After an introspective pause, he exhaled audibly and gave his analysis, apparently already thought out.

There were a few good units (the First Infantry, airborne and marine units, and a handful of ranger battalions he had trained and fought with), but most

ARVN units were badly led and poorly motivated. The best would be stretched too thin; the rest would eventually crack. Whole battalions and brigades would disintegrate, and then it would be over. There was nothing to prevent it: US ground troops would never return, airpower could only do so much next time. He judged it would take two years; twenty-four months after the last Americans left, Saigon would fall. The conversation fell off, as the two soldiers, raised in the post-World War II era but coming of age in Vietnam, pondered the waste of it all, as well as what America's first defeat might mean.

Between the departure of the last American troops and the fall of Saigon came Watergate, a far-reaching political scandal that further damaged beliefs and institutions. Watergate was in part the product of Nixon's style of politics, but it was also a product of recent history. It is difficult to imagine the scandal would have occurred had there been no unpopular war. A siege mentality, a sense that portions of the public were out to get the president, had taken hold in the Johnson administration. Both Johnson and Nixon viewed the antiwar movement as disloyal, subversive, in league with foreign powers, and they both used government assets to neutralize it. The shift from using agents against student groups to using them against political rivals came under the rationale of national security, a broad doctrine then, and one that could be broadened further amid a war. Had there been no war in Vietnam, it is difficult to imagine a major newspaper having the audacity to accuse a president of criminal activity. The war had undermined the credibility and integrity of every public figure, especially the president, and made his involvement in any wrongdoing seem at least possible. Who would have believed two young journalists over the President of the United States, had there not already been a number of lies on the war? More importantly, the widespread and intense hostility that pushed Nixon from office predated Watergate, and was based more on the dragged-out war than on a burglary and cover-up.

The end of the war had brought an easing of the crisis of public faith, but with Watergate the crisis flared again and took on new strength. Nixon had long presented himself and his administration as virtuous public servants, who lived the American dream, believed in it, and would restore the faith to all. Family and religion, law and order, honor and devotion, these were the themes of every public event and pronouncement, from the 1968 campaign to the White House dinner for returning POWs. He wrapped his administration in the American flag and wore a miniature one on his lapel. When the war ended, the opposition found itself disarmed, but with Watergate, they had a new weapon.

Nixon gave his opponents something the antiwar activists never had — solid evidence of criminal activity. Throughout 1973 and 1974 there was a steady stream of revelations about him and his administration: break-ins at a psychiatrist's office and the Democratic Party's headquarters, FBI participation in the cover-up, and patterns of illegal practices and perjury. The public seethed with an anger begun in Vietnam but now focusing on the White House. No longer a matter of debating the propriety of the war or mobilizing marches on the Mall, it was a matter of legal machinery, due process, subpoenas, indictments, and impeachment. In August 1974, Nixon resigned in disgrace, leaving the country he promised to restore worse than he found it.

The next year, events played themselves out to a dismal close. In early 1973, with Watergate still a minor story, Congress banned the use of American airpower in Southeast Asia. Returning ground troops to Southeast Asia was as unlikely as putting them on the moon. The war would be settled by the opposing Vietnamese armies, as well it might have been ten years and a million lives earlier. In the spring of 1975, after years of rebuilding and planning, North Vietnam launched an offensive to conquer the South. Sobered by failed offensives in 1968 and 1972, they planned for a long campaign, one lasting a couple of years or more, but it was soon clear, now to all, that the best ARVN forces were stretched too thin and the others were unwilling to play any part except one with an early exit.

The drama unfolded as much of it had already — on television. There were long lines of civilians fleeing down congested roads; ARVN soldiers leaving piles of rifles and equipment, running down tarmacs to scramble aboard the last plane out; streets with stores and bars bearing American names, deserted except for looters. Cities and bases fell one after the other. Airborne units stiffened around Saigon but were soon worn down, and eyes shifted for the final act near the American Embassy, where helicopters took the last Americans to ships offshore. The scene of helicopters thrown overboard conveyed a final sense of tragedy, waste, and senselessness that encapsulated a decade of the same dismal emotions. On 30 April 1975, twenty-five months after the last American troops had left, North Vietnamese troops took Saigon.

CHAPTER SEVEN

THE EXPERIENCE OF DEFEAT

But if the cause be not good,
The King himself hath a heavy reckoning to make
If these men do not die well,
It will be a black matter for the King
SHAKESPEARE, *Henry V* 4:1

"Middle America" . . . has come to symbolize everything that stands
in the way of progress: "family values," mindless patriotism, religious
fundamentalism, racism, homophobia, retrograde views of women.
CHRISTOPHER LASCH, *Revolt of the Elites* (not approvingly)

Americans felt they lived in a land of charm and grace. American exceptionalism was Providence's gift to a chosen nation that would enlighten the world and never lose a war. With each victory came further proof of the nation's uniqueness and righteousness. This cherished myth had been weakening, but, owing to the Great Event, it persisted into the 1960s. The dream and glory ended in Vietnam. The experience undermined long-standing beliefs and changed the nation into a postmodern country marked by malaise, weak family structure, fluid gender roles, atomized social relations, weakened beliefs, and mistrust of authority. Undoubtedly, the consequences of the war have been exaggerated by some for partisan purposes, but also minimized by others for their ends. And it should be borne in mind that the social problems of post-Vietnam America have been pointed out by thinkers from across the political spectrum.

MALAISE

Bitter experiences in war lead to malaise. Free-floating and dimly understood senses of dread and guilt pervade the country, along with confusion, cynicism, despair, and nostalgic searches for lost times. Until Vietnam, America as a whole had basked in victory, never knowing defeat, somehow unaware that within its boundaries lived people who had lost wars and endured the unendurable. After 1865, the South was a defeated land. A venerated social order had fallen; animosities toward the wealthy surfaced (a rich man's war); guilt was felt in much of life. Southerners sought relief in myths of a halcyon past and in patent medicines promising to lift spirits. Many were convinced that the end of the world was at hand.[1] In the 1890s, the Plains Indians, defeated and interned, lapsed into despair and millenarianism. They believed that floods and earthquakes would soon destroy the world, or that a messiah would come to restore the natural order of things.[2]

Following World War II, Americans witnessed the effects of defeat while presiding over Japan. Despair pervaded the lives of many; old certainties fell away; suicide rates rose sharply. Previously revered elites were now despised and blamed for millions of deaths. Traditional values and institutions were also held responsible, and radical reforms were needed to save the country. A popular novel of the period, *The Setting Sun,* inverted the once sacred symbol of Imperial Japan. The period's ablest historian notes, "Here was a world turned upside down."[3]

The pattern can be found elsewhere as well. In the nineteenth century, following a string of humiliating defeats that began with the Crimean War, Russia was swept by discontent. Many intellectuals and youths suddenly began to despise their country — Turgenev called them "nihilists" — and went off to live with peasants or joined revolutionary and terrorist organizations. Others saw salvation in a mythic past or in adopting foreign ways.[4] Following its defeat in the Franco-Prussian War (1871), France found itself plagued by pessimism, normlessness, suicide, drug use, crime, deracinated youth, doubt over its place in the world, and chronic divisiveness and directionlessness.[5] After defeat by the United States, Spain entered a period of self-disgust, epitomized by the "Generation of 1898," which blamed the country's culture for the disaster. Some claimed that the country had failed to modernize; others countered that the country had abandoned tradition, contradictory currents suggesting that fragmentation is another product of defeat.[6] In 1918, the imperial-military edifice of German nationhood collapsed, leaving the country in disarray. National beliefs and institutions could no longer provide meaning or coherence. Familiar surroundings took on alien, Kafkaesque qualities, and malaise spread like a dark cloud.[7]

The winning countries in 1918, if we can speak of any, experienced similar problems. Poets, writers, and composers gave expression to malaise, which replaced the supreme confidence of prewar years. Europe was a botched civilization, reduced to a wasteland and inhabited by hollow men.[8] Somerset Maugham wrote of a postwar generation lost in confusion, absorbed by greed, or, more benignly, in search of a new basis of spirituality in mysticism. Shortly after the lively waltzes of Strauss had resounded across Europe, the elegiac compositions of Vaughan Williams and Bax were heard, poignantly conveying disenchantment with the present and wistful yearning for the past. Alternately, musicians such as Bartók and Schoenberg explored dissonance and darkness — musical expressions of dread.

In the decades before Vietnam, Americans lived in confidence and pride. Leaders were regarded as high-minded, noble, and above reproach. The country knew no limits; nothing was beyond its reach. America never wanted war; it was slow to anger and only reluctantly unsheathed its sword. The American fighting man, the descendant of the Deerslayer, Alvin York, and Audie Murphy, would always win the day. Behind him stood a united people who would put aside partisan squabbles when the nation went to war.[9] Vietnam turned this upside down. Basic myths that bound Americans together were gone or in disarray, and the aura of national sacredness dissolved. National leaders and symbols no longer enjoyed an aura of romance and sanctity. Life became secular and rational-legal. Few could look at the flag or the White House and feel the enchantment they once elicited. People no longer felt part of a living national community. They related to each other more as strangers, competing interest groups, buyers and sellers, people who had lost trust with one another, or as antagonists who, though the source of animosity was past, could not be reconciled.

The country broke away from mooring points. Americans were no longer rooted in their nation, its history, and the sense of time and place it gave them. Only a few years earlier, the future was assured; families, schools, and myths provided a blueprint for life. Americans were part of an ongoing history of immigrants and settlers, average people and heroes, building a country and ensuring their children would do even better. No more.[10] Suicide rates had been relatively flat from the late 1930s to the mid-1960s but rose after 1968 (repeating the trend that followed World War I). Suicide among young people raised in post-Vietnam anomie soared to astounding levels.[11] Sociology and civics texts once emphasized principles of justice in a coherent social system, but now spoke of dangerous military and corporate power, social inequalities, racism, sexism, the flawed criminal justice system, and the powerlessness of average people.[12]

The cinema, once reluctant to deviate from the happy-ending standard, became pessimistic, obsessed with dreadful monsters and disasters. In one popular genre, orderly life suddenly collapses, usually owing to misdeeds by members of elites. Fearful forces are set loose, terrifying people, destroying established beliefs. Animals no longer behave as they should. Creatures from the deep become preternaturally evil and deadly. In horror films of the 1950s, science and the military swiftly came to the fore and saved the day, but now the system cannot cope with the problem, indeed its arrogance and meddling are responsible for it. Banding together, trying new ideas, average people triumph where putative superiors failed. They emerge from the crisis chastened, feeling a sense of limitation and respect for the powerful forces that had been upset.[13] A related genre tells of shipwrecks, earthquakes, and devastating fires. The first of these films involves a luxury liner capsized by a tidal wave. Stability is suddenly destroyed; the world is turned upside down. Authority figures should have seen the disaster coming and taken steps to avoid it, but through arrogance they blunder into it. People no longer abide by normal conventions; they must find new ways. Once again, an unconventional figure comes to the fore (a defrocked priest, an earnest working-class figure), convinces the survivors that old ways no longer work, and leads them through a harrowing escape. Survivors see the folly of trusting leaders and come away with a sense of limitation and hubris.[14]

The malaise was especially strong in certain groups. There was Middle America, who had been believers, even amid the turmoil of the war, but who now felt undermined, betrayed, and blamed for their blind allegiance to the country. They had served during the Second World War or in Korea, or perhaps were raised in working-class communities where American sacredness had been assumed. They believed in America, supported the war, and rallied to Nixon's appeal for patriotism and law and order. They felt sadness over the passing of a cherished world. They could no longer sustain an argument against those who mocked them and now felt that the war's tragic end had proved them right all along: that the country was flawed, racist, militarist.

Malaise was no more deeply felt than among the millions of Vietnam veterans. Most were relatively young and had believed in America, not from long experience, but from its promise of glory and honor in war — the guiding myth of their youth. Movies, backyard play, and television, they thought, had prepared them. More than any other generation, they thought they knew what to expect from war; more than any other generation, they returned disillusioned. Their writings and recollections describe the war's jarring effects on their beliefs. War was physical hardship and tedium interrupted by sniper fire, land mines, incoming rounds, and death. In moments of introspection, they looked for something in their pasts to help understand the hard realities, but found only a clutter of stock footage and clichés. They had to purge their minds of that adolescent foolishness, dissociate themselves from their upbringing, and embark upon a new, hard education for the next twelve months.

Returning home brought no respite. In 1865 and 1945, many veterans returned embittered and alienated, but ultimately buoyed by victory and the embrace of a grateful nation. Vietnam veterans returned to a divided country, neither side having much understanding of the war. It was difficult to communicate with people who saw the war in terms of a good cause and heroism, and so their praise was met with vacant stares. On the other side were the opponents of the war, certain they understood the war far better than simple soldiers did, befogged as they were by military indoctrination. Vacant stares came readily here too, especially when romantic views of the Viet Cong were heard, as they commonly were. It was best to avoid the whole subject. And after the defeat, avoiding the subject of Vietnam — avoiding the very word — was what Americans wanted anyway. For them, the war was not a political issue, it was the most meaningful and formative period of their lives. The education there was more important than all the years of family and school had been. But the experience, though often still surging and thundering, had to be put away or denied, except for their early appreciation for irony and tragedy, which would never be far from mind. Nagging many veterans was a sense of failure, of having broken faith with the past by losing America's first war.[15]

Not everyone felt malaise. A fragmented country could hardly respond to defeat in a homogeneous way. Many opponents of the war celebrated the fall of Saigon and congratulated themselves for their part in the Vietnamese people's triumph. One study of the antiwar movement ends by describing a V-V Day celebration:

> [A]nti-war activists shed tears of joy and relief. "It was a moment that many thought would never come," the radical *Guardian* newspaper observed. "Vietnam has won. And so have we." More than fifty thousand people filled Sheep Meadow in Central Park on May 11 to celebrate the war's end. Colorful streamers and gigantic balloons reflected the festive mood of the crowd, bathed by spring sunshine. A large banner on the speakers' platform proclaiming THE WAR IS OVER was flanked by huge pictures of the 1970 Kent State killings. Many of the celebrants hugged each other. Some reflected on the countless meetings and demonstrations of the past ten years. "There's lots of lumps in lots of throats," one said. "It's unbelievable." But it was true.[16]

Defeat would lead to a new day of genuine freedom and democracy, a society rid of hypocrisy, conformity, racism, militarism, and other burdens of the past. Others, not so politically engaged or even inclined toward social thinking, did not feel the malaise either. They too saw an opening. The war had freed them from stale rituals, mummery, and illusions of the old order, which had been long out of date, but which continued to impose a dreary regimen over the lives of people, especially the young. They were now free to live their lives as they chose. Life became a festival of leisure, consumption, and pleasure.

THE NEW FAMILY

By the mid-1970s, the family was no longer a meaningful institution. Its sanctity, authority, and formative influence were gone. There was no longer a sense of common purpose. Parental authority, like every form of authority, was punctured. There was little continuity between generations. The assumption that parents had decisive claims on the life choices of their children no longer held. Nor was the family even a locus of emotional warmth. By their early teens, if not earlier, children lived in a distinct and often antagonistic world of popular culture.

After 1945, parents, especially fathers, enjoyed an infusion of prestige. They were all part of a system that had proved itself. The opposite took place after Vietnam.[17] Parental authority, especially that of fathers, was the most immediate and localized part of the system responsible for the failed effort as well as for deception and repression at home. Familial authority was disregarded and mocked. Young people felt more informed and sophisticated than their parents, who were trapped in discredited thinking. Fathers no longer knew best; indeed, they never had. The media began to depict paternal authority as arrogant and insensitive, hypocritical and bigoted, uneducated and chauvinistic. The last term, which became a veritable catch-word, took a term for nationalist and militarist sentiment, and added to its meaning a sense of hostility to women and a disposition to subordinate them. Studies of popular culture show parental authority has become secondary or even peripheral to the main story of children or teens living in a world of their own, evading and outwitting parents, or avoiding the fears and prejudices parents try to instill. Parents are of little use in solving the child's problems. The answer lies within. The "normal" family holds some dark secret: alcoholism, abuse of some sort, or a pattern of neuroses that might be instilled in children. Children must break away, lest they end up like their parents.[18]

Traditional roles of women as only mothers and housewives had been changing for decades. Major wars had brought large numbers of women into the work force, and postwar prosperity further acquainted them with opportunities outside the home, but there was still a strong cultural current against independence. Vietnam put the assumption of male superiority on trial and found it guilty. During the trial, many young women had been active in the antiwar movement, which, despite its endorsement of equality and change, made the same patriarchal assumptions as the rest of the country. Resentful, many women left the movement for a new cause. The organizational skills, political styles, and militancy of the antiwar movement were redeployed in the feminist movement. The crisis of old beliefs, punctured male authority, and openness to change, made it more effective. The idea of a family comprising a working husband and a wife at home became part of a discredited past.[19]

The idea of manhood underwent change. It had traditionally connoted control or repression of emotions, superiority over women, assertiveness, and expertise in some form of violence (war service, contact sports, deer-hunting). Prominent in political and military elites, these characteristics were blamed for the bleak event. The inclination to use force, unwillingness to compromise, and certainty of judgment had led to disaster. Popular culture, at least sizable portions of it, began to press home the message of sharing decisions, willingness to compromise, the folly of armed force, the need to search one's soul and understand emotions.[20] A new generation of experts re-evaluated the function of the family. It was the nuclear family that transmitted the values essential to corporations and the military. The family had long performed the task of teaching the infallibility and providentially ordained nature of American beliefs and institutions. The family had traditionally taught pride in military symbols and organizations and instilled an exaggerated form of discipline that stifled creativity and limited life-choices. The nuclear family was a crucible in which various emotional problems formed.[21]

As the thrall of tradition fell away in the late 1960s, divorce rates shot up. Once a revered part of life, marriage lost its sense of sacredness and became almost trivialized. No longer bolstered by familial, religious, and community expectations, vows lost their binding force. From the late 1940s to the mid-1960s, divorce rates had been quite stable, but between 1966 and 1977 they rose one hundred percent.[22] Obtaining a divorce became easier; many were uncontested; some states no longer required evidence of irremediable damage. Marriage became little more than dating taken to a higher stage. Making a binding promise was no longer in tune with a society open to change, accepting of transience, and uncomfortable with commitment. Marriage is a contract that both parties can terminate with a moderate amount of effort and expense.[23]

The reduced role of the family attained the semblance of normalcy and became legitimized by a new generation of sociologists. They argue that the family in America has always been undergoing change, the "traditional family" never existed except in the minds of television writers of the 1950s, the family has always depended on government programs, work often mandated protracted familial separations, and abuse was rampant in family life over the years. They approve the transfer of functions to schools, the easing of parental and especially paternal authority, the attendant improvement in opportunities for women, and the claim that the creativity of children is now being stimulated.[24]

THE ECLIPSE OF COMMUNITY

Local community had been in decline well before Vietnam. Mobilization for the Second World War scattered people across the country. Most did not return, preferring to pursue new opportunities or move to suburbs. Communities gave way to areas with transient populations and conglomerations of people with little in common. Residential areas lost the moral pressures that older communities had exerted. Suburbanization continued unabated throughout the postwar period. The 1970 census showed for the first time that more than half the population lived in suburbs.

The Vietnam War had limited but important effects on local communities. As authorities in Washington lost credibility and prestige, so did local counterparts. With the growing cynicism of the period, it was widely believed, sometimes with good reason but often not, that local notables kept their sons out of the service, while those of the less fortunate had to risk their lives. The impact of a boy's death was more pronounced in small towns than elsewhere. Word spread quickly through neighbors, kin, and former classmates, making it more widely felt there than in less closely-knit suburbs and cities. During the turmoil of the war, local police attempted to keep a lid on things by harassing people with long hair and anyone who stood up to the system, suggesting to some that the decaying social order could only maintain itself through force. The spirit of the times brought a wave of investigations into local government. Many localities were thought of as rotten boroughs or robber-baron fiefs, which featured respect for the powerful but little for the law. Local tribunals looked for a Watergate right there in the hometown. Generational conflicts, passions, and incivility plagued public life. Debate was more quarrelsome, consensus a thing of the past.[25]

Themes from the 1920s returned. Small towns were regarded as cultural backwaters, bastions of bigotry, moribund forms of social organization best left to old folk. Movement was the order of the day. Young people fled from the Babbitts who benefited from the system, lived hopeless dreary lives, and supported the war while making money hand over fist. Films and music sent the message that it was better to keep moving and create a new life somewhere else. It was better to try California, a commune in Colorado, or a bohemian district in an entirely different part of the country. To stay still was to stagnate.

Expectations regarding appearance, manners, language, and decorum, once maintained by a range of sanctions, could no longer hold. A neighbor's scolding, a disapproving stare, a letter from a citizen's association, and sometimes a cop's rough hand traditionally preserved community standards. Moral pressures were far weaker in postwar society, especially in the suburbs, where they had been transplanted into less fertile soil anyway. In the 1970s, social control weakened further. Authority and tradition fell apart; anything unconventional and rebellious had appeal. Norms and conformity seemed archaic concepts, an invocation of a discredited past, which, even when heard, no longer carried legitimacy. Enforcement could no longer rely on informal pressures from the citizenry. An attempt to exert moral pressure on someone was likely to be ignored, or it might lead to an obscene reply or a lawsuit.[26]

Social control became the responsibility of police and courts. However, these rational-legal mechanisms had far less prestige now and were unable to assume the burden.[27] Years of unraveling followed; upholding standards of public behavior became as futile and absurd as maintaining standards of dress. There was neither the opportunity nor the will to find an agreeable middle ground between stifling conformity and civic decay. One had to learn to tolerate more and more, or withdraw into personal life.[28] Feelings of trust and mutual involvement fell away. One could no longer look to another person on the street or at a lunch counter and sense much in common. Participation in community life declined. Voter turnout decreased, as did attendance at town meetings, PTAs, churches, and the like. Community life, celebrated by de Tocqueville and chronicled by the Lynds, diminished. An exaggerated form of individualism arose that saw social norms as external impositions that had to be fended off.[29]

Ersatz forms of community arose, partially filling a void, but never becoming meaningful communities. The antiwar movement was itself a community of sorts. There were shared views and dogmas, very strong social control mechanisms, as well as common aspirations, activities, and symbols. But it was ad hoc, predicated on college life and the war, both of which, eventually, came to an end. The commune phenomenon flourished around this time, but a few hearty bastions notwithstanding, it too declined. Communards learned that scratching out a living from the soil was not an idyllic life, and that their upbringings had inculcated a preference for careers and creature comforts after all.

Pseudo-communities cropped up, such as the cult of citizen-band radios, whose devotees felt a sense of kinship with fellow enthusiasts as they chatted with each other and eluded authority. Oddly enough, but befitting the time, CBers typically remained anonymous, preferring pseudonyms when communicating with their putative good buddies, few of whom they ever met or wanted to meet. Another community of anonymous strangers was based on a shared fondness for particular television programs — an irony of immense proportions. Television, which in the 1950s did so much to do away with evening get-togethers and create atomized modern life, now became a basis for communities as shallow as the programs that inspired them.[30]

The 1970s saw a wave of cults, as people, especially young ones, fled the anomie around them and immersed themselves into a total organization. Cults mandated complete commitment, often requiring members to give up all possessions and totally embrace their ideology and lifestyle. With so much confusion, ambiguity, and violence about them, many young people found this agreeable. Many cults embraced eastern mysticism and folk rituals from the past. Life was joyful and ecstatic, a celebration of spiritual life, which members found a wondrous alternative to the sterile, atomized world outside.[31] In many senses, cults are authentic communities. However, an important difference stands out between a cult and a Middletown. Whereas traditional communities had been integrated into a larger American whole and inculcated beliefs found across the country, cults see themselves as refuges from the country, and stress separation from if not contempt for it. If there was any whole with which they identified, it was no mere nation-state. It was mankind, the cosmos, or something else abstract and spiritual. Inasmuch as cults teach distance from and the evil of the mainstream, they constitute a form of fragmentation, though a small one.

There was also a proliferation of clubs, associations, and organizations, more solid perhaps than other ersatz communities, but only somewhat more substantive. Support for a sports team, participation in a leisure club, or sending a check to an activist group offer the illusion of community, but without the bother of personal involvement. Social and political causes lure members with appeals to commitment, involvement, and common effort, but membership involves little more than paying dues and displaying a decal (optional). There are no common efforts or binding moral ties, though the illusion is comforting.[32]

A substantive and ironic form of community has developed among senior citizens. Many elderly people became detached from kinship ties during the Second World War and ensuing period of mobility. Their children no longer see care of the elderly as their responsibility. Raised in the old urban or small-town communities and tied by the experience of hard times and war, they share a common background with which they develop new forms of community. Fear of crime, brushes with swindlers, common problems of infirmity, and the need to help each other face the inevitable serve as important ties binding old folk together.[33]

PROGRESS

American history chronicled the rise of innovation and science, the growth of freedom and justice, expanding prosperity and wellbeing, and the spread of the country's ideas around the world. When war came, it provided an occasion to help less fortunate lands, placing them on the proper path of development. After 1945 and into the mid-1960s, Americans thought that, politically and economically, the world was becoming more like them, discarding outdated ways in favor of modern ones. The future was bright; possibilities were limitless. America determined to land on the moon before the end of the decade, and did.

As Americans reached the moon, faith in progress was disappearing. Confidence that world events would follow the American game plan fell apart. It was held to be a conceit, an ethnocentric arrogance, a fairy tale, the sort of folklore in which only children and rubes believed. Life lacked meaning and purpose; irony and sarcasm abounded. Consistent with the spirit of the time, the novels of Kurt Vonnegut, which stressed senselessness, anomie, and mordancy, became popular, as did the surreal art of Escher and Dali, which showed illogical continuities, meaningless cycles, and visual absurdities.

There had been a long line of critiques of material progress, from social critics of the post-Civil War era to novelists in the 1920s and the Beats thirty years later, but little of it influenced the general public. After the experience of defeat, however, such criticism became mainstream. Science no longer benefited humanity; it was sowing the seeds of global destruction. The world was plagued by pollution and nuclear weapons. The quest for material improvement had become an end in itself that came at the expense of creative and spiritual parts of life. Hard work was once honored as the means to achieving self-respect and improving the family's future. Now, it meant the denial of the self, becoming a cog in the machine. Two films of Elia Kazan, made only nine years apart, illustrate the rapid decline of this myth. *America, America* (1960) portrays the struggle of a young man to get to the New World and his sacrifices to raise enough money to bring his family from Anatolia. *The Arrangement* (1969) centers on the aging immigrant's son, whose work is part of the rat race and whose family has come undone. Breaking the Hollywood convention of a happy ending, *The Arrangement* ends with the old man's death and the son's contemplation of suicide.

Americans had once looked confidently to the future, believing that life would be better and change was always for the good. Better living would come through scientific advances and political leaders. The future promised shining cities of tomorrow, ever more abundance, even space travel. In the cinema, there was the occasional Martian invasion, but science deftly handled the unpleasantness and restored confidence. Beginning in the late 1960s and becoming more apparent in the next few years, the national mood fell. Old myths no longer worked. There was little faith in government, or anything else. The future was bleak, something to be feared.

There were parallels in Europe after the Great War. The nations of Europe had prided themselves on their advances over the last century. Industry had made great strides, bringing new wealth and opportunity. Middle classes arose and working classes were making good wages and benefits. Science was on the march; Reason was triumphing over superstition. The arts flourished and, with a few exceptions (Conrad and Hardy, for example), conveyed confidence and optimism. The Great War ended all that. European civilization was flawed and murderous. Revolutionary movements brought down or threatened old regimes. Even nominal victors experienced failing legitimacy. Science was the creature of the warlords, creating for its masters the machine-gun and poison gas. Postwar culture was filled with nostalgia, a search for lost times, and bleak depictions of the future. A British film, *Things To Come,* foretold (with uncanny accuracy as it turned out) another great war. Fearsome new weapons rain down on cities from immense aircraft, resulting in horrific civilian casualties and the virtual end of civilization. The German film *Metropolis* depicts, in dark expressionist images, a bleak, hyper-rationalized world, in which industrial magnates rule over a vast dehumanized working class. Populist demagogues, corporate cliques, and malevolent scientists engage in a power struggle that almost destroys civilization. Though both films ended in a contrived resolution, they left a sense of foreboding. High culture, too, lost its confidence. The historical studies of Toynbee and Spengler concluded that all civilizations followed an ineluctable pattern of growth, stagnation, and decline, and there was no doubt in which direction Europe was headed.

After Vietnam, America, for the first time, came up against limits. Continuity with the past came to an end, and uncertainty loomed. Books, magazine articles, and social thinkers proclaimed the end of a charmed past. The economy was no longer dynamic; technology had reached its limits; military spending had undercut competitiveness with other countries, especially Germany and Japan, whose cars and consumer electronics were everywhere. In pockets of traditional folk religion, there was an upsurge in dire predictions that Armageddon and the Second Coming were at hand. Secular thought was no more optimistic. Pollution had reached a point of no return; human and other life forms were doomed. Economic stagnation would lead to strife and breakdown. The military's influence made nuclear war likely. America had had its day, but now the sun was setting on it.[34]

Pessimism manifested itself in the films of the period, replacing the optimism and light-heartedness of the early 1960s with a dark vision of a dystopian future. Earth is an environmental disaster: horribly overpopulated, covered by dark clouds and ceaseless rain, devastated by nuclear war, and ruled by sinister corporations. In *Blade Runner,* Japan and Germany dominate the country — the post-1945 world turned upside down. *A Clockwork Orange* depicted a future in which norms had broken down completely. The night is ruled by gangs engaged in "ultraviolence;" youths in their early teens partake of casual sex with strangers. Attempts are made to hold society together through police repression and behavioral modification programs, but neither works.

Uncertain of the present and fearful of the future, many people looked wistfully to the past, appreciating the charm, innocence, and simplicity of earlier times. *American Graffiti* looked back only ten years earlier, but the quaint concerns and usages of 1962 were as distant as those of Huck Finn, and could be seen nostalgically or cynically. *The Way We Were,* whose very title evokes a lost past, remembered the romance and unity of the 1940s. *Gone With the*

Wind, which first played to Depression-era audiences facing a bleak future and yearning for the past, was re-released in 1972, tapping into similar emotions of the day.[35] *The Last Picture Show* gave an ambivalent image of small-town life, ending with the death of a beloved character and the closing of the local movie house, suggesting the end of an era and the beginning of an uncertain future.[36] But nostalgia was simply a daydream amid a disagreeable present. As a popular song suggested, however much the country looked for Joe DiMaggio, it was clear that Joltin' Joe had left and gone away.

There was also a resurgence of World War II movies (*Patton, MacArthur, Midway, A Bridge Too Far*). This is initially puzzling, for there was little respect for the military at the time and the quest for revenge in Southeast Asia had yet to make its screen debut. The key to the genre's popularity is probably the nature of the events the films depict. It is not the glorification of war or the military — that was the stuff of war movies of the 1950s. In these films, audiences plagued by uncertainty, disunity, and ambiguity over good and evil, look back on a lost time of consensus, order, clarity of purpose, and moral certainty. Amid the confusion, this had considerable appeal. And perhaps most importantly, we won.

TWILIGHT OF AUTHORITY

Success in war, when not entailing egregious losses, strengthens authority, making it more legitimate and sacred. Social problems become more tolerable: elites enjoy more prestige, attentions are diverted or properly directed, and social criticism is out of step, even seditious. The War of Independence endowed its leaders and their heirs with a reservoir of prestige. Similarly, victorious outcomes of later wars, especially the Civil War and World War II, infused the nation with powerful sentiments of sacredness and propriety. After 1945, authority figures throughout the social system took on the prestige of Roosevelt and Eisenhower; after Vietnam, they were stained by the sins of Nixon and Westmoreland.[37]

This is not a uniquely American phenomenon. The zenith of Athenian greatness came in large part from victories over Persia and Sparta. Roman generals from Scipio to Justinian won enormous prestige, for themselves as well as for the state and all its pillars. English nobles won honors for the social order at Agincourt, Minden, and Waterloo. Prussian force of arms repeatedly legitimized a military-bureaucratic state and a range of authority from harsh Junker landowners to the stern father of the household. Soviet authority, too, won legitimacy, perhaps for the first time, during the Great Patriotic War against Nazi invaders.[38] Catastrophic experiences — defeat, devastating casualties, loss of international standing — delegitimize authority and loosen society. Prussia had to mollify its suddenly unruly subjects with political and social reform when Napoleon bested its army, as did Russia following the Crimean War. France lurched from one political crisis to another after suffering a series of defeats during the nineteenth and twentieth centuries, from Waterloo to Sedan to Dien Bien Phu. Imperial Germany disintegrated in 1918. Authority was reviled as a curse from the past. Artists such as George Grosz depicted the powerful as grotesque swine, an act that might have led to imprisonment a few years earlier. Paternal authority dwindled as well; youth became disrespectful toward authority and gravitated toward nihilism and fringes of the left and right.[39]

Britain emerged from the Second World War on the winning side, but with its social order weakened. It had had its finest hour against the Luftwaffe, bested the Afrika Korps at El Alamein, and contributed significantly to the defeat of the Third Reich, but it could no longer claim to be a great power. Concern with reduced prestige was expressed in the wartime lament that GIs were overpaid, oversexed, and over here, but GIs got the better of it when they retorted that British men were underpaid, undersexed, and under Ike. Britain was a distant third in the great alliance and soon realized it could no longer rule the waves or its empire.[40] The aristocracy and monarchy became quaint vestiges of a bygone era of power and certainty. Old business and political leaders were stuffy remnants of the past, who still expected deference from a changing country. Youth was increasingly alienated from authority and tradition. They were "angry young men," hostile to their country's tradition and eager to follow trends from across the Atlantic.

Elites Discredited

How could a limited war halfway around the world figure highly in the crisis of American authority? Vietnam was not a major war by any means, but it came after a multitude of changes in American society since 1941 had already weakened traditional patterns of authority, making the impact of Vietnam far more significant. Consumerism and leisure had eroded dedication to duty and tradition; secularizing forces of science and materialism had diminished the aura of sacredness around authority. When defeat came, it delivered a devastating blow to authority.

Vietnam gravely damaged two presidents and numerous statesmen. Though in opposition to the war by the late 1960s, Congress fared little better. It was seen as an assembly of impotent critics, who, in their greatest moment of courage, repealed the Gulf of Tonkin Resolution but lacked the resolve to stop funding the war. The public came to regard official statements as lies, deceptions, and half-truths — and not without good reason. An official Pentagon history of the media during the war concludes by noting that press reports were generally more accurate than government statements.[41]

Popular books harshly criticized military and political leaders, claiming that presidents and their cabinet members had shown dismal judgment in Southeast Asia, from the early years of advising the South Vietnamese to the needlessly slow disengagement. With the publication of the Pentagon Papers (1971), it became clear that the Gulf of Tonkin Incident, the justification for deepening involvement, had not taken place as the administration claimed. The best minds from the revered heights of business, law, and academe deceived the public in order to obtain a blank check to wage war.[42]

Government efforts to discredit the antiwar movement did nothing to improve its relationship with the public. Agencies and bureaus gathered information on opponents of the war, collecting files and photographs that filled thousands of file cabinets. The movement was infiltrated by agents-provocateurs, illegally wiretapped, and subjected to dirty tricks. The government set up and funded pro-war organizations to orchestrate public opinion, as though the American people were unruly subjects.

Euphemism begat euphemism, and though they stemmed from bureaucratic zeal for argot, they appeared aimed at hiding something. A golden age of euphemism might have begun when an army code-name "Masher" was found impolitic and given the cheerful appellation "White Wing."[43] Unauthorized air strikes were "protective reaction strikes;" when "search and destroy" sounded too harsh, "clear and hold" was created; burning down villages was part of "pacification;" and, in a breathtaking bit of verbal legerdemain, Viet Cong suspects were "terminated with extreme prejudice" — with a bullet to the head.

The country experienced a resurgence of what Richard Hofstadter called a "paranoid style" of politics. Vietnam, the Cold War, and so much else took on the appearance of a conspiracy. Rumors — facts weren't needed — spread by word of mouth and through the cinema. Corporations led the country into war to reap huge profits; the military-industrial complex pulled strings behind the scenes; minorities were disproportionately exposed to combat to reduce their numbers. Politicians all got pieces of the action. LBJ's family made a fortune shipping matériel to Vietnam; the government maintained a secret system of internment camps in case of unrest; the Apollo moon landing in 1969 was a fraud.[44] Oil companies (demonic successors to the railroads of the nineteenth century) created artificial shortages to gouge the public and suppressed production of a new car that got a hundred miles per gallon.[45] And when oil was found off the Vietnamese coast . . . well, the real reason for the war was finally known. Two films of the mid-1970s, *Executive Action* and *The Parallax View*, depicted the CIA and business executives conspiring to assassinate progressive politicians. The former suggests that the CIA and oil companies collaborated in Kennedy's assassination. It became widely believed that the CIA assassinated John Kennedy after he decided to withdraw from Vietnam.[46]

Trust in government declined sharply. In 1964, twenty-two percent of respondents said they trusted the national government "only some of the time;" in 1972, forty-five percent gave that response. Voter turnout in national elections dropped from over sixty percent to fifty percent, far lower with only Congressional seats at stake.[47]

Deflation of authority ran throughout the social system. Corporate leaders were lords of the military-industrial complex and adepts in the machinations of government. The main work of scientists was the creation of instruments of death. The legal system muzzled lawful protest, failed to bring war criminals to justice, and enforced unfair conscription laws. Those who invoked law and order, tradition, and respect for the rules betrayed themselves as reactionary defenders of an old regime. A generation of young reporters looked everywhere for another My Lai or Watergate.[48] Members of Congress, police chiefs, judges, and any public official had their lives, public and private, scrutinized as never before. The discrediting process became a lark, a cynical pleasure.[49]

A Farewell to Arms

At the outset of the Vietnam War, the military was among the most respected of institutions. It had saved the world from the Third Reich and was containing the Soviet Union. Military service was honored, a part of an enviable vita. Postwar literature saw no dearth of incompetents and martinets in uniform, but most of it was light-hearted or focused on outliers, and the mainstream continued to revere the military. In the course of the long and painful conflict, respect for the military collapsed. In 1966, sixty-two percent of respondents expressed "a great deal of confidence" in the military; just five year later, only twenty-seven percent felt that way.[50]

Few thought the war would last long. The American fighting man versus a rag-tag guerrilla band was surely an unequal contest. The enemy would throw in the towel in a year or two at most. Two years later, there was no end in sight. The army was bogged down tracking elusive VC and NVA units along jungle trails and rugged mountains. The enemy — the term became increasingly difficult to use — was more resourceful than imagined. Gradually, beginning in late 1967 and accelerating with the shock of Tet, the military's image changed. It was arrogant and inept. Its heavy-handed methods led to needless civilian casualties, which furthered communist support. Incidents of torture, rape, death cards, and mutilation of corpses came to light, and it became difficult to overlook them as isolated cases or media sensationalism. Military discipline suffered, morale dwindled, and desertion rates soared. Stories of mutinies and fraggings made it seem the military was on the verge of collapse. Stateside events added to the problem. A Green Beret murdered his family and attempted to blame it on LSD-crazed hippies. NCO clubs were investigated for kickbacks. Cost overruns plagued many military contracts. Then there was the My Lai massacre.[51]

Even in moderate parts of the nation, the military's prestige diminished. It was regarded as an entrenched war interest, more willing to loose the sword than its predecessors had been. The military was a cold, impersonal machine, devouring resources and lives. Its commanders lived in air-conditioned luxury while the troops slogged through jungles and mountains. Very few generals saw combat, though they all got their Silver Stars and CIBs. They had all the bluster of front-line leaders, but only a few were wounded or killed (one, allegedly, when his Huey crashed while hunting tigers). The military became the focus of racial and social concerns. It was widely believed that minorities and the poor suffered disproportionately high casualties.[52] The military no longer had colorful figures such as "Bull" Halsey, "Lightning Joe" Collins, or "Howlin' Mad" Smith, whose plain speaking made for public relations coups during World War II. Most generals of the Vietnam era were dully bureaucratic and unable to capture the imagination of the public. Exceptions to the rule didn't help matters. One brigade commander commented that he didn't like war, but he sure liked "to see the arms and legs fly." He sent Christmas cards picturing mangled corpses with the inscription, *Peace on Earth*. Though hardly representative of the army, in a period not given to cautious reflection, he came to embody a callous, deranged caste.[53]

Even average soldiers, including draftees and national guardsmen, suffered from the deflation of prestige. Prior to Vietnam, servicemen wore their uniforms off base proudly. The public honored them, picked up the their tabs in restaurants, and gave them rides when they hitchhiked home. Young soldiers walked down Main Street the envy of their peers, the pride of the community. As discontent with the war in Vietnam grew, servicemen were mocked and insulted. They learned to leave their uniforms back in their footlockers and try to blend in the civilian world as best as their stigmatic haircuts allowed.

Vietnam popularized the view that war is futile and never solves anything. Whatever truth there is here, few Americans felt that way in 1945, when the issue of Nazi domination had been settled rather definitively. Such sentiments of futility, however, were widely encountered after the Great War in the writings of veterans of the Somme and Belleau Woods. The writings of veterans of Khe Sanh and Dak To, while less well known, convey the same disillusionment with war myth and the same aversion to the military. More importantly, much of the country was now opposed to armed force.

Numerous films of the period conveyed anti-military and antiwar messages. The film version of Joseph Heller's *Catch-22* had obvious resonance with popular opinion about Vietnam: insensitive and arrogant leaders, a profitable working relationship between the military and big business, and a war that dragged on. Perhaps best known were the film and television series *MASH,* situated in Korea, but obviously commenting on Vietnam. Military careerists are brutal, arrogant, and incompetent, obsessed with secrecy and suppressing communist hordes. Unconcerned with American casualties, they are chiefly interested in body counts and promotions. The morality of career military people is lampooned as viewers see them as hypocrites and adulterers. Counterpoised to the military stand the young protagonists — humanistic, irreverent, and unconventional. Sporting long hair and living in what seems more like a college dorm than a BOQ, they outwit the old guard and establish a modicum of sanity and decency amid the war.[54] *Johnny Got His Gun,* a tale of a horribly wounded soldier written shortly after World War I, became a film in 1971. *All Quiet on the Western Front* was remade for a public more in tune with post-1918 broodings than with post-1945 celebration.

When, after a period of conspicuous avoidance, films about Vietnam began to be made, they conveyed senselessness and disillusion. Protagonists typically break from the military and thereby liberate themselves. In *Apocalypse Now,* a young captain, after a voyage of self-discovery, breaks off communication with superiors. In *Platoon,* a young soldier cathartically kills his sadistic sergeant. In *The Deer Hunter,* a working-class veteran sees the destructiveness of his upbringing and tosses away his once cherished hunting rifle, a cleansing ritual that frees him from the hold of a militarist culture and helps humanize him. This was all part of a broad cultural reaction to the use of force. The people, no longer trusting the state, had to rein in the state and the military, though the gloomy mood of the time offered little confidence this could be done.

THE END OF THE AMERICAN IDEAL

Aside from the damage to beliefs and institutions, the war undermined the American idea. The country's name was long imbued with sacredness, but after Vietnam, "America" sounded antiquated and gimmicky, a verbal trick that hid an ugly history. The phrases "liberty and justice for all," "the American dream," "the land of the free," and the like were seldom used, except in sarcasm or irony — literary devices, as Paul Fussell notes, that find greater use after boasts and myth have been undermined.[55] The idea of America was once an amalgam of emotions, myths, traditions, and beliefs. America was an ongoing process from the colonial past to the present. The idea was questioned during the Depression, but it survived and grew stronger in World War II. Then it was remobilized and sent off to Vietnam.

Afterwards, few could still believe that America stood for goodness and acted out of noble intentions, that Providence inspired its leaders and institutions, the past had a moral influence on the present, justice was blind, the frontier heritage made our fighting men the finest in the world, and America was so blessed that it would never lose a war. The Vietnam experience was as shattering as learning of a loved one's infidelity. The framework of trust, commitment, and affection was gone, and an angry mood searched for the cause of the calamity. The military and politicians were obvious answers, but it wasn't just a blunder by power elites. There was something deeper. Literature, films, and public discussions looked into America's past and reported that America was a sick society, flawed from its inception. The frontier had indeed formed us, but not in the roseate ways Turner and Parkman suggested. The frontier made us violent and expansionist, eager to settle conflict with a flintlock, Winchester, or M-16.[56]

Puritanism was a baleful influence that imposed simplistic outlooks of good and evil, and a fiery zeal to stamp out wickedness in all its guises, from witches and adulteresses, to nonconformists and progressives. And of course, the energy behind fighting Communism had this same origin. The economic system put constant pressure on expansion, seizing resources and exploiting them, getting involved overseas, and suppressing any alternative system. The term "White Anglo-Saxon Protestant" once referred to an esteemed elite and to solid folk of colonial heritage, but it became a term of abuse. WASPs were stuffy economic royalists who ruled the country for their own benefit. They were behind-the-scenes manipulators, an arrogant power elite that restricted country club memberships and political participation.

In the decades after World War II, social scientists as well as the general public believed that American beliefs and institutions were models for the rest of the world. In some respects, this was the legacy of Puritan myths of America as the shining City on the Hill and of the post-1945 celebration. America would bring light to darker parts of the globe. Embellished with social science models and statistics, the idea of America as the model of world development reigned in the public and the academy.[57] It was turned on its head. The United States was responsible for the backwardness of much of the world; its foreign policy backed dictators and juntas around the world. Political and economic development in the Third World depended on breaking free of the fetters of American corporations, military aid, and cultural hegemony.[58]

RELIGION AND SOCIAL NORMS

Though church attendance remained high in the years after 1945, religion declined as a meaningful part of life. Consumer lifestyles cut into moral strictures. Scientific explanations were more respected than those based on religion, faith, and divine presence in the world. Vietnam had ambivalent effects on religion. It weakened the appeal of traditional religions, but also led to new forms of religious experience, and compelled many to seek spiritual comfort.

Religion and Defeat

It might be wondered how a secular event such as a military defeat could weaken religion. Weren't church and state separate in America, and didn't we render unto Caesar the things that were Caesar's, and so on? Historically, there have been important connections between temporal and spiritual realms in America. Most recently, religion and state had forged a working partnership during the Cold War. Many religious authorities had preached the evils of Communism and the need to fight it around the world. Secular politicians, for their part, presented the Cold War as a crusade against the forces of godlessness. True enough, but religious figures also figured prominently in the antiwar movement. Martin Luther King, William Sloane Coffin, and others, argued that the war was immoral and its burden fell unfairly on minorities and the poor. Religious figures were present at every rally, adding respectability and moderation.

Another explanation lies in the problems facing religion in times of upheaval or catastrophe. At such times, people ask, if God exists, why disasters occur, why God allows them to happen. This question of theodicy arises throughout history but is not always answered convincingly. More important though, is religion's integration with traditional authority, ways of life, and conventions. Religion, as Bellah has long told us, had been a basic part of the American idea since the founding of the Republic. God had surely guided the new nation through dire straits and had blessed the country with abundance and greatness. Now it shared blame for Vietnam. Americans no longer felt guidance from on high. That had been one of the delusions the country was now seeing through. The ensuing climate of cynicism and nihilism undermined all types of faith.[59]

American religion instilled a strict but simplistic delineation between good and evil. Whatever usefulness this had in the instruction of children, it was of no use in dealing with the complexities of the modern world. More importantly, American religions inculcated the virtuousness in destroying evil, root and branch, in all its guises: witches, savages, communists, and anyone else who did not conform. Religion was tied to expansionism. It legitimized the conquest of the West, the forcible conversion of the unwilling, and the spread of American ideas.

Disaffection did not necessarily lead to agnosticism or atheism; it also led to new forms of spirituality. One such form, already noted, was the cult, which was very strict, more so than traditional forms of religion. Most new forms of spirituality, however, were quite different. They were typically loose and undemanding, drawing from many sources, especially eastern mysticism and eclectic cosmologies. Right and wrong were not dogmatically differentiated, leaving considerable room for individual interpretation: the answer lies within. Doctrines had an easy-going quality, celebrating the individual and the self, and exalting in new found freedom and a holistic relationship to the world. It was just what many Americans were looking for: nontraditional and undemanding spirituality.[60]

Older forms of religion also relaxed. Dietary laws and Sabbath observances became less strict. Interpretation of right and wrong was allowed. Churches were more lenient in annulling marriages. Sermons became even friendlier and less scolding. It was essential in this time of transition to adapt or risk losing membership.[61] Between 1963 and 1976, the percentage of Americans who believed in the literal truth of the Bible dropped from sixty-five percent to thirty-eight percent.[62] Parables and the lives of the martyrs no longer guided day-to-day decisions. God no longer figured in the unfolding of history. Perhaps most importantly, religion could no longer provide a widely recognized standard of right and wrong. The country was now too fragmented to form any consensus based on moral values and authoritative interpreters. Determining right and wrong was increasingly a personal choice; disapproval could be dismissed as simply someone else's opinion or an attempt to impose values. As two keen observers of these changing norms disclosed: "Any attempt to articulate common beliefs and practices is an infringement on individual freedom."[63] Americans could look within and switch religions to find a moral message in keeping with their lifestyles. Alternately, they could find unguent and supportive thought in popular psychology, social philosophy, or in personal speculations.[64]

Previous generations of Americans were governed internally by beliefs, norms, and habits of the heart. Embedded in folklore, homilies, schoolbooks, and family stories, they constituted a moral order governing individual behavior and consensus on matters of right and wrong based on eternal truths. No longer bolstered by community pressures and religiousness, norms had been relaxing since World War II. With the decline in respect for authority and conventions in the late 1960s, the moral order all but fell away. Family and community pressures, national leaders and symbols, and numerous religious authorities could no longer maintain it. Values became a matter of personal taste.[65]

Vanity Fair

The nation was never without greed, selfishness, and eccentricity, but moderating pressures generally restrained and channeled them into acceptable directions. Those pressures began to disappear in the late 1960s. Consumption and self-absorption became the reigning values. People faced a new world with neither meaning nor coherence, and, like F. Scott Fitzgerald's generation that saw all gods dead, all creeds discredited, and all wars over, they plunged into it.

Another green light had been given. Like young Europeans after the Great War, they reveled in indulgence, as though in a Berlin cabaret, mocking a fallen order and caring little for what would follow.

The use of drugs exploded among mainstream youth. Experimentation with drugs had been part of artistically subgroups, the Beats, and early counterculture followers, who sought insight, inspiration, and spirituality from occasional use. There were few of these pretenses once drugs became mainstream. Drugs were routine parts of a lifestyle, a grasping for sensation, indulgence, and a celebration of new freedom. Specific drugs became tied to status levels. Marijuana, in time, became rather common and plebeian; heroin had unsavory lower-class connotations; and LSD was too debilitating for use by people with steady jobs. Cocaine, at least for a while, became prestigious, the drug of choice among lawyers, stockbrokers, and other high-income groups. Faltering social sanctions allowed more openness regarding drugs and their paraphernalia. Once sold only in counterculture enclaves, hookah pipes and rolling papers came to be sold in music shops and convenience stores. Shopkeepers were confident that authorities would look the other way.[66]

By the early 1970s, political involvement was for most young people only frustrating and fruitless. The new archetype of post-counterculture youth was no longer an activist. There was no higher compliment than to be described as "mellow and layback," that is to say, resigned to surrounding absurdities and content simply to enjoy life: a fine wine, novel cuisine, and, the centerpiece of dwellings of the period, a good stereo. Surprisingly quickly, in no more than a few years, the accoutrements got pricier. The lifestyle soon evolved into careerism, consumerism, and other forms of self-indulgence that, in the aggregate, constituted what Christopher Lasch called "the culture of narcissism."[67] They bought consumer products, which owing to their exoticness and sophistication, of course precluded any comparisons to their parents' lifestyles. Undemanding religions gave benediction to their new lives, or perhaps told them of greatness in past lives. They read and discussed popular psychology that assured them they were all okay, and that every day, in every way, they were getting better.

Work had little to do with feelings of efficacy or providing a better life for children. It certainly no longer had its old religious significance of identifying the elect over the damned. Work became a means of self-aggrandizement or of obtaining the money to support an increasingly expensive lifestyle. Marriage was devoid of the concepts of commitment and sanctity; it became little more than a transitory coincidence of tastes in food, music, and sex — a contract of mutual gratification. Throughout the 1970s, having a family meant lapsing into tradition, selling-out, or becoming like one's parents. Fertility rates fell and remained low for over a decade.[68]

Over the years, the culture of narcissism has become widespread and accepted — so much so, that much of it goes unnoticed. Sporting events, once displays of duty and heritage, have become arenas for individual exaltation. Teamwork and discipline of football have given way to egotistical displays, to the delight of spectators. Schools eschew discipline and authority as parts of the past. Every child has amazing and unique talents. Exploration and creativity, no matter the results, are lauded as great achievements. Everyone gets a prize. Students receive far better grades than did their predecessors who toiled under the old methods of memorization and precision. Civics classes once taught an array of duties and rights between individual and community. One civics textbook has only four pages on civic responsibilities.[69] Now students learn, perhaps even in schools named after John F. Kennedy, to ask only what their country can do for them. Schoolchildren, it must be admitted, enter the new society well prepared.[70]

The spirit of vanity dissociates people from their society and past. Blue laws had once proscribed various forms of business on Sundays, but by the mid-1970s they were disappearing. National holidays had once been solemn occasions when Americans recalled sacrifices in war and the ongoing history of their nation. Today, Veterans Day or Memorial Day might afford a fleeting glimpse of the meaning of duty, valor, and heritage. However, media coverage, vigilant that the public doesn't dwell on the past, quickly switches from a wreath-laying ceremony, somewhere or another, to backyard barbecues and sporting events.[71] Dates that had once been emblazoned into the national psyche no longer live in infamy or anything else. For the better part of the century, the country vacillated between duty and leisure, between tradition and consumerism. The matter has been settled.[72]

After the Sexual Revolution

The moral order of traditional America once imposed strict sexual norms. This is not to say that all Americans were once chaste innocents courting on the front porch and nervously looking forward to their wedding night, but important changes, beginning earlier in the century, have taken place. A new openness to sexuality came with the ferment of the 1920s. The Second World War brought long separation, sordid environments, and a sense of contingency that weakened sexual norms and set the stage for further change in the 1950s and the later revolution. Post-Vietnam society saw the dissolution of sexual norms among people under thirty or so, not only among young radicals, but in the mainstream as well. Old norms confining sexual relations were as obsolete as a call to the colors. Taboos became areas of exploration, daring, and creativeness; they were things one had been forced to internalize under the old regime, but could now throw off like an old cloak. Sex became another consumer product, complete with an array of "how-to" books.[73]

The carnival-like 1970s, with the discos, open marriages, and the like, are well known and require little description. Along with changing norms came an attendant decline in society's ability to enforce standards and laws. Again, this erosion did not begin with Vietnam. The cinema of the 1920s was filled with alluring content until public reaction led to the Hays Office and PCA, which watched over movie content until the 1950s, when a changed country demanded franker treatments of sex and social issues. By 1960, a few movies had been released without official approval, auguring the PCA's demise a few years later and replacement with a non-judgmental rating system. Ten years later, nudity and profanity had become obligatory in films, and studios avoided a "G" rating for fear it would keep audiences away.[74]

The public acquiesced to the increased presence of businesses previously relegated to rundown parts of town. Pornographic theaters, adult bookstores, and massage parlors sprang up in business districts, suburbs, and small towns — even in Muskogee, Oklahoma. Community efforts to prevent their spread usually failed. People simply shrugged their shoulders: few felt comfortable invoking old cries of danger to public morals; and no one could dispute that there was demand for such things. Censorship lost out to market forces. For a decade or so, pornographic movies enjoyed a measure of chicness and were shown in theaters that during the day might show a Disney film. Many welcomed the change as a long-needed break from dour Puritan norms.[75] Others were more circumspect. One filmmaker captured the historical context of *Deep Throat*: "That grubby little porno film coupled with its miserable success could almost stand as evidence of the state of the country at that particular time of our lives. There is some deep self-revulsion at work that no amount of legislation is going to stop."[76]

Incivility and Violence

The moral order once restrained human impulses. Between impulse and action stood an internal check on various forms of destructiveness. The decades following Vietnam witnessed its decline. Murder, assault, rape, and battery skyrocketed. Depictions of violence in popular culture suggest obsession. The public is fascinated by it and demands it in more and more "realistic" presentations.

Inasmuch as the war led to widespread revulsion with violence and warfare, there is an irony here. It might be argued that news coverage of Vietnam brought violence into the public eye and hence deserves a large measure of blame. There was indeed graphic footage of napalm victims, violent deaths, and other hideous images to which previous generations of Americans had not been exposed.

However, these images led to public disgust, and violent television content actually declined during the war.[77] There was violence in the antiwar movement, police efforts to stop it, as well as the terrorist campaign of the Weathermen. Yet, all in all, violence was a rather infrequent aspect of the movement, and the destructiveness that there was led to a sense that things were getting out of hand and that passions had to be checked.

Violence is undoubtedly a complicated phenomenon involving poverty, demographics, and other influences, but a significant contributor was the implosion of the moral order. Internal restraints were weakened and could no longer effectively govern behavior and intercede between impulse and action, instinct and deed, urge and crime. Commensurate with its decline came the ascendance of indulgence, less restrictive norms, incivility, and violence.[78] The murder rate was fairly steady from 1945 to 1965, but from 1965 to 1970 it increased thirty percent.[79] Reported rape went up a hundred eighteen percent in the 1970s.[80] One could recount various other statistics on rates of battery, armed robbery, and burglary, but few can be unaware that crime has shot up since the late 1960s. Many crimes are highly impulsive, done at the spur of the moment, without a plan, without any calculation of potential costs. Crime is often a spree or the satisfaction of a sudden whim.

Much of life is plagued by incivility: in public discourse, in stores, on streets, and on the road, where angry exchanges are daily occurrences and murderous ones on the rise.[81] Sporting events have become venues of boorish behavior, on the field and in the stands. One stadium now contains a courtroom to deal with unruly fans. Crowds roar their approval of fights, taunts, and needlessly hard hits. Sports segments on the local news devote a considerable portion of their limited time to violent episodes outside the play of the game. Serious injuries have a temporary sobering effect, but once the injured player is carted off (oddly, to polite applause), the Diocletian festival returns. The crowd regains its equilibrium and points its thumbs down.[82]

In film and television, killing is presented as exciting, titillating, something to relish in slow-motion and from several angles. There was no dearth of violence in films and television before Vietnam, but there was a moral message attached. Killing Nazi soldiers, dangerous criminals, lawless gunslingers, and the like linked violence to proper authority, good triumphing over evil, and the preservation of the moral order. Americans today see things in a more ambiguous way. Violence is no longer attached to justice; it is the province of unconventional figures, vigilantes, average people in whom rage has built to the breaking point — it's something anyone can do. Crime often goes unpunished; or when punished through the legal system, it is excessive or unfair. There is rarely restoration of the moral order.[83]

Dark memories of Vietnam manifest themselves in two cinematic forms: the deranged veteran exacting revenge on society; and the noble veteran destroying evil at home, or returning to Southeast Asia to settle a score (and rewrite history). Shifting from the cinema to the real world, it might be suspected that many no longer discern a difference. All too often, the country's attention is drawn to someone lost in a fantasy of camouflage fatigues, imagined war service, and amorphous senses of vengeance.[84] In the early 1980s, the military began sending medical personnel into urban areas to gain experience in treating gunshot wounds.

CHAPTER EIGHT

IMAGES OF THE PAST
IN POST-VIETNAM AMERICA

*America has a history. It is only that the tragic aspects and the ironic
implications of that history have been obscured by the national legend of
success and victory and by the perpetuation of infant illusions of innocence
and virtue.*

C. VANN WOODWARD, *The Irony of Southern History*

*It is with these shocking instruments that your great warriors and kings have
been doing their murderous work in the world. . . . What a number of items
of human crime, misery, slavery, to form that sum-total of glory!*

WILLIAM MAKEPEACE THACKERAY, *Barry Lyndon*

When a country's beliefs and institutions have been undermined, the public
no longer looks upon its past as it once did. The critical spirit of post-Vietnam
America had much in common with post-1918 outlooks: people recoiled from
the horror, lost respect for authority and tradition, and felt they were at last
seeing through an old ruse. Americans looked upon traditional histories with
the same skepticism and mistrust with which they had come to regard a
statement from the White House. Debunking and deconstructing were orders
of the day, and books, films, and documentaries obediently constructed a new
understanding of the past. Many of the themes of interwar progressivism and
in its heirs of the 1950s and early 1960s came to the fore. Defeat brought critical
views into the mainstream.

CHANGING VIEWS OF THE PAST

Keepers of a nation's memory are not value-free investigators, sifting through
archives and correspondences, above the influence of myth and passion. Nor are
they latter-day monastics or white-jacketed technicians dedicated to the search
for objective truth. More often than not, whether they admit it or not, they are
guided by forces that shape their understanding of evidence, the inferences they
make, and the conclusions they reach. At the outset of the nineteenth century,
American writers felt part of a noble effort to build a new nation, mythologize its

Great Events and leaders, and inspire public confidence. History was later used for other contemporary purposes, to marshal evidence to support or undermine partisan causes: providential support for the homeland, the evil of enemies, or the danger of concentrated wealth. Historical writings bear the unmistakable stamp of their time, as much as any other artifact from the period.

A romantic period of American historical writing began almost the day Cornwallis surrendered to Washington and carried on well after the Civil War. Written by gifted amateurs from the upper classes, these histories were part demolition and part construction: tearing lingering ties and sentiments favorable to Britain and forming a distinct American identity. The colonies were politically independent from Europe, but for them to be a great nation, an independent culture had to made. School texts from the 1790s show awareness of the problem: "They have not yet existed as a nation long enough for us to form an idea of what will be in its maturity, its prominent features."[1]

Into the breach marched a generation of writers devoted to differentiating America from Europe and building pride in the new nation. Europe was plagued by tyranny, aristocratic privilege, religious intolerance, and lack of opportunity. Historians and textbook writers celebrated natural beauty and the valorous deeds of great men. They forged a national identity based on a limitless frontier, marksmanship, progress, and the rising glory of the Republic. Americans were hardy and industrious, practical and highly moral; their leaders and institutions were sacred, guided by God to perform an historical mission. Receiving infusions of prestige from the War of 1812 and the Civil War, romantic history helped to build a new nation.[2]

The nation-building mandate often led to incautious examination of the evidence, as even one of the heroes of romantic history found. John Adams looked over the histories of his day and startled expectation by quipping:

> My history would so differ from the histories and traditions that I
> should give offence. I have no great objection to giving offence to
> people who take offence without just cause; but I have no ambition
> to be thought a liar by posterity, and I am sure nobody would
> believe my history who believed any other that I have seen.[3]

Discontent with mythic history gave rise in the late nineteenth century to the professionalization of history, or at least a considerable portion of it. Influenced by the rising power of science, and often trained in German universities, new historians stressed causal connections over romanticization, sound analysis over exhortation. They were capable of critical lines of thought, though their successors would hone that skill.[4]

The progressive historians of the early twentieth century launched a generation of new and often highly critical inquiries into the nation's past. By the turn of the century, the forces of industrialization had changed not only the nation's economy, but also its historians. Concentrated wealth, in the form of railroads, banks, and other trusts, endangered average people. Opportunities had dwindled since the closing of the frontier. Farmers and workers were in the clutches of railroad barons and other magnates. Government was no longer in the hands of the people; it had become the instrument of big business. In 1913, Charles Beard published a study that changed the study of American history and influenced generations of historians, including many of today. He saw the founding fathers not as selfless men of reason and faith, but as property owners, plutocrats, the Rockefellers and Morgans of the late eighteenth century. He saw the Constitution not as a sacred document embodying Enlightenment and Deist wisdom, but as an instrument to protect the interests of those who had lent money to the fledgling government, repress unruly debtors like Daniel Shays, and limit the franchise to men of property.[5]

Progressivism joined with the skepticism and relativism of the post-WWI mind. During the war, many historians had become part of the war effort, lionizing our allies and the cause, vilifying the Kaiser and his hosts. Every aspect of German history was filled with accounts of militarism and autocracy, leading inexorably to the barbarities of the day's headlines. The contrast to England and France was stark, dramatic, and filled with dubious reasoning. Our difficulties with Britain in 1776 stemmed not from a quarrel with the British people, but from the despotic designs of their headstrong monarch, who, it was duly noted, was German.[6] It was all very useful in inspiring a generation of youth to fight for their country, but in time it was seen as propaganda.

After the war, the progressive critique became more trenchant. Many concluded that previous historical works had been only somewhat more objective than wartime propaganda. The country had long been rent by divisions between common people and property holders: the early colonists and the great trading firms that ruled them, the small farmer and the Bank, slaves and the plantocracy, farmers and railroad barons, workers and industrialists. Years later, amid the more radical period of the Depression, Charles Beard branded the Constitution "the bulwark of every great national sin — from slavery to monopoly."[7] The idea of moral certainty, timeless truths, and objectivity, fell away, ushering in a period of cynicism and relativism. The noble search for Truth became an attempt to see "truth."[8] This form of history gained strength throughout the 1920s, and the Depression gave it more energy and cogency. Business leaders got by quite well while average folk went hungry and lost their farms. And as a new European war loomed in the late 1930s, the same diabolic forces that had led the country to war in 1918 were again beating drums and shouting rallying cries.

Despite the protests of progressives, America did go to war again, and emerged triumphant and revitalized by power prestige. Progressives were not untouched by the new spirit. During the war, Beard reassessed the founders and judged them pragmatic architects of an optimal middle ground between popular democracy and militaristic aristocracy.[9] After the war, there was a restored consensus that American civilization was ideal, a model of political and economic development for the world. The skepticism and relativism of progressive historians came under fire for contributing, albeit unwittingly, to the rise of National Socialism. The moral confusion and self-doubt of their school was said to have paralyzed the authority of democratic ideals, weakening the will to halt the Nazis early. The progressive historians' disregard for obvious interpretations and simplistic views of good and evil were silenced by the enormity of Hitler. Their tendency to search for balancing points of view and moral ambiguity found no mitigating circumstances for the Nazis and their aggressions. [10]

This is not to say that progressive history disappeared, only that, like the social policies of the New Deal, it became overshadowed by the war and the restored confidence that followed. Progressives still held academic positions and found a new band of followers among postwar youth who felt estranged from the society around them; but their views were out of step with the times, and less critical forms of history and social science came to the fore.[11]

POST-VIETNAM PERSPECTIVES

The turmoil and defeat of the war in Southeast Asia reinvigorated critical forms of history. New viewpoints emerged, expressed not only in academic publications and lectures, but also in school texts and popular media. Films, documentaries, and mini-series examined the leaders and events of the past and helped to reshape the public consciousness. In the decades after Vietnam, the popular media became increasingly important in forming the public's understanding of the past.[12]

New interpreters of history see previous works as constructs, as systems of beliefs, sentiments, and judgments based less on scientific investigation than on prevailing ideas of the time. Often, they argue that historical understandings are constructed by those who benefit most from dominant institutions, by those who have the most to win and the most to hide. Accordingly, the task of new historians is part demolition of the old, part construction of the new. They seek to take apart earlier historical models whose decrepitude recent events has revealed, and to construct in their place new historical models based on their beliefs.

Several themes stand out in post-Vietnam history, first among them *the primacy of economic forces.* Economic factors are thought to constitute the most important cause of human action and social change. Religious principles are downplayed, as would be expected in a secularizing society that had all but discarded religion as an ordering principle.[13] High-minded motivations such as idealism and reason have less prominence in today's history.

Discrediting elites is a second theme. Previous forms of history lionized political and economic leaders, building them into admirable figures, commanding respect, inspiring the young with tales of great achievements. Now their motives are generally seen as less noble and their achievements, though often important, are better seen as the products of larger social groups.

Accompanying this diminution of the roles of elites is appreciation of *the importance of less privileged classes.* Accordingly, more attention is paid to the laborers who built the railroads of Harriman and the workers who toiled on Ford's assembly line. The contributions of indentured servants and urban craftsmen in building the nation receive greater recognition than they received in books stressing the importance of John Winthrop and George Washington. The women whose lives were unjustly limited, but who nonetheless accomplished important things, now enjoy numerous pages in basic school texts and academic works. The slaves, abducted from their homelands, forced to endure the rigors of the Middle Passage, and ruthlessly exploited, similarly are given greater attention than older histories could bear to give.

The pervasiveness of racism is a fourth theme. New historians see the American past, from the early colonists' encounters with the Pequots and the Delaware to the injustices of today's inner cities, stained by the oppression of non-white peoples. Almost every achievement, great or small, they contend, was based on slavery, theft of land, or other injustices. The role of minorities in epic events such as the Revolution, Civil War, the settling of the West, and the World Wars had been unfairly neglected or downplayed, and correction is a working assumption of the new historian.

A fifth theme is that of *patterns of expansionism.* Americans long thought of themselves as peaceful isolationists, innocent of the evils of geopolitics and empire building. New history seeks to correct this by revealing the expansionist nature of colonization, the Mexican War, the movement West, and the acquisition of various lands in the Caribbean and Pacific. In short, there was a long history of imperial gambits that ultimately led to the war in Southeast Asia.

Implicit in post-Vietnam history is the effort to right the injustices of the past. It seeks to lift up those who had been held down and to win in the history books the battles they could not win in the past. It also seeks to indict, posthumously, wrongdoers and hold them up to the court of modern public opinion.[14]

GREAT MEN AND AVERAGE PERSONS

Traditional history stressed the importance of statesmen, generals, and inventors. Modern history, while not entirely dismissive of them, is more prone to emphasize the importance of ordinary people, average Americans whose voices and achievements had been ignored or underappreciated. The trend certainly predates the turmoil of the 1960s; it began in the interwar years as history began to study craftsmen, peasants, and artisans, whose lives had lacked the majesty of kings and warlords but whose work changed the world too.

The experience of Vietnam strengthened these trends of praising common people. It practically formed a new consensus. After the turmoil and defeat, most Americans thought they were beginning to see through the fog with which the powerful had long surrounded themselves. Attention turned to the past. The idea that great national figures acted out of idealism and far-sightedness no longer resonated with contemporary experience, while pursuit of self-interest and dishonesty were readily comprehensible, and easily attributed to the predecessors of Johnson and Nixon.

The spirit of the times was highly conducive to lampoonery and scorn for leaders, past and present, and whatever good they did was oft interred with their bones. Early explorers of the New World were seen as mercenaries, gold-hunters, and freebooters. The faults of the founding fathers were pointed out in popular articles and books. Paul Revere was remiss in his duty during his legendary midnight ride. George Washington took advantage of a rather generous expense account while his men shivered at Valley Forge and was a military mediocrity, who relied greatly on French and Dutch assistance. Thomas Paine profited nicely from privateering, an enterprise varying only a little from piracy. Benjamin Franklin had so many illegitimate children that he could well be called the father of our nation, or at least a goodly portion of it, and he may even have passed on shipping information to the British navy. Many of the founders used opiates. Henry Clay became wealthy from the production of hemp. Andrew Jackson was a brawling bigot whose attempts to exterminate the tribes of the South patterned later events. And most early leaders were guilty of the unpardonable sin of owning slaves.

The period did not look kindly upon traditional heroes. In the early 1970s, the diary of a Mexican veteran of the Alamo was discovered, containing an entry describing the aftermath of the mythic siege. The diarist asserts that the legendary Davy Crockett did not die a glorious death in the cause of freedom, valiantly immolating himself to prevent the fort's magazine from falling into the foe's hands. Taken prisoner, he swore he had nothing to do with the rebels, that he was on a hunting trip and had the misfortune of taking shelter in the old mission. He pleaded for his life. (Unconvinced, Santa Anna had him shot.) The report caused a furor among some Texans, but to much of the country, the story rang true. Debunking fit the spirit of the day as neatly as romanticization had fitted previous times.[15]

Captains of industry had long been detested in many quarters, but they enjoyed a period of enhanced reputation during and after World War II. A few decades later, they were once again considered robber barons, hoarders of wealth, exploiters of workers, who could no longer hide the crimes behind their fortunes. Even Thomas Edison's reputation diminished as history texts chose to point out that many of his alleged inventions he had actually bought and claimed for himself.[16]

In place of great men, histories now stress the importance of unsung people. The Revolutionary period serves as a case in point. The importance of notables such as Jefferson, Madison, and Washington is not absent, but independence required more than just a handful of disgruntled merchants and intellectuals. The energies and talents of craftsmen, artisans, and simple farmers were also brought to bear against the might of Great Britain. The economic boom caused by the French and Indian War had created a large working class along the Atlantic seaboard whose members became radicalized by an ensuing depression, which figured highly in the revolutionary ferment. Without them, the leaders would most surely have hanged — together or not. Independence found the rank and file of the Continental army deeply in debt and agitating for reform. Shays's Rebellion (1787) sought to redress their grievances, but fearful men of property who thought the Republic's polity should remain in the hands of the better sort suppressed it. Powerful interests thereby ended the potential for true democracy, and ushered in an era of oligarchy that has only grudgingly, and incompletely, given way to democratization over the centuries.[17]

Of course, traditional history had always had references to hearty settlers and immigrants, but it always took the main contours of American life to have been formed by elites. Histories of today seek to right this wrong. Accordingly, the struggles of working people have become common fare in the output of almost every history-oriented publishing house, as a cursory glance through any such catalog will show. Women and minorities are especially championed. Women were important laborers in the earliest colonies, contributed their labor in the textile mills of New England, and rode shotgun on Conestoga wagons. Political and social movements such as temperance leagues, abolitionism, and suffrage drives benefited from the energies of women and became foundations of progressive movements.[18]

Entrenched racism repressed minorities in the social order and obscured them in the history books, except as beneficiaries of white largesse. Slavery was always mentioned in traditional histories — there was no way around that — even in southern texts, in which the plantation came across almost as a community of brothers, that is, until the seeds of disharmony were sown by Union soldiers and carpetbaggers.[19] Even in northern texts, African-Americans were commonly described as inferior to whites and as passive products of history. They did not make their history, rather they had their history made for them, by whites. In older histories, the Civil War and Reconstruction settled the race question and eased white consciences.[20]

As odious as slavery is in the abstract, it is even more so in its day-to-day practice. New history takes a closer look at America's peculiar institution and tries to give it the proper amount of attention in school texts. Africans were torn from their homelands and stuffed into overcrowded ships in which they died in large numbers. Grueling work, brutal whippings, and sale of family members awaited them in the New World. Slave resistance is a common theme: accounts of courageous escapes, sabotage of plantation implements, and noble uprisings are found in many textbooks. Slavery's importance in economic development has been given more emphasis. It was agricultural surplus extracted in the South that financed the industrialization of the North. The lives of free blacks before the Civil War have proved to be an interesting but heretofore unexamined part of America's past. The inadequate solution at the end of the Civil War, which formally banned slavery but did little to ensure economic or political opportunities, is another source of study.[21]

The role of African-Americans in the country's wars gets considerable attention today, perhaps owing to the post-WWII atmosphere regarding racial injustice but probably more to racial problems exacerbated by Vietnam. School texts abound with reference to blacks (and other minorities) serving in wartime, from the Revolution to the Gulf War. Elementary students learn that a black soldier fell at Bunker Hill, over a hundred thousand former slaves fought in the Civil War, the all-black Ninth Cavalry patrolled the western frontier and served alongside Teddy's Rough Riders, and blacks distinguished themselves in World War II, Korea, and every other war. Implicit in these narrations is a sense of injustice, of people serving in the military of a nation that continues to deny them full citizenship.

THE LOSING OF THE WEST

Westward expansion provided basic myths of the American identity. There on the frontier, whether the Mohawk valley or the Great Plains, civilization triumphed over savagery, law and order won out over banditry and injustice, and opportunity abounded for individuals willing to take risks and work their claim. It came across in almost one voice, in the epic novels of James Fenimore

Cooper, in the news reports avidly read back East, and in Parkman's and Turner's studies.[22] Helen Hunt Jackson and James Mooney pointed out the long history of injustice toward indigenous peoples, but had only small audiences. Most Americans saw westward expansion as a national birthright, putting the land to proper service, extending democracy, natural growth, and many other ideologies of manifest destiny.[23] By the early 1960s, these myths, though still alive, had lost much of their power to inspire. The passage of time had made the epic more distant in the minds of most Americans. The mass media had turned the frontier experience into trite morality plays and melodrama broadcast nightly and repeated in summertime. Nonetheless, the template of righteousness was still in the American mind.

The Vietnam War caused many to look back on the old myths of the West and see troubling parallels. Inasmuch as the war had invoked so much western imagery (the Viet Cong held "Indian country," cavalry units had traded horses for helicopters and APCs, Kit Carson Scouts led patrols), Vietnam became western mythology's Last Stand, so to speak. The idea that foreign peoples must inevitably subscribe to American standards — once taken for granted — had been badly shaken, along with the confidence in the superiority of American ways. Simplistic views of good and evil could no longer find soil in post-My Lai America, except when inverted. Amid the controversy of the war, American Indians became increasingly militant, occupying Alacatraz and other government properties they claimed were theirs by treaty. To an increasingly sympathetic public, they pointed out unsettling similarities between the war on the Plains and the one in Vietnam, between Indians and Vietnamese, between Custer and Calley.[24] Books portraying the Indian Wars from their perspective found a sizable readership, eliciting feelings of guilt that came with growing disgust with the war.[25]

Older history texts had begun with the earliest explorations of Europeans, followed by the settlements in Virginia and Massachusetts. Before the advent of Europeans, the New World had no history, only the quaint superstitions and folklore of Indians, who, after a few vignettes at the first Thanksgiving and the rescue of John Smith, receded into obscurity until a brief and unpleasant reprise in the 1870s. Newer texts, however, devote many pages and often several chapters to Native Americans. In one textbook, white settlers appear only after a quarter of the book has looked at the Incas, Mayans, and other pre-Columbine civilizations.[26] The message is clear: the New World was not a howling wilderness; it was inhabited by numerous non-western cultures. They were here first.

Previously, textbooks depicted aboriginals as essentially ignorant and uncivilized, incapable of the cultural achievements of the West and hence predetermined to lose out. People who had no written language or farming skills could only benefit from the civilization across the big water, even if forced upon them. Newer texts find rich complexities in Native-American civilizations. Many had written languages and agrarian techniques, the latter freely given to new settlers facing famine. Many tribes had agricultural and social systems featuring periodic redivision of communal lands. The Algonquins had a highly developed political system, including a constitution containing passages on freedoms and liberties. Others had elaborate political arrangements that were far from the familiar images of them as uncivilized savages. Native Americans were typically peaceful and gentle, living harmoniously with nature and the environment.[27]

Early contacts between Native Americans and Europeans were not always amicable exchanges of beads and turkey parts. Because so many of the early Europeans were buccaneers and freebooters, it could hardly have been otherwise. Relations between the two civilizations were patterned quite early. Settlers pushed Indians aside, went to war with them, and often enslaved them. Some passages in recent texts bear the mark of Vietnam. In a vignette introducing the first chapter of a prominent college text, the Powhatan Indians look on as "land-hungry settlers swarm in." The Powhatans wage war to defend their homelands but lose to the Jamestown colonists. Their leader is taken prisoner, later shot in the back.[28] The next chapter on the Puritans has a similar introductory narrative:

> Captain Mason and his troops approached a Pequot village on the Mystic River. Supported by Naragansett allies, the English slipped into the town. After a few scuffles in the half-light, Mason cried out, "We must burn them," and his men began torching the Pequot wigwams. . . . As flames engulfed the huts, the Pequots fled the inferno, only to be cut down with musket and sword by the English soldiers who had ringed the community. Most of the terrified victims were noncombatants — old men, women, and children — for the Pequot warriors were preparing for war at another village about five miles away. . . . Mason himself wrote that God had "laughed at his enemies, . . . making them as a fiery oven." Captain John Mason was a God-fearing Puritan and a man highly esteemed by his fellow colonists. His actions . . . testify that the European colonization of America involved a violent confrontation of two cultures. We often speak of the "discovery" and "settlement" of North America by English and other European colonists. But the penetration of the eastern edge of what today is the United States might more accurately be called "the invasion of America."[29]

206

The narrative goes on to assure readers that many settlers were decent people, but a theme has been established.

Later events, the French and Indian War and the War of 1812, were cut from the same cloth. Indians sought to regain control of their homeland, sometimes by siding with the French, sometimes with the British, but in each case to no avail. Whereas early narratives chose to ignore Andrew Jackson's ouster of southern tribes from their homelands, the plight of the Five Nations is now a prominent part of early American history. The narrative is made more poignant by illustrations of Cherokee families fighting the bitter cold as they trek along the Trail of Tears from the Carolinas to the Oklahoma Territory.[30] The settling of the colonies is now seen as a brutal land grab that should not be transformed into pleasant homily, no matter how edifying it might be for children.

Older views of history romanticized the settling of the West. There, in books and movies, were hardy folk who endured great hardships as they crossed the prairie. By working their claim and building a house on it, they could get free land and rise or fall according to their abilities. Western history narrated the triumph of American virtues. Individualism, diligence, and family won the West, spread civilization into the wilderness, and expanded the nation's greatness from sea to shining sea. The entire process was mythic and sacred, as revered as the wisdom of the Founders and the trials of the Civil War.[31]

Following the lead of the Beards, who looked at the role of "merchant capitalists" in obtaining "real estate" in the Atlantic colonies, newer histories of the frontier bring out very different themes from those of older history.[32] Less emphasis is placed on individuals and families, and more on large businesses, though hardly in a congratulatory manner. Merchants of the mid-eighteenth century pressed into the Ohio valley, triggering a veritable world war known here as the French and Indian War, in Europe as the Seven Years War.

Wealthy speculators bought up huge tracts of land, lured unwary homesteaders, and reaped great revenue while others toiled under crushing debt. Similarly, railroad magnates were granted sprawling rights of way, from the Midwest to the Pacific, allowing them to enjoy the bulk of the bonanza. More importantly, they controlled the economic arteries through which commerce flowed. Prices were controlled, competitors driven out, and opponents quashed by cronies in government, a state of affairs that had the fortuitous result of giving rise to progressive movements of the late nineteenth century as well as to the beginning of government regulation and reform.[33]

Settling the West, whether by hearty settlers or corporate giants, continued the process of expropriating Native-American lands begun by the Puritans. The Pequot, Delaware, and Powhatan had all been conquered, and now the Sioux, Cheyenne, and other tribes of the Great Plains had to face the spread of white civilization. Settling the West brought conflict with the Plains Indians, and that meant the deployment of the cavalry. Enjoying a privileged status in the American mind, the cavalry was admired as dauntless warriors on horseback, hard-drinking and two-fisted, who arrived in the nick of time to rescue the besieged wagon train. By the early 1970s, however, Americans saw the West and the army in a new light.

A country that had lost its faith could hardly defend old conquests based on assertions of a superior civilization benefiting all. The expropriation of simple tribesmen and herding them into strategic reservations could no longer be defended. Sheridan's famous and once inspirational remark that the only good Indian was a dead one betrayed the racist assumptions behind the *Will nach Westen*. Accounts of cavalry attacks on peaceful Indian villages at Sand Creek and the Washita became common.[34] Visual reconstructions of these massacres occur in a recent documentary series *How the West Was Lost* (a syntactic inversion of Theodore Roosevelt's *The Winning of the West* and John Ford's *How the West Was Won*) and in films from the early 1970s, *Soldier Blue* and *Little Big Man*. These films, made shortly after My Lai, clearly drew parallels between the Indian Wars and Vietnam. In *Little Big Man*, soldiers shoot down the title character's Cheyenne wife (portrayed by an Asian actress) as she flees for her life, clutching their newborn baby.[35]

There was perhaps no more mythologized figure in the history of the West than George Armstrong Custer; today, there is no more vilified one. He was once the intrepid cavalry commander who had helped win the day at Gettysburg, a devoted husband, and defender of settlers from rampaging hostiles. His impetuous nature was no vice in the cavalry. He gained immortality when he attacked the Indian encampment along the Little Big Horn, rallied his men into a redoubt, and there made his legendary Last Stand. An enduring and vital myth came into being: Custer, clad in buckskins, heroically standing fast against the odds, urging his men on until an arrow silences him. The scene was immortalized in Buffalo Bill's Wild West Show, several Hollywood films, and popular paintings and lithographs adorning many a saloon, in which more than a few tipplers saluted the fallen colonel before downing another round.[36] Such was the power of the Custer myth that, in early 1942, the War Department purchased two thousand of these lithographs for posting on army bases, presumably as a morale booster.[37] In backyard play, many a lad imagined himself standing alongside the fearless colonel and somehow turning the tide that day.

The Custer myth has been stood on its head. Custer is seen now as foolhardy, power-hungry, even deranged. His men dashed across the Little Big Horn to perform the same barbarities they had done at the Washita a few years earlier. Accordingly, Custer and his command got what they deserved. One grade-school text notes, "Custer was greedy — greedy for glory." Another quotes Custer as "bragging" that his Seventh Cavalry "could whip all the Indians on the continent." Then, below an illustration of the last battle, the student is asked, "What happened to Custer and his men?"[38] A college text contains another illustration of the battle with the caption, "The spectacular Native American victory over General Custer's army in 1876 had little effect on the onslaught of white civilization."[39]

Old myths figure highly in the Vietnam-era book and film, *Little Big Man*. The central character, Jack Crabb, was raised by the Cheyenne after his parents are killed by Pawnee raiders (a tribe later seen as collaborators with the cavalry). Over the years, fortune's blows knock him back and forth between the two worlds. Jack's experiences with white society (a Bible-thumping hypocrite, a snake oil salesman, a cheating business partner) are invariably disagreeable, those with the Cheyenne almost always pleasant. When Jack first encounters Custer, he admires him. In time, he sees him as narcissistic, arrogant, and, following several scenes of slaughter, murderously insane. When Custer and his men venture into the Little Big Horn, the audience has long since seen through the myth and become sympathetic to those they had long been taught to consider the enemy. As doom nears, Custer goes mad — or rather his madness is finally revealed to all. His men, quite brave when cutting down women and children at the Washita, cower or flee in panic. The demise of Custer's cavalry troops is presented as wholly appropriate.[40]

AMERICA AT WAR

Americans had long prided themselves on their justness in war and peace. They did not start wars; other countries, by impressing sailors or waging unrestricted submarine warfare, forced us into it. Afterward, America created just treaties and enduring peace. When territory somehow came into American hands following a war, its people benefited from American stewardship. Vietnam damaged many myths, including these. The war left an enduring sense of disgust with the military and war. Historians looked back on a long line of military involvements with new sensibilities.

Older history saw the War of 1812 caused by violations of principles of freedom of the seas and the impressment of Americans into the British navy. Newer histories stress the practical economic matters intertwined with high principle. Merchant capitalists wished to trade with all sides in the Napoleonic Wars raging across the Atlantic. Antagonisms with England led to volatile senses of wounded pride among the War Hawks in the South and West, which plunged the nation into war. For this, armies clashed across the continent and navies traded salvoes on the high seas. Various Indian tribes were lured into the war by promises of a restoration of lost land, but in the end they found themselves defeated once more and pushed across the Mississippi.[41]

One could still plausibly argue that the United States had not sought war in 1812, that it had been forced upon us by European intrigues, and so America's essential peacefulness could still be asserted. With the Mexican War (1848), however, new texts argue that the United States provoked a war to gain territory. Statesmen such as Hamilton had long dreamed of mastering the continent and transforming the seaboard colonies into a great power. In 1848, leaders saw the opportunity to seize northern Mexico. President Polk dispatched General Zachary Taylor to the frontier with instructions to provoke war, an order the future president swiftly obeyed. The United States invaded Mexico, captured its capital, and forced the country to cede huge expanses of land that are now the American Southwest. Perhaps drawing from recent experience, writers often discuss at length domestic opposition to the war. Many Americans protested what they saw as a simple land grab and an attempt to spread slavery into the West. Many were imprisoned.[42]

Similar processes continued throughout the century, forcibly ending Japan's isolation and seizing the Samoas and Hawaii. Driving this wave of expansion was the need to find markets for American exports (especially grains), a need felt more acutely during one of the country's periodic depressions. Economic interests rallied support to the cause by playing upon jingoistic sentiments in the public. America must become a great power, and of course a great power needed a great navy, which they got as well. The most splendid acquisitions came from the Spanish-American War (1898) in which a feeble European country was forced to cede Cuba, Guam, and the Philippines. New histories foreshadow later passages by pointing out that the Filipinos put up fierce resistance:

> In what came to be a guerrilla war with some similarities to those
> fought later in the twentieth century in Asia and Central America,
> native nationalists tried to undermine the American will to fight by
> hit-and-run attacks. . . . In addition to the 18,000 killed in combat,
> an estimated 200,000 Filipinos (20 percent of the population) died
> of famine and disease because U.S. soldiers burned villages and
> destroyed crops and livestock to disrupt the economy and deny
> rebel fighters their food supply. [43]

Thus was American stewardship established.

Views on World War I needed no fundamental re-evaluation. Historians had never formed a roseate judgment on it. Owing to the celebration of the Second World War, the memory of its predecessor remained less than heroic and mythic. Perhaps as a result of constitutional infringements in the 1960s — especially those experienced by antiwar activists, more than a few of whom became academicians — many newer works on the Great War call attention to the curtailment of civil liberties during and after the war: the arrest of those who dared to speak out, suspicion of foreigners, and frenzied witch hunts following the Bolshevik Revolution. The attorney general said of opponents of intervention, "May God have mercy on them, for they need expect none from an outraged people and an avenging government."[44]

Post-Vietnam history has not reinterpreted World War II — the record of National Socialism precludes that. Even the war in the Pacific, though not unrelated to imperialist antagonisms, has yet to be widely reinterpreted in those terms. But the experience of Vietnam has caused many to emphasize flaws, and the passing of time has brought tarnish. The role of African-Americans and other minorities in the war is presented in a different light. Older histories, *Yank*, public relations events, and documentaries portrayed minorities as making important contributions to the war effort, showing themselves to be as American as the rest, and meriting acceptance as real Americans. Narratives of today invert this, from pride in dealing with the problem of race to another example of the racism that mars the country. Narratives recount episodes of segregated USOs and service clubs, harassment on leave (especially in the South), race riots in Detroit and Los Angeles, and courts-martial for minorities who protested dangerous or menial labor.[45]

Of particular salience is the racism exhibited toward the Japanese, a theme bound to emerge after a later Asian war. The internment of Japanese-Americans in camps receives considerable attention in today's textbooks, often taking up more space than that devoted to the European war. Japanese-Americans, whose loyalty was clearly on the right side of the hyphen, were robbed of their property, without compensation (until quite recently), by exploitive landholders purporting to be great patriots.[46] Wartime propaganda campaigns against Germany typically distinguished between Nazis and average Germans, who were not inherently evil — distinctions seldom drawn for Japanese. "Japs" were typically shown, in film and on posters, as rats, monkeys, repugnant sub-humans whose extermination would benefit the world. Accordingly, the war in the Pacific, as well as its depiction back home, took on a particularly brutal character. The Japanese were seen as diabolical and treacherous: feigning surrender then killing would-be captors, sadistically torturing American prisoners, launching fanatical banzai charges, and the like. Such people, wartime thinking went, simply had to be wiped out.[47]

The use of the atomic bombs on Hiroshima and Nagasaki is now often considered as at least partially motivated by racism. By the summer of 1945, it is often argued, Japan was on the verge of surrender, sending out peace feelers to the Soviet Union and meeting secretly with American officials in Switzerland. Such a weapon would never have been used on Germans, that is, on people who looked like us; but race hatred made the incineration of over a hundred and fifty thousand Asians easier on American sensibilities. It is also frequently argued that anti-Soviet sentiment contributed to the use of atomic weapons. Seeing the inevitability of postwar rivalry with the Soviet Union, American leaders dropped the bombs not so much to end the war — Japan was about to surrender anyway — as to intimidate the Soviet Union and make it more cooperative in the postwar era.[48]

The advent of nuclear weapons at the close of World War II was a transition to the senselessness of the Cold War, brought about by failure to maintain the wartime partnership with the Soviet Union. The collapse of accord between the two powers stemmed from mistrust of communism, an emerging national security state, and disputes over spheres of interest in Eastern Europe. This in turn set the stage for costly arms races that persisted for a half century, hysterical fears infringing on civil liberties, and the rise of an array of alliances with dictators around the world. And of course, it also led to Vietnam.[49]

NATIONALISM AND INTERNATIONALISM

Instilling patriotism was the very stuff of nineteenth-century schoolbooks and scholarly works, part of the socialization process that made the young into Americans. This was especially the case during waves of immigration, when educators worried about newcomers not assimilating American ways. The patriotic message came through on several levels: in textbooks, in general histories for the educated public, and in literature. Authors of these works were enamored by America and felt it their duty to instill the same feelings in others.[50]

Nationalism is now treated with considerable circumspection. At best, it is a naive provincialism that betrays a lack of sophistication; at worst, it is a totemic atavism that fosters racism, militarism, infringement of civil liberties, and recklessness in world affairs. Newer histories reflect these concerns in several ways. Older histories sought to involve students with their nation's heritage, accentuating arguments with romantic phrases and stirring images. An older textbook might describe the Revolution in heroic and inspiring prose, illustrated by romantic paintings from the period and the apotheosis of a great leader. Emphasis was on important events, noble leaders, and epic battles that forged a great nation. They made use of "we" and "our ancestors," simple words that drew students into the narrative and involved them with their country's events.

Later texts seek only to familiarize students with basic events and processes. There are almost no uses of "we" or "our."[51] Similarly, geography texts, reluctant to suggest primacy, seldom make the United States or North America the first area to be studied. Perhaps because it seems lacking in sophistication or perhaps because it reflects a certain gullibility toward official exhortation, the word "enemy" is rarely used. The reader is not struck by any outstanding moral worth of major historical figures. There is nothing exemplary or unique about American history, nor are there any noble and transcending ideals running through it. The United States is simply one of many countries that make up the world. The Constitution and other aspects of American culture are described not as providentially ordained or superior; there is nothing in which the student should feel any pride or loyalty. There are only certain political and cultural forms with which we happen to live.

Authors of older histories, naturally and unashamedly, wrote from an American point of view. There was no need to give balance to the other side of the Revolution by giving voice to George III's thoughts on colonial taxation, Benedict Arnold's views on war leadership, Santa Anna's perspective on the Texas question, or Jefferson Davis's on states rights (except in the South). There was general consensus on the contours of American history and on what was right and wrong in it. In the fragmented society of today, this confident consensus on right and wrong, fact and propaganda, is largely gone, and varying perspectives are presented. There has already been occasion to note that today's histories do not depict the settling of the West through the eyes of settlers and old Indian fighters who asserted the land would now be put to proper use. Indeed, Native-American points of view are now common. Similarly, the Mexican War is sometimes presented from Mexico's perspective. One text accentuates the narrative with a poignant account of a hundred Mexican youths (*Los Niños*) who fell while defending their native soil from invading Americans.[52]

Akin to downplaying nationalism is decreasing the importance of Western civilization, from ancient Greece to modern Britain. Again, this view, the Eurocentric view, is now thought to be provincial and narrow-minded, and to fall easily into racism. It is best to appreciate the importance of other nations and cultures and to see America and Europe as part of a greater world-historical process, without being judgmental about the superiority of one over another.[53]

***

American history has changed markedly since the turmoil and defeat of the Vietnam War. It no longer contains a basic consensus; it is no longer coherent. In this respect, it ably reflects the country. Both are highly fragmented, antagonistic, no longer confident as to what constitutes right and wrong, no longer searching for a restoration of consensus.

EPILOGUE

*Until the millennium arrives and countries cease trying to
enslave others, it will be necessary to accept one's
responsibilities and to be willing to make sacrifices for
one's country — as my comrades did. As the troops used to say,
"If the country is good enough to live in, it's good enough
to fight for." With privileges goes responsibility.*
E. B. SLEDGE, *With the Old Breed at Peleliu and Okinawa*

*This might sound selfish, but I think it would be a shame to
put America's best young minds on the front line.*
A college student during the Gulf War, quoted in
John Gregory Dunne, "Virtual Patriotism"

At the outset of the new century, when large-scale war has little relevance or
interest to most Americans, the importance of armed conflicts in the country's
history might seem implausible. But their effects are all around us. Wars have
brought rapid economic expansion, dislocated the population, changed the
social structure, altered norms and religious beliefs, and affected nationalist
sentiments. They have figured highly in breaking down traditional society and
pushing the country into modernity and post-modernity.

The transition, of course, is not complete, and it is unlikely to be so in the
foreseeable future. The rise of postmodern society has not done away with all
of traditional society. There are loci of tradition in rural areas (especially in
the South, Midwest, and West) as well as in the armed forces, where family,
religion, community, patriotism, and faith in the American idea are stronger
than elsewhere, though less than at the outset of the twentieth century and
probably less than professed. There is an uneasy tension between tradition-
oriented Americans and the rest of the country, which prefers a more diverse
and open way of life.

As a result, national issues are no longer debated within a context of relative
comity, based on shared heritage and common assumptions. Political discourse
has become vituperative and increasingly pointless. This is not to say that
political life was genteel before contagions from foreign wars infected the
Republic. The Northeast came close to secession during the War of 1812. Fights
broke out in Congress in the years before the Civil War. Political enemies were

ruined during the McCarthy years. But these periods of enmity were followed by restored comity: the Era of Good Feelings, the Gilded Age, and Camelot. Another period of restored comity is unlikely. Americans are deeply divided on many basic issues and have too few common bases. Differences, perhaps irreconcilable ones, have developed.

Debates go on not only in Washington, but also in schools as they argue over textbooks, in museums over presentations of the past, and in social gatherings when the conversation turns to issues of the day. Arguments go back and forth as in a tedious ping-pong volley. Without a common basis, there tends to be no dialogue, no exchange of ideas, no debate — only the marshaling of forces. Each side is incredulous at the other's "thinking." Exchanges of ideas lead to awkward silence, deepened polarization, and recognition that there is little point to discussion. Without common bases, in a period when national institutions have lost their prestige, romance, and unifying force, these fissures, which ominously coincide with regional divisions, could develop into secessionist sentiment in a few decades.

Whatever the long-term consequences may be, for the present it is clear that social change has not led to economic or military decline. At the outset of the new century, the U.S. economy, thought moribund after Vietnam, is powerful, dynamic, aggressive, and unstoppable. Its strength is forcing the rest of the world to emulate it or withdraw behind protectionism (where they are likely only to fall further behind). To much of the world, the United States is now an immense corporation on a hill. Domestically, economic growth is the principal source of political legitimacy. The dogma of patriotism, the tradition of courage, and the shrine of honor, *pace* Herzen, have been at least partially replaced by the rules of political economy.

The social changes described here are relevant to the rise of this economic juggernaut. The decline of the family has led to more people, men and women, especially professionals and managers, willing to work longer hours than nineteenth-century mill owners dared to demand of their workers. The family has lost most of its traditional tasks (education, socialization, welfare) and become essentially a consumer unit eager to sample new wares. Vanity has hyper-energized entrepreneurialism. The loosening of norms and beliefs has led to tremendous innovation and creativity that has revolutionized management and technology. Perhaps the clearest example of this is the California-based technology industries (significantly, not IBM), which every few years relegate earlier products to obsolescence. The decline of community has facilitated a greater mobility of capital — money, equipment, and people. Loyalty to towns and regions is largely gone; businesses pick up and move without qualms over the consequences for long-standing hosts. The decline of religion and norms has allowed more aggressive business practices. Law is the only restraint, and even here there is more willingness to explore gray areas and elide legal obstacles.

The military of the United States today is, relatively and absolutely, in conventional and nuclear arms, the most powerful in the world. Again, this is in contrast to post-Vietnam expectation, which saw it as inept and undisciplined. Now, its flotillas and regiments are said to stand to the entire world as the legions of Rome once did to the Mediterranean region, but even this analogy falls short. Whether a country devoid of traditional or any other moorings, and vulnerable to political and media exhortations, will use this power responsibly is likely to shape the history of the new century.

Military power rests in no small way on the technological developments just mentioned, which have provided new means of destruction, methods of communications, and organizational skills. There is a curious working relationship between a culture of tradition and honor in partnership with one of impermanence and silicon. Though this calls for some sort of satiric novel, it also underscores the cultural isolation of the armed forces, which is largely at odds with, if not contemptuous of mainstream society and many political leaders — in no small way, a legacy of Vietnam. And should regional and cultural fissures develop into secessionism, there is little doubt where the military's loyalties will lie.

After a decade or so of absence, Grenada, Panama, the Gulf Wars, and the Afghan Campaign have reacquainted Americans with their old military companion, who has been with them since the Revolution, but from whom they had become estranged since Vietnam. Owing to the painfulness and recentness of their falling out, it was only a reacquaintance and not a resumption of the ardor that followed Appomattox and V-J Day. But the country, or at least a large portion of it, once again enjoys the prestige of military power. They ask only that future affairs be short and uncostly. Most insist that their children know nothing of it.

NOTES

Preface

1. Karl Marx (and Friedrich Engels), "The Economic and Philosophic Manuscripts of 1844," "The German Ideology," and "The Communist Manifesto," in *Collected Works* (New York: International Publishers, 1976 [1844–48]).

2. Émile Durkheim, *Suicide: A Study in Sociology* (New York: Free Press, 1951).

3. Talcott Parsons, *The Social System* (New York: Free Press, 1951).

4. Barrington Moore, Jr., *Political Power and Social Theory* (Cambridge, Mass.: Harvard University Press, 1958).

5. Otto Hintze, *Die Hohenzollern und ihr Werk* (Berlin: Paul Parey, 1915); *Staat und Verfassung: Gesammelte Abhandlungen zur allgemeinen Verfassungsgeschichte*, ed. Fritz Hartung (Leipzig: Koehler & Amelang, 1941); *Regierung und Verwaltung: Gesammelte Abhandlungen zur Staats-, Rechts,- und Sozialgeschichte Preussens*, ed. Gerhard Oestreich (Göttingen: Vandenhoek und Ruprecht, 1967); Hans Delbrück, *History of the Art of War Within the Framework of Political History*, vols. 1–4 (Westport, Conn.: Greenwood Press, 1975–1985).

6. John Shy makes this point in his *A People Numerous and Armed: Reflections on the Military Struggle for American Independence* (New York: Oxford University Press, 1976), p. 124.

7. Charles A. Beard, *An Economic Interpretation of the Constitution of the United States* (New York: Macmillan, 1962 [1913]); Marc Bloch, *Feudal Society*, 2 vols. (Chicago: University of Chicago Press, 1961 [1940]); R. H. Tawney, "The Rise of the Gentry," *Economic History Review* 11 (1941): 1–38.

Chapter One

1. Helena M. Wall, *Fierce Communion: Family and Community in Early America* (Cambridge, Mass.: Harvard University Press, 1990), pp. 86–125; Carl N. Degler, *At Odds: Women and the Family in America from the Revolution to the Present* (New York: Oxford University Press, 1980), pp. 86–110; Philip J. Greven, Jr., *Four Generations: Population, Land, and Family in Andover, Massachusetts* (Ithaca: Cornell University Press, 1970), pp. 72–99.

2. W. I. Thomas and Florian Znaniecki, *The Polish Peasant in Europe and America* (Urbana: University of Illinois Press, 1984 [1918–20]), pp. 65–79; W. I. Thomas, Robert E. Park, and Herbert A. Miller, *Old World Traits Transplanted* (New York: Harper and Brothers, 1921); Steven Mintz and Susan Kellogg, *Domestic Revolutions: A Social History of American Family Life* (New York: Free Press, 1988), pp. 83–105.

3. John Bodnar, Roger Simon, and Michael P. Weber, *Lives of Their Own: Blacks, Italians, and Poles in Pittsburgh, 1900–1960* (Urbana: University of Illinois Press, 1982), pp. 89–108; Robert D. Slayton, *Back of the Yards: The Making of a Local Democracy* (Chicago: University of Chicago Press, 1986), pp. 80–89; Ruth B. Moynihan, Susan Armitage, and Christine Fischer Dichamp, eds., *So Much to Be Done: Women Settlers on the Mining and Ranching Frontiers* (Lincoln: University of Nebraska Press, 1990); Leslie Woodcock Tentler, *Wage-Earning Women: Industrial Work and Family Life in the United States, 1900–1930* (New York: Oxford University Press, 1979); Marlene Springer and Kaskell Springer, eds., *Plains Woman: The Diary of Martha Farnsworth, 1882–1992* (Bloomington: Indiana University Press, 1982), pp. 109–16.

4. Thomas and Znaniecki, *The Polish Peasant*, pp. 65–79.

5. See Maris A. Vinovskis, "Family and Schooling in Colonial and Nineteenth-Century America," in Tamara Hareven and Andrejs Plakans, eds., *Family History at the Crossroads* (Princeton: Princeton University Press, 1987), pp. 19–37; Robert Anthony Orsi, *The Madonna of 115th Street: Faith and Community in Italian Harlem, 1880–1950* (New Haven: Yale University Press, 1985), pp. 75–106; Herbert G. Gutman, *The Black Family in Slavery and Freedom, 1750–1925* (New York: Pantheon, 1976), pp. 185–229; Elizabeth H. Pleck, "The Two-Parent Household: Black Family Structure in Late Nineteenth-Century Boston," in Michael Gordon, ed., *The American Family in Social-Historical Perspective* (New York: St. Martin's, 1973), pp. 152–77.

6. On immigrant marriage see Slayton, *Back of the Yards,* pp. 65–66. On romantic love see Max Lerner, *America as a Civilization: Life and Thought in the United States Today* (New York: Simon & Schuster, 1957), pp. 582–84; Ellen K. Rothman, *Hands and Hearts: A History of Courtship in America* (Cambridge, Mass.: Harvard University Press, 1987); Springer and Springer, eds., *Plains Woman,* pp. 21–60; Christopher Lasch, *Haven in a Heartless World: The Family Besieged* (New York: W. W. Norton, 1977), pp. 3–4. Lasch and others argue that this affective role of the family came to be increasingly important as the family became less an economic unit and more a "haven in a heartless world." See also Thomas and Znaniecki, *The Polish Peasant,* pp. 94–95; Mintz and Kellogg, *Domestic Revolutions,* pp. 43–65.

7. Perry Miller, *Errand into the Wilderness* (New York: Harper & Row, 1964), pp. 5–7; Kai T. Erikson, *Wayward Puritans: A Study in the Sociology of Deviance* (New York: John Wiley, 1966), pp. 33–64; Richard Lingeman, *Small Town America: A Narrative History, 1620-the Present* (Boston: Houghton Mifflin, 1980), pp. 15–62; Winthrop S. Hudson, *Religion in America: An Historical Account of the Development of American Religious Life* 2nd ed. (New York: Scribner's, 1973), pp. 10–58.

8. Lingeman, *Small Town America,* pp. 25–48; Richard L. Bushman, *From Puritan to Yankee: Character and the Social Order in Connecticut, 1690–1765* (Cambridge, Mass.: Harvard University Press, 1967), pp. 54–134; Stephanie Grauman Wolf, *Urban Village: Population, Community, and Family Structure in Germantown, Pennsylvania, 1683–1800*

(Princeton: Princeton University Press, 1976), pp. 155–205; Vernon L. Parrington, *Main Currents in American Thought: An Interpretation of American Literature from the Beginnings to 1920* (New York: Harcourt, Brace, 1930), I: 62–75, 118–25, 233–47. Parrington, a progressive historian, saw these communities as ideal forms of democracy that had rid themselves of Puritan attempts at theocracy but had been stifled by the conservatism that the suppression of Shays's Rebellion ushered into political life. Perry Miller found this greatly overstated and typical of progressive historians. Miller bluntly states: "On this matter there is no middle. Parrington simply did not know what he was talking about." See *Errand into the Wilderness,* pp. 17–47.

9. De Tocqueville, *Democracy in America,* I: 53–91; Ray Allen Billington, *America's Frontier Heritage* (Albuquerque: University of New Mexico Press, 1991), pp. 75–145; Frederick Jackson Turner, *The Frontier in American History* (New York: Holt, Rinehart and Winston, 1962); Curti, *The Making of an American Community,* pp. 38–47, 297; Gutman, *The Black Family,* pp. 332–34; U. S. Grant, *Personal Memoirs* (New York: Library of America, 1990), pp. 152–53. De Tocqueville contrasts these settlements to European villages, where an aristocracy or central state handled matters and thwarted the development of local democracy. "I am of the opinion that a centralized administration is fit only to enervate the nations in which it exists, by incessantly diminishing their local spirit. . . . It may help admirably the transient greatness of a man, but not the durable prosperity of a nation." De Tocqueville, *Democracy in America,* I: 87. He describes the destruction of local government by the French state in his *Ancien Regime and the French Revolution,* which in this regard might be usefully read in conjunction with *Democracy in America.* The "transient greatness of a man" likely refers to Louis XIV, whom de Tocqueville faults for destroying the foundations of local government as well as ultimately, and unwittingly, the Bourbon monarchy.

10. Such continuity can also be found in early twentieth-century Russia. See Geroid Tanquary Robinson, *Rural Russia under the Old Régime: A History of the Landlord-Peasant World and a Prologue to the Peasant Revolution of 1917* (Berkeley and Los Angeles: University of California Press, 1972 [1932]), pp. 107–9; Robert Eugene Johnson, *Peasant and Proletarian: The Working Class of Moscow in the Late Nineteenth Century* (Leicester, U.K.: University of Leicester Press, 1979), pp. 28–31.

11. Slayton, *Back of the Yards,* pp. 78–80, 115–16; Thomas et al., *Old World Traits Transplanted,* pp. 124–40; David Brody, *Steelworkers in America: The Nonunion Era* (New York: Harper & Row, 1969), pp. 96–111; Thomas Lee Philpott, *The Slum and the Ghetto: Immigrants, Blacks, and Reformers in Chicago, 1880–1930* (Belmont, Calif.: Wadsworth, 1991), pp. 116–62; James R. Grossman, *Land of Hope: Chicago, Black Southerners, and the Great Migration* (Chicago: University of Chicago Press, 1989); Mintz and Kellogg, *Domestic Revolutions,* pp. 83–105; Oscar Handlin, *The Uprooted,* 2nd ed. (Boston: Little, Brown, 1973), pp. 150–58; John G. Clark et al. *Three Generations in Twentieth Century America: Family, Community, and Nation* (Homewood, Ill.: Dorsey Press, 1977), pp. 32–33.

12. Slayton, *Back of the Yards,* pp. 49–52; Handlin, *The Uprooted,* pp. 160–66; Jay P. Dolan, *The Immigrant Church: New York's Irish and German Catholics, 1815–1865* (Notre Dame: Notre Dame University Press, 1983 [1975]), pp. 45–86; Orsi, *The Madonna of 115th Street,* pp. 50–74; Clark et al., *Three Generations,* pp. 37–39; Morris Janowitz, *The Community Press in an Urban Setting: The Social Elements of Urbanism* 2nd ed. (Chicago: University of Chicago Press, 1967). Janowitz notes the gradual disappearance of the community press in the 1950s as the mass media played more important roles. He expresses concern for the continued vitality of ethnic communities.

13. Curti, *The Making of an American Community,* pp. 111–12; Wolf, *Urban Village,* pp. 236–38; James West, *Plainville, U.S.A.* (New York: Columbia University Press, 1945), pp. 30–31; Slayton, *Back of the Yards,* pp. 49–52; Herbert J. Gans, *The Urban Villagers: Group and Class in the Life of Italian-Americans* (New York: Free Press, 1962), pp. 160–61; Walter I. Trattner, *From Poor Law to Welfare State: A History of Social Welfare in America* (New York: Free Press, 1984), pp. 155–78. Charity and welfare remained community efforts until the Great Depression overwhelmed local agencies.

14. Wall, *Fierce Communion,* pp. 13–29. The bulk of her book consists of looking at cases of arbitration and litigation that she sees as exceptions to the rule.

15. Lewis Atherton, *Main Street on the Middle Border* (Chicago: Quadrangle, 1966 [1954]), pp. 3–64, 183–84; Curti, *The Making of an American Community,* pp. 111–36; Thomas and Znaniecki, *The Polish Peasant,* pp. 87–88; Margaret Jarman Hagood, *Mothers of the South: Portraiture of the White Tenant Farm Woman* (New York: W. W. Norton, 1977 [1939]), pp. 170–82; West, *Plainville, U.S.A.,* pp. 96–99; Robert S. Lynd and Helen M. Lynd, *Middletown* (New York: Harcourt Brace, 1929), pp. 3–17. See Colin M. Turnbull's discussion of settling disputes among central African communities in *The Forest People: A Study of the Pygmies of the Congo* (New York: Clarion, 1961), pp. 94–125. Turnbull shows drought and famine breaking down communal norms, resulting in an amoral, atomized social structure in *The Mountain People* (New York: Touchstone, 1972), pp. 155–82. (I thank Barrington Moore for these references.)

16. Atherton, *Main Street,* pp. 181–216; Richard D. Altick, *Of a Place and a Time: Remembering Lancaster* (Hamden, Conn.: Archon, 1991); Dolan, *The Immigrant Church,* pp. 27–44.

17. Adams quote from Hudson, *Religion in America,* p. 101. See also Merle Curti, *The Roots of American Loyalty* (New York: Columbia University Press, 1946), pp. 53–58, 92–121; Curti, *Growth of American Thought,* pp. 72–74; Carl Bridenbaugh, *The Spirit of '76: The Growth of American Patriotism before Independence* (New York: Oxford University Press, 1975), pp. 40–72.

18. Brooks, *The Flowering of New England, 1815–1865* (New York: Dutton, 1937), p. 86. See also pp. 135–46, 323–42.

19. Ruth Miller Elson, *Guardians of Tradition: American Schoolbooks of the Nineteenth Century* (Lincoln: University of Nebraska Press, 1964), pp. 166–85; Parrington, *Main*

Currents in American Thought, II; Curti, *The Roots of American Loyalty*, pp. 30–52; Michael Kammen, *Mystic Chords of Memory: The Transformation of Tradition in American Culture* (New York: Knopf, 1991), pp. 17–90; Roderick Nash, *Wilderness and the American Mind* (New Haven: Yale University Press, 1973), pp. 67–82.

20. Curti, *Growth of American Thought*, pp. 396–413; Curti, *The Roots of American Loyalty*, pp. 127–28; Henry Steele Commager, *The American Mind: An Interpretation of American Thought and Character since the 1880s* (New Haven: Yale University Press, 1978), pp. 39–48; Bessie Louise Pierce, *Public Opinion and the Teaching of History in the United States* (New York: Knopf, 1926); Bessie Louise Pierce, *Civic Attitudes in American School Textbooks* (Chicago: University of Chicago Press, 1930), pp. 3–67, 102–50; Handlin, *The Uprooted*, pp. 184–268.

21. William James, "The Moral Equivalence of War," in *Writings, 1902–1910*, ed. Bruce Kuklick (New York: The Library of America, 1987), pp. 1281–93. See also Robert Nisbet, *The Quest for Community* (Oxford: Oxford University Press, 1969 [1953]), pp. 38–44; Morris Janowitz, *The Reconstruction of Patriotism: Education for Civic Consciousness* (Chicago: University of Chicago Press, 1983), p. 84-85.

22. Dixon Wecter, *The Hero in America: A Chronicle of Hero Worship* (New York: Scribner's, 1969 [1941]), pp. 1–16, 50–147.

23. Curti, *Roots of American Loyalty*, p. 152; Steven Watts, *The Republic Reborn: War and the Making of Liberal America, 1790–1820* (Baltimore: Johns Hopkins University Press, 1987), pp. 283–98; Donald R. Hickey, *The War of 1812: A Forgotten Conflict* (Urbana: University of Illinois Press, 1989), pp. 29–51. Horace Mann, architect of public education in early America, decried the emphasis on war in schoolbooks. It served to "cultivate all the dissocial emotions, and turn the whole current of the mental forces into the channel of destructiveness." Quoted in Christopher Lasch, *The Revolt of the Elites and the Betrayal of Democracy* (New York: W. W. Norton, 1993), p. 149.

24. Grant, *Personal Memoirs*, p. 152. See also Thomas R. Kemp, "Community and War: The Civil War Experience of Two New Hampshire Towns," in Maris A. Vinovskis, ed., *Toward a Social History of the Civil War: Exploratory Essays* (New York: Cambridge University Press, 1990), pp. 31–77.

25. James M. McPherson, *For Cause and Comrades: Why Men Fought in the Civil War* (New York: Oxford University Press, 1997), pp. 14–29; Curti, *The Making of an American Community*, pp. 131–36; Commager, *The American Mind*, pp. 160–72; J. Matthew Gallman, "Voluntarism in Wartime: Philadelphia's Great Central Fair," in Vinovskis, ed., *Social History of the Civil War*, pp. 93–116.

26. Gerald F. Linderman, *Embattled Courage: The Experience of Combat in the American Civil War* (New York: Free Press, 1987), pp. 266–97; Charles William Wilson, *Baptized in Blood: The Religion of the Lost Cause* (Athens: University of Georgia Press, 1980), pp. 18–36. See also W. Lloyd Warner's look at Memorial Day rites in his *American Life: Dream and Reality* (Chicago: University of Chicago Press, 1964 [1953]), pp. 2–34.

27. David M. Kennedy, *Over Here: The First World War and American Society* (New York: Oxford University Press, 1980), pp. 45–50.

28. Commager, *The American Mind*, p. 39.

29. See Curti, *The Roots of American Loyalty*, pp. 55–60, 122–27; Kennedy, *Over Here*, pp. 70–83; Janowitz, *The Reconstruction of Patriotism*, pp. 1–42.

30. Russell F. Weigley, *The American Way of War: A History of United States Military Strategy and Policy* (Bloomington: Indiana University Press, 1973), p. 130; C. Vann Woodward, *The Future of the Past* (New York: Oxford University Press, 1989), p. 80; John D. McDermott, "Custer and the Little Big Horn Story: What It All Means," in Charles E. Rankin, ed., *Legacy: New Perspectives on the Battle of the Little Bighorn* (Helena: Montana Historical Society Press, 1996), p. 96.

31. De Tocqueville, *Democracy in America* I: 303; II: 6.

32. Hudson, *Religion in America*, p. 11.

33. Robert N. Bellah, *The Broken Covenant: American Civil Religion in Time of Trial* (Chicago: University of Chicago Press, 1992), pp. 5–35; Hudson, *Religion in America*, pp. 12–22; Merle Curti, *The Growth of American Thought*, 3rd ed. (New York: Harper & Row, 1964), pp. 4–6.

34. Bridenbaugh, *The Spirit of '76*, pp. 80–84; Paul R. Lucas, "The Origin of the Great Awakening in New England," *The Historian* 59 (1997): 741–58; Hudson, *Religion in America*, pp. 12–22, 101.

35. Carl Bridenbaugh, *Cities in Revolt: Urban Life in America, 1743–1776* (New York: Oxford University Press, 1971 [1955]), pp. 352–58, 373–417; Bridenbaugh, *The Spirit of '76*, pp. 84–92, 118–20; Bernhard Knollenberg, *Origin of the American Revolution: 1759–1766* (New York: Free Press, 1960), pp. 76–86; Curti, *The Growth of American Thought*, pp. 4–6; Bushman, *From Puritan to Yankee*, pp. 235–56.

36. John W. Blassingame, *The Slave Community: Plantation Life in the Antebellum South* (New York: Oxford University Press, 1972), pp. 126–30.

37. Adams, *The Education of Henry Adams* (New York: Modern Library, 1931 [1918]), p. 48.

38. Brooks, *The Flowering of New England*, pp. 388–89.

39. Arthur J. Vidich and Stanford M. Lyman, *American Sociology: Worldly Rejections of Religion and Their Directions* (New Haven: Yale University Press, 1985), pp. 22, 75–76.

40. Obviously, this draws from Max Weber's *The Protestant Ethic and the Spirit of Capitalism* (New York: Scribner's, 1976 [1905]). See also Daniel T. Rodgers, *The Work Ethic in Industrial America, 1850–1920* (Chicago: University of Chicago Press, 1978), pp. 1–64.

41. Allan Nevins, quoted in Commager, *The American Mind*, p. 426. See also Bodnar et al., *Lives of Their Own*, pp. 74–82.

42. Atherton, *Main Street*, pp. 65–105.

43. Quote from Lerner, *America as a Civilization*, pp. 10, 897. See also Parrington,

Main Currents in American Thought, I: 3–15; Bellah, *The Broken Covenant*, pp. 1–44; Barry Kosmin and Seymour P. Lachman, *One Nation under God: Religion in Contemporary American Society* (New York: Harmony Books, 1993), pp. 21–23; Perry Miller, *The New England Mind*, vol. 2 (Boston: Beacon Press, 1961), pp. 463–69; Lewis Perry, *Intellectual Life in America: A History* (Chicago: University of Chicago Press, 1984), pp. 4–5; Curti, *The Roots of American Loyalty*, pp. 53–55; Hudson, *Religion in America*, pp. 12–22.

    44. Carl Bridenbaugh, *Cities in Revolt*, pp. 172–209; De Tocqueville, *Democracy in America* II: 33–55; Curti, *Growth of American Thought*, pp. 335–57; Dolan, *The Immigrant Church*, pp. 99–120; Brooks, *The Flowering of New England*, pp. 172–95; Russell Blaine Nye, *The Cultural Life of the New Nation, 1776–1830* (New York: Harper & Row, 1960), pp. 150–70; Hudson, *Religion in America*, pp. 150–54.

    45. Thomas and Znaniecki, *The Polish Peasant in Europe and America*, pp. 210 ff; Billington, *America's Frontier Heritage*, pp. 73–95. Grossman, *Land of Hope*, pp. 246–58.

    46. Nye, *The Cultural Life of the New Nation*, pp. 54–95; James MacGregor Burns, *The Workshop of Democracy: The American Experiment*, vol. 2 (New York: Knopf, 1985), pp. 76–83.

    47. On the role of the frontier in mythic American thought see Francis Parkman, *The Oregon Trail* (New York: Library of America, 1991 [1847]); Frederick Jackson Turner, *The Frontier in American History* (New York: Holt, Rinehart and Winston, 1962); Billington, *America's Frontier Heritage*, pp. 1–22; Henry Nash Smith, *Virgin Land: The American West as Symbol and Myth* (Cambridge, Mass.: Harvard University Press, 1978 [1950]); Nash, *Wilderness and the American Mind*, pp. 141–60; George Dangerfield, *The Era of Good Feelings* (New York: Harcourt, Brace & World, 1963), pp. 105–21; William Tecumseh Sherman, *Memoirs of General W. T. Sherman* (New York: Library of America, 1990), pp. 35–152; Richard Slotkin, *Gunfighter Nation: The Myth of the Frontier in Twentieth-Century America* (New York: Atheneum, 1992); Perry Miller, *Life of the Mind*, pp. 99–104.

    48. See Weber, *The Protestant Ethic*; Edmund S. Morgan, ed., *Puritan Political Ideas, 1558–1794* (New York: Bobbs Merrill, 1965), pp. 35–59; *The Puritan Family: Religion and Domestic Relations in Seventeenth-Century New England* (New York: Harper & Row, 1966), pp. 3–12, 65–74; Warren I. Susman, *Culture as History: The Transformation of American Society in the Twentieth Century* (New York: Pantheon, 1984), pp. 41–43.

    49. De Tocqueville, *Democracy in America*, II: 128–33.

    50. Robert N. Bellah and Phillip E. Hammond, *Varieties of Civil Religion* (San Francisco: Harper & Row, 1980), pp. 16–17.

    51. David M. Potter, *People of Plenty: Economic Abundance and the American Character* (Chicago: University of Chicago Press, 1954), pp. 78–110.

    52. *Haven in a Heartless World*, pp. 3–4.

    53. On the sacred aspects of war in local ritual see Warner, *American Life*, pp. 5–19. See also Gary Laderman, *The Sacred Remains: American Attitudes toward Death, 1799–1883* (New Haven: Yale University Press, 1996), pp. 123–43.

54. G. P. Gooch, *History and Historians in the Nineteenth Century* (Boston: Beacon Press, 1959), pp. 377–83; Richard Hofstadter, *The Progressive Historians: Turner, Beard, Parrington* (New York: Knopf, 1969), pp. 3–43.

Chapter Two

1. *The Education of Henry Adams* (New York: Modern Library, 1931), pp. 499–500.

2. Quoted in Merle Curti, *The Growth of American Thought* 3rd ed. (New York: Harper & Row, 1964), p. 507. See also Michael Kimmel, *Manhood in America: A Cultural History* (New York: Free Press, 1996), pp. 82–84.

3. Adams, *The Education*, pp. 344–45.

4. On the populist and progressive movements see John D. Hicks, *The Populist Revolt: A History of the Farmers' Alliance and the Peoples' Party* (Lincoln: University of Nebraska Press, 1961 [1931]); C. Vann Woodward, *Tom Watson: Agrarian Rebel* (New York: Oxford University Press, 1963 [1938]); Richard Hofstadter, *The Age of Reform: From Bryan to F.D.R.* (New York: Knopf, 1955).

5. Cotton Mather, quoted in Richard L. Bushman, *From Puritan to Yankee: Character and the Social Order in Connecticut, 1690–1765* (Cambridge, Mass.: Harvard University Press, 1967), p. 23 (emphasis in original). Mather also warned that affluence would erode religiousness: "There is venom in *Riches* disposing our depraved Hearts to cast off their *Dependence* on *God*." op. cit., p. 188. Ironically, an important reason for the Puritans' departure from England was fear that the sect was becoming too materialistic. See Andrew Delbanco, *The Puritan Ordeal* (Cambridge, Mass: Harvard University Press, 1989), pp. 41–117.

6. Daniel T. Rodgers, *The Work Ethic in Industrial America, 1850–1920* (Chicago: University of Chicago Press, 1978), p. 95.

7. Rodgers, *The Work Ethic in Industrial America*, pp. 94–124; Lewis A. Erenberg, *Steppin' Out: New York Nightlife and the Transformation of American Culture, 1890–1930* (Chicago: University of Chicago Press, 1981), pp. 33–58; Thorstein Veblen, *The Theory of the Leisure Class* (Boston: Houghton Mifflin, 1973 [1899]); Lewis Atherton, *Main Street on the Middle Border* (Chicago: Quadrangle, 1966 [1954]), pp. 217–42.

8. Theodora Penny Martin, *The Sound of Our Own Voices: Women's Study Clubs, 1860–1910* (Boston: Beacon Press, 1987); Anne Ruggles Gere, *Intimate Practices: Literacy and Cultural Work in U. S. Women's Clubs, 1880–1920* (Urbana: University of Illinois Press, 1997).

9. Lincoln Steffens, *The Shame of the Cities* (New York: Hill and Wang, [1904] 1960), p. 7. The author of *Democracy*, it was later learned, was Henry Adams. See also C. Vann Woodward, "A Southern Critique of the Gilded Age," in his *The Burden of Southern History* 3rd ed. (Baton Rouge: Louisiana University Press, 1993), pp. 109–40; Mark Wahlgren Summers, *The Era of Good Stealings* (New York: Oxford University Press, 1993).

10. Jeremy Atack and Peter Passell, *A New Economic View of American History* (New

York: W. W. Norton, 1994), pp. 457–88; James L. Abrahamson, *The American Home Front: Revolutionary War, Civil War, World War I, World War II* (Washington D.C.: National Defense University Press, 1983), pp. 49–51, 69–71.

11. Russell F. Weigley, *The American Way of War: A History of United States Military Strategy and Policy* (Bloomington: Indiana University Press, 1973), pp. 128–52; Abrahamson, *The American Home Front*, pp. 44–71; Richard Franklin Bensel, *Yankee Leviathan: The Origins of Central State Authority in America, 1859–1877* (Cambridge: Cambridge University Press, 1990).

12. Quoted in Paul Fussell, *Wartime: Understanding and Behavior in the Second World War* (New York: Oxford University Press, 1989), pp. 10–11.

13. Robert Penn Warren, *The Legacy of the Civil War: Meditations on the Centennial* (New York: Random House, 1961), p. 46.

14. Quoted in Merle Curti, *The Growth of American Thought*, p. 465. Summers, though seeing the war as contributing to corruption, urges the reader not to exaggerate the influence of the war on public life. See *Era of Good Stealings*, pp. 16–29.

15. "Puritanism as a Literary Force," in George K. Anderson and Eda Lou Walton, eds., *This Generation: A Selection of British and American Literature from 1914 to the Present with Historical and Critical Essays* (Chicago: Scott, Foresman, 1939), pp. 118–19.

16. Warren, *The Legacy of the Civil War*, p. 64.

17. On growing discontent among women see Carl N. Degler, *At Odds: Women and the Family in America from the Revolution to the Present* (New York: Oxford University Press, 1980), pp. 178 ff.

18. Quoted in Arthur M. Schlesinger, Jr., *The Crisis of the Old Order, 1919–1933* (Boston: Houghton Mifflin, 1957), p. 75.

19. William James, "The Moral Equivalence of War," in *Writings, 1902–1910*, ed. Bruce Kuklick (New York: Library of America, 1987), pp. 1281–93; Gerald F. Linderman, *Embattled Courage: The Experience of Combat in the American Civil War* (New York: Free Press, 1987), pp. 290–94; Kimmel, *Manhood in America*, pp. 70–78.

20. Linderman, *Embattled Courage*, pp. 290–94.

21. Quoted in Edmund Wilson, *Patriotic Gore: Studies in the Literature of the American Civil War* (New York: Oxford University Press, 1962), p. 759.

22. Quoted in John Mueller, *Retreat from Doomsday: The Obsolescence of Major War* (New York: Basic Books, 1989), p. 39. See also *Hero Tales of the American Soldier and Sailor: The Unwritten History of American Chivalry* (n.p.: Hero Publishing, 1899).

23. Edward M. Coffman, *The War to End All Wars: The American Military Experience in World War I* (New York: Oxford University Press, 1968), pp. 54–85.

24. Quoted in Meirion and Susie Harries, *The Last Days of Innocence: America at War, 1917–1918* (New York: Random House, 1997), p. 193.

25. David M. Kennedy, *Over Here: The First World War and American Society* (New York: Oxford University Press, 1980), pp. 144–230.

26. Arno Mayer, *The Persistence of the Old Regime: Europe to the Great War* (New York: Pantheon, 1981), pp. 304–29; Mark Girouard, *The Return to Camelot: Chivalry and the English Gentleman* (New Haven: Yale University Press, 1981), pp. 276–93.

27. Quoted in David M. Kennedy, *Freedom from Fear: The American People in Depression and War, 1929–1945* (New York: Oxford University Press, 1999), p. 1.

28. Richard Bessel, *Germany after the First World War* (Oxford: Clarendon, 1993); Eugen Weber, *The Hollow Years: France in the 1930s* (New York: W. W. Norton, 1994).

29. From Wilfred Owen, *Dulce et Decorum Est.*

30. "Common Form," quoted in Paul Fussell, *The Norton Book of Modern War* (New York: W. W. Norton, 1991), p. 104.

31. Arnold Toynbee, *War and Civilization* (New York: Oxford University Press, 1950), p. 130. The volume is culled from essays written shortly after the Great War. On pessimism, especially reduced faith in reason, brought about by the destruction of the Napoleonic Wars, see Alfred Cobban, *In Search of Humanity: The Role of the Enlightenment in Modern History* (New York: George Braziller, 1960), pp. 214–21.

32. Toynbee, *War and Civilization*, pp. 164–65.

33. See Charles S. Maier, *Recasting Bourgeois Europe: Stabilization in France, Germany, and Italy in the Decade after World War I* (Princeton, N. J.: Princeton University Press, 1975), pp. 19–134. The mood is especially clear in literature. See Anderson and Walton, eds., *This Generation*, passim; Paul Fussell *The Great War and Modern Memory* (New York: Oxford University Press, 1975); Malcolm Cowley, *The Exile's Return: A Literary Odyssey of the 1920s* (New York: Viking, 1951 [1934]).

34. *Beyond the Pleasure Principle* (1920). Freud's development of the death instinct concept can be traced in his wartime changes to the "Little Hans" case history.

35. Quoted in Arthur Marwick, *The Deluge: British Society and the First World War* (New York: W. W. Norton, 1965), pp. 108–09.

36. Lancelot Law Whyte, quoted in Herbert J. Muller, *The Uses of the Past: Profiles of Former Societies* (New York: Oxford University Press, 1952), pp. 122–23.

37. Simone Weil, *The Need for Roots* (Boston: Beacon, 1952 [1943]), p. 130. See also Marwick, *The Deluge*, pp. 279–314.

38. Harold E. Stearns, ed., *Civilization in the United States: An Inquiry by Thirty Americans* (New York: Harcourt, Brace, 1922). See also Van Wyck Brooks, *New England: Indian Summer, 1865–1915* (Cleveland: World, 1946), pp. 250–75, 474–90; Samuel Hynes, *The Soldiers' Tale: Bearing Witness to Modern War* (Harmondsworth, U.K.: Penguin, 1997), pp. 31–107.

39. Sydney Bradshaw Fay, *The Origins of the World War*, 2 vols. (New York: Free Press, 1966 [1928–30]); Randolph S. Bourne, *War and the Intellectuals: Collected Essays, 1915–1919* (New York: Harper & Row, 1964), pp. 3–14. See also the antiwar aspects of populism in Woodward, *Tom Watson*, pp. 451–74. For romantic views of the causes of the war see John Jay Chapman, *Deutschland über Alles, or Germany Speaks* (New York: G. P. Putnam's Sons,

1914); Christian Gauss, *America in the War: Why We Went to War* (New York: Scribner's, 1918); Josiah Royce, *The Hope of the Great Community* (Freeport, N.Y.: Books for Libraries Press, 1967 [1916]).

40. Mencken, "Puritanism as a Literary Force," in Anderson and Walton, eds., *This Generation*, p. 118. Ostensibly, he speaks of the Civil War, but with an animus stemming from the Great War as well as an oblique reference to it.

41. Peter Novick, *That Noble Dream: The "Objectivity Question" and the American Historical Profession* (New York: Cambridge University Press, 1988), pp. 111–18.

42. Charles A. Beard, *An Economic Interpretation of the Constitution of the United States* (New York: Macmillan, 1962 [1913]). See also James Harvey Robinson, *The New History: Essays Illustrating the Modern Historical Outlook* (New York: Free Press, 1965 [1912]).

43. Quoted in Novick, *That Noble Dream*, p. 96 and Richard Hofstadter, *The Progressive Historians: Turner, Beard, Parrington* (New York: Knopf, 1969), pp. 212–13.

44. See Carl Becker, *The Declaration of Independence: A Study in the History of Political Ideas* (New York: Vintage Press, 1959 [1922]); Albert K. Weinberg, *Manifest Destiny: A Study of Nationalist Expansionism in American History* (Chicago: Quadrangle Books, 1963 [1935]); Frederick Lewis Allen, *Only Yesterday: An Informal History of the Nineteen-Twenties* (New York: Harper & Row, 1931), pp. 196–97; Novick, *That Noble Dream*, pp. 92–132; Gary B. Nash, Charlotte Crabtree, and Ross E. Dunn, *History on Trial: Culture Wars and the Teaching of the Past* (New York: Knopf, 1998), pp. 36–52.

45. Quoted in Kennedy, *Over Here*, p. 223 (see also pp. 220–30). See also Curti, *The Growth of American Thought*, pp. 667–78; Lewis Perry, *Intellectual Life in America: A History* (Chicago: University of Chicago Press, 1984), pp. 370–76; William E. Leuchtenburg, *The Perils of Prosperity, 1914–32* (Chicago: University of Chicago Press, 1958), pp. 142–44.

46. William March, *Company K* (Tuscaloosa: University of Alabama Press, 1989 [1933]), pp. 104–5.

47. Fussell, *The Great War*, pp. 21–23.

48. See Stanley Cooperman, *World War One and the American Novel* (Baltimore: Johns Hopkins University Press, 1967), pp. 5–13. On high- and low-culture accounts of the war see Kennedy, *Over Here*, pp. 228–29.

49. Erich Maria Remarque, *All Quiet on the Western Front* (Boston: Little, Brown, 1929); Arnold Zweig, *Education before Verdun* (New York: Viking, 1936). The former's impact on many interwar youths was wholly unintended. It was read as an action novel. See George L. Mosse, *Fallen Soldiers: Reshaping the Memory of the World Wars* (New York: Oxford University Press, 1990), p. 142. Hynes notes that the horrors of war described in literature and film were only dimly comprehended by boys and became an attraction. See *The Soldiers' Tale*, pp. 109–10.

50. Terry Christensen, *Reel Politics: American Political Movies from Birth of a Nation to Platoon* (Oxford: Basil Blackwell, 1987), pp. 24–29.

51. *The Wine of the Puritans: A Study of Present-Day America* (Folcroft, Penn.: Folcroft Press, 1958 [1908]), pp. 14–15. Had Brooks called for a more relevant curriculum, he might pass for a student activist from the 1960s.

52. Sydney E. Ahlstrom, *A Religious History of the American People* (New Haven: Yale University Press, 1972), pp. 877–89.

53. "The Archangel Woodrow," in *The Vintage Mencken*, ed. Alistair Cooke (New York: Vintage, 1990), pp. 116–20.

54. Quoted in Esmond Wright, "Historians and the Revolution," in his edited work, *Causes and Consequences of the Revolution* (Chicago: Quadrangle, 1966), p. 40.

55. Quoted in Malcolm Cowley, *The Exile's Return,* p. 60.

56. Vernon L. Parrington, *Main Currents in American Thought: An Interpretation of American Literature from the Beginnings to 1920* (New York: Harcourt, Brace, 1930), I: 21, 15.

57. Erenberg, *Steppin' Out,* pp. 234–35; Mabel A. Elliot and Francis E. Merrill, *Social Disorganization,* rev. ed. (New York: Harper & Brothers, 1941), pp. 864–96.

58. Quoted in Schlesinger, *The Crisis of the Old Order,* p. 74.

59. James J. Flink, *The Car Culture* (Cambridge, Mass.: MIT Press, 1975), pp. 140–51.

60. Ellis W. Hawley, *The Great War and the Search for a Modern Order: A History of the American People and Their Institutions, 1917-1933* (New York: St. Martin's Press, 1979), pp. 165–69.

61. David M. Potter, *People of Plenty: Economic Abundance and the American Character* (Chicago: University of Chicago Press, 1954), pp. 166–88; Leuchtenburg, *The Perils of Prosperity,* pp. 178–203; Atherton, *Main Street,* pp. 295–99; Stuart Ewen, *Captains of Consciousness: Advertising and the Social Roots of the Consumer Culture* (New York: McGraw-Hill, 1976), pp. 23–67; James Lincoln Collier, *The Rise of Selfishness in America* (New York: Oxford University Press, 1991), pp. 145–61. On similar events in postwar Britain see Robert Graves and Alan Hodge, *The Long Week-End: A Social History of Great Britain, 1918–1939* (New York: W. W. Norton, 1963 [1940]), pp. 171–90.

62. Lawrence W. Levine, *Defender of the Faith: William Jennings Bryan: The Last Decade, 1915–1925* (New York: Oxford University Press, 1965), pp. 128–31; Stanley Coben, *Rebellion against Victorianism: The Impetus for Cultural Change in 1920s America* (New York: Oxford University Press, 1991), pp. 91–111; Susan Ware, *Beyond Suffrage: Women in the New Deal* (Cambridge, Mass.: Harvard University Press, 1981), pp. 32, 61–63. Ware notes that wars tend to increase the numbers of women in government.

63. Hawley, *The Great War and the Search for a Modern Order,* pp. 28–29; Leuchtenburg, *The Perils of Prosperity,* pp. 158–77; Allen, *Only Yesterday,* pp. 73–101; Preston William Slosson, *The Great Crusade and After, 1914–1928* (New York: Macmillan, 1969 [1930]), pp. 154–61; Ewen, *Captains of Consciousness,* pp. 159–76. See also Graves and Hodge, *The Long Week-End,* pp. 36–49.

64. Ellen K. Rothman, *Hands and Hearts: A History of Courtship in America* (Cambridge, Mass.: Harvard University Press, 1987), pp. 203–44; Elliot and Merrill, *Social Disorganization*, pp. 845–46.

65. Robert S. Lynd and Helen M. Lynd, *Middletown* (New York: Harcourt Brace, 1929), pp. 110–78; Ewen, *Captains of Consciousness*, pp. 139–49; Rothman, *Hands and Hearts*, pp. 285–311; Steven Mintz and Susan Kellogg, *Domestic Revolutions: A Social History of American Family Life* (New York: Free Press, 1988), pp. 118–25.

66. Ahlstrom, *Religious History*, pp. 915–17. See also Jessie L. Weston, *From Ritual to Romance* (1919) and Sigmund Freud, *The Future of an Illusion* (1920).

67. Quotes from Leuchtenburg, *Perils of Prosperity*, pp. 187–89. See also Allen, *Only Yesterday*, pp. 146–50; Ewen, *Captains of Consciousness*, pp. 23–67.

68. Hawley, *The Great War and the Search for a Modern Order*, pp. 146–47. Max Weber, of course, noted the tension between material success and religion in *The Protestant Ethic and the Spirit of Capitalism* (New York: Scribner's, 1976 [1905]).

69. Quoted in Ahlstrom, *Religious History*, pp. 915–16.

70. Kennedy, *Freedom from Fear*, pp. 19–22; Atherton, *Main Street*, pp. 299–300; Lawrence W. Levine, *Defender of the Faith: William Jennings Bryan: The Last Decade, 1915–1925* (New York: Oxford University Press, 1965), pp. 254–60.

71. Meirion and Susie Harries, *The Last Days of Innocence*, pp. 135–41, 437–38.

72. Allen, *Only Yesterday*, pp. 38–72; Gregory D. Black, *Hollywood Censored: Morality Codes, Catholics, and the Movies* (Cambridge: Cambridge University Press, 1994), pp. 3–29.

73. See Mencken's essay in Stearns, ed., *Civilization in the United States*, and also his "Mush for the Multitude," in Roderick Nash, ed., *The Call of the Wild* (New York: George Braziller, 1970), pp. 132–36; Hawley, *The Great War and the Search for a Modern Order*, pp. 165–69. See also Graves and Hodge, *The Long Week-End*, pp. 56–63.

74. Atherton, *Main Street*, p. 181.

75. Abrahamson, *The American Home Front*, p. 94.

76. Kennedy, *Freedom from Fear*, pp. 16–17.

77. Elliot and Merrill, *Social Disorganization*, pp. 841–43; Max Lerner, *America as a Civilization: Life and Thought in the United States Today* (New York: Simon & Schuster, 1957), pp. 139–55; Richard Lingeman, *Small Town America: A Narrative History, 1620–the Present* (Boston: Houghton Mifflin, 1980), pp. 396–97.

78. Hawley, *The Great War and the Search for a Modern Order*, pp. 150–54. Hawley notes an increase in formal associations, which, in his view, compensated for the loss of traditional community. The present view is that such associations are unable to maintain social norms as older communities did.

79. Quoted in Flink, *The Car Culture*, p. 145.

80. Flink, *The Car Culture*, pp. 151–60.

81. See Hawley, *The Great War and the Search for a Modern Order*, pp. 137–38. Contemporary sources include: William Fielding Ogburn, *American Marriage and Family*

Relationships (New York: H. Holt, 1928); Ernest Groves, *The American Family* (Chicago: J. B. Lippincott, 1934).

82. Ewen, *Captains of Consciousness,* pp. 113–38.

83. On the demise of reform during the Great War see Hawley, *The Great War and the Search for a Modern Order,* pp. 23–24; David P. Thelen, *Robert M. La Follette and the Insurgent Spirit* (Madison: University of Wisconsin Press, 1985), pp. 125–54.

84. Archibald Wavell (a field marshal in World War II). Quoted in David Fromkin, *A Peace to End All Peace: The Fall of the Ottoman Empire and the Creation of the Modern Middle East* (New York: Henry Holt, 1989), p. 5. See also Kennedy, *Over Here,* pp. 231–95, 348–69.

85. Walter Karp, *The Politics of War: The Story of Two Wars which Altered Forever the Political Life of the American Republic (1890–1920)* (New York: Harper Collins, 1979), p. 325.

86. Levine, *Defender of the Faith,* pp. 218–92; Stanley Coben, *Rebellion against Victorianism,* pp. 136–56.

87. Suicide rates from *Vital Statistics Rates in the United States,* U.S. Dept. of Health, Education and Welfare, 1968, p. 99.

88. F. Scott Fitzgerald, *The Crack Up* (New York: New Directions, 1956), p. 20. Many economic historians argue that the crash of 1929 had little if anything to do with the Depression, and that the business cycle and faulty monetary policy were to blame. Inasmuch as most Americans believed the crash caused the downturn, it remains part of the present narrative.

89. Ahlstrom, *Religious History,* pp. 918–23.

90. Glen H. Elder, Jr., *Children of the Great Depression: Social Change in Life Experience* (Chicago: University of Chicago Press, 1974), pp. 49–117.

91. Robert S. and Helen M. Lynd, *Middletown in Transition* (New York: Harcourt Brace, 1965 [1937]), pp. 152–55.

92. Quoted in the Lynds, *Middletown in Transition,* pp. 146–47. This classic study of Depression-era Muncie found a general falling back on earlier values, though also increased social strains. Many community associations declined as people could no longer afford dues; community welfare programs were overwhelmed and replaced by federal relief agencies. See also W. Lloyd Warner, et al., *Democracy in Jonesville: A Study of Quality and Inequality* (New York: Harper & Brothers, 1949), pp. 115 ff. (The study's research was conducted during the Depression.)

93. Dan Morgan, *Rising in the West: The True Story of an 'Okie' Family from the Great Depression through the Reagan Years* (New York: Knopf, 1992), p. 133 (see also pp. 126–33). Morgan's study of an Okie family finds many differences with Steinbeck's fictional Joad family. Whereas the Joads find religion no longer providing any answers, Morgan's study finds continued if not strengthened faith. Morgan also found distrust of government and unions, again in contrast to the Joads.

94. See Charles R. Hearn, *The American Dream in the Great Depression* (Westport, Conn.: Greenwood Press, 1977), pp. 56–80; Emanuel Levy, *Small-Town America in Film: The Decline and Fall of Community* (New York: Continuum, 1991).

95. *Vital Statistics Rates in the United States* (U.S. Dept. of Health, Education and Welfare, 1968), p. 99. See also Robert S. McElvaine, ed., *Down and Out in the Great Depression: Letters from the Forgotten Man* (Chapel Hill: University of North Carolina Press, 1983).

96. Elliot and Merrill, *Social Disorganization*, pp. 838–89; Arthur J. Vidich and Joseph Bensman, *Small Town in Mass Society* (Princeton: Princeton University Press, 1958), pp. 11–13.

97. The Lynds, *Middletown in Transition*, pp. 102–43.

98. Kimmel, *Manhood in America,* pp. 216–221; Elliot and Merrill, *Social Disorganization*, pp. 425–54.

99. Ahlstrom, *Religious History*, pp. 918–31; The Lynds, *Middletown in Transition*, pp. 300–18. Elliott and Merrill noted a decline in church attendance in their "Centerville." See *Social Disorganization*, p. 787.

100. The Lynds, *Middletown in Transition*, pp. 317–18.

101. Kennedy, *Freedom from Fear*, pp. 62–103.

102. Quoted in McElvaine, *Down and Out*, p. 34. See also Hawley, *The Great War and the Search for a Modern Order*, pp. 180–86.

103. Charles A. and Mary R. Beard, *America in Midpassage* Vol. I (New York: Macmillan, 1939), pp. 69–83, 156–91. They also argued that the media were drumming up support for another foolhardy war in Europe, which would only profit big business, as had World War I. See also Thurman Arnold, *The Folklore of Capitalism* (New Haven: Yale University Press, 1937), pp. 46–82.

104. See also Morgan, *Rising in the West*; Kevin Starr, *Endangered Dreams: The Great Depression in California* (New York: Oxford University Press, 1996).

105. See Hearn, *The American Dream*, pp. 82–85.

106. Quoted in Catherine McNicol Stock, *Main Street in Crisis: The Great Depression and the Old Middle Class on the Northern Plains* (Chapel Hill: University of North Carolina Press, 1992), p. 140. See also her *Rural Radicals: Righteous Rage in the American Grain* (Ithaca: Cornell University Press, 1996), pp. 139–42.

107. Quote from Schlesinger, *The Crisis of the Old Order*, p. 256. See also William E. Leuchtenburg, *Franklin D. Roosevelt and the New Deal, 1932–1940* (New York: Harper & Row, 1963), pp. 1–40; Malcolm Cowley, *The Dream of the Golden Mountains: Remembering the 1930s* (New York: Viking, 1980), pp. 83–93, 149–66.

108. Schlesinger, *The Crisis of the Old Order*, pp. 67–69; Hawley, *The Great War and the Search for a Modern Order*, pp. 205–11.

109. Kennedy, *Freedom from Fear*, pp. 218–48; Schlesinger, *The Crisis of the Old Order*, pp. 258–63. A contemporary discussion of this political crossroads is found in Lyman

Bryson, *Which Way America? Communism, Fascism, Democracy* (New York: Macmillan, 1939). See also *Gabriel over the White House* (New York: Farrar and Rinehart, 1933).

110. Kennedy, *Freedom from Fear*, pp. 147–48, 177–78; Hawley, *The Great War and the Search for a Modern Order*, pp. 1–11, 219–29. It might be noted that the TVA, cornerstone of the New Deal, began as a power plant for a nitrate mine near Muscle Shoals, Alabama deemed essential for explosives production. On social mobilization during war see Walter Lippmann, *The Good Society* (Boston: Little, Brown, 1937), pp. 89–90.

111. Charles P. Kindleberger, *The World Depression, 1929–1939* (Berkeley and Los Angeles: University of California Press, 1973), pp. 262–77; Kennedy, *Freedom from Fear*, pp. 184–89.

112. Quoted in Robert Dallek, *Franklin Roosevelt and American Foreign Policy, 1932–1945* (New York: Oxford University Press, 1979), p. 182. See also Kennedy, *Freedom from Fear*, pp. 350–62.

113. See Alan Brinkley, *The End of Reform: New Deal Liberalism in Recession and War* (New York: Knopf, 1995), pp. 86–174.

114. David Schoenbaum, *Hitler's Social Revolution: Class and Status in Nazi Germany 1933–1939* (New York: W. W. Norton, 1980), pp. 73–151.

115. W. G. Beasley, *Japanese Imperialism, 1894–1945* (Oxford: Clarendon, 1987), pp. 198–219.

Chapter Three

1. David M. Kennedy, *Freedom from Fear: The American People in Depression and War, 1929–1945* (New York: Oxford University Press, 1999), pp. 426–54, 460–76.

2. On American entrance into World War II, see Robert Dallek, *Franklin Roosevelt and American Foreign Policy, 1932–1945* (New York: Oxford University Press, 1979), pp. 171–313; Joseph P. Lash, *Roosevelt and Churchill, 1939–1941: The Partnership that Saved the West* (New York: W. W. Norton, 1976); Robert E. Sherwood, *Roosevelt and Hopkins: An Intimate History* (New York: Harper & Brothers, 1948), pp. 429–38; W. G. Beasley, *Japanese Imperialism, 1894–1945* (Oxford: Clarendon Press, 1987), pp. 198–250.

3. Clayton R. Koppes and Gregory D. Black, *Hollywood Goes to War: How Politics, Profits and Propaganda Shaped World War II Movies* (Berkeley and Los Angeles: University of California Press, 1990), pp. 17–47; Michael S. Sherry, *In the Shadow of War: The United States since the 1930s* (New Haven: Yale University Press, 1995), pp. 53–55.

4. Quoted in Dallek, *Franklin Roosevelt and American Foreign Policy*, p. 259.

5. Geoffrey Perrett, *Days of Sadness, Years of Triumph: The American People, 1939–1945* (New York: Coward, Mcann, and Geoghegan, 1973), p. 203.

6. Quoted in Lawrence S. Wittner, *Rebels against War: The American Peace Movement, 1933–1983* (Philadelphia: Temple University Press, 1984), p. 36. (The author evidently provides space for opposing viewpoints.) See also W. Lloyd Warner et al., *Democracy in Jonesville: A Study in Quality and Inequality* (New York: Harper, 1964 [1949]), p. 266.

7. Henry L. Stimson and McGeorge Bundy, *On Active Service in Peace and War* (New York: Harper & Brothers, 1947), p. 393.

8. See Perrett, *Days of Sadness,* pp. 231–36; Judy Barrett Litoff and David C. Smith, eds., *Since You Went Away: World War II Letters from American Women on the Home Front* (New York: Oxford University Press, 1991); William M. Tuttle, Jr., *"Daddy's Gone to War:" The Second World War in the Lives of America's Children* (New York: Oxford University Press, 1993), pp. 112–47.

Francis E. Merrill, *Social Problems on the Home Front: A Study of War-time Influences* (New York: Harper & Brothers, 1948), pp. 26–63; Tuttle, *"Daddy's Gone to War,"* pp. 36–48.

9. Charles A. and Mary R. Beard, *The Basic History of the United States* (New York: Doubleday, 1944), pp. 474–75.

10. Merrill, *Social Problems on the Home Front,* p. 63; Kennedy, *Freedom from Fear,* pp. 747–48.

11. Kennedy, *Freedom from Fear,* pp. 634–47. Similar effects are described in John Barber and Mark Harrison, *The Soviet Home Front, 1941–1945: A Social and Economic History of the USSR in World War II* (London: Longman, 1991), pp. 90–96.

12. For statistics on the automotive and electrical industries see Ruth Milkman, *Gender at Work: The Dynamics of Job Segregation by Sex during World War II* (Urbana: University of Illinois Press, 1987), pp. 49–52.

13. See Susan M. Hartmann, *The Home Front and Beyond: American Women in the 1940s* (Boston: Twayne, 1982); D'Ann Campbell, *Women at War with America: Private Lives in a Patriotic Era* (Cambridge, Mass.: Harvard University Press, 1984). See also Angus Calder, *The People's War: Britain, 1939–1945* (New York: Pantheon, 1969), pp. 331–35.

14. Carl N. Degler, *At Odds: Women and the Family in America from the Revolution to the Present* (New York: Oxford University Press, 1980), pp. 418–35; Geraldine Youcha, *Minding the Children: Child Care in America from Colonial Times to the Present* (New York: Scribner's, 1995), pp. 307–35. Youcha points out a number of federal programs that provided childcare during the war, many of which evolved from the WPA.

15. Merrill, *Social Problems on the Home Front,* pp. 80–162; Richard R. Lingeman, *Don't You Know There's a War On?: The American Home Front, 1941–1945* (New York: Putnam, 1970), pp. 88–91; Marc Scott Miller, *The Irony of Victory: World War II and Lowell, Massachusetts* (Urbana: University of Illinois Press, 1988), pp. 166–87. On parallel events in Britain see Arthur Marwick, *The Deluge: British Society and the First World War* (New York: W. W. Norton, 1965), pp. 116–19; David Reynolds, *Rich Relations: The American Occupation of Britain, 1941–1945* (New York: Random House, 1995), pp. 267–70.

16. Kennedy, *Freedom from Fear,* pp. 632–33.

17. Warner et al., *Democracy in Jonesville,* pp. 268–72; W. Lloyd Warner, *American Life: Dream and Reality* (Chicago: University of Chicago Press, 1964 [1953]), pp. 24–30;

William Serrin, *Homestead: The Glory and Tragedy of an American Steel Town* (New York: Times, 1992), pp. 234–35.

18. Ernie Pyle, *Brave Men* (New York: Henry Holt, 1944), pp. 467–74.

19. Bill Gold, quoted in Roy Hoopes, *Americans Remember the Home Front: An Oral Narrative* (New York: Hawthorn, 1977), p. xii.

20. Quoted in Hoopes, *Americans Remember the Home Front*, p. 93. See also Serrin, *Homestead*, pp. 222–23.

21. See Robert J. Havighurst, *The Social History of a War-Boom Community* (New York: Longmans, Green, 1951); John Morton Blum, V *Was for Victory: Politics and American Culture during World War II* (New York: Harcourt, Brace, Jovanovich, 1976), pp. 53–64; Warner *American Life*, pp. 26–30; Richard Polenberg, ed., *America at War: The Home Front, 1941–1945* (Englewood Cliffs, N.J.: Prentice-Hall, 1968), pp. 11–12; Polenberg, *War and Society: The United States, 1941–1945* (New York: J. B. Lippincott, 1972), pp. 131–35; Perrett, *Days of Sadness*, pp. 203–35.

22. John L. Shover, *First Majority – Last Minority: The Transformation of Rural Life in America* (De Kalb: Northern Illinois University Press, 1976), p. 6.

23. James L. Abrahamson, *The American Home Front: Revolutionary War, Civil War, World War I, World War II* (Washington D.C.: National Defense University Press, 1983), p. 149; Kim McQuaid, *Uneasy Partners: Big Business in American Politics, 1945–1990* (Baltimore: Johns Hopkins University Press, 1994), pp. 14–15. Abrahamson notes that the government attempted to help small businesses by allowing them to reconvert to consumer goods ahead of their large rivals.

24. Quoted in Polenberg, ed., *America at War*, p. 28. See also Blum, V *Was for Victory*, pp. 124–31; John Dos Passos, *State of the Nation* (Boston: Houghton Mifflin, 1943), pp. 24–26.

25. See Blum, V *Was for Victory*, pp. 125–27; McQuaid, *Uneasy Partners*, pp. 12–17; Bruce Catton, *The Warlords of Washington* (New York: Harcourt Brace, 1948); The Beards, *Basic History*, pp. 478–79; Gerald D. Nash, *World War II and the West: Reshaping the Economy* (Lincoln: University of Nebraska Press, 1990).

26. Quoted in Reynolds, *Rich Relations*, p. 47.

27. Warner et al., *Democracy in Jonesville*, pp. 267–69; Everett M. Rogers, *Social Change in Rural Society* (New York: Appleton-Century-Crofts, 1960), pp. 11–15; Lowell Juilliard Carr and James Edson Stermer, *Willow Run: A Study of Industrialization and Cultural Inadequacy* (New York: Harper & Brothers, 1952).

28. W. Lloyd Warner, "The American Town," in William Fielding Ogburn, ed., *American Society in Wartime* (Chicago: University of Chicago Press, 1943), pp. 41–42. Carl Bridenbaugh noted a similar process in colonial towns during the wars of the mid-eighteenth century: "During these years of conflict, vastly complicated by wartime abnormalities, ordinary municipal peace officers found it difficult — indeed, often impossible — to ensure quiet and public safety. Large accretions of population, including

large proportions of floaters — sailors, soldiers, runaways from the country, immigrants, and rougher elements — exerted more pressure on the feeble guarantors of law and order than they could withstand." *Cities in Revolt: Urban Life in America, 1743–1776* (London: Oxford University Press, 1971 [1955]), p. 107. Bridenbaugh argues that these wars broke down traditional social patterns and opened Americans to revolutionary sentiments in the next few decades. See also Frederick Lewis Allen's observations on war and social change during World War I in *Only Yesterday: An Informal History of the Nineteen-Twenties* (New York: Harper & Row, 1931), pp. 38–72.

29. Statistics on population growth in cities from Lingeman, *Don't You Know There's a War On*, pp. 69–70. See also Havighurst, *War-Boom Community*; Carr and Stermer, *Willow Run*; Dos Passos, *State of the Nation*, pp. 43–6, 89–95. Many contemporary sociologists, including Warner and Havighurst, felt that communities would return to normalcy after the war. I don't believe that happened and shall argue the point in the next chapter. On demographic shifts in the wartime Soviet Union see Susan J. Linz, "World War II and Soviet Economic Growth, 1940–1953" and Alec Nove, "Soviet Peasantry in World War Two," in Susan J. Linz, ed., *The Impact of World War II on the Soviet Union* (Totowa, N.J.: Rowman & Allanheld, 1985), pp. 11–46, 77–90. Dislocations were exacerbated by forced migrations of suspect populations such as Poles and Volga Germans. See Amy Knight, *Beria: Stalin's First Lieutenant* (Princeton: Princeton University Press, 1993), pp. 126–29. For British dislocations see Calder, *The People's War*, pp. 315–17.

30. See Max Weber, *Ancient Judaism*, trans. and ed. by Hans H. Gerth and Don Martindale (New York: Free Press, 1952), pp. 127-46; Gwilym H. Jones, "The Concept of Holy War," in R. E. Clements, ed., *The World of Ancient Israel: Sociological Anthropological and Political Perspectives* (Cambridge: Cambridge University Press, 1989), pp. 299-321; Thomas B. Dozeman, *God at War: Power in the Exodus Tradition* (New York: Oxford University Press, 1996), pp. 42–70.

31. Numa Denis Fustel de Coulange, *The Ancient City: A Study on the Religion, Laws, and Institutions of Greece and Rome* (Garden City, N.Y.: Doubleday, 1956), pp. 164–67; Ramsay MacMullen, *Constantine* (London: Croom Helm, 1987), pp. 65–78. When one of his commanders feared the auguries from a calf, Hannibal replied, "Do you put more faith in a slice of veal than in an old general?" See R. M. Ogilvie, *The Romans and Their Gods in the Age of Augustus* (New York: W. W. Norton, 1969), p. 67.

32. Serge A. Zenkovsky, ed., *Medieval Russia's Epics, Chronicles, and Tales* (New York: E. P. Dutton, 1974).

33. Michael Howard, quoted in John Mueller, *Retreat from Doomsday: The Obsolescence of Major War* (New York: Basic Books, 1989), p. 24.

34. Steven Watts, *The Republic Reborn: War and the Making of Liberal America, 1790–1820* (Baltimore: Johns Hopkins University Press, 1987), pp. 151–60; James M. McPherson, *For Cause and Comrades: Why Men Fought in the Civil War* (New York: Oxford University Press, 1997), pp. 62–74; Charles William Wilson, *Baptized in Blood:*

The Religion of the Lost Cause (Athens: University of Georgia Press, 1980), pp. 37–57; Gary Laderman, *The Sacred Remains: American Attitudes toward Death, 1799–1883* (New Haven: Yale University Press, 1996), pp. 123–43.

35. Reynolds, *Rich Relations*, p. 370. See also Robert Anthony Orsi, *The Madonna of 115th Street: Faith and Community in Italian Harlem, 1880–1950* (New Haven: Yale University Press, 1985), pp. 67–70, 166–67.

36. Quoted in Debs Myers, Jonathan Kilbourn and Richard Harrity, eds., *Yank – the GI Story of the War* (New York: Duell, Sloan & Pearce, 1947), p. 90. Seeing the utility of religion in the war effort, Stalin mobilized Orthodoxy during the war. See John Shelton Curtiss, *The Russian Church and the Soviet State, 1917–1950* (Gloucester, Mass.: Peter Smith, 1965), pp. 291 ff. This of course contrasts with earlier attempts to stamp out religion.

37. Stouffer, *The American Soldier* II: pp. 173–91. Numbers range among enlisted men in different theaters of operation and were always higher among combat soldiers than among non-combat soldiers. Length of combat did not affect responses. For similar religious dynamics in the Soviet Union see William C. Fletcher, "The Soviet Bible Belt: World War II's Effects on Religion," in Linz, ed., *The Impact of World War II*, pp. 91–106. See also Reid Mitchell, *Civil War Soldiers: Their Expectations and Their Experiences* (New York: Viking, 1988), pp. 77–79.

38. Paul Fussell, *Wartime: Understanding and Behavior in the Second World War* (New York: Oxford University Press, 1989), pp. 66–70. See also T. E. Lawrence, *The Mint: A Day-Book of the R.A.F. Depot between August and December 1922 with Later Notes* (London: Jonathan Cape, 1955); Gerhard Ritter, *The Sword and the Scepter: The Problem of Militarism in Germany* (Princeton Junction, N.J.: The Scholar's Bookshelf, 1988 [1954]), pp. 94–95.

39. Norman Mailer, *The Naked and the Dead* (New York: Rinehart, 1948), pp. 703–4.

40. James Jones, *The Thin Red Line* (New York: Scribner's, 1964), p. 267. Similar complaints have been noted among Civil War soldiers. See McPherson, *For Cause and Comrades*, pp. 47–49.

41. Quoted in James T. Patterson, *Grand Expectations: The United States, 1945–1974* (New York: Oxford University Press, 1996), p. 7. Ironically, McNair was killed by friendly fire while observing a carpet-bombing of German positions near St. Lô in July 1944.

42. Fussell, *Wartime*, p. 138. See also J. Glenn Gray, *The Warriors: Reflections on Men in Battle* (New York: Harper & Row, 1967 [1959]), pp. 131–69.

43. Twenty-three percent of medical evacuations were for psychiatric reasons. See Ronald H. Spector, *After Tet: The Bloodiest Year in Vietnam* (New York: Free Press, 1993), p. 63. By comparison, only six percent of such evacuations from Vietnam were for those reasons.

44. Mailer, *The Naked and the Dead*, pp. 122–23, 708.

45. Kurt Vonnegut, *Slaughterhouse-Five, or the Children's Crusade: A Duty Dance with Death* (New York: Delacorte, 1969). See also Gray, *The Warriors*, pp. 97–129; Gerald F.

Linderman, *Embattled Courage: The Experience of Combat in the American Civil War* (New York: Free Press, 1987), pp. 113–265.

46. Wyndham Lewis, quoted in Paul Fussell, *Doing Battle: The Making of a Skeptic* (Boston: Little, Brown, 1996), p. 63.

47. Fussell, *Wartime*, pp. 3–13, 129–43; Paul Fussell, *The Norton Book of Modern War* (New York: W. W. Norton, 1991), pp. 17–25. See also Mitchell, *Civil War Soldiers*, pp. 24–55.

48. Thomas Howell, "U.S. Domestic Propaganda in World War II," *The Historian* 59 (1997): 806.

49. Fussell, *Wartime*, pp. 92–95, 254–67. Note the observations of two writers after the Great War: "The habit of continuous obscene language, which a long and miserable war has always induced, persisted four or five years more and had even spread to the younger women." See Robert Graves and Alan Hodge, *The Long Week-End: A Social History of Great Britain, 1918–1939* (New York: W. W. Norton, 1963 [1940]), pp. 26–27.

50. See Richard Slotkin, *Gunfighter Nation: The Myth of the Frontier in Twentieth-Century America* (New York: Atheneum, 1992), pp. 313–43.

51. Quotes from Milton Mayer and Carl Friedrich, in Howell, "U.S. Domestic Propaganda in World War II," p. 807.

52. Quoted in Meirion and Susie Harries, *The Last Days of Innocence: America at War, 1917–1918* (New York: Random House, 1997), p. 293.

53. See Ernie Pyle, *Brave Men* (New York: Henry Holt, 1944); Margaret Bourke-White, *Purple Heart Valley: A Combat Chronicle of the War in Italy* (New York: Simon & Schuster, 1944); Richard Tregaskis, *Guadalcanal Diary* (New York: Random House, 1943); and various others in *Reporting World War II*, 2 vols. (New York: Library of America, 1995).

54. Tregaskis, *Guadalcanal Diary;* John Hersey, *Into the Valley: A Skirmish of the Marines* (Garden City, N.Y.: Sun Dial Press, 1943).

55. Myers et al., *Yank – the GI Story of the War*, p. 41.

56. Bill Mauldin, *Up Front* (Cleveland: World, 1945), pp. 12–14.

57. Ernie Pyle, "A Small Assembly Plant," in *Reporting World War II*, II: 198.

58. Harry Brown, *A Walk in the Sun* (New York: Knopf, 1944), p. 99.

59. See George L. Mosse, *Fallen Soldiers: Reshaping the Memory of the World Wars* (New York: Oxford University Press, 1990), pp. 8, 76, 130.

60. James L. Baughman, *The Republic of Mass Culture: Journalism, Filmmaking, and Broadcasting in America since 1941* (Baltimore: Johns Hopkins University Press, 1992), pp. 4–7; William Manchester, *Goodbye Darkness: Memoirs of the Pacific War* (Boston: Little, Brown, 1979), pp. 242–43; Fussell, *Wartime*, pp. 12–13.

61. See Slotkin, *Gunfighter Nation*, pp. 323–26.

62. See Ernest Burgess, "The Family," in Ogburn, ed., *American Society in Wartime*, pp. 18 ff; Costello, *Virtue under Fire*, pp. 73–89; Blum, V *Was for Victory*, pp. 79–80. On

parallel cultural coarsening in Germany from the Great War see Mosse, *Fallen Soldiers*, pp. 159–60. There were limits on what could be presented. Aside from *The Fighting Sullivans*, John Houston's documentary on nervous breakdowns (*Let There Be Light*) was kept under wraps until after the war, though much of it looks staged.

63. Quoted in Fussell, *The Norton Book of Modern War*, p. 458. See also J. Glenn Gray, *The Warriors*, pp. 59–95.

64. Quoted in Reynolds, *Rich Relations*, pp. 413–14. For loosening sexual norms in Britain during the First World War see Marwick, *The Deluge*, pp. 108–09.

65. See Costello, *Virtue under Fire*, passim. On similar changes during and after World War I see Allen, *Only Yesterday*, pp. 38–72. On the experience in Britain: "It was pretty painful business — the evacuation of children, the life in the shelters, the black-out, the separation of husbands and wives, the frantic embarkation leave marriages, the have-a-good-time-tonight-because-you-may-get-bumped-off tomorrow atmosphere." David Mace, quoted in Sheila Jeffreys, *Anticlimax: A Feminist Perspective on the Sexual Revolution* (New York: New York University Press, 1990), p. 7. See also Calder, *The People's War*, pp. 312–15.

66. Reynolds, *Rich Relations*, pp. 200–37; Philip Wylie, *Generation of Vipers* (New York: Farrar and Rinehart, 1942), p. 68. Wylie is given to sarcastic overstatement, but he hits home often. On loosening sexual norms in Britain during the previous war see Marwick, *The Deluge*, pp. 106–13.

67. Quoted in Reynolds, *Rich Relations*, p. xxiii.

68. Wylie, *Generation of Vipers*, pp. 52–77; Merrill, *Social Problems on the Home Front*, pp. 93–144; Lingeman, *Don't You Know There's a War On*, pp. 88–95; Fussell, *Wartime*, pp. 105–14; Edwin P. Hoyt, *The GI's War: American Soldiers in Europe during World War II* (New York: Da Capo, 1988), pp. 131, 138–39, 568–69. Costello and Wylie assert that the war brought on increased homosexuality but provide little evidence. Novels from the period (Burns's *The Gallery* and Jones's *The Thin Red Line*) refer to homosexuality, as do Manchester's work, *Goodbye Darkness*, and (obliquely in the Cummings character) Mailer's *The Naked and the Dead*. It might be safer to say that GIs were widely exposed to *rumors* of homosexuality. It might be noted that, in the service, anyone displaying aloofness and reluctance to drink heavily and visit brothels is suspected of homosexuality. Bridenbaugh saw sexual norms relaxing during the wars of the mid-eighteenth century. See *Cities in Revolt*, pp. 121–22.

69. Jeremy Atack and Peter Passell, *A New Economic View of American History* (New York: W. W. Norton, 1994), pp. 631–33.

70. Charles P. Kindleberger, *The World Depression, 1929–1939* (Berkeley and Los Angeles: University of California Press, 1973), pp. 278–90; Alan S. Milward, *War, Economy and Society, 1939–1945* (Berkeley and Los Angeles: University of California Press, 1977), pp. 63–74; Abrahamson, *The American Home Front*, pp. 139–53.

71. Kennedy, *Freedom from Fear*, pp. 645–66; Sherry, *In the Shadow of War*, pp. 69–80;

Lingeman, *Don't You Know There's a War On,* pp. 91–101; Blum, V *Was for Victory,* pp. 91–124.

72. Gerald D. Nash, *The American West in the Twentieth Century: A Short History of an Urban Oasis* (Englewood Cliffs. N.J.: Prentice-Hall, 1973), pp. 195–216; Nash, *World War II and the West,* passim.

73. Statistics on income from Perrett, *Days of Sadness,* pp. 352–56. See also Arthur Marwick, *Class: Image and Reality in Britain, France, and the USA since 1930* (Glasgow, U.K.: Collins, 1980), pp. 256–89.

74. Lionel Edie, quoted in John U. Nef, *War and Human Progress: An Essay on the Rise of Industrial Civilization* (Cambridge, Mass.: Harvard University Press, 1950), p. 167.

75. On technological innovation during the war see Milward, *War, Economy and Society,* pp. 169–207. For a broader historical treatment of war and scientific advances see Nef's classic, *War and Human Progress.*

76. *Vital Statistics Rates in the United States.* U.S. Dept. of Health, Education and Welfare, 1968, p. 99. See also Ogburn, ed., *American Society in Wartime,* passim; Polenberg, ed., *America at War,* pp. 131–53.

77. Myers, Kilbourn, and Harrity, eds., *Yank* p. 25.

78. Fussell, *Wartime,* pp. 140–42; Manchester, *Goodbye Darkness,* p. 375; Sherwood, *Roosevelt and Hopkins,* p. 438. See also Samuel Hynes, *The Soldiers' Tale: Bearing Witness to Modern War* (Harmondsworth, U.K.: Penguin, 1997), pp. 108–15; Cabell Phillips, *The 1940s: Decade of Triumph and Trouble* (New York: Macmillan, 1975), p. 175.

79. See Mosse, *Fallen Soldiers,* p. 142.

80. See Ramsay MacMullen, *Soldier and Civilian in the Later Roman Empire* (Cambridge, Mass.: Harvard University Press, 1963); J. B. Campbell, *The Emperor and the Roman Army, 31 BC – AD 235* (Oxford: Clarendon Press, 1984), pp. 157–203; Fritz Redlich, *The German Military Enterpriser and His Workforce: A Study in European Economic and Social History,* 2 vols. (Wiesbaden: Franz Steiner Verlag, 1964); Richard Severo and Lewis Milford, *The Wages of War: When America's Soldiers Came Home – From Valley Forge to Vietnam* (New York: Simon & Schuster, 1989), pp. 21–118.

81. The wellspring of the primary-group analysis is Edward A. Shils and Morris Janowitz, "Cohesion and Disintegration in the Wehrmacht in World War II," *Public Opinion Quarterly* 12 (1948): 280–315. See also McPherson, *For Cause and Comrades,* pp. 77–89; Anthony Kellett, *Combat Motivations: The Behavior of Soldiers in Battle* (Boston: Kluwer, 1982), pp. 41–58; William Darryl Henderson, *Cohesion, The Human Element in Combat: Leadership and Societal Influence in the Armies of the Soviet Union, the United States, North Vietnam, and Israel* (Washington, D.C.: National Defense University Press, 1985). For a critique see Cameron, *American Samurai,* pp. 191–202.

82. Samuel Stouffer, *The American Soldier* II: 108.

83. Warner's study of a small Illinois town found much higher military participation in upper and upper-middle strata. See Warner et al., *Democracy in Jonesville,* pp. 273–74.

Reid Mitchell has ably sketched the importance of community norms in the Union army in his "The Northern Soldier and His Community," in Maris A. Vinovskis, ed., *Toward a Social History of the Civil War: Exploratory Essays* (New York: Cambridge University Press, 1990), pp. 78–92. On this view, societies with amoral familism, religious and caste divisions, and political schisms would be far less able to field effective, modern armies.

84. Glen H. Elder, Jr., *Children of the Great Depression: Social Change in Life Experience* (Chicago: University of Chicago Press, 1974), esp. pp. 28–29.

85. Manchester, *Goodbye Darkness*, p. 395. Cameron also sees the cynicism of the post-WWI era as well as the hard times of the Depression as important in forming the character of marines and soldiers of World War II. See *American Samurai*, p. 246. The theme is also conveyed in Mailer's *The Naked and the Dead*, in which characters from southern (Croft and Ridges) and Jewish (Goldstein and Roth) backgrounds exhibit personal needs to complete an arduous recon patrol and bring a badly wounded soldier to the beachhead.

86. See E. Digby Baltzell, *The Protestant Establishment: Aristocracy and Caste in America* (New York: Vintage, 1964), pp. 22–25, 277–93; William R. Hutchison, ed., *Between the Times: The Travail of the Protestant Establishment in America, 1900–1960* (New York: Cambridge University Press, 1989).

87. Quoted in Polenberg, ed., *America at War*, p. 109. See also letters in *Yank* on the injustice of American racism in *Reporting World War II*, II: 470–73. It is significant that most of the letters are from ethnic Americans, who themselves were not considered real Americans.

88. Quoted in Studs Terkel, *'The Good War:' An Oral History of World War Two* (New York: Pantheon, 1984), p. 70n.

89. Hondon B. Hargrove, *Buffalo Soldiers in Italy: Black Americans in World War II* (Jefferson, N.C.: McFarland and Co., 1985).

90. Quoted in Kennedy, *Freedom from Fear*, p. 772.

91. Stouffer et al., *The American Soldier* I: 530–35; Morris Janowitz, *The Reconstruction of Patriotism: Education for Civic Consciousness* (Chicago: University of Chicago Press, 1983), pp. 123–26; *American Military History* (Washington, D.C.: Center of Military History), p. 494; Stephen E. Ambrose, "Grant and Eisenhower," in Gabor S. Boritt, ed., *War Comes Again: Comparative Vistas on the Civil War and World War II* (New York: Oxford University Press, 1995), p. 47. Ambrose also notes that following the heavy losses of the Wilderness Campaign (Summer 1864), Grant began to use more black troops. Ironically, in November of 1864, Jefferson Davis, facing superior Union numbers, black and white, proposed to the Confederate Congress that slaves who fought for the South be emancipated after the war. Davis's program, needless to say, met a chilly response. The governor of Georgia objected: "Whenever we establish the fact that they are a military race, we destroy our whole theory that they are unfit to be free." Lee's army was ground down the following spring. See Emory Thomas, *The Confederate Nation: 1861–1865*

(New York: Harper & Row, 1979), pp. 290–93. Quote from Joseph T. Glatthaar, "Black Glory: The African-American Role in Union Victory," in Gabor S. Boritt, ed., *Why the Confederacy Lost* (New York: Oxford University Press, 1992), p. 140.

92. Kennedy, *Freedom from Fear*, pp. 764–70.

93. Howell, "U.S. Domestic Propaganda in World War II," pp. 808–10.

94. Patterson, *Grand Expectations*, p. 20; C. Vann Woodward, *The Strange Career of Jim Crow* (New York: Oxford University Press, 1966), pp. 130–34; Manning Marable, *Race, Reform, and Rebellion: The Second Reconstruction in Black America, 1945–1990* (Jackson: University Press of Mississippi, 1991), pp. 13–39.

95. Koppes and Black, *Hollywood Goes to War*, pp. 179–80.

96. Fussell, *Doing Battle*, pp. 123 and 119. After a Jewish soldier was badly wounded, Fussell noticed that "anti-semitic innuendoes stopped dramatically."

97. See Samuel Stouffer et al., *The American Soldier*, vol. 1 *Adjustment during Army Life* (Princeton: Princeton University Press, 1949), pp. 590–99. Racial tolerance was highest in integrated combat units, less so in segregated combat units, and the least in segregated rear-echelon units. Soldiers who expressed increased tolerance toward blacks did not necessarily feel that integration outside combat zones was desirable. Stouffer's findings and quotes might well sound like the answers public relation officers would pressure GIs to give, but that could be said of many other topics, some of which show marked animosity toward officers and the service. See also Woodward, *Jim Crow*, p. 137.

98. Quoted in Sherry, *In the Shadow of War*, p. 108.

99. Reynolds, *Rich Relations*, pp. 302–34.

100. Quoted in Dan Morgan, *Rising in the West: The True Story of an "Okie" Family from the Great Depression through the Reagan Years* (New York: Knopf, 1992), p. 151.

101. Quoted in Baltzell, *The Protestant Establishment*, p. 23; Reynolds, *Rich Relations*, pp. 441–43. See also Bill Mauldin, *The Brass Ring: A Sort of Memoir* (New York: W. W. Norton, 1971); Sherry, *In the Shadow of War*, p. 108. On the declining significance of ethnicity in the postwar years see Warner, *American Life*, pp. 179–205.

102. See Mailer, *The Naked and the Dead*, pp. 702–11. Mailer served in a reconnaissance platoon in the Philippines during the war, and his powerful book is in many ways reportage. He asserts he did not even change the names of several characters.

103. See Alan Brinkley, *The End of Reform: New Deal Liberalism in Recession and War* (New York: Knopf, 1995), pp. 86–174.

104. During the First World War, progressive animus toward big business waned and the Justice Department granted anti-trust immunity to corporations contributing to the war effort. See Ellis W. Hawley, *The Great War and the Search for a Modern Order: A History of the American People and Their Institutions, 1917–1933* (New York: St. Martin's Press, 1979), pp. 23–24.

105. On resentment toward military authority see Stouffer et al., *The American Soldier* II: 54–81, 362–429. The study shows greater respect for officers in combat units than

in support units. R. Ernest Dupuy, "Pass in Review," *The Army Combat Forces Journal* 4 (1954), p. 43; Cameron, *American Samurai,* pp. 54–62. See also Wylie, *Generation of Vipers,* pp. 256–72; Mauldin, *Up Front,* passim.

106. Fussell, *Wartime,* pp. 19–35; Ronald H. Spector, *Eagle against the Sun: The American War with Japan* (New York: Free Press, 1985), pp. 420–22.

107. "Things Are Really Fouled Up," "Fouled Up Beyond All Recognition," and, in tribute to inter-service operations, "Joint Army-Navy Foul Up."

108. Arnold Toynbee, *The Prospects of Western Civilization* (New York: Columbia University Press, 1949), p. 8.

109. See Correlli Barnett, *The Pride and the Fall: The Dream and Illusion of Britain as a Great Nation* (New York: Free Press, 1986).

Chapter Four

1. See W. Lloyd Warner et al., *Democracy in Jonesville: A Study in Quality and Inequality* (New York: Harper, 1964 [1949]), pp. 276–77; Samuel Hynes, *The Soldiers' Tale: Bearing Witness to Modern War* (Harmondsworth, U.K.: Penguin, 1997), p. 23; J. Glenn Gray, *The Warriors: Reflections on Men in Battle* (New York: Harper & Row, 1967 [1959]), pp. 3–58.

2. See Reid Mitchell, *Civil War Soldiers: Their Expectations and Their Experiences* (New York: Viking, 1988), pp. 68–70; Gerald F. Linderman, *Embattled Courage: The Experience of Combat in the American Civil War* (New York: Free Press, 1987), pp. 266–97; Paul Fussell, *Abroad: British Literary Traveling between the Wars* (New York: Oxford University Press, 1980); and *Doing Battle: The Making of a Skeptic* (Boston: Little, Brown, 1996), pp. 185-86. For a survey of veterans since the War of Independence see Richard Severo and Lewis Milford, *The Wages of War: When America's Soldiers Came Home — From Valley Forge to Vietnam* (New York: Simon & Schuster, 1989).

3. Quoted in John L. Shover, *First Majority – Last Minority: The Transformation of Rural Life in America* (De Kalb: Northern Illinois University Press, 1976), p. 8. See also Robert Anthony Orsi, *The Madonna of 115th Street: Faith and Community in Italian Harlem, 1880–1950* (New Haven: Yale University Press, 1985), pp. 71–74.

4. Philip Roth, *American Pastoral* (Boston: Houghton Mifflin, 1997), pp. 40–41.

5. For an overview of postwar changes see Frederick Lewis Allen, *The Big Change: America Transforms Itself, 1900–1950* (New York: Harper & Row, 1952), pp. 139–257. On change in the Soviet Union after 1945 see Sheila Fitzpatrick, "Postwar Soviet Society: The 'Return to Normalcy,' 1945–1953," in Susan J. Linz, ed., *The Impact of World War II on the Soviet Union* (Totowa, N.J.: Rowman & Allanheld, 1985), pp. 129–56.

6. Ernest W. Burgess and Harvey J. Locke, *The Family from Institution to Companionship* (New York: American Book, 1945); Carle Zimmerman, *The Family of Tomorrow: The Cultural Crisis and the Way Out* (New York: Harper, 1949); Ruth Nanda Anshen, ed., *The Family: Its Function and Destiny* (New York: Harper and Brothers, 1959 [1949]). On the persistence of traditional family patterns in certain areas see Jack E. Weller, *Yesterday's*

People: Life in Contemporary Appalachia (Lexington: University of Kentucky Press, 1965), pp. 59–68.

7. Michael Kimmel, *Manhood in America: A Cultural History* (New York: Free Press, 1996), pp. 82–84.

8. Richard Polenberg, ed., *America at War: The Home Front, 1941–1945* (Englewood Cliffs, N.J.: Prentice-Hall, 1968), p. 28. See also John Dos Passos, *State of the Nation* (Boston: Houghton Mifflin, 1943), pp. 24–26.

9. Allen, *The Big Change*, p. 151.

10. On postwar growth of white-collar work see Everett Carll Ladd, Jr., *Ideology in America: Change and Response in City, a Suburb, and a Small Town* (Ithaca: Cornell University Press, 1969), pp. 49–52; Joseph Bensman and Bernard Rosenberg, *Mass, Class, and Bureaucracy: The Evolution of Contemporary Society* (New York: Prentice-Hall, 1963), pp. 255–78; C. Wright Mills, *White Collar* (New York: Oxford University Press, 1951); William H. Whyte, *The Organization Man* (Garden City, N.Y.: Anchor Doubleday, 1957).

11. On weakened paternal authority see Steven Mintz and Susan Kellogg, *Domestic Revolutions: A Social History of American Family Life* (New York: Free Press, 1988), pp. 184–86; Everett M. Rogers, *Social Change in Rural Society* (New York: Appleton-Century-Crofts, 1960), pp. 171–205; Christopher Lasch, *Haven in a Heartless World: The Family Besieged* (New York: W. W. Norton, 1977), pp. 123–28; Robin M. Williams, Jr., *American Society: A Sociological Interpretation* (New York: Knopf, 1955), pp. 54–55; Jules Henry, *Culture against Man* (New York: Vintage, 1963), pp. 130–46.

12. Kimmel, *Manhood in America*, pp. 223–58.

13. James S. Coleman, "The Adolescent Society," in Derek L. Phillips, ed., *Studies in American Society* (New York: Crowell, 1965), p. 113. See also Bensman and Bernard Rosenberg, *Mass, Class, and Bureaucracy*, pp. 107–33; Ruth Nanda Anshen, "The Family in Transition," in her edited work, *The Family*, pp. 3–19.

14. Herbert J. Gans, *The Urban Villagers: Group and Class in the Life of Italian-Americans* (New York: Free Press, 1962), pp. 64–75; Weller, *Yesterday's People*, pp. 68–72.

15. David Riesman, *The Lonely Crowd: A Study in the Changing American Character* (New Haven: Yale University Press, 1950), p. 49. See also Orsi, *The Madonna of 115th Street*, pp. 71–74.

16. Bensman and Rosenberg, *Mass, Class, and Bureaucracy*, pp. 93–95. On the retention of traditional child-rearing practices in rural and ethnic neighborhood settings see Moira Komarovsky, *Blue-Collar Marriage* (New York: Vintage, 1962), pp. 33–37; Weller, *Yesterday's People*, pp. 64–68; Gans, *The Urban Villagers*, pp. 54–64.

17. Herbert H. Lyman, quoted in Komarovsky, *Blue-Collar Marriage*, p. 37.

18. Obviously, the most popular of these works was Benjamin Spock, *The Common Sense Book of Baby and Child Care* (New York: Duell, Sloan and Pearce, 1946), which sold millions of copies by the end of the 1940s. See also Williams, *American Society*, pp. 65–66.

19. Christopher Lasch notes, not with approval, this stance among the new experts. See his *Haven in a Heartless World*, pp. 171–74.

20. On popular images of the period see Paul Fussell, *The Norton Book of Modern War* (New York: W. W. Norton, 1991), pp. 23–24; Kenneth Keniston, *Youth and Dissent: The Rise of a New Opposition* (New York: Harcourt Brace Jovanovich, 1971), pp. 68–69; Raymond M. Olderman, *Beyond the Wasteland: The American Novel in the Nineteen-Sixties* (New Haven: Yale University Press, 1972); Todd Gitlin, *The Sixties: Years of Hope, Days of Rage* (New York: Bantam, 1987), pp. 31–36; Karal Ann Marling, *As Seen on TV: The Visual Culture of Everyday Life in the 1950s* (Cambridge, Mass.: Harvard University Press, 1994), pp. 165–201.

21. Rogers, *Social Change in Rural Society*, p. 38.

22. Popular books of this type include Margaret Mead, *Coming of Age in Samoa: A Psychological Study of Primitive Youth for Western Civilization* (New York: William Morrow, 1928); Ruth Benedict, *Patterns of Culture* (Boston: Houghton Mifflin, 1934); Clyde Kluckhohn, *Mirror for Man: Anthropology for Modern Life* (New York: McGraw-Hill, 1949); Geoffrey Gorer, *The American People: A Study in National Character* (New York: W. W. Norton, 1948); Erik H. Erikson, *Childhood and Society* (New York: W. W. Norton, 1950).

23. Riesman, *The Lonely Crowd*, pp. 38–55. See also Rogers, *Social Change in Rural Society*, pp. 15–16, 171–205; Mintz and Kellogg, *Domestic Revolutions*, pp. 162–67; Morris Janowitz, *The Last Half-Century: Societal Change and Politics in America* (Chicago: University of Chicago Press, 1978), pp. 264–65; Henry, *Culture against Man*, pp. 147–282.

24. This point, often made rather clumsily, is skillfully made by Mintz and Kellogg in *Domestic Revolutions*, pp. 179–80.

25. Richard Pells, *Not Like Us: How Europeans Have Loved, Hated, and Transformed American Culture since World War II* (New York: Basic Books, 1997), pp. 166–67; Maurice R. Stein, *The Eclipse of Community: An Interpretation of American Studies* (Princeton: Princeton University Press, 1960), pp. 275–303.

26. Shover, *First Majority*, p. 6.

27. Arthur J. Vidich and Joseph Bensman, *Small Town in Mass Society* (Princeton: Princeton University Press, 1958), pp. 18, 85; James T. Patterson, *Grand Expectations: The United States, 1945–1974* (New York: Oxford University Press, 1996), p. 18.

28. Rogers, *Social Change in Rural Society*, p. 4.

29. On weakened communities in the postwar period, see Vidich and Bensman, *Small Town in Mass Society*, esp. pp. 41–2, 290–92; Art Gallaher, *Plainville Fifteen Years Later* (New York: Columbia University Press, 1961), pp. 3–37.

30. Packard, *A Nation of Strangers*, pp. 92–93.

31. Rogers, *Social Change in Rural Society*, p. 28.

32. Rogers, *Social Change in Rural Society*, pp. 129–66, 212–32, 396–422.

33. Kenneth T. Jackson, *Crabgrass Frontier: The Suburbanization of the United States* (New York: Oxford University Press, 1985), pp. 234–45.

34. See Lewis Mumford, *The City in History: Its Origins, Its Transformations and Its Prospects* (New York: Harcourt, Brace and World, 1961), pp. 482–86.

35. See David Riesman, "The Suburban Dislocation," in Philip Olson, ed., *America as a Mass Society: Changing Community and Identity* (New York: Free Press, 1963), pp. 283–312; Jackson, *Crabgrass Frontier*, pp. 265–66, 272–74. On general trends away from local community see Morris Janowitz, *The Last Half-Century: Societal Change and Politics in America* (Chicago: University of Chicago Press, 1978), pp. 264–66; Percival Goodman and Paul Goodman, *Communitas* (New York: Vintage, 1960). Herbert Gans's study of postwar suburbs saw a rise in community associations, which gave the author hope that suburbia would develop into strong communities along the lines of the small town and ethnic neighborhoods. Such formal organizations, however, are quite distinct from the moral rooting of the old neighborhoods. See his *The Levittowners: Ways of Life and Politics in a New Suburban Community* (New York: Vintage, 1967), pp. 52–67.

36. Jackson, *Crabgrass Frontier*, pp. 280–82.

37. Gans, *The Levittowners*, pp. 159–60; Lasch, *Haven in a Heartless World*, pp. 123–28. Glen Elder, following Alex Inkeles, argues that the Depression impressed adaptability and openness to change on those who went through it. See *Children of the Great Depression: Social Change in Life Experience* (Chicago: University of Chicago Press, 1974), pp. 3–17. The present perspective sees the war, with all its training, dislocations, and adjustments, as more important.

38. On the decline of local government see Vidich and Bensman, *Small Town in Mass Society*, pp. 113–26, 132–36; Ladd, *Ideology in America*, pp. 41–43, 82–84; Nisbet, *The Quest for Community*, p. xvi; Samuel Pratt, "Metropolitan Community Development and Change in Sub-Center Economic Functions," in Olson, ed., *America as a Mass Society*, pp. 220–231; Rogers, *Social Change in Rural Society*, pp. 296–98; Shover, *First Majority*, pp. 229–63.

39. James L. Baughman, *The Republic of Mass Culture: Journalism, Filmmaking, and Broadcasting in America since 1941* (Baltimore: Johns Hopkins University Press, 1992), pp. 1–2.

40. Wilbur Schramm, Jack Lyle, and Edwin B. Parker, *Television in the Lives of Our Children* (Stanford, Calif.: Stanford University Press, 1961); Vidich and Bensman, *Small Town in Mass Society*, pp. 84–85, 101–3; Joseph Bensman and Bernard Rosenberg, "Mass Media and Mass Culture," Olson, ed., *America as a Mass Society*, pp. 166–184; Donald Horton and R. Richard Wohl, "Mass Communication and Para-Social Interaction: Observations on Intimacy at a Distance," in ibid., pp. 548–68; Rogers, *Social Change in Rural Society*, pp. 8–11; Marling, *As Seen on TV*, pp. 96–97.

41. Erik Barnouw, *Tube of Plenty: The Evolution of American Television* (New York: Oxford University Press, 1990), pp. 99–148; Morris Janowitz, *The Community Press in an*

Urban Setting: The Social Elements of Urbanism 2nd ed. (Chicago: University of Chicago Press, 1967); Gallaher, *Plainville Fifteen Years Later.*

42. A masterful look at the small town in the cinema is Emanuel Levy's, *Small-Town America in Film: The Decline and Fall of Community* (New York: Continuum, 1991).

43. See Ladd, *Ideology in America*, pp. 82–91, 138–40; and Lewis Atherton's eulogy for the small town, *Main Street on the Middle Border* (Chicago: Quadrangle, 1966 [1954]), pp. 353–57.

44. Citing a clerical error, the Pentagon, in June 2000, revised downward the casualty figures for the Korean War, from 54,246 killed to 36,516 (both numbers include combat and non-combat deaths). The higher figure included soldiers and sailors killed worldwide during the conflict, as was the practice in World War II. The higher number is used here because it is the one Americans were familiar with at the time.

45. John Lewis Gaddis, *We Now Know: Rethinking Cold War History* (Oxford: Clarendon Press, 1997), pp. 103–10.

46. On postwar income levels see Ladd, *Ideology in America*, pp. 18–52. See also Eric F. Goldman, *The Crucial Decade – and After: America, 1945–1960* (New York: Vintage, 1960), pp. 19–28; James Lincoln Collier, *The Rise of Selfishness in America* (New York: Oxford University Press, 1991), pp. 85–88. On parallel trends in England during the Great War see Arthur Marwick, *The Deluge: British Society and the First World War* (New York: W. W. Norton, 1965), p. 109.

47. Quoted in John Morton Blum, V *Was for Victory: Politics and American Culture during World War II* (New York: Harcourt, Brace, Jovanovich, 1976), p. 101. For some of the crasser wartime advertisements see Michael S. Sherry, *In the Shadow of War: The United States since the 1930s* (New Haven: Yale University Press, 1995), pp. 89–91. Sherry notes that a truss manufacturer suggested that "freedom from rupture" was one of the great freedoms for which the nation was fighting.

48. David M. Potter, *People of Plenty: Economic Abundance and the American Character* (Chicago: University of Chicago Press, 1954).

49. Tom Wolfe, *The Kandy-Kolored Tangerine-Flake Streamline Baby* (New York: Farrar, Straus and Giroux, 1965); Marling, *As Seen on TV*, pp. 87–126.

50. Robert Penn Warren, *The Legacy of the Civil War: Meditations on the Centennial* (New York: Random House, 1961), pp. 46–64.

51. See Martin E. Marty, *Modern American Religion*, vol. 3: *Under God, Indivisible, 1941–1960* (Chicago: University of Chicago Press, 1996), pp. 330–32. Lawrence W. Levine notes similar blurring during the Great War in his *Defender of the Faith: William Jennings Bryan: The Last Decade, 1915–1925* (New York: Oxford University Press, 1965), p. 102.

52. Orsi, *The Madonna of 115th Street*, pp. 72–73.

53. Marty, *Modern American Religion* III: 130–56; Robert Wuthnow, "Science and the Sacred," in Phillip E. Hammond, ed., *The Sacred in a Secular Age: Toward Revision in the Scientific Study of Religion* (Berkeley and Los Angeles: University of California Press,

1985), pp. 187–203.

54. Marty, *Modern American Religion* III: 89–102, 211–30.

55. For an historical parallel see J. H. W. G. Liebeschuetz, *Continuity and Change in Roman Religion* (Oxford: Clarendon, 1979). An ancient historian (Velleius Paterculus) noted a similar phenomenon on Augustus's return from his triumph over Antonius in Egypt: "Thereafter men could hope from nothing from the gods, the gods could give nothing to men, nothing could be the object of prayer and the gift of good fortune, which Augustus did not bestow upon the Republic and upon the world after his return to the city." Quoted in A. H. M. Jones, *Augustus* (New York: W. W. Norton, 1970), p. 47.

56. Sydney E. Ahlstrom, *A Religious History of the American People* (New Haven: Yale University Press, 1972), pp. 951–52.

57. Vidich and Bensman, *Small Town in Mass Society*, pp. 234–39.

58. Marty, *Modern American Religion* III: 280–2, 313.

59. See Weller, *Yesterday's People*, pp. 121–33.

60. Will Herberg, *Protestant – Catholic – Jew: An Essay in American Religious Sociology* (New York: Doubleday, 1955), pp. 74–81.

61. From *A Modern Instance*. Quoted in Joseph F. Kett, *Rites of Passage: Adolescence in America, 1790 to the Present* (New York: Basic Books, 1977), p. 121.

62. Martin Marty makes this point in *Modern American Religion* III: 317–30.

63. Marty, *Modern American Religion,* III: 313–15; Bensman and Rosenberg, *Mass, Class, and Bureaucracy*, pp. 459–95; Arthur L. Swift, "Religious Values," in Anshen, ed., *The Family*, pp. 313–27; Warren A. Nord, *Religion and American Education: Rethinking an American Dilemma* (Chapel Hill: University of North Carolina Press, 1995), pp. 1–62. Riesman explores a shift from "morality to morale" in *The Lonely Crowd*, pp. 37–65.

64. George Creel, quoted in Ellis W. Hawley, *The Great War and the Search for a Modern Order: A History of the American People and Their Institutions, 1917–1933* (New York: St. Martin's Press, 1979), p. 22.

65. Paul Fussell, *Wartime: Understanding and Behavior in the Second World War* (New York: Oxford University Press, 1989), p. 164.

66. Wakeman, *The Hucksters* (New York: Rinehart, 1946).

67. Mumford, *The City in History*, p. 494. See also Patterson, *Grand Expectations*, pp. 12–15, 61–81; Riesman, *The Lonely Crowd*, pp. 116–25; Vance Packard, *The Status Seekers* (New York: McKay, 1959). Reinhold Niebuhr notes the tension between material prosperity and religion in *The Irony of American History* (New York: Scribner's, 1962), pp. 43–64.

68. John Hersey, *A Bell for Adano* (New York: Knopf, 1944); Kurt Vonnegut, *Slaughterhouse-Five, or the Children's Crusade: A Duty Dance with Death* (New York: Delacorte, 1969).

69. John Horne Burns, *The Gallery* (New York: Harper and Brothers, 1948), p. 262; Irwin Shaw, *The Young Lions* (New York: Random House, 1948). Burns's book is also

noteworthy for its veiled references to homosexuality — another taboo that could then be broached, albeit cautiously. It might also be noted that the film *Crossfire* (1947), in which a bigoted sergeant murders a Jewish veteran, was originally written about the murder of a homosexual later discovered to have been a decorated veteran.

70. Norman Mailer, *The Naked and the Dead* (New York: Rinehart, 1948), pp. 718–19. Kurt Vonnegut, too, was struck by the "mop-up" euphemism: "It is, in the imagination of combat's fans, the divinely listless loveplay that follows the orgasm of victory." See *Slaughterhouse-Five*, p. 51.

71. Carl Rollyson, *The Lives of Norman Mailer* (New York: Paragon, 1991), pp. 40–41. There is an often heard story that, on being introduced to Mailer, Tallulah Bankhead said, "Oh, you're the young man who can't spell 'f—.'" Mailer says it is a wonderful anecdote but untrue.

72. *From Here to Eternity* (New York: Scribner's, 1951).

73. On postwar literature see John Aldridge, *After the Lost Generation: A Critical Study of the Writers of Two Wars* (Freeport, N.Y.: Books for Libraries Press, 1971 [1951]), pp. 133–69. Note also an observations from just after the Great War: "The habit of continuous obscene language, which a long and miserable war has always induced, persisted four or five years more and had even spread to the younger women." Robert Graves and Alan Hodge, *The Long Week-End: A Social History of Great Britain, 1918–1939* (New York: W. W. Norton, 1963 [1940]), pp. 26–27.

74. Barnouw, *Tube of Plenty*, p. 142; David T. Courtwright, *Violent Land: Single Men and Social Disorder from the Frontier to the Inner City* (Cambridge, Mass.: Harvard University Press, 1996), pp. 103–7.

75. Richard Slotkin notes this gun "fetish" in his *Gunfighter Nation: The Myth of the Frontier in Twentieth-Century America* (New York: Atheneum, 1992), pp. 379–486.

76. See Gitlin, *The Sixties*, pp. 37–44; Patterson, *Grand Expectations*, pp. 355–61; Paul Goodman, *Growing Up Absurd: Problems of Youth in the Organized System* (New York: Random House, 1960 [1956]), pp. 119–32; Sheila Jeffreys, *Anticlimax: A Feminist Perspective on the Sexual Revolution* (New York: New York University Press, 1990), pp. 58–90.

77. Baughman, *The Republic of Mass Culture*, pp. 68–74; W. T. Lhamon, Jr., *Deliberate Speed: The Origins of a Cultural Style in the American 1950s* (Washington, D.C.: Smithsonian Institution Press, 1990), pp. 38–97.

78. See Gregory D. Black, *Hollywood Censored: Morality Codes, Catholics, and the Movies* (Cambridge: Cambridge University Press, 1994), p. 299; Baughman, *The Republic of Mass Media*, pp. 80–83; Robert Sklar, *Movie-Made America: A Cultural History of the Movies* (New York: Random House, 1975), pp. 294–96; Terry Christensen, *Reel Politics: American Political Movies from Birth of a Nation to Platoon* (Oxford: Basil Blackwell, 1987), p. 99; Collier, *The Rise of Selfishness in America*, pp. 194–200.

79. See Edward Shils's essay on war and authority, "American Society and the War in Indochina," in Anthony Lake, ed., *The Legacy of Vietnam: The War, American Society and the*

Future of American Foreign Policy (New York: New York University Press, 1976), pp. 40–65.

80. Quoted in David Reynolds, *Rich Relations: The American Occupation of Britain, 1941–1945* (New York: Random House, 1995), p. 441.

81. Charles A. Beard, *President Roosevelt and the Coming of War, 1941: A Study in Appearances and Realities* (New Haven: Yale University Press, 1948).

82. Fussell, *Wartime*, pp. 149–50.

83. Quoted in Patterson, *Grand Expectations*, p. 8. See also Goldman, *The Crucial Decade*, pp. 28–40.

84. See Adam Yarmolinsky, *The Military Establishment: Its Impact on American Society* (New York: Harper & Row, 1971), pp. 302–23.

85. Ronald H. Spector, *Advice and Support: The Early Years of the U.S. Army in Vietnam 1941–1960* (New York: Free Press, 1985), pp. 219–379; Sigmund Diamond, *Compromised Campus: The Collaboration of Universities with the Intelligence Community, 1945–1955* (New York: Oxford University Press, 1992), pp. 111–37.

86. Quoted in Lawrence S. Wittner, *Rebels against War: The American Peace Movement, 1933–1983* (Philadelphia: Temple University Press, 1984), p. 98.

87. On the militarization of youth culture see Tom Englehardt, *The End of Victory Culture: Cold War America and the Disillusioning of a Generation* (New York: Basic Books, 1994), pp. 69–171; Richard Slotkin, *Gunfighter Nation*, pp. 347–486; William M. Tuttle, Jr., *"Daddy's Gone to War:" The Second World War in the Lives of America's Children* (New York: Oxford University Press, 1993), pp. 159–60. Many Vietnam veterans note the importance of postwar culture in preparing them for military service. See Tim O'Brien, *If I Die in a Combat Zone* (New York: Delacorte, 1975), pp. 11–13; Ron Kovic, *Born on the Fourth of July* (New York: Pocket, 1977), pp. 54–56.

88. See H. Paul Jeffers and Dick Levitan, *See Parris and Die: Brutality in the U. S. Marines* (New York: Hawthorn, 1971).

89. See Allen Guttmann *From Ritual to Record: The Nature of Modern Sports* (New York: Columbia University Press, 1978), pp. 117–36; David Riesman "Football in America," *American Quarterly* 3 (1951): 309–25. Of related interest are Arnold Toynbee, *War and Civilization* (New York: Oxford University Press, 1950), pp. 14–15; Michael B. Poliakoff, *Combat Sports in the Ancient World: Competition, Violence, and Culture* (New Haven: Yale University Press, 1987); Peter Gay, *The Cultivation of Hatred: The Bourgeois Experience, Victoria to Freud*, vol. 3 (New York: W. W. Norton, 1993), pp. 9–33.

90. Simone Weil saw interwar France as an essentially deracinated country loosely held together by national myths and symbols. See *The Need for Roots* (Boston: Beacon, 1952 [1943]), pp. 99 ff.

91. A wartime study found that soldiers were more inclined to be involved in community activities than they were before the war. See Samuel Stouffer et al., *The American Soldier*, vol. 2, *Combat and Its Aftermath* (Princeton: Princeton University Press, 1949), pp. 641–43.

92. See W. Lloyd Warner, *American Life: Dream and Reality* (Chicago: University of Chicago Press, 1964 [1953]), pp. 8–19. See also Nina Tumarkin, *The Living and the Dead: The Rise and Fall of the Cult of World War II in Russia* (New York: Basic, 1994), pp. 125–57; David I. Kertzer, *Ritual, Politics, and Power* (New Haven: Yale University Press, 1988), pp. 69–70. Morris Janowitz notes the declining importance of such rituals during the 1950s. See *The Reconstruction of Patriotism: Education for Civic Consciousness* (Chicago: University of Chicago Press, 1983), p. 94.

Chapter Five

1. See C. Wright Mills, *White Collar: The American Middle Classes* (Oxford: Oxford University Press, 1953), pp. 161–88; Kenneth Keniston, *Youth and Dissent: The Rise of a New Opposition* (New York: Harcourt Brace Jovanovich, 1971), pp. 3–80.

2. See Martin E. Marty, *Modern American Religion,* vol. 3, *Under God, Indivisible, 1941–1960* (Chicago: University of Chicago Press, 1996), pp. 211–30.

3. E. Digby Baltzell makes this point in his *The Protestant Establishment: Aristocracy and Caste in America* (New York: Vintage, 1964), pp. 260–93. See also Joseph Bensman and Bernard Rosenberg, "Mass Media and Mass Culture," in Philip Olson, ed., *America as a Mass Society: Changing Community and Identity* (New York: Free Press, 1963), pp. 166–184.

4. Alfred C. Kinsey, Wardell B. Pomeroy, and Clyde E. Martin, *Sexual Behavior in the Human Male* (Philadelphia: W. B. Saunders, 1948); Kinsey et al., *Sexual Behavior in the Human Female* (Philadelphia: W. B. Saunders, 1953).

5. Paul Goodman, *Growing Up Absurd: Problems of Youth in the Organized System* (New York: Random House, 1960 [1956]), pp. 3–16; Eric F. Goldman, *The Crucial Decade – and After: America, 1945–1960* (New York: Vintage, 1960), pp. 187–201, 316–26.

6. On secularizing trends see Warren A. Nord, *Religion and American Education: Rethinking an American Dilemma* (Chapel Hill: University of North Carolina Press, 1995), pp. 15–62; Everett M. Rogers, *Social Change in Rural Society* (New York: Appleton-Century-Crofts, 1960), pp. 207–9.

7. See Bruno Bettelheim, *The Uses of Enchantment: The Meaning and Importance of Fairy Tales* (New York: Vintage, 1977), pp. 3–53; Vigen Guroian, *Tending the Heart of Virtue: How Classic Stories Awaken a Child's Moral Imagination* (New York: Oxford University Press, 1998).

8. On war movies of the period and the trivialization of war experiences see Lawrence H. Suid, *Guts and Glory: Great American War Movies* (Reading, Mass.: Addison-Wesley, 1978); Craig M. Cameron, *American Samurai: Myth, Imagination, and the Conduct of Battle in the First Marine Division, 1941–1951* (New York: Cambridge University Press, 1994), pp. 241–72. Goodman notes weakening patriotism in *Growing Up Absurd*, pp. 96–118.

9. Nathanael West, *Miss Lonely Hearts* (New York: New Directions, 1962 [1933]), p. 39.

10. Marty, *Modern American Religion* III: 130–56.

11. David Riesman, *The Lonely Crowd: A Study in the Changing American Character* (New Haven: Yale University Press, 1950), pp. 3–36. Riesman sees this shift from inner-directedness to other-directedness as the result of economic and demographic changes. The present view is that it stemmed more from the breakdown of local communities, dislocations in population, rapid mobility, and other changes brought on by the war.

12. Numerous studies examined the problems of rapid social change in postwar America. Mills, *White Collar*; William Kornhauser, *The Politics of Mass Society* (Glencoe, Ill.: Free Press, 1959); Robert E. Lane, *Political Ideology: Why the American Common Man Believes What He Does* (New York: Free Press, 1962); Philip Olson, ed., *America as a Mass Society: Changing Community and Identity* (New York: Free Press, 1963); Seymour Martin Lipset and Theodore Raab, *The Politics of Unreason: Right-Wing Extremism in America, 1790–1977* 2nd ed. (Chicago: University of Chicago Press, 1978), pp. 209–47; Robert Jay Lifton, *The Protean Self: Human Resilience in an Age of Fragmentation* (New York: Basic, 1993). There were of course important differences on the causes and consequences of anomie among these authors. Some saw it as a sign of decay, others saw it as an opening to a new order.

13. Robert Penn Warren, *The Legacy of the Civil War: Meditations on the Centennial* (New York: Random House, 1961), p. 64. Warren's interpretation of post-Civil War America was likely shaped by the similar climate in the years following World War II, during which it was written.

14. On discontent with post-Civil War sanctimony see Merle Curti, *The Growth of American Thought* 3rd ed. (New York: Harper & Row, 1964), pp. 465–507; Stuart McConnell, *Glorious Contentment: The Grand Army of the Republic, 1865–1900* (Chapel Hill: University of North Carolina Press, 1992).

15. See Christopher Lasch, *The New Radicalism in America, 1889–1963: The Intellectual As a Social Type* (New York: Knopf, 1965), pp. 286–349; Dwight Macdonald, *Against the Grain: Essays on the Effect of Mass Culture* (New York: Random House, 1962).

16. On the dismantling of New Deal agencies during the war see Alan Brinkley, *The End of Reform: New Deal Liberalism in Recession and War* (New York: Knopf, 1995), pp. 140–42; David M. Kennedy, *Freedom from Fear: The American People in Depression and War, 1929–1945* (New York: Oxford University Press, 1999), pp. 782–87; John Dos Passos, *State of the Nation* (Boston: Houghton Mifflin, 1943), pp. 154–57.

17. Goldman, *The Crucial Decade*, pp. 38–40. For weakening of progressivism during and after the Great War see Ellis W. Hawley, *The Great War and the Search for a Modern Order: A History of the American People and Their Institutions, 1917–1933* (New York: St. Martin's Press, 1979), pp. 23–24; David P. Thelen, *Robert M. La Follette and the Insurgent Spirit* (Madison: University of Wisconsin Press, 1985), pp. 125–54.

18. Popular books on this include J. K. Galbraith, *The Affluent Society* (London: Hamish Hamilton, 1958); Michael Harrington, *The Other America: Poverty in the United*

States (New York: Macmillan, 1963); Jules Henry, *Culture against Man* (New York: Vintage, 1963). These voices of protest might not be giving the war its due in bringing about important social change. The war ended widespread poverty, created expansive middle classes, gave millions access to college education, and saw the beginning of housing standards, rent control, and child care.

19. Rachel Carson, *Silent Spring* (Boston: Houghton Mifflin, 1962).

20. Joseph Bensman and Bernard Rosenberg, *Mass, Class, and Bureaucracy: The Evolution of Contemporary Society* (New York: Prentice-Hall, 1963), pp. 93–95.

21. Moira Komarovsky, *Blue-Collar Marriage* (New York: Vintage, 1962), p. 49.

22. Komarovsky, *Blue-Collar Marriage*, pp. 49–56.

23. Cynthia Fuchs Epstein, *Woman's Place: Options and Limits in Professional Careers* (Berkeley and Los Angeles: University of California Press, 1971), p. 7.

24. Bensman and Rosenberg, *Mass, Class, and Bureaucracy*, pp. 99–104; Carl N. Degler, *At Odds: Women and the Family in America from the Revolution to the Present* (New York: Oxford University Press, 1980), pp. 418–35; James T. Patterson, *Grand Expectations: The United States, 1945–1974* (New York: Oxford University Press, 1996), pp. 31–38, 361–69. Popular books from the time include Simone de Beauvoir, *The Second Sex* (New York: Knopf, 1953); Betty Friedan, *The Feminine Mystique* (New York: W. W. Norton, 1963). For background see Lasch, *The New Radicalism in America*, pp. 38–69; William H. Whyte, Jr., "The Wives of Management," in Olson, ed., *America as a Mass Society*, pp. 478–91.

25. Quote from Manning Marable, *Race, Reform, and Rebellion: The Second Reconstruction in Black America, 1945–1990* (Jackson: University Press of Mississippi, 1991), p. 14; C. Vann Woodward, *The Strange Career of Jim Crow* (New York: Oxford University Press, 1966), pp. 134–35. Morris Janowitz says of the war experience, "The preconditions for a more effective civil rights movement were created." See *The Reconstruction of Patriotism: Education for Civic Consciousness* (Chicago: University of Chicago Press, 1983), p. 126.

26. Woodward, *The Strange Career of Jim Crow*, p. 128; Frederick Lewis Allen, *The Big Change: America Transforms Itself, 1900–1950* (New York: Harper & Row, 1952), p. 162; Patterson, *Grand Expectations*, p. 19. On black migration to northern cities during the Great War see Thomas Lee Philpott, *The Slum and the Ghetto: Immigrants, Blacks, and Reformers in Chicago, 1880–1930* (Belmont, Calif.: Wadsworth, 1991), pp. 116–62; James R. Grossman, *Land of Hope: Chicago, Black Southerners, and the Great Migration* (Chicago: University of Chicago Press, 1989).

27. See Patterson, *Grand Expectations*, p. 20; Dos Passos, *State of the Nation*, pp. 95–103.

28. David Reynolds, *Rich Relations: The American Occupation of Britain, 1941–1945* (New York: Random House, 1995), pp. 302–34.

29. See Samuel Stouffer et al., *The American Soldier*, vol. 1: *Adjustment during Army Life* (Princeton: Princeton University Press, 1949), pp. 514–19.

30. Quoted in Joseph C. Goulden, *The Best Years, 1945–1950* (New York: Atheneum, 1976), p. 353.

31. Quoted in Reynolds, *Rich Relations,* p. 443. See also Neil R. McMillen, *Dark Journey: Black Mississippians in the Age of Jim Crow* (Urbana: University of Illinois Press, 1990), pp. 317–18.

32. Rosa Parks and Jim Haskins, *Rosa Parks: My Story* (New York: Dial, 1992), pp. 65–94.

33. Jules Tygiel, *Baseball's Great Experiment: Jackie Robinson and His Legacy* (New York: Oxford University Press, 1983), pp. 37–64.

34. Quoted in Goldman, *The Crucial Decade,* p. 185. McAuliffe, it might be remembered, was the commander at Bastogne during the Battle of the Bulge who delivered the famous "Nuts!" response to German demands for surrender. See also Janowitz, *The Reconstruction of Patriotism,* pp. 123-27.

35. Woodward, *Jim Crow,* pp. 136–39.

36. Quoted in Woodward, *Jim Crow,* p. 132.

37. On the changed postwar atmosphere see Woodward, *Jim Crow,* pp. 130–47; Marable, *Race, Reform, and Rebellion,* pp. 13–39; Patterson, *Grand Expectations,* pp. 20–31, 385–406; Michael S. Sherry, *In the Shadow of War: The United States since the 1930s* (New Haven: Yale University Press, 1995), pp. 144–51, 208–14; Ira Berlin, "Fighting on Two Fronts: War and the Struggle for Racial Equality in Two Centuries," in Gabor S. Boritt, ed., *War Comes Again: Comparative Vistas on the Civil War and World War II* (New York: Oxford University Press, 1995), pp. 125–41. Bill Mauldin conveys the changed racial climate following the war in his *Back Home* (New York: William Sloane, 1947), pp. 154–89.

38. See Paul Fussell, *Wartime: Understanding and Behavior in the Second World War* (New York: Oxford University Press, 1989), pp. 79–95.

39. Despite the victory and ensuing celebration, forty-eight percent of veterans interviewed in 1947 answered that the war had made their lives worse. See Samuel Stouffer et al., *The American Soldier,* vol. II: *Combat and Its Aftermath* (Princeton: Princeton University Press, 1949), pp. 631–32. Similar resentments can be found in the writings of Civil War soldiers. See James M. McPherson, *For Cause and Comrades: Why Men Fought in the Civil War* (New York: Oxford University Press, 1997), pp. 56–61.

40. "On the enlisted men's side the stresses of war and the sudden heady blooming of temporary rank produced sufficient injustices and unnecessary hardships to rankle. . . . Some of them found themselves to be better educated than the leaders assigned to them by the fortunes of war." R. Ernest Dupuy, "Pass in Review," *The Army Combat Forces Journal* 4 (1954): 43. (I thank Peter Sweda for this reference.) See also Cameron, *American Samurai,* pp. 54–62.

41. *Brave Men* (New York: Henry Holt, 1944), p. 465. Mauldin had much praise for Ike and Brad (none for most other officers) in his *Back Home,* pp. 15–16, 95–96. Bradley's memoirs are none too kind to Patton. See Omar N. Bradley, *A Soldier's Story* (New York: Henry Holt, 1951), pp. 52–63. (Bradley once told Patton that his pearl-handled pistols made him look like a pimp in a New Orleans bordello.)

NOTES, pp. 133–136

42. Bill Mauldin, *The Brass Ring: A Sort of Memoir* (New York: W. W. Norton, 1971), pp. 353–64.

43. John Hersey, *A Bell for Adano* (New York: Knopf, 1944); James Jones, *From Here to Eternity* (New York: Scribner's, 1948) and *The Thin Red Line* (New York: Scribner's, 1962); Norman Mailer, *The Naked and the Dead* (New York: Rinehart, 1948); Irwin Shaw, *The Young Lions* (New York: Random House, 1948).

44. See Max Schulman's *Rally Round the Flag, Boys!* (New York: Doubleday, 1957), later made into a film. Films and television shows of this genre include *Sgt. Bilko, McHale's Navy, F Troop, Soldier in the Rain,* and *No Time for Sergeants.*

45. C. Wright Mills, *The Causes of World War Three* (New York: Simon & Schuster, 1958), p 23. See also Henry, *Culture against Man,* pp. 100–23.

46. For discontent with the cant of postwar America see Paul Fussell, *Doing Battle: The Making of a Skeptic* (Boston: Little, Brown, 1996), pp. 211-13, 228-29; Cameron, *American Samurai,* pp. 241–72; Mauldin, *Back Home,* pp. 154–315.

47. See Lawrence S. Wittner, *Rebels against War: The American Peace Movement, 1933–1983* (Philadelphia: Temple University Press, 1984), pp. 151–275; Goodman, *Growing Up Absurd,* pp. 100–03; Reinhold Niebuhr pointed out the tension between traditional American virtue and the new power realities of the postwar world in *The Irony of American History* (New York: Scribner's, 1962).

48. See Stouffer et al., *The American Soldier* II: 228–31. Dave Grossman argues that after the war the military developed techniques to break down the human resistance to killing and thus were better able to turn citizens into effective combat soldiers. See *On Killing: The Psychological Cost of Learning to Kill in War and Society* (Boston: Little, Brown, 1995), pp. 231–80. I think postwar youth's adulation of the military might have been more important.

49. Major General W. H. Rupertus, "Rifleman's Creed," quoted in Gustav Hasford, *The Short-Timers* (New York: Bantam, 1980), pp. 22–23.

50. David T. Courtwright, *Violent Land: Single Men and Social Disorder from the Frontier to the Inner City* (Cambridge, Mass.: Harvard University Press, 1996), pp. 43–45. See also Hasford, *The Short-Timers*; Adam Yarmolinsky, *The Military Establishment: Its Impact on American Society* (New York: Harper & Row, 1971), pp. 324–408; H. Paul Jeffers and Dick Levitan, *See Parris and Die: Brutality in the U.S. Marines* (New York: Hawthorn, 1971). Hasford's book was the basis for the 1986 film *Full Metal Jacket.* The latter three works reflect changing views regarding the military brought on by Vietnam. On post-Vietnam changes in the marines see Thomas E. Ricks, *Making the Corps* (New York: Simon & Schuster, 1997).

51. William Appleman Williams, *The Contours of American History* (Chicago: Quadrangle Books, 1966 [1961]), p. 17.

52. John Hersey's might have planted the seed of discontent with atomic weapons shortly after the war with his *Hiroshima* (New York: Knopf, 1946), originally published

254

in *The New Yorker.*

53. Two of the better-known books of this genre are Herman Kahn's, *On Thermonuclear War* (Princeton: Princeton University Press, 1960) and *Thinking about the Unthinkable* (New York: Horizon, 1962).

54. See Paul Boyer, *By the Bomb's Early Light: American Thought and Culture at the Dawn of the Atomic Age* (New York: Pantheon, 1985), pp. 3–26; John Lewis Gaddis, *We Now Know: Rethinking Cold War History* (Oxford: Clarendon Press, 1997), pp. 221–59. For anti-nuclear sentiment's role in the development of the counterculture see Todd Gitlin, *The Sixties: Years of Hope, Days of Rage* (New York: Bantam, 1987), pp. 22–26; David Horowitz, *Radical Son: A Generational Odyssey* (New York: Simon & Schuster, 1997), pp. 35–119.

55. See Mills, *The Causes of World War Three*, pp. 56–67.

56. See Reynolds, *Rich Relations*, pp. 363–66; Stephen E. Ambrose, *Band of Brothers: E Company, 506th Regiment, 101st Airborne, from Normandy to Hitler's Nest* (New York: Simon & Schuster, 1992), pp. 57–58.

57. It is often alleged that this pact secured local support for the invasion of Sicily (1943), but disparate Mafia groups there had long been at odds with the Mussolini regime, and parts of them, many of whom were essentially mountain-dwelling bandits, acted as scouts and intelligence sources. See Christopher Duggan, *Fascism and the Mafia* (New Haven: Yale University Press, 1989), pp. 53–91.

58. Edward S. Corwin, *Total War and the Constitution* (New York: Alfred A. Knopf, 1947) and *The Constitution and What It Means Today* (New York: Atheneum, 1963), pp. 64–68; Arthur Schlesinger, Jr., "War and the Constitution: Abraham Lincoln and Franklin Roosevelt," in Gabor S. Boritt, ed., *War Comes Again: Comparative Vistas on the Civil War and World War II* (New York: Oxford University Press, 1995), pp. 143–65; Cabell Phillips, *The 1940s: Decade of Triumph and Trouble* (New York: Macmillan, 1975), pp. 122–34. See also Harold Lasswell, "The Garrison State and the Specialists on Violence," *American Journal of Sociology* 47 (1941): 455–68.

59. Gaddis, *We Now Know*, pp. 179–91; H. W. Brands, *The Devil We Knew: Americans and the Cold War* (New York: Oxford University Press, 1993), pp. 31–58.

60. David Burner, *Making Peace with the 60s* (Princeton: Princeton University Press, 1997), pp. 108–12; Gaddis, *We Now Know*, pp. 260–80.

61. Fletcher Knebel and Charles W. Bailey II, *Seven Days in May* (New York: Harper & Row, 1962). Ironically, Walker commanded the troops charged with integrating the Little Rock public schools — a task he performed professionally despite his segregationalist views. See Fred J. Cook, *The Warfare State* (New York: Macmillan, 1962), pp. 264–83.

62. Eugene Burdick and Harvey Wheeler, *Fail Safe* (New York: McGraw-Hill, 1962). C. Wright Mills, sketched a very similar scenario in his 1958 work *The Causes of World War Three*, pp. 44–46.

63. Peter Bryant, *Red Alert* (New York: Ace, 1958). The director of *Dr. Strangelove,*

Stanley Kubrick, began to adapt the novel as a serious drama but found the subject so surreal as to demand presentation as dark comedy.

64. Mark Rascovich, *The Bedford Incident* (New York: Atheneum, 1963).

65. On growing discontent with militarism see Sherry, *In the Shadow of War*, pp. 237–49; Brands, *The Devil We Knew*, pp. 59–85; Lawrence S. Wittner, *Rebels against War: The American Peace Movement, 1933–1983* (Philadelphia: Temple University Press, 1984), pp. 151–275.

66. On estranged youth of the period see Kenneth Keniston, *The Uncommitted: Alienated Youth in American Society* (New York: Harcourt, Brace and World, 1965 [1960]), as well as his follow-up study, *Young Radicals: Notes on Committed Youth* (New York: Harcourt Brace and World, 1968); Goodman, *Growing Up Absurd*. For counterparts among young adults see Norman Mailer's 1959 essay "The White Negro," reprinted in *The Time of Our Time* (New York: Random House, 1998), pp. 211–30; Charles Webb, *The Graduate* (n.p.: New American Library, 1963).

67. Quoted in Curti, *The Growth of American Thought*, p. 465.

68. See Gitlin, *The Sixties*, pp. 11–21; Paul Jacobs and Saul Landau, *The New Radicals: A Report with Documents* (New York: Random House, 1966), pp. 3–64.

69. Many studies of the 1950s, quite puzzlingly, see the period as plagued by stifling conformity. Notable exceptions are John Patrick Diggins, *The Proud Decades: America in War and Peace, 1941–1960* (New York: W. W. Norton, 1988); W. T. Lhamon, Jr., *Deliberate Speed: The Origins of a Cultural Style in the American 1950s* (Washington, D.C.: Smithsonian Institution Press, 1990); Gitlin, *The Sixties*, pp. 1–77; and David Halberstam, *The Fifties* (New York: Villard, 1993).

70. These sentiments linger to this day. See Karal Ann Marling, *As Seen on TV: The Visual Culture of Everyday Life in the 1950s* (Cambridge, Mass.: Harvard University Press, 1994).

71. Erik Barnouw, *Tube of Plenty: The Evolution of American Television* (New York: Oxford University Press, 1990), pp. 193–98.

72. B. A. Botkin, *A Treasury of American Folklore: Stories, Ballads, and Traditions of the People* (New York: Crown, 1944), p. 6.

73. Botkin, *A Treasury of American Folklore*, pp. 2–32, 134–50, and passim; James Atkins Shackford, *David Crockett: The Man and the Legend* (Chapel Hill: University of North Carolina Press, 1986), pp. 3–72; Dixon Wecter, *The Hero in America: A Chronicle of Hero Worship* (New York: Scribner's, 1969 [1941]), pp. 189–93.

74. Janowitz notes the declining quality of public school teachers (as well as the attendant weakening of civic education in *The Reconstruction of Patriotism*, p. 65. See also Robin M. Williams, Jr., *American Society: A Sociological Interpretation* (New York: Knopf, 1955), pp. 275–80; Goodman, *Growing Up Absurd*, pp. 71–95; Henry, *Culture against Man*, pp. 283–321.

75. Burner, *Making Peace with the 60s*, pp. 135–36; Lewis S. Feuer, *The Conflict of*

Generations: The Character and Significance of Student Movements (New York: Basic Books, 1969), pp. 385–435.

76. Peter Novick, *That Noble Dream: The "Objectivity Question" and the American Historical Profession* (New York: Cambridge University Press, 1988), pp. 281–85; Brinkley, *The End of Reform,* pp. 137–64; Gary B. Nash, Charlotte Crabtree, and Ross E. Dunn, *History on Trial: Culture Wars and the Teaching of the Past* (New York: Knopf, 1998), pp. 25–74.

77. See James Burnham, *The Managerial Revolution* (New York: John Day, 1941); Friedrich von Hayek, *The Road to Serfdom* (Chicago: University of Chicago Press, 1944).

78. Richard Hofstadter, *The Progressive Historians: Turner, Beard, Parrington* (New York: Knopf, 1969), pp. 437–66.

79. Talcott Parsons, *The Social System* (New York: Free Press, 1964 [1951]); Talcott Parsons and Edward A. Shils, eds., *Toward a General Theory of Action* (Cambridge, Mass.: Harvard University Press, 1951); David Easton, *A Systems Analysis of Political Life* (New York: Wiley, 1965).

80. Critics of prevailing social science included Barrington Moore, Jr., *Political Power and Social Theory* (Cambridge, Mass.: Harvard University Press, 1958); William Appleman Williams, *The Tragedy of American Diplomacy* 2nd ed. (New York: Dell, 1972 [1959]); C. Wright Mills, *The Sociological Imagination* (New York: Oxford University Press, 1959).

81. Morris Dickstein, *Gates of Eden: American Culture in the Sixties* (New York: Basic Books, 1977), pp. 25–88; James Miller, *Democracy Is in the Streets: From Port Huron to the Siege of Chicago* (Cambridge, Mass.: Harvard University Press, 1994), pp. 83–93; Diggins, *The Proud Decades,* pp. 247–57; Georg G. Iggers, *Historiography in the Twentieth Century: From Scientific Objectivity to the Postmodern Challenge* (Hanover, N.H.: Wesleyan University Press, 1997), pp. 41–47.

82. See Hofstadter, *The Progressive Historians,* pp. 437–66; Gitlin, *The Sixties,* pp. 26–30; Keniston, *Youth and Dissent,* pp. 81–98, 127–42; Theodore Roszak, *The Making of a Counter Culture: Reflections on the Technocratic Society and Its Youthful Opposition* (New York: Anchor, 1969).

83. Keniston, *Young Radicals,* p. 139; Tom Wolfe, *The Electric Kool-Aid Acid Test* (New York: Farrar, Straus and Giroux, 1968), pp. 34–67.

84. See Kerouac's books (*On the Road, Big Sur, The Dharma Bums*) as well as Alan W. Watts, *The Spirit of Zen: A Way of Life, Work and Art in the Far East* (New York: Grove Press, 1958); William Plummer, *The Holy Goof: A Biography of Neal Cassady* (Englewood Cliffs, N.J.: Prentice-Hall, 1981); David Burner, *Making Peace with the 60s,* pp. 113–33; Reece McGee, *Social Disorganization in America* (San Francisco, Calif.: Chandler, 1962), pp. 66–74. Kerouac, unlike most of his fellow Beats, admired the American past and felt alienated from the modern country it was becoming.

85. Burner, *Making Peace with the 60s,* pp. 134–66; Gitlin, *The Sixties,* pp. 81–170; Clayborne Carson, *In Struggle: SNCC and the Black Awakening of the 1960s* (Cambridge,

Mass.: Harvard University Press, 1981); Roszak, *The Making of a Counter Culture*, pp. 1–41.

86. Dickstein, *Gates of Eden*, pp. 188–90; James L. Baughman, *The Republic of Mass Culture: Journalism, Filmmaking, and Broadcasting in America since 1941* (Baltimore: Johns Hopkins University Press, 1992), pp. 132–34; R. Serge Denisoff and Richard A. Peterson, eds., *The Sounds of Social Change: Studies in Popular Culture* (Rand McNally, 1972); Gitlin, *The Sixties*, pp. 74–77.

87. Dickstein, *Gates of Eden*, pp. 205–10; Baughman, *The Republic of Mass Culture*, pp. 134–37.

Chapter Six

1. Robert Dallek, *Franklin Roosevelt and American Foreign Policy, 1932–1945* (New York: Oxford University Press, 1979), pp. 269–75.

2. John W. Dower, *War without Mercy: Race and Power in the Pacific War* (New York: Pantheon, 1987), pp. 3–14, 203–317; Saburo Ienaga, *The Pacific War, 1931–1945: A Critical Perspective on Japan's Role in World War II* (New York: Pantheon, 1978), pp. 178–80.

3. Ronald H. Spector, *Advice and Support: The Early Years of the U.S. Army in Vietnam 1941–1960* (New York: Free Press, 1985), pp. 37–50; Archimedes L. A. Patti, *Why Viet Nam? Prelude to America's Albatross* (Berkeley and Los Angeles: University of California Press, 1980), pp. 28–71.

4. See Joseph Buttinger, *Vietnam: A Dragon Embattled*, vol. 1, *From Colonialism to the Viet Minh* (New York: Praeger, 1967); David G. Marr, *Vietnamese Tradition on Trial, 1920–1945* (Berkeley and Los Angeles: University of California Press, 1981), pp. 327–420.

5. John Lewis Gaddis, *We Now Know: Rethinking Cold War History* (Oxford: Clarendon Press, 1997), pp. 155–58. France embarked on imperialist adventures after defeats in the Napoleonic Wars and the Franco-Prussian War. See V. G. Kiernan, *Colonial Empires and Armies, 1815-1960* (London: Sutton, 1998), pp. 13-14, 167-78.

6. Spector, *Advice and Support*, pp. 191–214.

7. Quoted in Stephen E. Ambrose, *Eisenhower*, vol. 2, *The President* (New York: Simon and Schuster, 1984), p. 176. He deleted the passage shortly before publication in 1964, as the country's involvement was deepening.

8. See Gaddis, *We Now Know*, pp. 161–63; Bernard B. Fall, *Street Without Joy* (New York: Schocken, 1972); Joseph Buttinger, *The Smaller Dragon: A Political History of Vietnam* (New York: Praeger, 1958).

9. See Walt W. Rostow, *The Stages of Economic Growth: A Non-Communist Manifesto* (Cambridge: Cambridge University Press, 1960); Robert A. Packenham, *Liberal America and the Third World: Political Development Ideas in Foreign Aid and Social Science* (Princeton: Princeton University Press, 1973), pp. 59–110; Gaddis, *We Now Know*, pp. 183–85.

10. Roy L. Prosterman and Jeffrey M. Riedinger, *Land Reform and Democratic Development* (Baltimore: Johns Hopkins University Press, 1987), pp. 121–26. See also Roy

L. Prosterman, "Land Reform in South Vietnam: A Proposal for Turning the Tables on the Vietcong," *Cornell Law Review* 53 (1967): 26–44; Robert L. Sansom, *The Economics of Insurgency in the Mekong Delta* (Cambridge, Mass.: MIT Press, 1970), pp. 53–74.

11. Spector, *Advice and Support*, pp. 219–379; J. J. Zasloff, "Origins of the Insurgency in South Vietnam, 1954–1960: The Role of the Southern Vietminh Cadres," (Santa Monica, Calif.: Rand Memorandum 5163/2-ISA/ARPA, May 1968).

12. On the growing insurgency see the local studies of Jeffrey Race, *War Comes to Long An: Revolutionary Conflict in a Vietnamese Province* (Berkeley and Los Angeles: University of California Press, 1972); William R. Andrews, *The Village War: Vietnamese Communist Revolutionary Activities in Dinh Tuong Province, 1960–1964* (Columbia: University of Missouri Press, 1973).

13. Harold P. Ford, *CIA and the Vietnam Policymakers: Three Episodes, 1962–1968* (McLean, Va.: Center for the Study of Intelligence, 1998), pp. 25–84.

14. On the path to war in Vietnam see George McT. Kahin, *Intervention: How America Became Involved in Vietnam* (New York: Knopf, 1986), pp. 347–401; Leslie H. Gelb and Richard K. Betts, *The Irony of Vietnam: The System Worked* (Washington D. C.: Brookings Institution, 1979), pp. 116–130; John C. Donnell, Guy J. Pauker, and Joseph J. Zasloff, "Viet Cong Motivation and Morale in 1964: A Preliminary Report," (Santa Monica, Calif.: Rand Corporation Research Memorandum RM4507/3–15A, March 1965); J. J. Zasloff, "Origins of the Insurgency in South Vietnam, 1954–1960: The Role of the Southern Vietminh Cadres," (Santa Monica, Calif.: Rand Memorandum 5163/2-ISA/ARPA, May 1968).

15. Daniel C. Hallin, *The "Uncensored War:" The Media and Vietnam* (New York: Oxford University Press, 1986), pp. 126–58.

16. Hans J. Morgenthau, *Vietnam and the United States* (Washington D. C.: Public Affairs Press, 1965), p. 12. See also Gelb and Betts, *The Irony of Vietnam*, p.213.

17. For polling data on support and opposition see John E. Mueller, *Wars, Presidents, and Public Opinion* (New York: John Wiley, 1973). Mueller sees eroding support stemming from mounting casualty figures. The present view is that the public would likely have maintained support if there had been signs of progress and if South Vietnam had been a worthy ally.

18. Stanley Karnow, *Vietnam: A History* (New York: Viking, 1983), pp. 320–21; Phillip B. Davidson, *Vietnam at War: The History, 1946–1975* (New York: Oxford University Press, 1991), pp. 451–52.

19. On the early years of the American phase of the war see John C. Donnell, "Viet Cong Recruitment: Why and How Men Join," (Santa Monica, Calif.: Rand Corporation Research Memorandum RM 5486–1, 1967); Harold G. Moore and Joseph L. Galloway, *We Were Soldiers Once . . . and Young* (New York: Random House, 1993).

20. For criticism of the strategy of attrition see Andrew F. Krepinevich, Jr., *The Army and Vietnam* (Baltimore: Johns Hopkins University Press, 1983).

21. See Bernard William Rogers, *Cedar Falls – Junction City: A Turning Point* (Washington, D.C. Government Printing Office, 1974); John A. Cash, John Albright, and Allan W. Sandstrum, *Seven Firefights in Vietnam* (Washington, D.C.: Center of Military History, 1989).

22. On the early antiwar movement see Adam Garfinkle, *Telltale Hearts: The Origins and Impact of the Vietnam Antiwar Movement* (New York: St Martin's Griffin, 1997), pp. 85–148; Todd Gitlin, *The Sixties: Years of Hope, Days of Rage* (New York: Bantam, 1987), pp. 242–82; Todd Gitlin, *The Whole World Is Watching: Mass Media in the Making and Unmaking of the New Left* (Berkeley and Los Angeles: University of California Press, 1980), pp. 1–179; Paul Jacobs and Saul Landau, *The New Radicals: A Report with Documents* (New York: Random House, 1966), pp. 65–73.

23. Christian G. Appy, *Working-Class War: American Combat Soldiers and Vietnam* (Chapel Hill: University of North Carolina Press, 1993), pp. 206–49.

24. For opposition to earlier wars see Robert L. Beisner, *Twelve against Empire: The Anti-Imperialists, 1898–1900* (New York: McGraw-Hill, 1968); Samuel Eliot Morison, Frederick Merk, and Frank Friedel, *Dissent in Three American Wars* (Cambridge, Mass.: Harvard University Press, 1970); Roger H. Brown, *The Republic in Peril: 1812* (New York: W. W. Norton, 1971), pp. 131–91.

25. See Mueller, *Wars, Presidents, and Public Opinion*, pp. 23–65. On the inability to stem the flow of supplies from the North see Mark Clodfelter, *The Limits of Airpower: The American Bombing of North Vietnam* (New York: Free Press, 1989), pp. 123–28.

26. Philip Roth conveys this atmosphere in his novel, *American Pastoral* (Boston: Houghton Mifflin, 1997), pp. 93–174. See also John A. Clausen, *American Lives: Looking Back at the Children of the Great Depression* (New York: Free Press, 1993), pp. 103–5; Donald Katz, *Home Fires: An Intimate Portrait of One Middle-Class Family in Postwar America* (New York: Harper Collins, 1992), pp. 231–305.

27. Appy, *Working-Class War*, pp. 38–43.

28. Morris Dickstein, *Gates of Eden: American Culture in the Sixties* (New York: Basic Books, 1977), pp. 154–82; David Burner, *Making Peace with the 60s* (Princeton: Princeton University Press, 1997), pp. 49–83.

29. Steven Mintz and Susan Kellogg, *Domestic Revolutions: A Social History of American Family Life* (New York: Free Press, 1988), pp. 203–37; Gitlin, *The Sixties*, pp. 362–76; Ruth Rosen, "The Day They Buried Traditional Womanhood," in D. Michael Shafer, ed., *The Legacy: The Vietnam War in the American Imagination* (Boston: Beacon Press, 1990), pp. 233–61.

30. For general discussion of the counterculture see David Horowitz, *Radical Son: A Generational Odyssey* (New York: Simon & Schuster, 1997), pp. 157–202; Tom Wolfe, *The Electric Kool-Aid Acid Test* (New York: Farrar, Straus and Giroux, 1968); Rosabeth Moss Kanter, *Commitment and Community: Communes and Utopias in Sociological Perspective* (Cambridge, Mass.: Harvard University Press, 1972).

31. The passions and confusion of these demonstrations are conveyed in Norman Mailer's *The Armies of the Night* (New York: New American Library, 1968); Richard A. Siggelkow, *Dissent and Disruption: A University under Siege* (Buffalo, N.Y.: Prometheus, 1991); Roger Rosenblatt, *Coming Apart: A Memoir of the Harvard Wars of 1969* (Boston: Little, Brown, 1997).

32. See Garfinkle, *Telltale Hearts,* pp. 117–48; Gitlin, *The Sixties,* pp. 242–82; Tom Wells, *The War Within: America's Battle over Vietnam* (Berkeley and Los Angeles: University of California Press, 1994), pp. 115–222; Seymour Martin Lipset and Philip G. Altbach, *Students in Revolt* (Boston: Beacon Press, 1970); Gitlin, *The Whole World Is Watching,* pp. 180–204.

33. By contrast, support for World War II increased each year. See Mueller, *Wars, Presidents, and Public Opinion,* pp. 6, 168–75.

34. American intelligence had captured plans outlining a major attack on many cities and bases. Commanders canceled scheduled operations in remote areas and shifted troops to major cities such as Saigon and Hue. When the pope requested that Johnson order a bombing halt, he told him that, because of an impending offensive, he could not. See Davidson, *Vietnam at War,* pp. 468–70; James J. Wirtz, *The Tet Offensive: Intelligence Failure in War* (Ithaca: Cornell University Press, 1991), pp. 72–84.

35. Forty-seven thousand Viet Cong deserted in 1969; thirty-two thousand the following year. See Douglas S. Blaufarb, *The Counterinsurgency Era: U. S. Doctrine and Performance, 1950 to the Present* (New York: Free Press, 1977), p. 267.

36. Ronald H. Spector, *After Tet: The Bloodiest Year in Vietnam* (New York: Free Press, 1993), pp. 76–78; Truong Nhu Tang, *A Viet Cong Memoir: An Inside Account of the Vietnam War and Its Aftermath* (New York: Vintage, 1986), pp. 154–55, 192–93; Michael Lee Lanning and Dan Cragg, *Inside the VC and the NVA* (New York: Fawcett Columbine, 1992), pp. 26–29; Wirtz, *The Tet Offensive,* p. 252.

37. NBC decided not to air a report suggesting that Tet had been a defeat for the communists, because it was convinced the public would not believe it. See Michael X. Delli Carpini, "Vietnam and the Press," in Shafer, ed., *The Legacy,* p. 146. This is not to blame the media for poor reporting of Tet, leading to the collapse of support for the war. As counterintuitive as it may be, support for the war *increased* slightly during Tet. Inasmuch as the same is true of the Cambodian invasion in 1970, it might be suspected that an upsurge in fighting led to hope that a decisive battle was being fought that would end the war. In each case, increased support was short-lived and support again dwindled, as it became clear that the fighting was not decisive and stalemate had returned.

38. Don Oberdorfer, *Tet!: The Turning Point in the Vietnam War* (New York: Da Capo, 1971), pp. 245–46; Karnow, *Vietnam,* pp. 545–47.

39. Quotes from Oberdorfer, *Tet,* pp. 245–46.

40. Clark Clifford, "A Viet Nam Reappraisal," *Foreign Affairs* 47 (1969): 601–22; Herbert Y. Schandler, *Lyndon Johnson and Vietnam: The Unmaking of a President*

(Princeton: Princeton University Press, 1977), pp. 121–76.

41. Townsend Hoopes, *The Limits of Intervention* (New York: David McKay, 1973), pp. 202–24; Schandler, *Lyndon Johnson and Vietnam*, pp. 256–65.

42. Gitlin, *The Whole World Is Watching*, pp. 205–232; Wells, *The War Within*, pp. 223–86; Lynn Eden, *Crisis in Watertown: The Polarization of an American Community* (Ann Arbor: University of Michigan Press, 1972), p. 47.

43. For contemporary views see Norman Mailer, *Why Are We in Vietnam?* (New York: Holt, Rinehart and Winston, 1967), an odd novella on gun culture, vestiges of the frontier, and virility, woven into a story about a young man about to go to war.

44. Richard Hofstadter, *The Progressive Historians: Turner, Beard, Parrington* (New York: Knopf, 1969), p. 150.

45. William Appleman Williams, "Rise of an American World Power Complex," in N. D. Houghton, ed., *Struggle against History: U.S. Foreign Policy in an Age of Revolution* (New York: Clarion, 1968), pp. 1–19. (Quote from p. 1.)

46. Garfinkle, *Telltale Hearts*, pp. 148–90; Gitlin, *The Sixties*, pp. 285–340; Horowitz, *Radical Son*, pp. 157–202; Richard H. Rovere, *Waist Deep in the Big Muddy* (Boston: Atlantic Monthly, 1968); Robert V. Daniels, *Year of the Heroic Guerrilla: World Revolution and Counterrevolution in 1968* (New York: Basic Books, 1989), pp. 3–147.

47. Mueller, *Wars, Presidents, and Public Opinion*, pp. 164–65.

48. Spector, *After Tet*, p. 315.

49. Guenter Lewy, *America and Vietnam* (New York: Oxford University Press, 1978), pp. 144–47.

50. It is widely thought that the army covered up the massacre and that the public only became aware of it when Seymour Hersh broke the story. Hersh, however, states that he had never heard of Calley or My Lai until hearing, on the network news, of the army's indictment of Calley. Local commanders in Vietnam attempted to cover up the massacre but were later indicted for doing so. Hersh does criticize the Pentagon for not adequately publicizing Calley's indictment, yet notes that the networks and wire services carried the story. See Hersh, *My Lai 4: A Report on the Massacre and Its Aftermath* (New York: Vintage, 1970), pp. 128–34.

51. See Michael Bilton and Kevin Sim, *Four Hours in My Lai* (New York: Penguin, 1992), pp. 248–357.

52. This "partisan effect" is noted by Mueller, *Wars, Presidents, and Public Opinion*, pp. 116–22.

53. Joan Didion provides insight into the movement's blending into an alternative consumer culture in *Slouching towards Bethlehem* (New York: Touchstone, 1979), pp. 84–128.

54. See Tom Wolfe, *Radical Chic & Mau-Mauing the Flak Catchers* (New York: Farrar, Straus and Giroux, 1970), pp. 3–94.

55. Quoted in Gitlin, *The Sixties*, p. 401. See also Dickstein, *Gates of Eden*, pp.

269–70.

56. On the rise of violence in the movement see Tom Bates, *Rads: The 1970 Bombing of the Army Math Research Center at the University of Wisconsin and Its Aftermath* (New York: Harper Collins, 1992); Ron Jacobs, *The Way the Wind Blew: A History of the Weather Underground* (London: Verso, 1997); Garfinkle, *Telltale Hearts,* pp. 180–207; Gitlin, *The Sixties,* pp. 384–408.

57. Telford Taylor, *Nuremberg and Vietnam: An American Tragedy* (Chicago: Quadrangle, 1970). The moderate voice of opposition is well put in Hans J. Morgenthau, *Truth and Power: Essays of a Decade, 1960–70* (New York: Praeger, 1970), pp. 398–425; Milton J. Rosenberg, Sidney Verba, and Philip E. Converse, *Vietnam and the Silent Majority: The Dove's Guide* (New York: Harper & Collins, 1970).

58. On the decline of the antiwar movement see Gitlin, *The Sixties,* pp. 409–40; Garfinkle, *Telltale Hearts,* pp. 181–207.

59. Peter Braestrup, ed., *Vietnam as History: Ten Years after the Paris Peace Accords* (Washington D.C.: University Press of America, 1984), pp. 163–69.

60. *The Pentagon Papers: The Defense Department History of the United States Decisionmaking on Vietnam,* The Senator Gravel ed. (Boston: Beacon Press, 1971).

61. Frances Fitzgerald, *Fire in the Lake: The Vietnamese and the Americans in Vietnam* (Boston: Atlantic Monthly, 1972); David Halberstam, *The Best and the Brightest* (New York: Random House, 1972).

Chapter Seven

1. C. Vann Woodward *The Future of the Past* (New York: Oxford University Press, 1989), pp. 100–14; Charles William Wilson, *Baptized in Blood: The Religion of the Lost Cause* (Athens: University of Georgia Press, 1980), pp. 63–65; Robert Penn Warren, *The Legacy of the Civil War: Meditations on the Centennial* (New York: Random House, 1961), p. 53.

2. See James Mooney, *The Ghost-Dance Religion and Wounded Knee* (Mineola, N.Y.: Dover, 1973 [1896]); Ruth M. Underhill, *Red Man's Religion: Beliefs and Practices of the Indians North of Mexico* (Chicago: University of Chicago Press, 1965), pp. 254–69.

3. John W. Dower, *Embracing Defeat: Japan in the Wake of World War II* (New York: New Press, 1999), pp. 34–253. ("Upside down" quote from p. 108.) See also Michio Takeyama, *Harp of Burma,* trans. by Howard Hibbett (Rutland, Vt.: Charles E. Tuttle, 1966 [1946]).

4. James H. Billington, *The Icon and the Axe: An Interpretive History of Russian Culture* (New York: Vintage, 1970), pp. 360–70; Dietrich Geyer, *Russian Imperialism: The Interaction of Domestic and Foreign Policy, 1860-1914* (New Haven: Yale University Press, 1987), pp. 66-85.

5. Eugen Weber, *France, Fin de Siècle* (Cambridge, Mass.: Belknap Press, 1986), pp. 9–26, 105–29.

6. Raymond Carr, *Spain, 1808–1975* (New York: Oxford University Press, 1982), pp. 473–523.

7. Walter Laqueur, *Weimar: A Cultural History, 1918–1933* (New York: G. P. Putnam, 1974); Alfred Döblin, *A People Betrayed, November 1918: A German Revolution* (New York: Fromm, 1983). In Vietnam, millenarian cults such as the Hoa Hao appeared after the French conquest. See David G. Marr, *Vietnamese Anticolonialism 1885–1925* (Berkeley and Los Angeles: University of California Press, 1971).

8. See Robert Graves, *Goodbye to All That* (New York: Anchor, 1985 [1929]); Eugen Weber, *The Hollow Years: France in the 1930s* (New York: W. W. Norton, 1994), esp. pp. 3-25; Richard Bessell, *Germany after the First World War* (Oxford: Clarendon, 1993), pp. 220-53. Bessell notes that concerns with social decay were exaggerated by many (p. 222) but provides ample evidence of ills brought on after defeat.

9. See Woodward, *The Future of the Past*, pp. 113–14; John Hellmann, *American Myth and the Legacy of Vietnam* (New York: Columbia University Press, 1986).

10. See Richard Slotkin, *Gunfighter Nation: The Myth of the Frontier in Twentieth-Century America* (New York: Atheneum, 1992), pp. 534–660; Tom Englehardt, *The End of Victory Culture: Cold War America and the Disillusioning of a Generation* (New York: Basic Books, 1994), pp. 175–303.

11. Suicide rates from U.S. Dept. of Health, Education and Welfare, *Vital Statistics Rates in the United States* 1968, p. 99; Department of Commerce *Historical Abstract of the United States: Colonial Times to 1970*, part 1, 1975, p. 414; Herbert Hendin, *Suicide in America* (New York: W. W. Norton, 1982), p. 31.

12. See Jerome Skolnick and Elliott Currie, eds., *Crisis in American Institutions* (Boston: Little, Brown, 1973); Maurice Zeitlin, ed., *American Society, Inc.* (Chicago: Markham, 1970); Larry T. Reynolds and James M. Henslin, eds., *American Society: A Critical Analysis* (New York: McKay, 1973); Gene L. Mason and Fred Vetter, eds., *The Politics of Exploitation* (New York: Random House, 1973). See also Irving Louis Horowitz, *The Decomposition of Sociology* (New York: Oxford University Press, 1993), esp. pp. 9–21.

13. On the relationship between defeat and themes of dread in the cinema see Siegfried Kracauer's classic work, *From Caligari to Hitler: A Psychological Study of the German Cinema* (Princeton: Princeton University Press, 1947), esp. pp. 61–96.

14. Cf. the Marxian interpretation of Robin Cook in his *Hollywood from Vietnam to Reagan* (New York: Columbia University Press, 1986), pp. 26–38.

15. Pertinent veteran literature includes Philip Caputo, *A Rumor of War* (New York: Holt, Rinehart & Winston, 1977); Tim O'Brien, *If I Die in a Combat Zone* (New York: Delacorte, 1973); Gustav Hasford, *The Short-Timers* (New York: Harper & Row, 1979); Al Santoli, *Everything We Had: An Oral History of the Vietnam War* (New York: Random House, 1981). See also Samuel Hynes, *The Soldiers' Tale: Bearing Witness to Modern War* (Harmondsworth, U.K.: Penguin, 1997), pp. 177–222; Jonathan Shay, *Achilles in Vietnam: Combat Trauma and the Undoing of Character* (New York: Atheneum, 1994).

16. Tom Wells, *The War Within: America's Battle over Vietnam* (Berkeley and Los Angeles: University of California Press, 1994), pp. 577–78.

17. See Edward Shils, "American Society and the War in Indochina," in Anthony Lake, ed., *The Legacy of Vietnam: The War, American Society and the Future of American Foreign Policy* (New York: New York University Press, 1976), pp. 40–65.

18. See S. Robert Lichter, Linda S. Lichter, and Stanley Rothman, *Watching Television: What Television Tells Us about Our Lives* (New York: Prentice-Hall, 1991), pp. 80–104; Paul C. Vitz, *Psychology as Religion: The Cult of Self-Worship* (Grand Rapids, Mich.: Eerdmans, 1977), pp. 83–90.

19. Steven Mintz and Susan Kellogg, *Domestic Revolutions: A Social History of American Family Life* (New York: Free Press, 1988), pp. 203–37; Todd Gitlin, *The Sixties: Years of Hope, Days of Rage* (New York: Bantam, 1987), pp. 362–76; Ruth Rosen, "The Day They Buried Traditional Womanhood," in D. Michael Shafer, ed., *The Legacy: The Vietnam War in the American Imagination* (Boston: Beacon Press, 1990), pp. 233–61. On discontent with women's roles and radical ferment in Russia following defeat in the Crimean War (1853–1856) see Barbara Alpern Engel, *Mothers and Daughters: Women of the Intelligentsia in Nineteenth-Century Russia* (New York: Cambridge University Press, 1983).

20. See Kay M. Tooley, "*Johnny, I Hardly Knew Ye*: Toward Revision of the Theory of Male Psychosexual Development," in Arlene and Jerome H. Skolnick, eds., *Family in Transition: Rethinking Marriage, Sexuality, Child Rearing, and Family Organization* 3rd ed. (Boston: Little, Brown, 1980), pp. 194–204; Mirra Komarovsky, "Cultural Contradictions and Sex Roles: The Masculine Case," in ibid., pp. 205–16; the Lichters and Rothman, *Watching Television*, pp. 80–104.

21. See Dana Mack, *The Assault on Parenthood: How Our Culture Undermines the Family* (New York: Simon & Schuster, 1997), pp. 29–53; Sar A. Levitan and Richard S. Belous, *What's Happening to the American Family?* (Baltimore: Johns Hopkins University Press, 1981), p. 7.

22. National divorce rates from *Vital Statistics of the United States*, vol. 3, *Marriage and Divorce*, U.S. Department of Health and Human Services (1986), pp. 2–5; Levitan and Belous, *The American Family*, pp. 28–33; Theodore Caplow, et al., *Middletown Families: Fifty Years of Change and Continuity* (Minneapolis: University of Minnesota Press, 1982), p. 16.

23. See Barbara Dafoe Whitehead, *The Divorce Culture* (New York: Knopf, 1992); Riane Tennenhaus Eisler, *Dissolution: No-Fault Divorce, Marriage, and the Future of Women* (New York: McGraw-Hill, 1977). Eisler provides an appendix entitled "Divorce Checklist," which provides a guide to obtaining a divorce.

24. The late Christopher Lasch skillfully traces the decline of the family in the last hundred years in *Haven in a Heartless World: The Family Besieged* (New York: W. W. Norton, 1977). For debunkers of the old family see John R. Gillis, *A World of Their Own Making: Myth, Ritual, and the Quest for Family Values* (New York: Basic Books, 1996);

Stephanie Coontz, *The Way We Never Were: American Families and the Nostalgia Trap* (New York: Basic Books, 1993); Stephanie Coontz, *The Way We Really Are: Coming to Terms With America's Changing Families* (New York: Basic Books, 1998); Viqi Wagner, ed., *The Family in America: Opposing Viewpoints* (San Diego, Calif.: Greenhaven Press, 1992).

25. Lynn Eden, *Crisis in Watertown: The Polarization of an American Community* (Ann Arbor: University of Michigan Press, 1972). Eden looks at social tensions arising over housing, integration, church activism, and loss of cohesion amid the turmoil of the war.

26. On the decline of informal social controls see Mack, *Assault on Parenthood*, pp. 18–19.

27. Samuel P. Huntington notes the increased resort to litigation during this period in his *American Politics: The Promise of Disharmony* (Cambridge, Mass.: Belknap, 1981), p. 183. See also Bryan Wilson, "Secularization: The Inherited Model," in Phillip E. Hammond, ed., *The Sacred in a Secular Age: Toward Revision in the Scientific Study of Religion* (Berkeley and Los Angeles: University of California Press, 1985), pp. 14–15.

28. Christopher Lasch notes this retreat in *The Minimal Self: Psychic Survival in Troubled Times* (New York: W. W. Norton, 1984), pp. 60–64.

29. On declining community life, though not necessarily caused by the war, see Robert D. Putnam, "Bowling Alone, Revisited," *The Responsive Community* (Spring, 1995), pp. 18–33. William Damon, *Greater Expectations: Overcoming the Culture of Indulgence in America's Homes and Schools* (New York: Free Press, 1995), pp. 223–46.

30. On ersatz communities, what Bellah et al call "lifestyle enclaves" see Putnam, "Bowling Alone, Revisited;" Robert N. Bellah et al., *Habits of the Heart: Individualism and Commitment in American Life* (Berkeley and Los Angeles: University of California Press, 1985), pp. 72–75. Robert Nisbet saw the beginnings of this trend in his *The Quest for Community* (Oxford: Oxford University Press, 1969 [1953]), p. 31.

31. See Eileen Barker, "New Religious Movements: Yet Another Great Awakening?" in Hammond, ed., *The Sacred in a Secular Age*, pp. 26–57; Tom Wolfe, *The Electric Kool-Aid Acid Test* (New York: Farrar, Straus and Giroux, 1968); Rosabeth Moss Kanter, *Commitment and Community: Communes and Utopias in Sociological Perspective* (Cambridge, Mass.: Harvard University Press, 1972); Richard Fairfield, *Communes USA: A Personal Tour* (Baltimore: Penguin, 1972).

32. By the Vietnam era, the study of community had fallen significantly from its heyday before World War II. Useful studies include Putnam, "Bowling Alone, Revisited;" Eden, *Crisis in Watertown*; M. P. Baumgartner, *The Moral Order of a Suburb* (New York: Oxford University Press, 1988), esp. pp. 72–100; Peter Osnos, "The War and Riverdale," in Lake, ed., *The Legacy of Vietnam*. Bellah et al.'s *Habits of the Heart* is set in a period of lost community and the absence of shared values. See also the late Christopher Lasch's comments in *Revolt of the Elites and the Betrayal of Democracy* (New York: W. W. Norton, 1995), pp. 92–128.

33. See Arlie Russell Hochschild, *The Unexpected Community: Portrait of an Old Age Subculture* (Berkeley and Los Angeles: University of California Press, 1973).

34. See Marvin Harris, *America Now: The Anthropology of a Changing Culture* (New York: Simon & Schuster, 1981); Paul Blumberg, *Inequality in an Age of Decline* (New York: Oxford University Press, 1980); Paul Erdman, *The Coming Collapse of America* (New York: Simon & Schuster, 1980); Rufus C. Miles, Jr., *Awaking from the American Dream: The Social and Political Limits to Growth* (New York: Universe, 1976). An enormously popular, religiously inspired view of imminent apocalypse is Hal Lindsey, *The Late Great Planet Earth* (Grand Rapids, Mich.: Zondervan, 1970) in which a nuclear Armageddon (foretold in the Bible) signals the return of Jesus.

35. John Dower notes that the book was translated into Japanese after 1945 and enjoyed considerable readership there, as many saw their recent experiences paralleling those of the defeated South. See *Embracing Defeat*, pp. 527–28.

36. See Christopher Lasch, *The True and Only Heaven: Progress and Its Critics* (New York: W. W. Norton, 1991), pp. 82–119.

37. See Shils, "American Society and the War in Indochina," pp. 40–65; Gerald Grant, *The World We Created at Hamilton High* (Cambridge, Mass.: Harvard University Press, 1988), pp. 45–76. For parallel sentiment in interwar France see Weber, *The Hollow Years*, pp. 111–12.

38. Donald Kagan, *Pericles of Athens and the Birth of Democracy: The Triumph of Vision in Leadership* (New York: Touchstone, 1991); J. B. Campbell, *The Emperor and the Roman Army, 31 BC– AD 235* (Oxford: Clarendon Press, 1984), pp. 120–56; Gerhard Ritter, *The Sword and the Scepter: The Problem of Militarism in Germany* (Princeton Junction, N.J.: The Scholar's Bookshelf, 1988 [1954]), pp. 81–84.

39. R. Bruce Lincoln, *In the Vanguard of Reform: Russia's Enlightened Bureaucrats, 1825–61* (DeKalb: Northern Illinois University Press, 1984); Walter Laqueur, *Weimar: A Cultural History, 1918–1933* (New York: G. P. Putnam, 1974).

40. Correlli Barnett, *The Pride and the Fall: The Dream and Illusion of Britain as a Great Nation* (New York: Free Press, 1986). The theme runs throughout David Reynolds's *Rich Relations: The American Occupation of Britain, 1941–1945* (New York: Random House, 1995).

41. William C. Hammond, *Public Affairs: The Military and the Media, 1962–1968* (Washington D.C.: Center of Military History, 1988), p. 388.

42. Frances Fitzgerald, *Fire in the Lake: The Vietnamese and the Americans in Vietnam* (Boston: Atlantic Monthly, 1972); David Halberstam, *The Best and the Brightest* (New York: Random House, 1972); *The Pentagon Papers: The Defense Department History of the United States Decisionmaking on Vietnam,* The Senator Gravel ed. (Boston: Beacon Press, 1971); Townsend Hoopes, *The Limits of Intervention* (New York: David McKay, 1973).

43. See Guenter Lewy, *America and Vietnam* (New York: Oxford University Press, 1978), p. 57.

44. On popular culture's depiction of authority see James L. Baughman, *The Republic of Mass Culture: Journalism, Filmmaking, and Broadcasting in America since 1941* (Baltimore: Johns Hopkins University Press, 1992), pp. 148–50; the Lichtmans and Rothman, *Watching America*, pp. 115–24, 260–86.

45. Daniel Yergin, *The Prize: The Epic Quest for Oil, Money and Power* (New York: Simon & Schuster, 1991), pp. 656–69.

46. On conspiracies see the work of the former SDS leader, Carl Oglesby, *The Yankee and Cowboy War: Conspiracies from Dallas to Watergate* (Kansas City, Mo.: Sheed Andrews and McMeel, 1976). It is curious to note that, despite polling data showing that over fifty percent of Americans believe that Kennedy was killed by a conspiracy, there is little interest in looking into the matter. Döblin notes the prevalence of conspiracy theories in post-1918 Germany in his *A People Betrayed*.

47. Samuel P. Huntington, "The United States," in Michael J. Crozier, Samuel P. Huntington, and Joji Watanuki, *The Crisis of Democracy* (New York: New York University Press, 1975), p. 81; Huntington, *American Politics*, p. 201–2; Norman Nie, Sidney Verba, and John R. Petrocik, *The Changing American Voter* (Cambridge, Mass.: Harvard University Press, 1976), pp. 270–88.

48. Samuel P. Huntington, "The Democratic Distemper," *Public Interest* 41 (1975): 9–38; Baughman, *The Republic of Mass Culture*, pp. 165–70, 175–81.

49. See Huntington, *American Politics*, pp. 188–96. On similar processes in France after World War I see Weber, *The Hollow Years*, pp. 129–38.

50. Huntington, "The United States," p. 83. By the early 1980s, the military enjoyed a measure of increased respect, but did not re-attain pre-Vietnam levels.

51. Michael S. Sherry, *In the Shadow of War: The United States since the 1930s* (New Haven: Yale University Press, 1995), pp. 321–23. See also Marc Bloch, *Strange Defeat: A Statement of Evidence Written in 1940* (New York: W. W. Norton, 1968 [1940]).

52. The debate goes on. See Maurice Zeitlin et al., "Death in Vietnam: Class Poverty and the Risks of War," *Politics and Society* Vol. 3 (1973): 313–28; Charles C. Moskos, Jr., "The American Combat Soldier in Vietnam," *Journal of Social Issues* 31 (1975): 25–38; Gilbert Badillo and G. David Curry, "The Social Incidence of Vietnam Casualties," *Armed Forces and Society* 2 (1976); Arnold Barnett, "America's Vietnam Casualties: Victims of a Class War?" *Operations Research* 40 (1992); James Fallows, "Low Class Conclusions," *Atlantic Monthly* 271 (1993): 38–44. Owing to downed aircraft and the vulnerability to sniper and small-arms fire, pilots and company-grade officers suffered disproportionately high casualties. Inasmuch as officers were more often than not college educated, and minorities had less access to higher education then, this might explain the possibly counterintuitive argument (advanced by Moskos) that minorities did not suffer disproportionately high casualties.

53. Popular anti-military works from the period include James A. Donovan, *Militarism, U.S.A.* (New York: Scribner's, 1970); Adam Yarmolinsky, *The Military Establishment: Its*

Impact on American Society (New York: Harper & Row, 1971). It is interesting to note the backgrounds of these authors. Donovan was a career officer in the marines. The introduction to his book was written by Daniel M. Shoup, a former Commandant of the Corps, who won the Medal of Honor at Tarawa. He became an acerbic critic, not only of the war in Vietnam, but also of military influence in American life. Yarmolinsky was an assistant secretary of defense in the Johnson administration. See also Peter Tauber, *The Sunshine Soldiers* (New York: Simon & Schuster, 1971); H. Paul Jeffers and Dick Levitan, *See Parris and Die: Brutality in the U. S. Marines* (New York: Hawthorn, 1971). For similar dynamics in interwar France see Weber, *The Hollow Years*, pp. 15–18.

54. On popular culture's depiction of the military see the Lichtmans and Rothman, *Watching America*, pp. 268–86.

55. *The Great War and Modern Memory* (New York: Oxford University Press, 1975), pp. 7–18.

56. Early popular indictments of America can be found in Norman Mailer's allegorical hunting novel, *Why Are We in Vietnam?* (New York: Holt, Rinehart and Winston, 1967); Richard J. Barnet, *Intervention and Revolution: The United States in the Third World* (New York: Mentor, 1968). For parallel dynamics see Friedrich Meinecke's look into the Prussian roots of the Third Reich in *The German Catastrophe: Reflections and Recollections*, trans. by Sidney B. Fay (Boston: Beacon, 1963 [1950]); and Arnold Toynbee's post-1918 essays, *War and Civilization* (New York: Oxford University Press, 1950).

57. Some important works in this field include Walt W. Rostow, *The Stages of Economic Growth: A Non-Communist Manifesto* (Cambridge: Cambridge University Press, 1960); Daniel Lerner, *The Passing of Traditional Society: Modernizing the Middle East* (New York: Free Press, 1958); Seymour Martin Lipset, "Some Social Requisites of Democracy," *American Political Science Review* 53 (1959): 69–105; Talcott Parsons, "Evolutionary Universals in Society," *American Sociological Review* 29 (1964): 339–357.

58. See Andre Gunder Frank, *Capitalism and Underdevelopment in Latin America: Historical Studies of Chile and Brazil* (New York: Monthly Review, 1967); *Lumpenbourgeoisie, Lumpendevelopment: Dependence, Class, and Politics in Latin America* (New York: Monthly Review Press, 1972); Fernando Henrique Cardoso and Enzo Faletto, *Dependency and Development in Latin America* (Berkeley and Los Angeles: University of California Press, 1979).

59. See Robert N. Bellah, *The Broken Covenant: American Civil Religion in Time of Trial* (Chicago: University of Chicago Press, 1992), pp. 139–51; Sydney E. Ahlstrom, *A Religious History of the American People* (New Haven: Yale University Press, 1972), pp. 1091–96. See also Herbert Butterfield, *Christianity and History* (New York: Scribner's, 1949), pp. 48–67.

60. Bellah et al. note this trend toward personal forms of spirituality in *Habits of the Heart*; Bryan Wilson, "Secularization: The Inherited Model," pp. 19–20; Nisbet saw it beginning as a consequence of declining community. See *The Quest for Community*, p. 31.

Tom Wolfe noted the beginnings of this amorphous spirituality in his *The Electric Kool-Aid Acid Test*, pp. 125–49.

61. On declining religiousness see Lasch, *Revolt of the Elites*, pp. 197–246; Stephen L. Carter, *The Culture of Disbelief: How American Law and Politics Trivialize Religious Devotion* (New York: Basic Books, 1993), pp. 3–101.

62. William G. Mayer, *The Changing American Mind: How and Why American Public Opinion Changed between 1960 and 1988* (Ann Arbor: University of Michigan, 1992), p. 31.

63. Robert N. Bellah and Phillip E. Hammond, *Varieties of Civil Religion* (San Francisco: Harper & Row, 1980), p. 36.

64. Harold Bloom, *The American Religion: The Emergence of the Post-Christian Nation* (New York: Simon & Schuster, 1992), pp. 181–88; Robert D. Heslep, *Moral Education for Americans* (Westport, Conn.: Praeger, 1995), pp. 1–2; James Lincoln Collier, *The Rise of Selfishness in America* (New York: Oxford University Press, 1991), pp. 231–33.

65. See Gertrude Himmelfarb, *The De-Moralization of Society: From Victorian Virtues to Modern Values* (New York: Knopf, 1995), pp. 221–57; Daniel Patrick Moynihan, "Defining Deviancy Down," *The American Scholar* (1993): 245–61; Heslep, *Moral Education*, pp. 1–25.

66. Collier, *The Rise of Selfishness in America*, pp. 224–38.

67. Christopher Lasch, *The Culture of Narcissism: American Life in an Age of Diminishing Expectations* (New York: W. W. Norton, 1978). See also his *The Minimal Self*, pp. 23–59.

68. *Statistical Abstract of the United States* (1997), p. 77; Levitan and Belous, *The American Family*, pp. 37–46.

69. John J. Patrick and Richard C. Remy, *Civics for Americans* (Glenview, Ill.: Scott, Foresman, 1980), pp. 106–9. Morris Janowitz notes that earlier textbooks had stressed civic obligations but that after Vietnam the emphasis declined. See *The Reconstruction of Patriotism: Education for Civic Consciousness* (Chicago: University of Chicago Press, 1983), pp. 84-85, 146-48, 152-69.

70. Damon, *Greater Expectations*, esp. pp. 65–93; Mack, *Assault on Parenthood*, pp. 109–19, 137–48; Collier, *The Rise of Selfishness in America*, pp. 262–64; Joseph J. Tobin, David Y. H. Yu, and Dana H Davidson, *Preschool in Three Cultures: Japan, China, and the United States* (New Haven: Yale University Press, 1989), pp. 126–87. Compare this to a study of the inculcation of "other-directedness" in Philip Olson and Carlton Daley, "The Education of the 'Individual,'" in Philip Olson, ed., *America as a Mass Society: Changing Community and Identity* (New York: Free Press, 1963), pp. 419–34.

71. Cf W. Lloyd Warner's look at Memorial Day rites in his *American Life: Dream and Reality* (Chicago: University of Chicago Press, 1964 [1953]), pp. 2–34.

72. See Lasch, *The Culture of Narcissism*; William Damon has made a valuable contribution with his *Greater Expectations*. Paul Fussell's *Class: A Guide through the*

American Status System (New York: Summit, 1883) contains a satirical but insightful exploration of American society and each stratum's consumerism. On the beginnings of this trend see Thorstein Veblen, *The Theory of the Leisure Class* (Boston: Houghton Mifflin, 1973 [1899]). See also Janowitz, *The Reconstruction of Patriotism*, which, though coming from a different political perspective from Lasch, has a similar concern with social trends away from senses of duty and obligation, esp. pp. 152-69.

73. See Collier, *The Rise of Selfishness in America*, pp. 225–29; Sheila Jeffreys, *Anticlimax: A Feminist Perspective on the Sexual Revolution* (New York: New York University Press, 1990), p. 90. Jeffreys, who identifies herself as "a lesbian and a revolutionary feminist," sees the sexual revolution as having made women more amenable to whatever their male partners wished. See also the many consumer-sex books, including Alex Comfort, *The Joy of Sex: A Gourmet Guide to Love Making* (New York: Simon & Schuster, 1972).

74. Robert Sklar, *Movie-Made America: A Cultural History of the Movies* (New York: Random House, 1975), pp. 294–304; Gregory D. Black, *Hollywood Censored: Morality Codes, Catholics, and the Movies* (Cambridge: Cambridge University Press, 1994).

75. Linda Williams, *Hard Core: Power, Pleasure, and the "Frenzy of the Visible"* (Berkeley and Los Angeles: University of California Press, 1989), pp. 99–100.

76. Peter Bogdanovich, *Time Pieces: Bogdanovich on the Movies, 1961–1985* (New York: Arbor House, 1985), p. 165. See also the Lichtmans and Rothman, *Watching America*, pp. 25–49; Baughman, *The Republic of Mass Culture*, pp. 150–52.

77. George Comstock et al., *Television and Human Behavior* (New York: Columbia University Press, 1978), pp. 72–74.

78. Collier, *The Rise of Selfishness in America*, pp. 258–59.

79. Dept. of Commerce, *Historical Abstracts of the United States: Colonial Times to 1970*, part 1, 1975, p. 414.

80. Dept. of Commerce, *Statistical Abstract of the United States* (1997), p. 205.

81. See Tom Wolfe, *Radical Chic & Mau-Mauing the Flak Catchers* (New York: Farrar, Straus and Giroux, 1970), pp. 97-153; Stephen Carter, *Civility: Manners, Morality, and the Etiquette of Democracy* (New York: Basic Books, 1998).

82. Sissela Bok, *Mayhem: Violence as Public Entertainment* (Reading, Mass.: Addison-Wesley, 1998), pp. 22–45.

83. Comstock et al., *Television and Human Behavior*, pp. 64–83; Mack, *Assault on Parenthood*, pp. 210–17; David T. Courtwright, *Violent Land: Single Men and Social Disorder from the Frontier to the Inner City* (Cambridge, Mass.: Harvard University Press, 1996), pp. 225–69.

84. On culture and violence see James William Gibson, *Warrior Dreams: Paramilitary Culture in Post-Vietnam America* (Boston: Hill and Wang, 1994), pp. 17–32; Dave Grossman, *On Killing: The Psychological Cost of Learning to Kill in War and Society* (Boston: Little, Brown, 1995), pp. 299–322.

Chapter Eight

1. Quoted in Ruth Miller Elson, *Guardians of Tradition: American Schoolbooks of the Nineteenth Century* (Lincoln: University of Nebraska Press, 1964), p. 167, from a geography text by Jedidiah Morse published in 1794. The theme continues in schoolbooks into the early nineteenth century.

2. See Richard Hofstadter, *The Progressive Historians: Turner, Beard, Parrington* (New York: Knopf, 1969), pp. 3–43; Elson, *Guardians of Tradition*, pp. 166–85 and passim; Michael Kammen, *Mystic Chords of Memory: The Transformation of Tradition in American Culture* (New York: Knopf, 1991), pp. 17–100; Esmond Wright, "Historians and the Revolution," in his edited work, *Causes and Consequences of the American Revolution* (Chicago: Quadrangle, 1966), pp. 20–25.

3. Quoted in Merrill Jensen, "Historians and the Nature of the American Revolution," in Ray Allen Billington, *The Reinterpretation of Early American History* (New York: W. W. Norton, 1968), pp. 101–2.

4. See Peter Novick, *That Noble Dream: The "Objectivity Question" and the American Historical Profession* (New York: Cambridge University Press, 1988), pp. 47–60.

5. Charles A. Beard, *An Economic Interpretation of the Constitution of the United States* (New York: Macmillan, 1962 [1913]); as well as his *Economic Origins of Jeffersonian Democracy* (New York: Free Press, 1965 [1915]). See also James Harvey Robinson, *The New History: Essays Illustrating the Modern Historical Outlook* (New York: Free Press, 1965 [1912]); Hofstadter, *The Progressive Historians*, pp. 167–346.

6. Novick, *That Noble Dream*, pp. 111–18.

7. Quoted in Novick, *That Noble Dream*, p. 98.

8. Novick, *That Noble Dream*, pp. 86–249; Gary B. Nash, Charlotte Crabtree, and Ross E. Dunn, *History on Trial: Culture Wars and the Teaching of the Past* (New York: Knopf, 1998), pp. 25–52; Ernst Breisach, *Historiography: Ancient, Medieval, and Modern* (Chicago: University of Chicago Press, 1983), pp. 313–36. Other important works from this period include Carl Becker, *The Declaration of Independence: A Study in the History of Political Ideas* (New York: Vintage Press, 1959 [1922]); John D. Hicks, *The Populist Revolt: A History of the Farmers' Alliance and the Peoples' Party* (Lincoln: University of Nebraska Press, 1961 [1931]); Albert K. Weinberg, *Manifest Destiny: A Study of Nationalist Expansionism in American History* (Chicago: Quadrangle Books, 1963 [1935]).

9. Hofstadter, *The Progressive Historians*, pp. 220–22. Hofstadter suggests that Beard's reappraisal stemmed from his concern with foreign militarism, opposition to the war, and concern with the growing influence of the military in American life.

10. See Novick, *That Noble Dream*, pp. 281–85; Nash et al., *History on Trial:* pp. 53–67; C. Vann Woodward, *The Future of the Past* (New York: Oxford University Press, 1989), pp. 3–12. Eugen Weber notes that French writings of the interwar period similarly made France less vigilant regarding the rise of the Third Reich. See his *The Hollow Years: France*

in the 1930s (New York: W. W. Norton, 1994), pp. 20–25.

11. Hofstadter, *The Progressive Historians: Turner, Beard, Parrington*, pp. 437–66.

12. C. Vann Woodward notes this state of affairs in his *The Future of the Past*, p. vii.

13. Carl Bridenbaugh cautioned against this trend in a lecture delivered at the time of the Bicentennial: "The sustained secular drift of our own times must not be permitted through sheer ignorance or cynicism to black out of history the potent fact that religion was the central concern for most Americans." See his *The Spirit of '76: The Growth of American Patriotism before Independence* (New York: Oxford University Press, 1975), p. 118.

14. See Herbert Butterfield on this type of history in his *The Whig Interpretation of History* (New York: W. W. Norton, 1965 [1931]), pp. 1-8.

15. The Crockett story is mentioned in Gary Wills, *John Wayne's America: The Politics of Celebrity* (New York: Simon & Schuster, 1997), pp. 213–15. Most eyewitnesses asserted that Crockett was killed by Mexican fire early in the siege. See James Atkins Shackford, *David Crockett: The Man and the Legend* (Chapel Hill: University of North Carolina Press, 1986), pp. 223–40.

16. The account of Edison is from a recent elementary school text: Barry K. Beyer, *United States and Its Neighbors: The World around Us* (New York: Macmillan/McGraw-Hill, 1991), p. 452. Most recent texts give less attention to the inventiveness of great Americans such as Franklin, Fulton, Whitney, Colt, and the like — the old embodiments of Yankee Ingenuity — in favor of emphasizing the achievements of common people.

17. These basic arguments are found in the earlier progressive works of the Beards and Vernon Parrington, but find new voice in Gary B. Nash, *The Urban Crucible: The Northern Seaports and the Origins of the American Revolution* (Cambridge, Mass.: Harvard University Press, 1986); Eric Foner, *Tom Paine and Revolutionary America* (New York: Oxford University Press, 1976). See also Nash's textbook, Gary Nash et al., *The American People: Creating a Nation and Society*, vol. 1 (New York: Harper & Row, 1986), pp. 225–29. (Nash appreciates the importance of war in historical change, a view obviously shared here.)

18. Women have twenty-seven headings in Nash et al., *The American People* I, more than the Constitution and Civil War combined. See also reissues of Margaret Jarman Hagood, *Mothers of the South: Portraiture of the White Tenant Farm Woman* (New York: W. W. Norton, 1977 [1939]); Eleanor Flexner, *Century of Struggle: The Woman's Rights Movement in the United States* (Cambridge, Mass.: Harvard University Press, 1975 [1959]); as well as Carol Lasser, "Century of Struggle, Decades of Revision: A Retrospective on Eleanor Flexner's Suffrage History," in Stanley I. Kutler, ed., *American Retrospectives: Historians on Historians* (Baltimore: Johns Hopkins University Press, 1995), pp. 117–27; Ruth B. Moynihan, Susan Armitage, and Christine Fischer Dichamp, eds., *So Much to Be Done: Women Settlers on the Mining and Ranching Frontiers* (Lincoln: University of Nebraska Press, 1990); Susan Ware, *Beyond Suffrage: Women in the New Deal* (Cambridge, Mass.: Harvard University Press, 1981); D'Ann Campbell, *Women at War with America:*

Private Lives in a Patriotic Era (Cambridge, Mass.: Harvard University Press, 1984); Linda Gordon, "U.S. Women's History," in Eric Foner, ed., *The New American History* (Philadelphia: Temple University Press, 1990), pp. 185–210.

19. See Elson, *Guardians of Tradition*, pp. 98–100.

20. Elson, *Guardians of Tradition*, pp. 87–100; Nash et al., *History on Trial*, pp. 58–60.

21. See Thomas C. Holt, "African-American History," in Foner, ed., *New American History*, pp. 211–31; John W. Blassingame, *The Slave Community: Plantation Life in the Antebellum South* (New York: Oxford University Press, 1972); Eugene D. Genovese, *Roll, Jordan, Roll: The World the Slaves Made* (New York: Random House, 1976); Herbert G. Gutman, *The Black Family in Slavery and Freedom, 1750–1925* (New York: Pantheon, 1976); Douglas R. Egerton, *Gabriel's Rebellion: The Virginia Slave Conspiracies of 1800 and 1802* (Chapel Hill: University of North Carolina Press, 1993). Slavery and its legacy are much discussed in Nash's widely used text, meriting fifty-one headings and sub-headings in the index. By contrast the Revolution gets twenty-six, the Constitution eleven, and Civil War ten. See Nash et al., *The American People* I.

22. Francis Parkman, *The Oregon Trail* (New York: Library of America, 1991 [1847]); Frederick Jackson Turner, *Frontier and Section: Selected Essays of Frederick Jackson Turner* (Englewood Cliffs, N.J.: Prentice-Hall, 1961); *The Frontier in American History* (New York: Holt, Rinehart and Winston, 1962).

23. Helen Hunt Jackson, *A Century of Dishonor: The Early Crusade for Indian Reform* (New York: Harper, 1965 [1881]); James Mooney, *The Ghost-Dance Religion and Wounded Knee* (Mineola, N.Y.: Dover, 1973 [1896]); George Bird Grinnell, *The Fighting Cheyennes* (Norman: University of Oklahoma Press, 1985 [1915]).

24. Brian W. Dippie, *Custer's Last Stand: The Anatomy of an American Myth* (Lincoln: University of Nebraska Press, 1976), pp. 137–40; Stanley David Lyman, *Wounded Knee 1973: A Personal Account* (Lincoln: University of Nebraska Press, 1991).

25. Vine Deloria, Jr., *Custer Died for Your Sins: An Indian Manifesto* (New York: Avon, 1969); Dee Brown, *Bury My Heart at Wounded Knee: An Indian History of the American West* (New York: Holt, Rinehart & Winston, 1971). A somewhat earlier work, Merrill D. Beal's *I Will Fight No More Forever: Chief Joseph and the Nez Perce War* (Seattle: University of Washington Press, 1966), also enjoyed popular success and was made into a television mini-series in the mid-1970s. See also Tom Engelhardt, *The End of Victory Culture: Cold War America and the Disillusioning of a Generation* (New York: Basic Books, 1994), pp. 234–303.

26. Francis Jennings, *The Invasion of America: Indians, Colonialism, and the Cant of Conquest* (New York: W. W. Norton, 1975), pp. 58–127.

27. Beyer, *United States and Its Neighbors*, pp. 68–125. There is an extensive quote from Geronimo stressing harmony with the environment on p. 97. See also Nash et al., *The American People* I: 3–9.

28. Nash et al., *The American People* I: 3–4. See also Francis Jennings, *Empire of Fortune: Crowns, Colonies and Tribes in the Seven Years War in America* (New York: W. W. Norton, 1990 [1988]), pp. 21–69.

29. Nash et al., *The American People* I: 31–32. See also Jennings, *The Invasion of America*, pp. 128–227; Russell Bourne, *The Red King's Rebellion: Racial Politics in New England, 1675–1678* (New York: Oxford University Press, 1990); John M. Murrin, "Beneficiaries of Catastrophe: The English Colonies in America," in Foner, ed., *New American History*, pp. 3–23.

30. Beyer, *United States and Its Neighbors*, pp. 354–56; Nash et al., *The American People* I: 438–40; Jack Abramowitz, *American History* 6th ed. (Boston: Allyn and Bacon, 1983), pp. 255–57.

31. For a summary see Richard Slotkin, *Gunfighter Nation: The Myth of the Frontier in Twentieth-Century America* (New York: Atheneum, 1992), pp. 1–87.

32. Charles A. and Mary R. Beard, *Basic History of the United States* (New York: Doubleday, 1944), pp. 1–45.

33. Jennings, *Empire of Fortune*, pp. 109–38; Patricia Nelson Limerick, *The Legacy of Conquest: The Unbroken Past of the American West* (New York: W. W. Norton, 1987), pp. 61–77, 82–129; William G. Robbins, *Colony and Empire: The Capitalist Transformation of the American West* (Lawrence: University Press of Kansas, 1994), pp. 61–82; Nash et al., *The American People* II: 586–92. The cinema took up these themes of business interests dominating the West in several popular films including *Butch Cassidy and the Sundance Kid*, *The Wild Bunch*, *McCabe and Mrs Miller*, *Once upon a Time in the West*, and *Pat Garrett and Billy the Kid*.

34. See "The Second Great Removal," in Nash et al., *The American People* II: 574–78; Abramowitz, *American History*, pp. 388–403. It may be of interest to note that John Ford's classic *The Searchers* (1956) depicts the aftermath of one such massacre in which a central character's Indian wife has been slaughtered and survivors have gone insane. Ford's *Cheyenne Autumn* (1964) recounts cavalry attacks on a helpless band of Indians seeking to return to their homeland. Even his "cavalry trilogy" (*Fort Apache*, *She Wore a Yellow Ribbon*, and *Rio Grande*) exhibits sympathy for Indians. Protagonists, played by John Wayne, face a dilemma of sympathy for the Indians and duty to their country. Accordingly, the plight of Native Americans was not wholly absent in films prior to Vietnam. As noted earlier, the experience of World War II brought about a measure of respect for other races that had taken part in the Great Event. Ford even made a film (*Sergeant Rutledge* [1960]) about the all-black Ninth Cavalry and the prejudice it encountered.

35. The film's director observed, "Although I am focusing on history, I believe the film is contemporary because . . . history does repeat itself." Quoted in Paul Andrew Hutton, "'Correct in Every Detail:' General Custer in Hollywood," in Charles E. Rankin, ed., *Legacy: New Perspectives on the Battle of the Little Bighorn* (Helena: Montana Historical Society Press, 1996), pp. 259–60. A French film of the early 1970s, *Touche pas la Femme*,

used Vietnamese in place of American Indians in its depiction of the Little Big Horn. See also Dippie, *Custer's Last Stand*, p. 139.

36. See Brian W. Dippie, "'What Valor Is:' Artists and the Mythic Moment," in Rankin, *Legacy*, pp. 208–230; Dippie, *Custer's Last Stand*, pp. 12–61.

37. Slotkin, *Gunfighter Nation*, p. 319.

38. Beyer, *United States and Its Neighbors*, p. 442.

39. Nash et al., *The American People* II: 576. Cf. the account in Bernard Bailyn et al., *The Great Republic: A History of the American People*, vol. 2, 4th ed. (Lexington, Mass.: D. C. Heath, 1992), pp. 103–4. The authors mention the massacres of Indians at the Washita and elsewhere but avoid praise or blame, romanticization or vilification. They describe events as simply following from the clash of civilizations.

40. On cinematic presentations of the Little Big Horn see Paul Andrew Hutton, "'Correct in Every Detail:' General Custer in Hollywood," in Rankin, *Legacy*, pp. 321–70. Cf. Robert M. Utley, *Cavalier in Buckskin: George Armstrong Custer and the Western Military Frontier* (Norman: University of Oklahoma Press, 1988); Slotkin, *Gunfighter Nation*, pp. 534–623.

41. Nash et al., *The American People* I: 318–26; Beyer, *United States and Its Neighbors*, pp. 348–52. Expansionist aspects of American history had been stressed in a few histories written just prior to Vietnam. See Richard W. Van Alstyne, *The Rising American Empire* (New York: Oxford University Press, 1960). This line of thinking also benefited from William Appleman Williams's, *The Roots of the Modern American Empire: A Study of the Growth and Shaping of Social Consciousness in a Marketplace Society* (New York: Random House, 1969), which was written at the height of the Vietnam War, reinterpreting much of American foreign policy in economic terms. A more recent work is Michael H. Hunt, *Ideology and U.S. Foreign Policy* (New Haven: Yale University Press, 1987), pp. 19–45, 125–198.

42. Nash et al., *The American People* I: 444–50; Beyer, *United States and Its Neighbors*, pp. 380–81. "Polk provoked weak Mexico into open conflict. . . . To secure that border (and to acquire California in the process), Polk was willing to shed American blood." Charles M. Dollar et al., *America: Changing Times*, vol. 1 (New York: Wiley, 1982), p. 346. A recent (1998) Public Broadcasting System documentary similarly presented the war as an act of aggression. See also, Hunt, *Ideology and U.S. Foreign Policy*, pp. 32–35.

43. Nash et al., *The American People* II: 659–60, see also pp. 659–85.

44. Quoted in David M. Kennedy, *Over Here: The First World War and American Society* (New York: Oxford University Press, 1980), p. 78. See also Paul L. Murphy, *World War One and the Origin of Civil Liberties in the United States* (New York: W. W. Norton, 1979); Ronald Schaffer, *America in the Great War: The Rise of the War Welfare State* (New York: Oxford University Press, 1991), pp. 13–30. Jennings sees the Seven Years War as leading to intolerance toward Quakers and Catholics. See *Empire of Fortune*, pp. 223–47.

45. Nash's treatment mentions prejudice but, at least as often, also the opportunities

that military service offered minorities. See Nash et al., *The American People* II: 836–41. He is clearly one of the most sophisticated of the post-Vietnam historians. Unlike many of his colleagues who, in keeping with the sustained secular drift, downplay the importance of religion, he appreciates the role of religion in social change, especially in the Revolution and the Civil War. It might also be noted that he has been excoriated by minorities and women for insensitivity toward them. Such are today's polarizations in the presentation of history, especially in textbooks. See Todd Gitlin, *The Twilight of Common Dreams: Why America is Wracked by Culture Wars* (New York: Henry Holt, 1996), pp. 7–36.

46. Beyer, *United States and Its Neighbors*, pp. 509–12; Nash et al., *The American People* II: 832–33, 845–47; Richard Polenberg, *War and Society: The United States, 1941–1945* (New York: J. B. Lippincott, 1972), pp. 37–72; Studs Terkel, *"The Good War:" An Oral History of World War Two* (New York: Pantheon, 1984), pp. 33–35.

47. See John W. Dower, *War without Mercy: Race and Power in the Pacific War* (New York: Pantheon, 1987), pp. 77–93; Sam Keen, *Faces of the Enemy: Reflections of the Hostile Imagination* (San Francisco, Calif.: Harper & Row, 1986), pp. 33, 76, 115. Curators of the National Air and Space Museum, "The Crossroads: The End of World War II, the Atomic Bomb and the Origins of the Cold War," in Philip Nobile, ed., *Judgment at the Smithsonian* (New York: Marlowe, 1995), pp. 3–22. Nobile (happily not a Smithsonian figure) argues in the preface that Truman should be tried posthumously as a war criminal and compares the pilot of the Enola Gay to an SS killer. See pp. l-lxxi.

48. See Gar Alperovitz, *The Decision to Use the Atomic Bomb and the Architecture of an American Myth* (New York: Knopf, 1995). Nash et al. give four reasons for the use of atomic weapons: the high casualties of Iwo Jima and fear of high casualties from an invasion of the mainland; vindictiveness over the treachery of Pearl Harbor; justification for the huge expenses of developing the bomb; and the desire to intimidate the Soviet Union. See *The American People* II: 849–50. Cf. Robert J. C. Butow, *Japan's Decision to Surrender* (Stanford, Calif.: Stanford University Press, 1954); Pacific War Research Society, *Japan's Longest Day* (Tokyo: Kodarsha International, 1968).

49. Robert G. Paterson, ed., *The Origins of the Cold War* 2nd ed. (Lexington, Mass.: D. C. Heath, 1974); Polenberg, *War and Society*, pp. 37–72; Gabriel Kolko, *The Politics of War: The World and the United States Foreign Policy, 1943–45* (New York: Random House, 1968); Curators of the National Air and Space Museum, "The Crossroads," pp. 117–26; Elaine Tyler May contends that the Cold War served to keep women in traditional roles in her *Homeward Bound: American Families in the Cold War Era* (New York: Basic Books, 1988). Cf. John Lewis Gaddis, *The United States and the Origins of the Cold War, 1941–1947* (New York: Columbia University Press, 1972).

50. See Bessie Louise Pierce, *Public Opinion and the Teaching of History in the United States* (New York: Knopf, 1926), pp. 70–131; Pierce, *Civic Attitudes in American School Textbooks* (Chicago: University of Chicago Press, 1930), passim. Even later general histories such as those edited or written by Henry Steele Commager, Max Lerner, and

Merle Curti, though written in a time less conducive to romantic phrases than earlier times, were discernibly patriotic.

51. During the First World War, the government urged newspapers to use "our" and "we" in their coverage after American entry. See Preston William Slosson, *The Great Crusade and After, 1914–1928* (New York: Macmillan, 1969 [1930]), p. 64.

52. Beyer, *United States and Its Neighbors,* p. 380. Another aspect of the fragmented nature of American history is the tendency for professional historians to avoid general study of American history and to specialize in the history of women or a particular minority group. Here, a romantic form of narrative still finds voice. See Novick, *That Noble Dream,* pp. 469–629.

53. Nash notes problems with scholarship based on American sub-groups and opposed to basic Western principles: "Militant multiculturalists . . . have romanticized the history of their particular group, or world regions other than Europe, out of all recognition, and stigmatized Western civilization as the world's oldest evil empire." Nash et al., *History on Trial,* p. 99. See also Arthur M. Schlesinger, Jr., *The Disuniting of America: Reflections on a Multicultural Society* (New York: W. W. Norton, 1992), pp. 61–138.

BIBLIOGRAPHY

Social Theory

Allport, Gordon. *The Nature of Prejudice.* New York: Addison-Wesley, 1954.

Banfield, Edward C. *The Moral Basis of a Backward Society.* New York: Free Press, 1958.

Bell, Norman, and Ezra F. Vogel, eds. *A Modern Introduction to the Family.* Glencoe, Ill.: Free Press, 1960.

Berger, Peter L. *The Sacred Canopy: Elements of a Sociological Theory of Religion.* Garden City, N.Y.: Anchor, 1969.

———. *A Rumor of Angels: Modern Society and the Rediscovery of the Supernatural.* New York: Doubleday, 1969.

Bettelheim, Bruno. *The Uses of Enchantment: The Meaning and Importance of Fairy Tales.* New York: Vintage, 1977.

Bok, Sissela. *Mayhem: Violence as Public Entertainment.* Reading, Mass.: Addison-Wesley, 1998,

Breisach, Ernst. *Historiography: Ancient, Medieval, and Modern.* Chicago: University of Chicago Press, 1983.

Butterfield, Herbert. *The Whig Interpretation of History.* New York: W. W. Norton, 1965 [1931].

———. *Christianity and History.* New York: Scribner's, 1949.

Durkheim, Emile. *Suicide: A Study in Sociology.* New York: Free Press, 1951.

Feuer, Lewis S. *The Conflict of Generations: The Character and Significance of Student Movements.* New York: Basic Books, 1969.

Fustel de Coulange, Numa Denis. *The Ancient City: A Study on the Religion, Laws, and Institutions of Greece and Rome.* Garden City, N.Y.: Doubleday.

Guroian, Vigen. *Tending the Heart of Virtue: How Classic Stories Awaken a Child's Moral Imagination.* New York: Oxford University Press, 1998.

Guttmann, Allen. *From Ritual to Record: The Nature of Modern Sports.* New York: Columbia University Press, 1978.

Hintze, Otto. *The Historical Essays of Otto Hintze.* Edited by Felix Gilbert. New York: Oxford University Press, 1975.

Horowitz, Irving Louis. *The Decomposition of Sociology.* New York: Oxford University Press, 1993.

Iggers, Georg G. *Historiography in the Twentieth Century: From Scientific Objectivity to the Postmodern Challenge.* Hanover, N.H.: Wesleyan University Press, 1997.

James, William. *Writings, 1902-1910.* Edited by Bruce Kuklick. New York: The Library of America, 1987.

Kluckhohn, Clyde. *Mirror for Man: Anthropology for Modern Life*. New York: McGraw-Hill, 1949.

Lane, Robert E. *Political Life: Why People Get Involved in Politics*. Glencoe, Ill.: Free Press, 1951.

———. *Political Ideology: Why the American Common Man Believes What He Does* New York: Free Press, 1962.

Lasswell, Harold. "The Garrison State and the Specialists on Violence." *American Journal of Sociology* 47 (1941): 455-68.

Moore, Barrington, Jr. *Political Power and Social Theory*. Cambridge, Mass.: Harvard University Press, 1958.

Muller, Herbert J. *The Uses of the Past: Profiles of Former Societies*. New York: Oxford University Press, 1952.

Mumford, Lewis. *The City in History: Its Origins, Its Transformations and Its Prospects*. New York: Harcourt, Brace and World, 1961.

Nef, John U. *War and Human Progress: An Essay on the Rise of Industrial Civilization*. Cambridge, Mass.: Harvard University Press, 1950.

Nisbet, Robert. *The Quest for Community*. Oxford: Oxford University Press, 1969 [1953].

———. *Twilight of Authority*. New York: Oxford University Press, 1975.

Novick, Peter. *That Noble Dream: The "Objectivity Question" and the American Historical Profession*. New York: Cambridge University Press, 1988.

Park, Robert E. *Human Communities*. Glencoe, Ill.: Free Press, 1952.

———. *Society*. Glencoe, Ill.: Free Press, 1954.

Parsons, Talcott. *The Social System*. New York: Free Press, 1951.

———. *The Structure of Social Action*. New York: Free Press, 1968.

Robinson, James Harvey. *The New History: Essays Illustrating the Modern Historical Outlook*. New York: Free Press, 1965 [1912].

Schumpeter, Joseph. *Imperialism and Social Classes*. Translated by Heinz Norden. New York: Augustus M. Kelley, 1951 [1919].

Sorokin, Pitirim A. *The Crisis of Our Age*. New York: E. P. Dutton, 1957 [1941].

Spengler, Oswald. *The Decline of the West*. New York: Knopf, 1929.

Tocqueville, Alexis de. *The Old Regime and the French Revolution*. Garden City, N.Y. Anchor, 1955.

———. *Democracy In America*. New York: Knopf, 1980.

Toynbee, Arnold. *War and Civilization*. New York: Oxford University Press, 1950.

Weber, Max. *Economy and Society*. 2 vols. Edited by Guenther Roth and Claus Wittich. Berkeley and Los Angeles: University of California Press, 1978.

———. *The Protestant Ethic and the Spirit of Capitalism*. New York: Scribner's, 1976 [1905.

———. *Ancient Judaism*. Translated and edited by Hans H. Gerth and Don Martindale. New York: Free Press, 1967 [1917-19].

Weil, Simone. *The Need for Roots*. Boston: Beacon, 1952 [1943].

Weston, Jessie L. *From Ritual to Romance*. Princeton: Princeton University Press, 1993.

American History and Society

Abrahamson, James L. *The American Home Front: Revolutionary War, Civil War, World War I, World War II*. Washington D.C.: National Defense University Press, 1983.

Abramowitz, Jack. *American History*. 6th ed. Boston, Mass.: Allyn and Bacon, 1983.

Adams, Charles Francis. *The Autobiography of Charles Francis Adams*. New York: Chelsea, 1983.

Adams, Henry. *The Education of Henry Adams*. New York: Modern Library, 1931 [1918].

———. *Democracy: An American Novel*. New York: Library of America, 1983 [1880].

Ahlstrom, Sydney E. *A Religious History of the American People*. New Haven: Yale University Press, 1972.

Allen, Frederick Lewis. *Only Yesterday: An Informal History of the Nineteen-Twenties*. New York: Harper & Row, 1931.

———. *The Big Change: America Transforms Itself, 1900-1950*. New York: Harper & Row, 1952.

Ambrose, Stephen E. *Eisenhower*. Vol. 2, *The President*. New York: Simon and Schuster, 1984.

Anderson, George K., and Eda Lou Walton, eds. *This Generation: A Selection of British and American Literature from 1914 to the Present with Historical and Critical Essays*. Chicago: Scott, Foresman, 1939.

Anshen, Ruth Nanda, ed. *The Family: Its Function and Destiny*. New York: Harper and Brothers, 1959 [1949].

Arnold, Thurman. *The Folklore of Capitalism*. New Haven: Yale University Press, 1937.

Atack, Jeremy, and Peter Passell. *A New Economic View of American History* New York: W. W. Norton, 1994.

Atherton, Lewis. *Main Street on the Middle Border*. Chicago: Quadrangle, 1966 [1954].

Baltzell, E. Digby. *The Protestant Establishment: Aristocracy and Caste in America*. New York: Vintage, 1964.

Barnouw, Erik. *Tube of Plenty: The Evolution of American Television*. New York: Oxford University Press, 1990.

Baughman, James L. *The Republic of Mass Culture: Journalism, Filmmaking, and Broadcasting in America since 1941*. Baltimore: The Johns Hopkins University Press, 1992.

Beard, Charles A. *An Economic Interpretation of the Constitution of the United States*. New York: Macmillan, 1962 [1913].

———. *Economic Origins of Jeffersonian Democracy*. New York: Free Press, 1965 [1915].

———. and Mary R. Beard. *America in Midpassage*. 2 vols. New York: Macmillan, 1939.

————. *Basic History of the United States.* New York: Doubleday, 1944.

————. *President Roosevelt and the Coming of War, 1941: A Study in Appearances and Realities.* New Haven: Yale University Press, 1948.

Becker, Carl. *The Declaration of Independence: A Study in the History of Political Ideas.* New York: Vintage Press, 1959 [1922].

Becker, Howard S. *Outsiders: Studies in the Sociology of Deviance.* Glencoe, Ill: Free Press, 1963.

Beisner, Robert L. *Twelve against Empire: The Anti-Imperialists, 1898-1900.* New York: McGraw-Hill, 1968.

Bellah, Robert N., and Phillip E. Hammond, *Varieties of Civil Religion.* San Francisco: Harper & Row, 1980.

Bellah, Robert N. et al. *Habits of the Heart: Individualism and Commitment in American Life.* Berkeley and Los Angeles: University of California Press, 1985.

————. et al. *The Good Society.* New York: Vintage, 1991.

Bellah, Robert N., *The Broken Covenant: American Civil Religion in Time of Trial.* Chicago: University of Chicago Press, 1992.

Bensel, Richard Franklin. *Yankee Leviathan: The Origins of Central State Authority in America, 1859–1877.* Cambridge: Cambridge University Press, 1990.

Bensman, Joseph, and Bernard Rosenberg. *Mass, Class, and Bureaucracy: The Evolution of Contemporary Society.* New York: Prentice-Hall, 1963.

Benson, Susan Porter, Stephen Brier, and Roy Rosenzweig, eds. *Presenting the Past: Essays on History and the Public.* Philadelphia, Pa.: Temple University Press, 1986.

Bercovitch, Sacvan. *The Puritan Origins of the American Self.* New Haven: Yale University Press, 1975.

Beyer, Barry K. *United States and Its Neighbors: The World around Us.* New York: Macmillan/McGraw-Hill, 1991.

Billington, Ray Allen. *America's Frontier Heritage.* Albuquerque: University of New Mexico Press, 1991.

Blakely, Edward J., and Mary Gail Snyder. *Fortress America: Gated Communities in the United States.* Washington, D. C.: Brookings Institution, 1998.

Blassingame, John W. *The Slave Community: Plantation Life in the Antebellum South.* New York: Oxford University Press, 1972.

Bloom, Harold. *The American Religion: The Emergence of the Post-Christian Nation.* New York: Simon & Schuster, 1992.

Blumberg, Paul. *Inequality in an Age of Decline.* New York: Oxford University Press, 1980.

Bodnar, John, Roger Simon, and Michael P. Weber. *Lives of Their Own: Blacks, Italians, and Poles in Pittsburgh, 1900–1960.* Urbana: University of Illinois Press, 1982.

Boritt, Gabor S., ed. *Why the Confederacy Lost.* New York: Oxford University Press, 1992.

————. *War Comes Again: Comparative Vistas on the Civil War and World War II.* New York: Oxford University Press, 1995.

Botkin, B. A. *A Treasury of American Folklore: Stories, Ballads, and Traditions of the People.* New York: Crown, 1944.

Bourne, Russell. *The Red King's Rebellion: Racial Politics in New England, 1675–1678.* New York: Oxford University Press, 1990.

Boyer, Paul. *By the Bomb's Early Light: American Thought and Culture at the Dawn of the Atomic Age.* New York: Pantheon, 1985.

Brands, H. W. *The Devil We Knew: Americans and the Cold War.* New York: Oxford University Press, 1993.

Bridenbaugh, Carl. *Cities in Revolt: Urban Life in America, 1743–1776.* London: Oxford University Press, 1971 [1955].

———. *The Spirit of '76: The Growth of American Patriotism before Independence.* New York: Oxford University Press, 1975.

Brinkley, Alan. *Voices of Protest: Huey Long, Father Coughlin, and the Great Depression.* New York: Vintage Press, 1982.

———. *The End of Reform: New Deal Liberalism in Recession and War.* New York: Knopf, 1995.

Brody, David. *Steelworkers in America: The Nonunion Era.* New York: Harper & Row, 1969.

Brooks, Van Wyck. *The Wine of the Puritans: A Study of Present-Day America.* Folcroft, Pa.: Folcroft Press, 1969 [1908].

———. *The Flowering of New England, 1815–1865.* New York: Dutton, 1937.

Brown, Richard Maxwell. *No Duty to Retreat: Violence and Values in American History and Society.* New York: Oxford University Press, 1991.

Brown, Roger H. *The Republic in Peril: 1812.* New York: W. W. Norton, 1971.

Bryson, Lyman. *Which Way America? Communism, Fascism, Democracy.* New York: Macmillan, 1939.

Burner, David. *Making Peace with the 60s.* Princeton: Princeton University Press, 1997.

Burns, James MacGregor. *The Deadlock of Democracy: Four Party Politics in America.* Englewood Cliffs, N. J.: Prentice-Hall, 1963.

———. *The Vineyard of Liberty.* Vol 1 of *The American Experiment.* New York: Vintage, 1983.

———. *The Workshop of Democracy.* Vol 2 of *The American Experiment.* New York: Knopf, 1985.

Bushman, Richard L. *From Puritan to Yankee: Character and the Social Order in Connecticut, 1690–1765.* Cambridge, Mass.: Harvard University Press, 1967.

Carson, Clayborne. *In Struggle: SNCC and the Black Awakening of the 1960s.* Cambridge, Mass.: Harvard University Press, 1981.

Caplow, Theodore, et al. *Middletown Families: Fifty Years of Change and Continuity.* Minneapolis: University of Minnesota Press, 1982.

Carter, Stephen L. *The Culture of Disbelief: How American Law and Politics Trivialize*

Religious Devotion. New York: Basic Books, 1993.

———. *Civility: Manners, Morality, and the Etiquette of Democracy.* New York: Basic Books, 1998.

Cash, W. J. *The Mind of the South.* New York: Vintage, 1969 [1941].

Chapman, John Jay. *Deutschland über Alles, or Germany Speaks.* New York: G.P. Putnam's Sons, 1914.

Clark, John G., et al. *Three Generations in Twentieth Century America: Family, Community, and Nation.* Homewood, Ill.: Dorsey Press, 1977.

Clausen, John A. *American Lives: Looking Back at the Children of the Great Depression.* New York: Free Press, 1993.

Coben, Stanley. *Rebellion against Victorianism: The Impetus for Cultural Change in 1920s America.* New York: Oxford University Press, 1991.

Coffman, Edward M. *The War to End All Wars: The American Military Experience in World War I.* New York: Oxford University Press, 1968.

Collier, James Lincoln. *The Rise of Selfishness in America.* New York: Oxford University Press, 1991.

Commager, Henry Steele. *The American Mind: An Interpretation of American Thought and Character since the 1880s.* New Haven: Yale University Press, 1978.

Comstock, George, et al. *Television and Human Behavior.* New York: Columbia University Press, 1978.

Cook, Fred J. *The Warfare State.* New York: Macmillan, 1962.

Coontz, Stephanie. *The Way We Never Were: American Families and the Nostalgia Trap.* New York: Basic Books, 1993.

———. *The Way We Really Are: Coming to Terms With America's Changing Families.* New York: Basic Books, 1998.

Courtwright, David T. *Violent Land: Single Men and Social Disorder from the Frontier to the Inner City.* Cambridge, Mass.: Harvard University Press, 1996.

Cowley, Malcolm. *The Dream of the Golden Mountains: Remembering the 1930s.* New York: Viking, 1980.

Crozier, Michael, Samuel P. Huntington, Joji Watanuki. *The Crisis of Democracy.* New York: New York University Press, 1975.

Curti, Merle. *The Roots of American Loyalty.* New York: Columbia University Press, 1946.

———. *The Making of an American Community: A Case Study of Democracy in a Frontier County.* Stanford, Calif.: Stanford University Press, 1959.

———. *The Growth of American Thought.* 3rd ed. New York: Harper & Row, 1964.

Damon, William. *Greater Expectations: Overcoming the Culture of Indulgence in America's Homes and Schools.* New York: Free Press, 1995.

Dangerfield, George. *The Era of Good Feelings.* New York: Harcourt, Brace & World, 1963.

Degler, Carl N. *Out of Our Past: The Forces That Shaped Modern America.* Rev. ed. New York: Harper Colophon, 1970.

———. *At Odds: Women and the Family in America from the Revolution to the Present.* New York: Oxford University Press, 1980.

Delbanco, Andrew. *The Puritan Ordeal.* Cambridge, Mass: Harvard University Press, 1989.

Deloria, Vine, Jr. *Custer Died for Your Sins: An Indian Manifesto.* New York: Avon, 1969.

Demos, John. *A Little Commonwealth: Family Life in Plymouth Colony.* Oxford: Oxford University Press, 1971.

Denisoff, R. Serge, and Richard A. Peterson, eds. *The Sounds of Social Change: Studies in Popular Culture.* Rand McNally, 1972.

Diamond, Sigmund. *Compromised Campus: The Collaboration of Universities with the Intelligence Community, 1945–1955.* New York: Oxford University Press, 1992.

Dickstein, Morris. *Gates of Eden: American Culture in the Sixties.* New York: Basic Books, 1977.

Didion, Joan. *Slouching towards Bethlehem.* New York: Touchstone, 1979.

Diggins, John Patrick. *The Proud Decades: America in War and Peace, 1941–1960.* New York: W. W. Norton, 1988.

Dippie, Brian W. *Custer's Last Stand: The Anatomy of an American Myth.* Lincoln: University of Nebraska Press, 1976.

Dolan, Jay P. *The Immigrant Church: New York's Irish and German Catholics, 1815–1865.* Notre Dame: Notre Dame University Press, 1983 [1975].

Dollar, Charles M. et al. *America: Changing Times.* Vol. 1. New York: Wiley, 1982.

Donovan, James A. *Militarism, U.S.A.* New York: Charles Scribner's, 1970.

Dupuy, R. Ernest. "Pass in Review." *The Army Combat Forces Journal* 4 (1954).

Eden, Lynn. *Crisis in Watertown; The Polarization of an American Community.* Ann Arbor: University of Michigan Press, 1972.

Egerton, Douglas R. *Gabriel's Rebellion: The Virginia Slave Conspiracies of 1800 and 1802.* Chapel Hill: University of North Carolina Press, 1993.

Eisler, Riane Tennenhaus. *Dissolution: No-Fault Divorce, Marriage, and the Future of Women.* New York: McGraw-Hill, 1977.

Elder, Glen H., Jr. *Children of the Great Depression: Social Change in Life Experience.* Chicago: University of Chicago Press, 1974.

Elliot, Mabel A., and Francis E. Merrill. *Social Disorganization.* Rev. ed. New York: Harper & Brothers, 1941.

Elson, Ruth Miller. *Guardians of Tradition: American Schoolbooks of the Nineteenth Century.* Lincoln: University of Nebraska Press, 1964.

Englehardt, Tom. *The End of Victory Culture: Cold War America and the Disillusioning of a Generation.* New York: Basic Books, 1994.

Erenberg. Lewis A. *Steppin' Out: New York Nightlife and the Transformation of American Culture, 1890–1930.* Chicago: University of Chicago Press, 1981.

Erikson, Kai T. *Wayward Puritans: A Study in the Sociology of Deviance.* New York: John

Wiley, 1966.

Ewen, Stuart. *Captains of Consciousness: Advertising and the Social Roots of the Consumer Culture.* New York: McGraw-Hill, 1976.

Fairfield, Richard. *Communes USA: A Personal Tour.* Baltimore: Penguin, 1972.

Flexner, Eleanor. *Century of Struggle: The Woman's Rights Movement in the United States.* Cambridge, Mass.: Harvard University Press, 1975 [1959].

Flink, James J. *The Car Culture.* Cambridge, Mass.: MIT Press, 1975.

Fogel, Robert William, and Stanley L. Engerman. *Time on the Cross: The Economics of American Negro Slavery.* Boston: Little, Brown, 1974.

Foner, Eric. *Free Soil, Free Labor, Free Men: The Ideology of the Republican Party before the Civil War.* New York: Oxford University Press, 1970.

———. *Tom Paine and Revolutionary America.* New York: Oxford University Press, 1976.

———, ed. *The New American History.* Philadelphia: Temple University Press, 1990.

Fussell, Paul. *Class: A Guide through the American Status System.* New York: Summit, 1883.

———. *BAD: Or, the Dumbing of America.* New York: Summit. 1991.

———. *Doing Battle: The Making of a Skeptic.* Boston: Little, Brown, 1996.

Gaddis, John Lewis. *The United States and the Origins of the Cold War, 1941–1947.* New York: Columbia University Press, 1972.

———. *We Now Know: Rethinking Cold War History.* Oxford: Clarendon Press, 1997.

Galambos, Louis, ed. *The New American State: Bureaucracies and Policies since World War II.* Baltimore: Johns Hopkins University Press, 1987.

Gallaher, Art. *Plainville Fifteen Years Later.* New York: Columbia University Press, 1961.

Gans, Herbert J. *The Urban Villagers: Group and Class in the Life of Italian-Americans.* New York: Free Press, 1962.

———. *The Levittowners: Ways of Life and Politics in a New Suburban Community.* New York: Vintage, 1967.

———. *Popular Culture and High Culture: An Analysis and Evaluation of Taste.* New York: Basic Books, 1974.

Gauss, Christian. *America in the War: Why We Went to War.* New York: Scribner's, 1918.

Genovese, Eugene D. *Roll, Jordan, Roll: The World the Slaves Made.* New York: Random House, 1976.

Gere, Anne Ruggles. *Intimate Practices: Literacy and Cultural Work in U. S. Women's Clubs, 1880–1920.* Urbana: University of Illinois Press, 1997.

Gibson, James William. *Warrior Dreams: Paramilitary Culture in Post-Vietnam America.* Boston: Hill and Wang, 1994.

Gillis, John R. *A World of Their Own Making: Myth, Ritual, and the Quest for Family Values.* New York: Basic Books, 1996.

Gitlin, Todd. *The Whole World Is Watching: Mass Media in the Making and Unmaking of the New Left.* Berkeley and Los Angeles: University of California Press, 1980.

———. *The Sixties: Years of Hope, Days of Rage.* New York: Bantam, 1987.

———. *The Twilight of Common Dreams: Why America is Wracked by Culture Wars.* New York: Henry Holt, 1996.

Goldman, Eric F. *The Crucial Decade – and After: America, 1945–1960.* New York: Vintage, 1960.

Goodman, Paul. *Growing Up Absurd: Problems of Youth in the Organized System.* New York: Random House, 1960 [1956].

Goodman, Percival, and Paul Goodman. *Communitas: Means of Livelihood and Ways of Life.* New York: Vintage, 1960.

Goodwyn, Lawrence. *The Populist Moment: A Short History of the Agrarian Revolt in America.* New York: Oxford University Press, 1978.

Gordon, Michael, ed. *The American Family in Social-Historical Perspective.* New York: St. Martin's Press, 1973.

Grant, Gerald. *The World We Created at Hamilton High.* Cambridge, Mass.: Harvard University Press, 1988.

Grant, U. S. *Personal Memoirs.* New York: Library of America, 1990.

Greven, Philip J., Jr. *Four Generations: Population, Land, and Family in Andover, Massachusetts.* Ithaca: Cornell University Press, 1970.

Grinnell, George Bird. *The Fighting Cheyennes.* Norman: University of Oklahoma Press, 1985 [1915].

Grossman, Dave. *On Killing: The Psychological Cost of Learning to Kill in War and Society.* Boston: Little, Brown, 1995.

Grossman, James R. *Land of Hope: Chicago, Black Southerners, and the Great Migration.* Chicago: University of Chicago Press, 1989.

Gutman, Herbert G. *The Black Family in Slavery and Freedom, 1750–1925.* New York: Pantheon, 1976.

Hacker, Louis M. *The Triumph of American Capitalism: The Development of Forces in American History to the Beginning of the Twentieth Century.* New York: McGraw Hill, 1965 [1940].

Hagood, Margaret Jarman. *Mothers of the South: Portraiture of the White Tenant Farm Woman.* New York: W. W. Norton, 1977 [1939].

Halberstam, David. *The Fifties.* New York: Villard, 1993.

Hammond, Phillip E., ed. *The Sacred in a Secular Age: Toward Revision in the Scientific Study of Religion.* Berkeley and Los Angeles: University of California Press, 1985.

Handlin, Oscar. *The Uprooted.* Second edition. Boston: Little, Brown, 1973.

———, and Lillian Handlin. *Liberty and Power, 1600–1760.* New York: Harper and Row, 1986.

Hareven, Tamara, and Andrejs Plakans, eds. *Family History at the Crossroads.* Princeton: Princeton University Press, 1987.

Harries, Meirion and Susie. *The Last Days of Innocence: America at War, 1917–1918.* New York: Random House, 1997.

Harris, Marvin. *America Now: The Anthropology of a Changing Culture.* New York: Simon & Schuster, 1981.

Hawley, Ellis W. *The Great War and the Search for a Modern Order: A History of the American People and Their Institutions, 1917–1933.* New York: St. Martin's Press, 1979.

Hays, Samuel P. *The Response to Industrialism, 1885–1914.* Chicago: University of Chicago Press, 1957.

Hearn, Charles R. *The American Dream in the Great Depression.* Westport, Conn.: Greenwood Press, 1977.

Hendin, Herbert. *Suicide in America.* New York: W. W. Norton, 1982.

Henry, Jules. *Culture against Man.* New York: Vintage, 1963.

Herberg, Will. *Protestant–Catholic–Jew: An Essay in American Religious Sociology.* New York: Doubleday, 1955.

Hero Tales of the American Soldier and Sailor: The Unwritten History of American Chivalry. Hero Publishing, 1899.

Hickey, Donald R. *The War of 1812: A Forgotten War.* Urbana: University of Illinois Press, 1989.

Hicks, John D. *The Populist Revolt: A History of the Farmers' Alliance and the Peoples' Party.* Lincoln: University of Nebraska Press, 1961 [1931].

Himmelfarb, Gertrude. *The De-Moralization of Society: From Victorian Virtues to Modern Values.* New York: Knopf, 1995.

Hochschild, Arlie Russell. *The Unexpected Community: Portrait of an Old Age Subculture.* Berkeley and Los Angeles: University of California Press, 1973.

Hofstadter, Richard. *The Age of Reform: From Bryan to F. D. R.* New York: Knopf, 1955.

———. *Anti-Intellectualism in American Life.* New York: Vintage, 1962.

———. *The Progressive Historians: Turner, Beard, Parrington.* New York: Knopf, 1969.

Horowitz, David. *Radical Son: A Generational Odyssey.* New York: Simon & Schuster, 1997.

Hudson, Winthrop S. *Religion in America: An Historical Account of the Development of American Religious Life.* 2nd ed. New York: Scribner's, 1973.

Hunt, Michael H. *Ideology and U.S. Foreign Policy.* New Haven: Yale University Press, 1987.

Huntington, Samuel P. "The Democratic Distemper," *Public Interest* 41 (1975): 9-38.

———. *American Politics: The Promise of Disharmony.* Cambridge, Mass.: Belknap, 1981.

Hutchison, William R., ed. *Between the Times: The Travail of the Protestant Establishment in America, 1900-1960.* New York: Cambridge University Press, 1989.

Jackman, Jarrell, and Carla Borden, eds. *The Muses Flee Hitler: Cultural Transfer and Adaptation, 1930–1945.* Washington, D.C.: Smithsonian Institution Press, 1983.

Jackson, Helen Hunt. *A Century of Dishonor: The Early Crusade for Indian Reform.* New York: Harper, 1965 [1881].

Jackson, Kenneth T. *Crabgrass Frontier: The Suburbanization of the United States.* New York: Oxford University Press, 1985.

Jacobs, Paul, and Saul Landau. *The New Radicals: A Report with Documents.* New York: Random House, 1966.

Jacobs, Ron. *The Way the Wind Blew: A History of the Weather Underground.* London: Verso, 1997.

Janowitz, Morris. *The Community Press in an Urban Setting: The Social Elements of Urbanism.* 2nd ed. Chicago: University of Chicago Press, 1967.

———. *The Last Half-Century: Societal Change and Politics in America.* Chicago: University of Chicago Press, 1978.

———. *The Reconstruction of Patriotism: Education for Civic Consciousness.* Chicago: University of Chicago Press, 1983.

Jeffers, H. Paul, and Dick Levitan. *See Parris and Die: Brutality in the U. S. Marines.* New York: Hawthorn, 1971.

Jeffreys, Sheila. *Anticlimax: A Feminist Perspective on the Sexual Revolution.* New York: New York University Press, 1990.

Jennings, Francis. *The Invasion of America: Indians, Colonialism, and the Cant of Conquest.* New York: W. W. Norton, 1975.

———. *Empire of Fortune: Crowns, Colonies and Tribes in the Seven Years War in America.* New York: W. W. Norton, 1990 [1988].

Johnson, Charles A. *The Frontier Camp Meeting: Religion's Harvest Time.* Dallas: Southern Methodist University Press, 1985 [1955].

Kammen, Michael. *Mystic Chords of Memory: The Transformation of Tradition in American Culture.* New York: Alfred A. Knopf, 1991.

———. *In the Past Lane: Historical Perspectives on American Culture.* New York: Oxford University Press, 1997.

Kanter, Rosabeth Moss. *Commitment and Community: Communes and Utopias in Sociological Perspective.* Cambridge, Mass.: Harvard University Press, 1972.

Karl, Barry D. *The Uneasy State: The United States from 1915 to 1945.* Chicago: University of Chicago Press, 1983.

Karp, Walter. *The Politics of War: The Story of Two Wars which Altered Forever the Political Life of the American Republic 1890–1920.* New York: Harper Collins, 1979.

Katz, Donald. *Home Fires: An Intimate Portrait of One Middle-Class Family in Postwar America.* New York: Harper Collins, 1992.

Kennedy, David M. *Over Here: The First World War and American Society.* New York: Oxford University Press, 1980.

———. *Freedom from Fear: The American People in Depression and War, 1929–1945.* New York: Oxford University Press, 1999.

Keniston, Kenneth. *The Uncommitted. Alienated Youth in American Society.* New York: Harcourt, Brace and World, 1965 [1960].

———. *Young Radicals: Notes on Committed Youth.* New York: Harcourt Brace and World, 1968.

———. *Youth and Dissent: The Rise of a New Opposition.* New York: Harcourt Brace Jovanovich, 1971.

Kett, Joseph F. *Rites of Passage: Adolescence in America, 1790 to the Present.* New York: Basic Books, 1977.

Kimmel, Michael. *Manhood in America: A Cultural History.* New York: Free Press, 1996.

Kindleberger, Charles P. *The World Depression, 1929–1939.* Berkeley and Los Angeles: University of California Press, 1973.

Kittner, James H. *The Development of American Citizenship, 1608–1870.* Chapel Hill: University of North Carolina Press, 1970.

Knollenberg, Bernhard. *Origin of the American Revolution: 1759–1766.* New York: Free Press, 1960.

Komarovsky, Moira. *Blue-Collar Marriage.* New York: Vintage, 1962.

Kosmin, Barry A., and Seymour P. Lachman, *One Nation under God: Religion in Contemporary American Society.* New York: Harmony Books, 1993.

Kutler, Stanley I., ed. *American Retrospectives: Historians on Historians.* Baltimore: Johns Hopkins University Press, 1995.

Ladd, Everett Carll, Jr. *Ideology in America: Change and Response in City, a Suburb, and a Small Town.* Ithaca: Cornell University Press, 1969.

Laderman, Gary. *The Sacred Remains: American Attitudes toward Death, 1799–1883.* New Haven: Yale University Press, 1996.

La Feber, Walter. *The New Empire: An Interpretation of American Expansion, 1860–1898.* Ithaca: Cornell University Press, 1963.

———, and Richard Polenberg. *The American Century: A History of the United States since the 1890s.* New York: John Wiley & Sons, 1975.

Lasch, Christopher. *The New Radicalism in America, 1889–1963: The Intellectual As a Social Type.* New York: Knopf, 1965.

———. *Haven in a Heartless World: The Family Besieged.* New York: W. W. Norton, 1977.

———. *The Culture of Narcissism: American Life in an Age of Diminishing Expectations.* New York: W. W. Norton, 1978.

———. *The Minimal Self: Psychic Survival in Troubled Times.* New York: W. W. Norton, 1984.

———. *The True and Only Heaven: Progress and Its Critics.* New York: W. W. Norton, 1991.

———. *The Revolt of the Elites and the Betrayal of Democracy.* New York: W. W. Norton, 1993.

Leach, William. *Land of Desire: Merchants, Power, and the Rise of a New American Culture.* New York: Pantheon, 1993.

Lerner, Max. *America as a Civilization: Life and Thought in the United States Today.* New York: Simon & Schuster, 1957.

Leuchtenburg, William E. *The Perils of Prosperity, 1914–32.* Chicago: University of Chicago Press, 1958.

———. *Franklin D. Roosevelt and the New Deal, 1932–1940.* New York: Harper & Row, 1963.

———. *A Troubled Feast: American Society since 1945.* Boston: Little, Brown, 1979.

Levine, Lawrence W. *Defender of the Faith: William Jennings Bryan: The Last Decade, 1915–1925.* New York: Oxford University Press, 1965.

Levitan, Sar A., and Richard S. Belous. *What's Happening to the American Family?* Baltimore: Johns Hopkins University Press, 1981.

Lhamon. W. T., Jr. *Deliberate Speed: The Origins of a Cultural Style in the American 1950s.* Washington, D. C.: Smithsonian Institution Press, 1990.

Lichter, S. Robert, Linda S. Lichter, and Stanley Rothman, *Watching Television: What Television Tells Us about Our Lives.* New York: Prentice-Hall, 1991.

Lifton, Robert Jay. *The Protean Self: Human Resilience in an Age of Fragmentation.* New York: Basic, 1993.

Limerick, Patricia Nelson. *The Legacy of Conquest: The Unbroken Past of the American West.* New York: W. W. Norton, 1987.

Linderman, Gerald F. *Embattled Courage: The Experience of Combat in the American Civil War.* New York: Free Press, 1987.

Lindsey, Hal. *The Late Great Planet Earth.* Grand Rapids, Mich.: Zondervan, 1970.

Linenthal, Edeward T., and Tom Englehardt, eds. *History Wars: The Enola Gay and Other Battles for the American Past.* New York: Metropolitan, 1996.

Lingeman, Richard. *Small Town America: A Narrative History, 1620 - the Present.* Boston: Houghton Mifflin, 1980.

Lippmann, Walter. *The Good Society.* Boston: Little, Brown, 1937.

Lipset, Seymour Martin. *The First New Nation: The United States in Historical and Comparative Perspective.* New York: W. W. Norton, [1963] 1979.

———. and Philip G. Altbach. *Students in Revolt.* Boston: Beacon Press, 1970.

Lowi, Theodore J. *The End of Liberalism: Ideology, Policy, and the Crisis of Public Authority.* New York: W. W. Norton, 1969.

Lucas, Paul R. "The Origin of the Great Awakening in New England." *The Historian* 59 (1997): 741–58.

Lyman, Stanley David, *Wounded Knee 1973: A Personal Account.* Lincoln: University of Nebraska Press, 1991.

Lynd, Robert S., and Helen M. Lynd. *Middletown.* New York: Harcourt Brace, 1929.

———. *Middletown in Transition.* New York: Harcourt Brace, 1937.

Lynd, Staughton. *Intellectual Origins of American Radicalism.* Cambridge, Mass.: Harvard University Press, 1982.

Macdonald, Dwight. *Against the Grain: Essays on the Effects of Mass Culture.* New York: Random House, 1962.

McConnell, Stuart. *Glorious Contentment: The Grand Army of the Republic, 1865–1900.* Chapel Hill: University of North Carolina Press, 1992.

McElvaine, Robert S., ed. *Down and Out in the Great Depression: Letters from the Forgotten Man.* Chapel Hill: University of North Carolina Press, 1983.

McGee, Reece. *Social Disorganization in America.* San Francisco: Chandler, 1962.

McPherson, James M. *Battle Cry of Freedom: The Civil War Era.* New York: Oxford University Press, 1988.

———. *For Cause and Comrades: Why Men Fought in the Civil War.* New York: Oxford University Press, 1997.

McQuaid, Kim. *Uneasy Partners: Big Business in American Politics, 1945–1990.* Baltimore: Johns Hopkins University Press, 1994.

Mack, Dana. *The Assault on Parenthood: How Our Culture Undermines the Family.* New York: Simon & Schuster, 1997.

Maddox, Robert James. *The New Left and the Origins of the Cold War.* Princeton: Princeton University Press, 1973.

Mailer, Norman. *Advertisements for Myself.* New York: Putnam's. 1959.

———. *The Time of Our Time.* New York: Random House, 1998.

Marling, Karal Ann. *As Seen on TV: The Visual Culture of Everyday Life in the 1950s.* Cambridge, Mass.: Harvard University Press, 1994.

Martin, Theodora Penny. *The Sound of Our Own Voices: Women's Study Clubs, 1860–1910.* Boston: Beacon Press, 1987.

Marty, Martin E. *Modern American Religion,* Vol. 1: *The Irony of It All, 1893–1919.* Chicago: University of Chicago Press, 1986.

———. *Modern American Religion.* Vol. 3: *Under God, Indivisible, 1941–1960.* Chicago: University of Chicago Press, 1996.

May, Elaine Tyler. *Homeward Bound: American Families in the Cold War Era.* New York: Basic Books, 1988.

May, Ernest R. *The World War and American Isolation, 1914–1917.* Chicago: Quadrangle, 1966 [1959].

———. *Imperial Democracy: The Emergence of America as a Great Power.* New York: Harper & Row, 1973.

Mayer, William G. *The Changing American Mind: How and Why American Public Opinion Changed between 1960 and 1988.* Ann Arbor: University of Michigan Press, 1992.

Mead, Margaret. *And Keep Your Powder Dry: An Anthropologist Looks at America.* New York: Morrow, 1942.

Mead, Walter Russell. *Mortal Splendor: The American Empire in Transition.* Boston: Houghton Mifflin, 1987.

Miles, Rufus C., Jr. *Awaking from the American Dream: The Social and Political Limits to Growth.* New York: Universe, 1976.

Miller, James. *Democracy is in the Street: From Port Huron to the Siege of Chicago.* Cambridge, Mass.: Harvard University Press, 1994.

Miller, Perry. *The New England Mind.* 2 vols. Boston: Beacon Press, 1961.

———. *Errand into the Wilderness.* New York: Harper & Row, 1964.

———. *The Life of the Mind in America: From the Revolution to the Civil War.* New York: Harcourt Brace Jovanovich, 1965.

Mills, C. Wright. *White Collar.* New York: Oxford University Press, 1951.

———. *The Power Elite.* Oxford: Oxford University Press, 1956.

———. *The Causes of World War Three.* New York: Simon & Schuster, 1958.

———. *The Sociological Imagination.* New York: Oxford University Press, 1959.

Mintz, Steven, and Susan Kellogg. *Domestic Revolutions: A Social History of American Family Life.* New York: Free Press, 1988.

Mitchell, Reid. *Civil War Soldiers: Their Expectations and Their Experiences.* New York: Viking, 1988.

———. *The Vacant Chair: The Northern Soldier Leaves Home.* New York: Oxford University Press, 1993.

Mooney, James. *The Ghost-Dance Religion and Wounded Knee.* Mineola, N.Y.: Dover, 1973 [1896].

Morgan, Dan. *Rising in the West: The True Story of an 'Okie' Family from the Great Depression through the Reagan Years.* New York: Knopf, 1992.

Morgan, Edmund, ed. *Puritan Political Ideas, 1558–1794.* New York: Bobbs Merrill, 1965.

———. *The Puritan Family: Religion and Domestic Relations in Seventeenth-Century New England.* New York: Harper & Row, 1966.

Morgenthau, Hans J. *Truth and Power: Essays of a Decade, 1960–70.* New York: Praeger, 1970.

Morison, Samuel Eliot, Frederick Merk, and Frank Friedel. *Dissent in Three American Wars.* Cambridge, Mass.: Harvard University Press, 1970.

Moynihan, Daniel Patrick. "Defining Deviancy Down," *The American Scholar* 62 (1993): 245–61.

Moynihan, Ruth B., Susan Armitage, and Christine Fischer Dichamp, eds. *So Much to Be Done: Women Settlers on the Mining and Ranching Frontiers.* Lincoln: University of Nebraska Press, 1990.

Mueller, John. *Retreat from Doomsday: The Obsolescence of Major War.* New York: Basic Books, 1989.

Mykitiuk, Roxanne, Martha Albertson, and Martha A. Fineman, eds. *The Public Nature of Private Violence: The Discovery of Domestic Abuse.* New York: Routledge, 1994.

Nash, Gary B. *The Urban Crucible: The Northern Seaports and the Origins of the American Revolution.* Cambridge, Mass.: Harvard University Press, 1986.

————, et al. *The American People: Creating a Nation and Society.* 2 vols. New York: Harper & Row, 1986.

————. Charlotte Crabtree, and Ross E. Dunn. *History on Trial: Culture Wars and the Teaching of the Past.* New York: Knopf, 1998.

Nash, Gerald D. *The American West in the Twentieth Century: A Short History of an Urban Oasis.* Englewood Cliffs, N. J.: Prentice-Hall, 1973.

Nash, Roderick, ed. *The Call of the Wild.* New York: George Braziller, 1970.

————. *Wilderness and the American Mind.* New Haven: Yale University Press, 1973.

Nie, Norman, Sidney Verba, and John R. Petrocik. *The Changing American Voter.* Cambridge, Mass.: Harvard University Press, 1976.

Niebuhr, Reinhold. *The Irony of American History.* New York: Scribner's, 1962.

Nisbet, Robert. *The Quest for Community.* London: Oxford University Press, 1953.

————. *Twilight of Authority.* New York: Oxford University Press, 1975.

————. *The Present Age: Progress and Anarchy in Modern America.* New York: Harper & Row, 1988.

Nobile, Philip, ed. *Judgment at the Smithsonian.* New York: Marlowe, 1995.

Nord, Warren A. *Religion and American Education: Rethinking an American Dilemma.* Chapel Hill: University of North Carolina Press, 1995.

Nye, Russell Blaine. *The Cultural Life of the New Nation, 1776–1830.* New York: Harper & Row, 1960.

Oglesby, Carl. *The Yankee and Cowboy War: Conspiracies from Dallas to Watergate.* Kansas City: Sheed Andrews and McMeel, 1976.

Olderman, Raymond M. *Beyond the Wasteland: The American Novel in the Nineteen-Sixties.* New Haven: Yale University Press, 1972.

Olson, Philip, ed. *America as a Mass Society: Changing Community and Identity.* New York: Free Press, 1963.

Orsi, Robert Anthony. *The Madonna of 115th Street: Faith and Community in Italian Harlem, 1880–1950.* New Haven: Yale University Press, 1985.

Packard, Vance. *The Status Seekers.* New York: McKay, 1959.

————. *A Nation of Strangers.* New York: McKay, 1972.

Packenham, Robert A. *Liberal America and the Third World: Political Development Ideas in Foreign Aid and Social Science.* Princeton: Princeton University Press, 1973.

Parks, Rosa, and Jim Haskins. *Rosa Parks: My Story.* New York: Dial, 1992.

Parrington, Vernon L. *Main Currents in American Thought: An Interpretation of American Literature from the Beginnings to 1920.* New York: Harcourt, Brace, 1930.

Paterson, Robert G. ed. *Cold War Critics: Alternatives to American Foreign Policy in the Truman Years.* Chicago: Quadrangle, 1971.

————, ed. *The Origins of the Cold War.* Second ed.. Lexington, Mass.: D. C. Heath, 1974.

Patrick, John J., and Richard C. Remy. *Civics for Americans*. Glenview, Ill.: Scott, Foresman, 1980.

Patterson, James T. *Grand Expectations: The United States, 1945–1974*. New York: Oxford University Press, 1996.

Pells, Richard. *Not Like Us: How Europeans Have Loved, Hated, and Transformed American Culture since World War II*. New York: Basic Books, 1997.

Perry, Lewis. *Intellectual Life in America: A History*. Chicago: University of Chicago Press, 1984.

Phillips, Derek L. ed. *Studies in American Society*. New York: Crowell, 1965.

Philpott, Thomas Lee. *The Slum and the Ghetto: Immigrants, Blacks, and Reformers in Chicago, 1880–1930*. Belmont, Calif.: Wadsworth, 1991.

Pierce, Bessie Louise. *Public Opinion and the Teaching of History in the United States*. New York: Knopf, 1926.

———. *Civic Attitudes in American School Textbooks*. Chicago: University of Chicago Press, 1930.

Plummer, William. *The Holy Goof: A Biography of Neal Cassady* Englewood Cliffs, N. J.: Prentice-Hall, 1981.

Potter, David M. *People of Plenty: Economic Abundance and the American Character*. Chicago: University of Chicago Press, 1954.

Putnam, Robert. "Bowling Alone." paper, Center for International Affairs, Harvard University, 1994.

Rankin. Charles E., ed. *Legacy: New Perspectives on the Battle of the Little Bighorn*. Helena: Montana Historical Society Press, 1996.

Ricks, Thomas E. *Making the Corps*. New York: Simon & Schuster, 1997.

Riesman, David. *The Lonely Crowd: A Study in the Changing American Character*. New Haven: Yale University Press, 1951.

———. "Football in America." *American Quarterly* 3 (1951): 309–25.

———. *Individualism Reconsidered, and Other Essays*. Glencoe, Ill.: Free Press, 1954.

Rodgers, Daniel T. *The Work Ethic in Industrial America, 1850–1920*. Chicago: University of Chicago Press, 1978.

Rogers, Everett M. *Social Change in Rural Society*. New York: Appleton-Century-Crofts, 1960.

Rosenblatt, Roger. *Coming Apart: A Memoir of the Harvard Wars of 1969*. Boston: Little, Brown, 1997.

Roszak, Theodore. *The Making of a Counter Culture: Reflections on the Technocratic Society and Its Youthful Opposition*. New York: Anchor, 1969.

Rothman, Ellen K. *Hands and Hearts: A History of Courtship in America*. Cambridge, Mass.: Harvard University Press, 1987.

Royce, Josiah. *The Problem of Christianity*. Chicago: University of Chicago Press, 1968 [1913].

————. *The Hope of the Great Community*. Freeport, N.Y.: Books for Libraries Press, 1967 [1916].

Shackford, James Atkins. *David Crockett: The Man and the Legend*. Chapel Hill: University of North Carolina Press, 1986.

Schaffer, Ronald. *America in the Great War: The Rise of the War Welfare State*. New York: Oxford University Press, 1991.

Schlesinger, Arthur M., Jr. *The Crisis of the Old Order, 1919-1933*. Boston: Houghton Mifflin, 1957.

Schlissel, Lillian. *Women's Diaries of the Westward Journey*. New York: Schocken, 1982.

Schrecker, Ellen W. *No Ivory Tower: McCarthyism and the Universities*. New York: Oxford University Press, 1986.

Schramm, Wilbur, Jack Lyle, and Edwin B. Parker, *Television in the Lives of Our Children*. Stanford: Stanford University Press, 1961.

Selesky, Harold E. *War and Society in Colonial Connecticut*. New Haven: Yale University Press, 1990.

Serrin, William. *Homestead: The Glory and Tragedy of an American Steel Town*. New York: Times, 1992.

Severo, Richard, and Lewis Milford. *The Wages of War: When America's Soldiers Came Home – From Valley Forge to Vietnam*. New York: Simon & Schuster, 1989.

Sherman, William Tecumseh. *Memoirs of General W. T. Sherman*. New York: Library of America, 1990.

Sherry, Michael S. *In the Shadow of War: The United States since the 1930s*. New Haven: Yale University Press, 1995.

Shover, John L. *First Majority – Last Minority: The Transformation of Rural Life in America*. De Kalb: Northern Illinois University Press, 1976.

Shy, John. *A People Numerous and Armed: Reflections on the Military Struggle for American Independence*. New York: Oxford University Press, 1976.

Siggelkow, Richard A. *Dissent and Disruption: A University under Siege*. Buffalo: Prometheus, 1991.

Skolnick, Arlene, and Jerome H. Skolnick, eds. *Family in Transition: Rethinking Marriage, Sexuality, Child Rearing, and Family Organization*. 3rd ed. Boston: Little, Brown, 1980.

Starr, Kevin. *Endangered Dreams: The Great Depression in California*. New York: Oxford University Press, 1996.

Skowronek, Stephen. *Building a New American State: The Expansion of National Administrative Capacity, 1877-1920*. Cambridge: Cambridge University Press, 1982.

Slayton, Robert D. *Back of the Yards: The Making of a Local Democracy*. Chicago: University of Chicago Press 1986.

Slosson, Preston William. *The Great Crusade and After, 1914-1928*. New York: Macmillan, 1969 [1930].

Slotkin, Richard. *Regeneration through Violence: The Mythology of the American Frontier, 1600-1860.* Middletown, Conn.: Wesleyan University Press, 1973.

———. *Gunfighter Nation: The Myth of the Frontier in Twentieth-Century America.* New York: Atheneum, 1992.

Smith, Henry Nash. *Virgin Land: The American West as Symbol and Myth.* Cambridge, Mass.: Harvard University Press, 1978 [1950].

Springer, Marlene, and Kaskell Springer, eds. *Plains Woman: The Diary of Martha Farnsworth, 1882-1992.* Bloomington: Indiana University Press, 1982.

Stearns, Harold E., ed. *Civilization in the United States: An Inquiry by Thirty Americans.* New York: Harcourt, Brace, 1922.

Stein, Maurice R. *The Eclipse of Community: An Interpretation of American Studies.* Princeton: Princeton University Press, 1960.

Steffens, Lincoln. *The Shame of the Cities.* New York: Hill and Wang, 1960.

Stock, Catherine McNicol. *Main Street in Crisis: The Great Depression and the Old Middle Class on the Northern Plains.* Chapel Hill: University of North Carolina Press, 1992.

———. *Rural Radicals: Righteous Rage in the American Grain.* Ithaca: Cornell University Press, 1996.

Struna, *People of Prowess: Sport, Leisure, and Labor in Early Anglo-America.* Urbana: University of Illinois Press, 1996.

Summers, Mark Wahlgren. *The Era of Good Stealings.* New York: Oxford University Press, 1993.

Susman, Warren I. *Culture as History: The Transformation of American Society in the Twentieth Century.* New York: Pantheon, 1984.

Tarbell, Ida M. *The History of the Standard Oil Company.* Edited by David M. Chalmers. New York: W. W. Norton, 1969 [1904].

Tauber, Peter. *The Sunshine Soldiers.* New York: Simon & Schuster, 1971.

Taylor, William R. *Cavalier and Yankee: The Old South and American National Character.* New York: Harper and Row, 1961.

Teixeira, Ruy A. *The Disappearing American Voter.* Washington, D.C.: Brookings Institution, 1992.

Tentler, Leslie Woodcock. *Wage-Earning Women: Industrial Work and Family Life in the United States, 1900-1930.* New York: Oxford University Press, 1979.

Thelen, David P. *Robert M. La Follette and the Insurgent Spirit.* Madison: University of Wisconsin Press, 1985.

Thomas, Emory, *The Confederate Nation: 1861-1865.* New York: Harper & Row, 1979.

Thomas, W. I., and Florian Znaniecki. *The Polish Peasant in Europe and America.* Urbana: University of Illinois Press, 1984 [1918-20].

———. Robert E. Park, and Herbert A. Miller. *Old World Traits Transplanted.* New York: Harper and Brothers, 1921.

Tobin, Joseph J., David Y. H. Yu, and Dana H Davidson. *Preschool in Three Cultures: Japan, China, and the United States*. New Haven: Yale University Press, 1989.

Trattner, Walter I. *From Poor Law to Welfare State: A History of Social Welfare in America*. New York: Free Press, 1984.

Turner, Frederick Jackson. *Frontier and Section: Selected Essays of Frederick Jackson Turner*. Englewood Cliffs. N. J.: Prentice-Hall, 1961.

———. *The Frontier in American History*. New York: Holt, Rinehart and Winston, 1962.

Tygiel, Jules. *Baseball's Great Experiment: Jackie Robinson and His Legacy*. New York: Oxford University Press, 1983.

Underhill, Ruth M. *Red Man's Religion: Beliefs and Practices of the Indians North of Mexico*. Chicago: University of Chicago Press, 1965.

Utley, Robert M. *Cavalier in Buckskin: George Armstrong Custer and the Western Military Frontier*. Norman: University of Oklahoma Press, 1988.

Van Alstyne, Richard W. *The Rising American Empire*. New York: Oxford University Press, 1960.

Veblen, Thorstein. *The Theory of the Leisure Class*. Boston: Houghton Mifflin, 1973 [1899].

Vidich, Arthur J., and Joseph Bensman. *Small Town in Mass Society*. Princeton: Princeton University Press, 1958.

Vidich, Arthur J., and Stanford M. Lyman. *American Sociology: Worldly Rejections of Religion and Their Directions*. New Haven: Yale University Press, 1985.

Vinovskis, Maris A. ed. *Toward a Social History of the Civil War: Exploratory Essays*. New York: Cambridge University Press, 1990.

Vitz, Paul C. *Psychology as Religion: The Cult of Self-Worship*. Grand Rapids: Eerdmans, 1977.

Wade, Richard C. *The Urban Frontier: Pioneer Life in Early Pittsburgh, Cincinatti, Lexington, and St. Louis*. Chicago: University of Chicago Press, 1976.

Wagner, Viqi, ed. *The Family in America: Opposing Viewpoints*. San Diego: Greenhaven Press, 1992.

Wall, Helena M. *Fierce Communion: Family and Community in Early America*. Cambridge, Mass.: Harvard University Press, 1990.

Ward, John William. *Andrew Jackson -- Symbol for an Age*. New York: Oxford University Press, 1955.

Ware, Susan. *Beyond Suffrage: Women in the New Deal*. Cambridge, Mass.: Harvard University Press, 1981.

Warner, W. Lloyd, and Paul S. Lunt. *The Social Life of a Modern Community: Class, Religion and Power in a Rural Community*. New Haven: Yale University Press, 1941.

———. *American Life: Dream and Reality*. Chicago: University of Chicago Press, 1964 [1953].

Warner, W. Lloyd et al. *Democracy in Jonesville: A Study of Quality and Inequality.* New York: Harper & Brothers, 1949.

———. Marcia Meeker, and Kenneth Eells. *Social Class in America: The Evaluation of Status.* New York: Harper & Row, 1960.

———. *The Family of God: A Symbolic Study of Christian Life in America.* New Haven: Yale University Press, 1961.

Warren, Robert Penn. *The Legacy of the Civil War: Meditations on the Centennial.* New York: Random House, 1961.

Watts, Alan W. *The Spirit of Zen: A Way of Life, Work and Art in the Far East.* New York: Grove Press, 1958.

Watts, Steven. *The Republic Reborn: War and the Making of Liberal America, 1790-1820.* Baltimore: Johns Hopkins University Press, 1987.

Webb, Charles. *The Graduate.* N.p.: New American Library, 1963.

Wecter, Dixon. *The Hero in America: A Chronicle of Hero Worship.* New York: Scribner's, 1969 [1941].

Weigley, Russell F. *The American Way of War: A History of United States Military Strategy and Policy.* Bloomington: Indiana University Press, 1973.

Weinberg, Albert K. *Manifest Destiny: A Study of Nationalist Expansionism in American History.* Chicago: Quadrangle Books, 1963 [1935].

Weller, Jack E. *Yesterday's People: Life in Contemporary Appalachia.* Lexington: University of Kentucky Press, 1965.

West, James. *Plainville, U.S.A.* New York: Columbia University Press, 1945.

Whitehead, Barbara Dafoe. *The Divorce Culture.* New York: Knopf, 1992.

Whyte, William H. *The Organization Man.* Garden City, N.Y.: Anchor Doubleday, 1957.

Wiebe, Robert H. *The Search for Order, 1877-1920.* New York: Hill and Wang, 1967.

Williams, Robin M., Jr. *American Society: A Sociological Interpretation.* New York: Knopf, 1955.

Williams, William Appleman. *The Tragedy of American Diplomacy.* Second edition. New York: Dell, 1972 [1959].

———. *The Contours of American History.* Chicago: Quadrangle Books, 1966 [1961].

———. *The Roots of the Modern American Empire: A Study of the Growth and Shaping of Social Consciousness in a Marketplace Society.* New York: Random House, 1969.

———. *History as a Way of Learning.* New York: New Viewpoints, 1973.

Wills, Garry. *John Wayne's America: The Politics of Celebrity.* New York: Simon & Schuster, 1997.

Wilson, Charles William, *Baptized in Blood: The Religion of the Lost Cause.* Athens: University of Georgia Press, 1980.

Wilson, Edmund. *Patriotic Gore: Studies in the Literature of the American Civil War.* New York: Oxford University Press, 1962.

Wittner, Lawrence S. *Rebels against War: The American Peace Movement, 1933-1983.* Philadelphia: Temple University Press, 1984.

Wolf, Stephanie Grauman. *Urban Village: Population, Community, and Family Structure in Germantown, Pennsylvania, 1683-1800.* Princeton: Princeton University Press, 1976.

Wolfe, Tom. *The Kandy-Kolored Tangerine-Flake Streamline Baby.* New York: Farrar, Straus and Giroux, 1965.

———. *The Electric Kool-Aid Acid Test.* New York: Farrar, Straus and Giroux, 1968.

———. *Radical Chic & Mau-Mauing the Flak Catchers.* New York: Farrar, Straus and Giroux, 1970.

Woodward, C. Vann. *Tom Watson: Agrarian Rebel.* New York: Oxford University Press, 1963 [1938].

———. *The Strange Career of Jim Crow.* New York: Oxford University Press, 1966.

———. *Origins of the New South, 1877-1913.* Baton Rouge: Louisiana State University Press, 1980.

———. *The Future of the Past.* New York: Oxford University Press, 1989.

———. *The Burden of Southern History.* 3rd ed. Baton Rouge: Louisiana State University Press, 1993.

Wreszin, Michael. *A Rebel in Defense of Tradition: The Life and Politics of Dwight Macdonald.* New York: Basic, 1994.

Wright, Esmond, ed. *Causes and Consequences of the American Revolution.* Chicago: Quadrangle, 1966.

Wylie, Philip. *Generation of Vipers.* New York: Farrar and Rinehart, 1942.

Yarmolinsky, Adam. *The Military Establishment: Its Impact on American Society.* New York: Harper & Row, 1971.

Youcha, Geraldine. *Minding the Children: Child Care in America from Colonial Times to the Present.* New York: Scribner's, 1995.

Zelinsky, Wilbur. *Nation into State: The Shifting Symbolic Foundations of American Nationalism.* Chapel Hill: University of North Carolina Press, 1988.

World War II

Alperovitz, Gar. *The Decision to Use the Atomic Bomb and the Architecture of an American Myth.* New York: Knopf, 1995.

Ambrose, Stephen E. *Band of Brothers: E Company, 506th Regiment, 101st Airborne, from Normandy to Hitler's Nest.* New York: Simon & Schuster, 1992.

Beasley, W. G. *Japanese Imperialism, 1894-1945.* Oxford: Clarendon, 1987.

Blum, John Morton. V *Was for Victory: Politics and American Culture during World War II.* New York: Harcourt, Brace, Jovanovich, 1976.

Bourke-White, Margaret. *Purple Heart Valley: A Combat Chronicle of the War in Italy.* New York: Simon & Schuster, 1944.

Butow, Robert J. C. *Japan's Decision to Surrender.* Stanford: Stanford University Press, 1954.

Cameron, Craig M. *American Samurai: Myth, Imagination, and the Conduct of Battle in the First Marine Division, 1941-1951.* New York: Cambridge University Press, 1994.

Campbell, D'Ann. *Women at War with America: Private Lives in a Patriotic Era.* Cambridge, Mass.: Harvard University Press, 1984.

Carr, Lowell Juilliard, and James Edson Stermer. *Willow Run: A Study of Industrialization and Cultural Inadequacy.* New York: Harper & Brothers, 1952.

Catton, Bruce. *The Warlords of Washington.* New York: Harcourt Brace, 1948.

Corwin, Edward S. *Total War and the Constitution.* New York: Knopf, 1947.

Costello, John. *Virtue under Fire: How World War II Changed our Social and Sexual Attitudes.* Boston: Little, Brown, 1985.

Dallek, Robert. *Franklin Roosevelt and American Foreign Policy, 1932-1945.* New York: Oxford University Press, 1979.

Dos Passos, John. *State of the Nation.* Boston: Houghton Mifflin, 1943.

Dower, John. W. *War without Mercy: Race and Power in the Pacific War.* New York: Pantheon, 1987.

Fairchild, Byron, and Jonathan Grossman. *The Army and Industrial Manpower.* Washington, D. C.: Government Printing Office, 1959.

Fussell, Paul. *Wartime: Understanding and Behavior in the Second World War.* New York: Oxford University Press, 1989.

Goulden, Joseph C. *The Best Years, 1945–1950.* New York: Atheneum, 1976.

Gray, J. Glenn. *The Warriors: Reflections on Men in Battle.* New York: Harper & Row, 1967 [1959].

Hargrove, Hondon B. *Buffalo Soldiers in Italy: Black Americans in World War II.* Jefferson, N.C.: McFarland and Co., 1985.

Hartmann, Susan M. *The Home Front and Beyond: American Women in the 1940s.* Boston: Twayne, 1982.

Havighurst, Robert J. *The Social History of a War-Boom Community.* New York: Longmans, Green, 1951.

Hersey, John. *Into the Valley: A Skirmish of the Marines.* Garden City, N.Y.: Sun Dial Press, 1943.

Hoopes, Roy. *Americans Remember the Home Front: An Oral Narrative.* New York: Hawthorn, 1977.

Howell, Thomas. "U.S. Domestic Propaganda in World War II." *The Historian* 59 (1997): 795-813.

Hoyt, Edwin P. *The GI's War: American Soldiers in Europe during World War II.* New York: Da Capo, 1988.

Ienaga, Saburo. *The Pacific War, 1931-1945: A Critical Perspective on Japan's Role in World War II.* New York: Pantheon, 1978.

Lash, Joseph P. *Roosevelt and Churchill, 1939-1941: The Partnership that Saved the West.* New York: W. W. Norton, 1976.

Lingeman, Richard R. *Don't You Know There's a War On?: The American Home Front, 1941–1945.* New York: Putnam, 1970.

Litoff, Judy Barrett, and David C. Smith, eds. *Since You Went Away: World War II Letters from American Women on the Home Front.* New York: Oxford University Press, 1991.

Manchester, William. *American Caesar: Douglas MacArthur, 1880-1964.* Boston: Little, Brown, 1978.

———. *Goodbye Darkness: Memoirs of the Pacific War.* Boston: Little, Brown, 1979.

Mauldin, Bill. *Up Front.* Cleveland: World, 1945.

———. *Back Home.* New York: William Sloane, 1945.

———. *The Brass Ring: A Sort of Memoir.* New York: W. W. Norton, 1971.

Merrill, Francis E., *Social Problems on the Home Front: A Study of War-time Influences.* New York: Harper & Brothers, 1948.

Milkman, Ruth. *Gender at Work: The Dynamics of Job Segregation by Sex during World War II.* Urbana: University of Illinois Press, 1987.

Miller, Marc Scott. *The Irony of Victory: World War II and Lowell, Massachusetts.* Urbana: University of Illinois Press, 1988.

Myers, Debs, Jonathan Kilbourn and Richard Harrity, eds. *Yank – the GI Story of the War.* New York: Duell, Sloan & Pearce, 1947.

Nash, Gerald D. *World War II and the West: Reshaping the Economy.* Lincoln: University of Nebraska Press, 1990.

Ogburn, William Fielding, ed. *American Society in Wartime.* Chicago: University of Chicago Press, 1943.

Perret, Geoffrey. *Days of Sadness, Years of Triumph: The American People, 1939-1945.* New York: Coward, Mcann, and Geoghegan: 1973.

———. *A Country Made by War.* New York: Random House, 1989.

———. *There's a War to be Won: The United States Army in World War II.* New York: Random House, 1991.

Phillips, Cabell. *The 1940s: Decade of Triumph and Trouble.* New York: Macmillan, 1975.

Polenberg, Richard, ed. *America at War: The Home Front, 1941-1945.* Englewood Cliffs, N.J.: Prentice-Hall, 1968.

———. *War and Society: The United States, 1941-1945.* New York: J. B. Lippincott, 1972.

Pyle, Ernie. *Here is Your War: The Story of G.I. War.* New York: Henry Holt, 1943.

———. *Brave Men.* New York: Henry Holt, 1944.

Reynolds, David. *Rich Relations: The American Occupation of Britain, 1941-1945.* New York: Random House, 1995.

Sherwood, Robert E. *Roosevelt and Hopkins: An Intimate History.* New York: Harper & Brothers, 1948.

Sledge, E. B. *With the Old Breed at Peleliu and Okinawa.* Novato, Calif.: Presidio, 1990.

Stimson, Henry L., and McGeorge Bundy. *On Active Service in Peace and War.* New York: Harper & Brothers, 1947.

Terkel, Studs. *'The Good War:' An Oral History of World War Two.* New York: Pantheon, 1984.

Tuttle, William M., Jr. *"Daddy's Gone to War:" The Second World War in the Lives of America's Children.* New York: Oxford University Press, 1993.

Tregaskis, Richard. *Guadalcanal Diary.* New York: Random House, 1943.

The Vietnam War

Andrews, William R. *The Village War: Vietnamese Communist Revolutionary Activities in Dinh Tuong Province, 1960-1964.* Columbia: University of Missouri Press 1973.

Appy, Christian G. *Working-Class War: American Combat Soldiers and Vietnam.* Chapel Hill: University of North Carolina Press, 1993.

Bates, Tom. *Rads: The 1970 Bombing of the Army Math Research Center at the University of Wisconsin and Its Aftermath.* New York: Harper Collins, 1992.

Bilton, Michael, and Kevin Sim. *Four Hours in My Lai.* New York: Penguin, 1992.

Braestrup, Peter, ed. *Vietnam as History: Ten Years after the Paris Peace Accords.* Washington, D. C.: University Press of America, 1984.

Bredo, William. "Agrarian Reform in Vietnam: Vietcong and Government of Vietnam Strategies in Conflict." *Asian Survey* 10 (1970): 738-50.

Callison, Charles Stuart. *Land-to-the Tiller in the Mekong Delta: Economic, Social and Political Effects of Land Reform in Four Villages of South Vietnam.* Lanham, Md.: University Press of America, 1983.

Cash, John A., John Albright, and Allan W. Sandstrum. *Seven Firefights in Vietnam* Washington, D. C.: Center of Military History, 1989.

Clifford, Clark. "A Viet Nam Reappraisal." *Foreign Affairs* 47 (1969): 601-22.

Clodfelter, Mark. *The Limits of Airpower: The American Bombing of North Vietnam.* New York: Free Press, 1989.

Davidson, Phillip B. *Vietnam at War: The History, 1946-1975.* New York: Oxford University Press, 1991.

Davison, W. P. "Some Observations on Viet Cong Operations in the Villages." Santa Monica, Calif.: Rand Corporation Research Memorandum RM 5267/2, 1968.

Donnell, John C., Guy J. Pauker, and Joseph J. Zasloff. "Viet Cong Motivation and Morale in 1964: A Preliminary Report." Santa Monica, Calif.: Rand Corporation Research Memorandum RM4507/3-15A, March 1965.

Donnell, John C. "Viet Cong Recruitment: Why and How Men Join." Santa Monica, Calif.: Rand Corporation Research Memorandum RM 5486-1, 1967.

Donovan, David. *Once a Warrior King: Memories of an Officer in Vietnam.* New York: McGraw-Hill, 1985.

Dung, Van Tien. *Our Great Spring Victory: An Account of the Liberation of South Vietnam.* New York: Monthly Press, 1977.

Fall, Bernard B. *The Two Viet-Nams: A Political and Military Analysis.* New York: Praeger, 1963.

———. *Street Without Joy.* New York: Schocken, 1972.

Fitzgerald, Frances. *Fire in the Lake: The Vietnamese and the Americans in Vietnam.* Boston: Atlantic Monthly, 1972.

Fligstein, Neil D. "Who Served in the Military, 1940-73?" *Armed Forces and Society* 6 (1980): 297-312.

Ford, Harold P. *CIA and the Vietnam Policymakers: Three Episodes, 1962-1968.* McLean, Va.: Center for the Study of Intelligence, 1998.

Gardner, Lloyd C. *Approaching Vietnam: From World War II through Dienbienphu.* New York: W. W. Norton, 1988.

Garfinkle, Adam. *Telltale Hearts: The Origins and Impact of the Vietnam Antiwar Movement.* New York: St Martin's Griffin, 1997.

Gelb, Leslie H. and Richard K. Betts. *The Irony of Vietnam: The System Worked.* Washington, D. C.: Brookings Institution, 1979.

Halberstam, David. *The Best and the Brightest.* New York: Random House, 1972.

Hallin, Daniel C. *The "Uncensored War:" The Media and Vietnam.* New York: Oxford University Press, 1986.

Hammond, William M. *Public Affairs: The Military and the Media, 1962-1968.* Washington, D. C.: Government Printing Office, 1988.

Hellmann, John. *American Myth and the Legacy of Vietnam.* New York: Columbia University Press, 1986.

Henderson, William Darryl. *Why the Vietcong Fought: A Study of Motivation and Control in a Modern Army in Combat.* Westport, Conn.: Greenwood Press, 1979.

Hoopes, Townsend. *The Limits of Intervention.* New York: David McKay, 1973.

Houghton, N. D., ed. *Struggle against History: U.S. Foreign Policy in an Age of Revolution.* New York: Clarion, 1968.

Kahin, George McT. *Intervention: How America Became Involved in Vietnam.* New York: Knopf, 1986.

Karnow, Stanley. *Vietnam: A History.* New York: Viking, 1983.

Krepinevich, Andrew F., Jr. *The Army and Vietnam.* Baltimore: Johns Hopkins University Press, 1983.

Lake, Anthony, ed. *The Legacy of Vietnam: The War, American Society and the Future of American Foreign Policy.* New York: New York Univerity Press, 1976.

Lewy, Guenter. *America and Vietnam.* New York: Oxford University Press, 1978.

Mailer, Norman. *Why Are We in Vietnam?* New York: Holt, Rinehart and Winston, 1967.

———. *The Armies of the Night.* New York: New American Library, 1968.

Marr, David G. *Vietnamese Anticolonialism 1885-1925.* Berkeley and Los Angeles: University of California Press, 1971.

———. *Vietnamese Tradition on Trial, 1920-1945.* Berkeley and Los Angeles: University of California Press, 1981.

Moore, Harold G., and Joseph L. Galloway. *We Were Soldiers Once . . . and Young.* New York: Random House, 1993.

Morgenthau, Hans J. *Vietnam and the United States.* Washington, D.C.: Public Affairs Press, 1965.

Mueller, John E. *Wars, Presidents, and Public Opinion.* New York: John Wiley, 1973.

Oberdorfer, Don. *Tet!: The Turning Point in the Vietnam War.* New York: Da Capo, 1971.

Patti, Archimedes L. A. *Why Viet Nam? Prelude to America's Albatross.* Berkeley and Los Angeles: University of California Press, 1980.

Prosterman, Roy L. "Land Reform in South Vietnam: A Proposal for Turning the Tables on the Vietcong." *Cornell Law Review* 53 (1967): 26-44.

Prosterman, Roy L., and Jeffrey M. Riedinger. *Land Reform and Democratic Development.* Baltimore: Johns Hopkins University Press, 1987.

Race, Jeffrey. *War Comes to Long An: Revolutionary Conflict in a Vietnamese Province.* Berkeley and Los Angeles: University of California Press, 1972.

Rosenberg, Milton J., Sidney Verba, and Philip E. Converse. *Vietnam and the Silent Majority: The Dove's Guide.* New York: Harper & Collins, 1970.

Rovere, Richard H. *Waist Deep in the Big Muddy.* Boston: Atlantic Monthly, 1968.

Rotter, Andrew J. *The Path to Vietnam: Origins of the American Commitment to Southeast Asia.* Ithaca: Cornell University Press, 1987.

Sansom, Robert L. *The Economics of Insurgency in the Mekong Delta.* Cambridge, Mass.: MIT Press, 1970.

Santoli, Al. *Everything We Had: An Oral History of the Vietnam War.* New York: Random House, 1981.

Shafer, D. Michael, ed. *The Legacy: The Vietnam War in the American Imagination.* Boston: Beacon Press, 1990.

Schandler, Herbert Y. *Lyndon Johnson and Vietnam: The Unmaking of a President.* Princeton: Princeton University Press, 1977.

Spector, Ronald H. *Advice and Support: The Early Years of the U.S. Army in Vietnam 1941-1960.* New York: Free Press, 1985.

———. *After Tet: The Bloodiest Year in Vietnam.* New York: Free Press, 1993.

Taylor, Telford. *Nuremberg and Vietnam: An American Tragedy.* Chicago: Quadrangle, 1970.

Thompson, W. Scott, and Donaldson D. Frizell, eds. *The Lessons of Vietnam.* New York: Crane, Russack, 1977.

Wells, Tom. *The War Within: America's Battle over Vietnam.* Berkeley and Los Angeles: University of California Press, 1994.

Wirtz, James J. *The Tet Offensive: Intelligence Failure in War.* Ithaca, N.Y.: Cornell University Press, 1991.

Zasloff, J. J. "Origins of the Insurgency in South Vietnam, 1954-1960: The Role of the Southern Vietminh Cadres." Santa Monica, Calif.: Rand Memorandum 5163/ 2-ISA/ARPA, May 1968.

Comparative History

Barber, John, and Mark Harrison. *The Soviet Home Front, 1941-1945: A Social and Economic History of the USSR in World War II.* London: Longman, 1991.

Barnett, Correlli. *The Pride and the Fall: The Dream and Illusion of Britain as a Great Nation.* New York: Free Press, 1986.

Bessel, Richard. *Germany after the First World War.* Oxford: Clarendon, 1993.

Billington, James H. *The Icon and the Axe: An Interpretive History of Russian Culture.* New York: Vintage, 1970.

Bradley, Joseph. *Muzhik and Muscovite: Urbanization in Late Imperial Russia.* Berkeley and Los Angeles: University of California Press, 1985.

Bloch, Marc. *Strange Defeat: A Statement of Evidence Written in 1940.* New York: W. W. Norton, 1968 [1940].

Buruma, Ian, *The Wages of War: Memories of War in Germany and Japan.* New York: Meridian, 1995.

Calder, Angus. *The People's War: Britain, 1939-1945.* New York: Pantheon, 1969.

Campbell, J. B. *The Emperor and the Roman Army, 31 BC – AD 235.* Oxford: Clarendon Press, 1984.

Carr, Raymond. *Spain, 1808-1975.* New York: Oxford University Press, 1982.

Clements, R. E., ed. *The World of Ancient Israel: Sociological Anthropological and Political Perspectives.* Cambridge: Cambridge University Press, 1989.

Cobban, Alfred. *In Search of Humanity: The Role of the Enlightenment in Modern History.* New York: George Braziller, 1960.

Dozeman, Thomas B. *God at War: Power in the Exodus Tradition.* New York: Oxford University Press, 1996.

Dower, John W. *Embracing Defeat: Japan in the Wake of World War II.* New York: New Press, 1999.

Duggan, Christopher. *Fascism and the Mafia.* New Haven: Yale University Press, 1989.

Engel, Barbara Alpern. *Mothers and Daughters: Women of the Intelligentsia in Nineteenth-Century Russia.* New York: Cambridge University Press, 1983.

Fromkin, David. *A Peace to End All Peace: The Fall of the Ottoman Empire and the Creation of the Modern Middle East.* New York: Henry Holt, 1989.

Gay, Peter. *The Cultivation of Hatred.* Vol. 3 of *The Bourgeois Experience, Victoria to Freud.* New York: W. W. Norton, 1993.

Girouard, Mark. *The Return to Camelot: Chivalry and the English Gentleman.* New Haven:

Yale University Press, 1981.

Graves, Robert, and Alan Hodge. *The Long Week-End: A Social History of Great Britain, 1918–1939.* New York: W. W. Norton, 1963 [1940].

Harris, William V. *War and Imperialism in Republican Rome 327–70 B.C.* Oxford: Clarendon Press, 1989.

Henderson, William Darryl. *Cohesion, The Human Element in Combat: Leadership and Societal Influence in the Armies of the Soviet Union, the United States, North Vietnam, and Israel.* Washington, D. C.: National Defense University Press, 1985.

Holmes, Richard. *Acts of War: The Behavior of Men in Battle.* New York: Free Press, 1989.

Hynes, Samuel. *The Soldiers' Tale: Bearing Witness to Modern War.* Harmondsworth, U.K.: Penguin, 1997.

Jones, A. H. M. *Augustus.* New York: W. W. Norton, 1970.

Kagan, Donald. *Pericles of Athens and the Birth of Democracy: The Triumph of Vision in Leadership.* New York: Touchstone, 1991.

Keen, Sam. *Faces of the Enemy: Reflections of the Hostile Imagination.* San Francisco, Calif.: Harper & Row, 1986.

Kellett, Anthony. *Combat Motivations: The Behavior of Soldiers in Battle.* Boston: Kluwer, 1982.

Kennedy, Paul M. *The Rise and Fall of the Great Powers: Economic Change and Military Conflict from 1500 to 2000.* New York: Random House, 1987.

Knight, Amy. *Beria: Stalin's First Lieutenant.* Princeton: Princeton University Press, 1993.

Lambert, E. *Sons against Fathers: Studies in Russian Radicalism and Revolution.* Oxford: Clarendon Press, 1965.

Laqueur, Walter. *Weimar: A Cultural History, 1918-1933.* New York: G. P. Putnam, 1974.

Lawrence, T. E. *The Mint: A Day-Book of the R.A.F. Depot between August and December 1922 with Later Notes.* London: Jonathan Cape, 1955.

Liebeschuetz, J. H. W. G. *Continuity and Change in Roman Religion.* Oxford: Clarendon, 1979.

Lincoln, R. Bruce. *In the Vanguard of Reform: Russia's Enlightened Bureaucrats, 1825–61.* DeKalb: Northern Illinois University Press, 1984.

Linz, Susan J. ed. *The Impact of World War II on the Soviet Union.* Totowa, N. J.: Rowman & Allanheld, 1985.

MacMullen, Ramsay. *Soldier and Civilian in the Later Roman Empire.* Cambridge, Mass.: Harvard University Press, 1960.

———. *Constantine.* London: Croom Helm, 1987.

McCormick, Michael. *Eternal Victory: Triumphal Rulership in Late Antiquity, Byzantium, and the Early Medieval West.* Cambridge: Cambridge University Press, 1986.

Maier, Charles S. *Recasting Bourgeois Europe: Stabilization in France, Germany, and Italy in the Decade after World War I.* Princeton: Princeton University Press, 1975.

Mayer, Arno. *The Persistence of the Old Regime: Europe to the Great War.* New York: Pantheon, 1981.

Marwick, Arthur. *The Deluge: British Society and the First World War.* New York: W. W. Norton, 1965.

———. *War and Social Change in the Twentieth Century.* London: Macmillan, 1974.

———. *Class: Image and Reality in Britain, France, and the USA since 1930.* Glasgow, U.K.: Collins, 1980.

———. *British Society since 1945.* Harmondsworth, U.K.: Penguin, 1982.

Meinecke, Friedrich. *The German Catastrophe: The Social and Historical Influences Which led to the Rise and Ruin of Hitler and Germany.* Translated by Sidney B. Fay. Boston: Beacon Press, 1963.

Milward, Alan. S. *War, Economy and Society, 1939-1945.* Berkeley and Los Angeles: University of California Press, 1977.

Mosse, George L. *The Crisis of German Ideology: Intellectual Origins of the Third Reich.* New York: Universal, 1964.

———. *Fallen Soldiers: Reshaping the Memory of the World Wars.* New York: Oxford University Press, 1990.

Ritter, Gerhard. *The Sword and the Scepter: The Problem of Militarism in Germany.* Princeton Junction, N.J.: The Scholar's Bookshelf, 1988 [1954].

Schoenbaum, David. *Hitler's Social Revolution: Class and Status in Nazi Germany 1933–1939.* New York: W. W. Norton, 1980.

Shils, Edward A., and Morris Janowitz. "Cohesion and Disintegration in the Wehrmacht in World War II." *Public Opinion Quarterly* 12 (1948): 280-315.

Stern, Fritz. *The Politics of Cultural Despair: A Study in the Rise of the Germanic Ideology.* Berkeley and Los Angeles: University of California Press, 1961.

Strachan, Hew. *European Armies and the Conduct of War.* London: George Allen and Unwin, 1983.

Syme, Ronald. *The Roman Revolution.* Oxford: Oxford University Press, 1939.

Takeyama, Michio. *Harp of Burma.* Translated by Howard Hibbett. Rutland, Vt.: Charles E. Tuttle, 1966 [1946].

Tumarkin, Nina. *The Living and the Dead: The Rise and Fall of the Cult of World War II in Russia.* New York: Basic, 1994.

Walicki, Andrzej. *A History of Russian Thought from the Enlightenment to Marxism.* Stanford: Stanford University Press, 1979.

Weber, Eugen. *France, Fin de Siècle.* Cambridge, Mass.: Belknap Press, 1986.

———. *The Hollow Years: France in the 1930s.* New York: W. W. Norton, 1994.

Werth, Alexander. *Russia at War, 1941–1945.* New York: E. P. Dutton, 1964.

Film Studies

Black, Gregory D. *Hollywood Censored: Morality Codes, Catholics, and the Movies.*

Cambridge: Cambridge University Press, 1994.

Bogdanovich, Peter. *Time Pieces: Bogdanovich on the Movies, 1961-1985.* New York: Arbor House, 1985.

Christensen, Terry, *Reel Politics: American Political Movies from Birth of a Nation to Platoon.* Oxford: Basil Blackwell, 1987.

Koppes, Clayton R., and Gregory D. Black. *Hollywood Goes to War: How Politics, Profits and Propaganda Shaped World War II Movies.* Berkeley and Los Angeles: University of California Press, 1990.

Kracauer, Sigfried. *From Caligari to Hitler: A Psychological Study of the German Cinema.* Princeton: Princeton University Press, 1947.

Levy, Emanuel. *Small-Town America in Film: The Decline and Fall of Community.* New York: Continuum, 1991.

Medved, Michael. *Hollywood versus America: Popular Culture and the War on Traditional Values.* New York: Harper Collins, 1992.

Sklar, Robert. *Movie-Made America: A Cultural History of the Movies.* New York: Random House, 1975.

Smith, Paul. *The Historian and Film.* Cambridge: Cambridge University Press, 1976.

Suid, Lawrence H. *Guts and Glory: Great American War Movies.* Reading, Mass.: Addison-Wesley, 1978.

Williams, Linda. *Hard Core: Power, Pleasure, and the "Frenzy of the Visible."* Berkeley and Los Angeles: University of California Press, 1989.

Zuker, William. *Arthur Penn: A Guide to References and Resources.* Boston: G. K. Hall, 1980.

War and Literature

Brown, Harry. *A Walk in the Sun.* New York: Knopf, 1944.

Burns, John Horne. *The Gallery.* New York: Harper and Brothers, 1948.

Cobb, Humphrey. *Paths of Glory.* Athens: University of Georgia Press, 1987 [1935].

Cowley, Malcolm. *The Exile's Return: A Literary Odyssey of the 1920s.* New York: Viking, 1951 [1934].

Döblin, Alfred. *A People Betrayed, November 1918: A German Revolution.* New York: Fromm, 1983.

Faulkner, William. *Soldiers' Pay.* New York: New American Library, 1968 [1926].

Forester, C. S. *The General.* New York: Bantam, 1967 [1936].

Fussell, Paul. *The Great War and Modern Memory.* New York: Oxford University Press, 1975.

———. *The Norton Book of Modern War.* New York: W. W. Norton, 1991.

Graves, Robert. *Goodbye to All That.* New York: Anchor, 1985 [1929].

Hasford, Gustav. *The Short-Timers.* New York: Bantam, 1980.

Heinrich, Willi. *The Cross of Iron.* Indianapolis: Bobbs-Merrill, 1956.

Heller, Joseph. *Catch-22*. New York: Simon and Schuster, 1961.

Hersey, John. *A Bell for Adano*. New York: Knopf, 1944.

———. *The War Lover*. New York: Knopf, 1959.

Jones, James. *From Here to Eternity*. New York: Scribner's, 1951.

———. *The Thin Red Line*. New York: Scribner's, 1962.

Kovic, Ron. *Born on the Fourth of July*. New York: Pocket, 1977.

Mailer, Norman. *The Naked and the Dead*. New York: Rinehart, 1948.

March, William. *Company K*. Tuscaloosa: University of Alabama Press, 1989 [1933].

Maugham, W. Somerset. *The Razor's Edge*. New York: Doubleday, 1944.

O'Brien, Tim. *If I Die in a Combat Zone*. New York: Delacorte, 1975.

Remarque, Erich Maria. *All Quiet on the Western Front*. Boston: Little, Brown, 1929.

———. *A Time to Love and a Time to Die*. New York: Harcourt, Brace, 1954.

Shaw, Irwin. *The Young Lions*. New York: Random House, 1948.

Vonnegut, Kurt. *Slaughterhouse-Five, or the Children's Crusade: A Duty Dance with Death*. New York: Delacorte, 1969.

Zweig, Arnold. *Education before Verdun*. New York: Viking, 1936.

Index

Index

blues, the, 146
Bogdanovich, Peter, 194
Bonanza, 99
Bonus Army, 61
Book of Martyrs, 27
Boone, Daniel, 31
Bourke-White, Margaret, 78
Bourne, Randolph, 46
Bowie, Jim, 143
Brandeis, Louis, 41
Brady Bunch, The, 156
Brando, Marlon, 100
Bridenbaugh, Carl, 124, 234 n. 28, 238 n.
  68, 273 n. 13
Bridge Too Far, A, 183
Brooks, Van Wyck, 20, 27, 48–49
Brown, Harry, 79
Bryan, William Jennings, 56
Bryant, William Cullen, 24
Buffalo Bill's Wild West Show, 208
Bundy, McGeorge, 155–56, 159, 161
Bunker Hill, 21–22
Burns, John Horne, 76, 111–12
Butch Cassidy and the Sundance Kid, 275
  n. 33

Caldwell, Erskine, 60–61
Calley, William C., 164–65, 205
Calvin, John, 28
Calvinism, 15, 30–31
Capra, Frank, 75, 104
Carbine Williams, 114
Carson, Rachel, 129, 142
Casablanca, 116
Cat on a Hot Tin Roof, 104
Catch-22, 187–88
Catholics, 25
Catton, Bruce, 40
Channing, William Ellery, 26
Chautauqua, 29

Cheyenne Autumn, 275 n. 34
Chicago, University of, 19
Chicago Tribune, 62
Chickamauga, 23
child-rearing, 99–100
CIA, 118, 151, 138, 168, 185
Citizen Kane, 61
Civil War: Beards' reinterpretation
  of, 47; economic boom, 37–40; and
  nationalism, 22; postwar discontent,
  40; religious fusion, 27–28
Clay, Henry, 202
Cleveland, Grover, 59
Clifford, Clark, 161
Clockwork Orange, A, 182
coarsening: after WWI, 52–53, 77–78;
  and WWII, 74–80, 110–13; after
  Vietnam, 194–96
Coffin, William Sloane, 190
Cold War: 105–6; and social progress,
  131–32; unease with, 137–39, 212
Coleman, James, 99
Collins, J. Lawton, 187
Colt .45, 114
Columbia the Gem of the Ocean, 21
Combat motivation, 85–86
Commager, Henry Steele, 24
community: after WWII, 101–7; anti-war
  movement as, 157–59; decline after
  Vietnam, 177–80; discontent after
  WWI, 53–54; during the Depression,
  57–58; during Vietnam, 156–57; during
  WWII, 68–71; ersatz, 179–80; ethnic,
  18–19; integration, 19–20; in traditional
  society, 17–19; and war, 22–23
Con Thien, 159
Congregationalism, 26
Constantine, 183
Constitution, U.S., 21; and WWII,
  137–38; Beard on, 199; in postmodern

Index

INDEX

INDEX

Printed in the United States
18536LVS00004B/9